MW01627559

Christmas 2015
Sean + Mary
XOX
Mela + Jay

AUDACIOUS

AUDACIOUS
THE FINE ART OF WOOD
THE MONTALTO BOHLEN COLLECTION

Peabody Essex Museum, Salem, Massachusetts
Distributed by University Press of New England, Hanover and London

Audacious: The Fine Art of Wood from the Montalto Bohlen Collection accompanies the exhibition of the same name, organized by the Peabody Essex Museum, Salem, Massachusetts, on view February 21, 2015-June 21, 2015.

The East India Marine Associates of the Peabody Essex Museum provided support for this project.

Peabody Essex Museum
East India Square
Salem, Massachusetts 01970
www.pem.org

Distributed by University Press
of New England
1 Court Street
Lebanon, New Hampshire 03766

Library of Congress Control Number:
2014917646

ISBN: 978-0-87577-228-8

Front jacket: Stuart Mortimer, *Squid Series #2,* 2002, page 46
Back jacket: Hal Metlitzky, *Double Helix,* 2012, pages 114-15

Designed by Jena Sher
Jena Sher Graphic Design, Wisconsin
www.jenasher.com

Color separations/prepress by
Professional Graphics, Inc., Illinois
www.pgiworldwide.com

Printed in the United States
by Puritan Capital, New Hampshire
www.puritancapital.com

Dimensions are given height by width by depth or height by diameter.

Photography Credits

Page 16 (top) Courtesy of the National Gallery of Art; (bottom) © Peabody Essex Museum; (right) Art © 2014 Artists Rights Society (ARS), New York/ADAGP, Paris. Digital Image © The Museum of Modern Art. Licensed by SCALA/Art Resource, NY. Page 18 © Erich Lessing/Art Resource, NY. Page 19: Donald Judd, *Untitled,* 1976. Courtesy Dia Art Foundation, New York; Gift of The Brown Foundation. © Donald Judd Foundation. Licensed by VAGA, New York, NY. Photo by Bill Jacobson Studio, New York. Page 24 (right) Courtesy of The Nelson-Atkins Museum of Art, Kansas City, Missouri. Photo by Jamison Miller

Pages 20, 28, 44-45, 46, 49, 52-53, 75, 79, 86, 104, 107, 120, 127-28, 140, 168-69, 177, 184, and 188, photos by Dirk Bakker

Pages 22-23, 30-37, 39-41, 47-48, 51, 54-55, 57-59, 61-63, 65-74, 76-78, 80-81, 84, 87-99, 100-101, 103, 106, 108-13, 116-19, 124-26, 129-32, 134-36, 138-39, 141-49, 150-53, 155-59, 162-67, 172-76, 179-83, 185, 187, and 189-95, photos by Terry Martin

Pages 5, 6, 196, and 200 © 2014 Jena Sher

Pages 8, 12, 14, 21, 24 (left), 26, 38, 42, 50, 56, 60, 64, 82, 85, 102, 114-15, 121-22, 133, 137, 154, 160, 170-71, 178, and 186, photos by Walter Silver/PEM

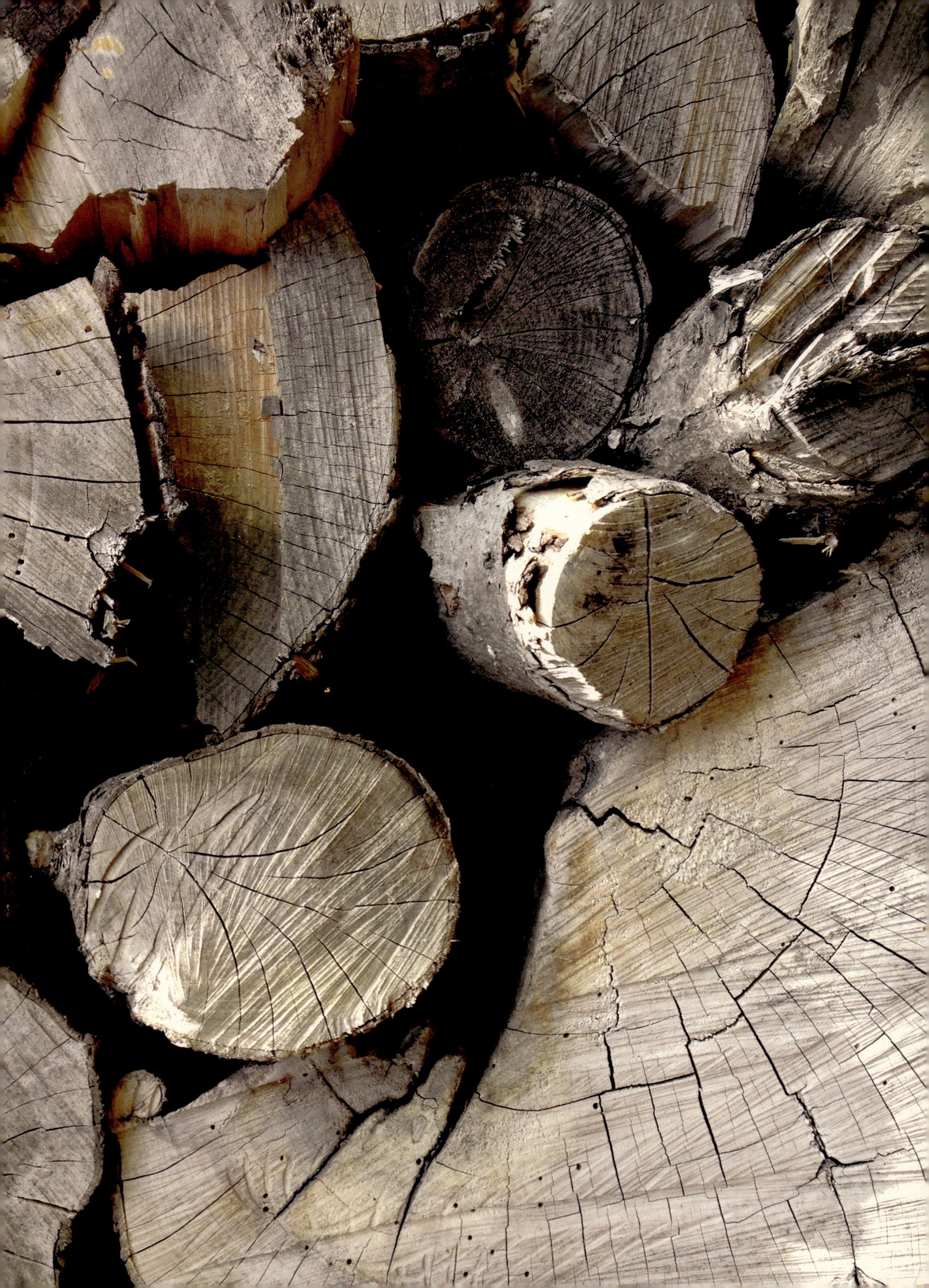

CONTENTS

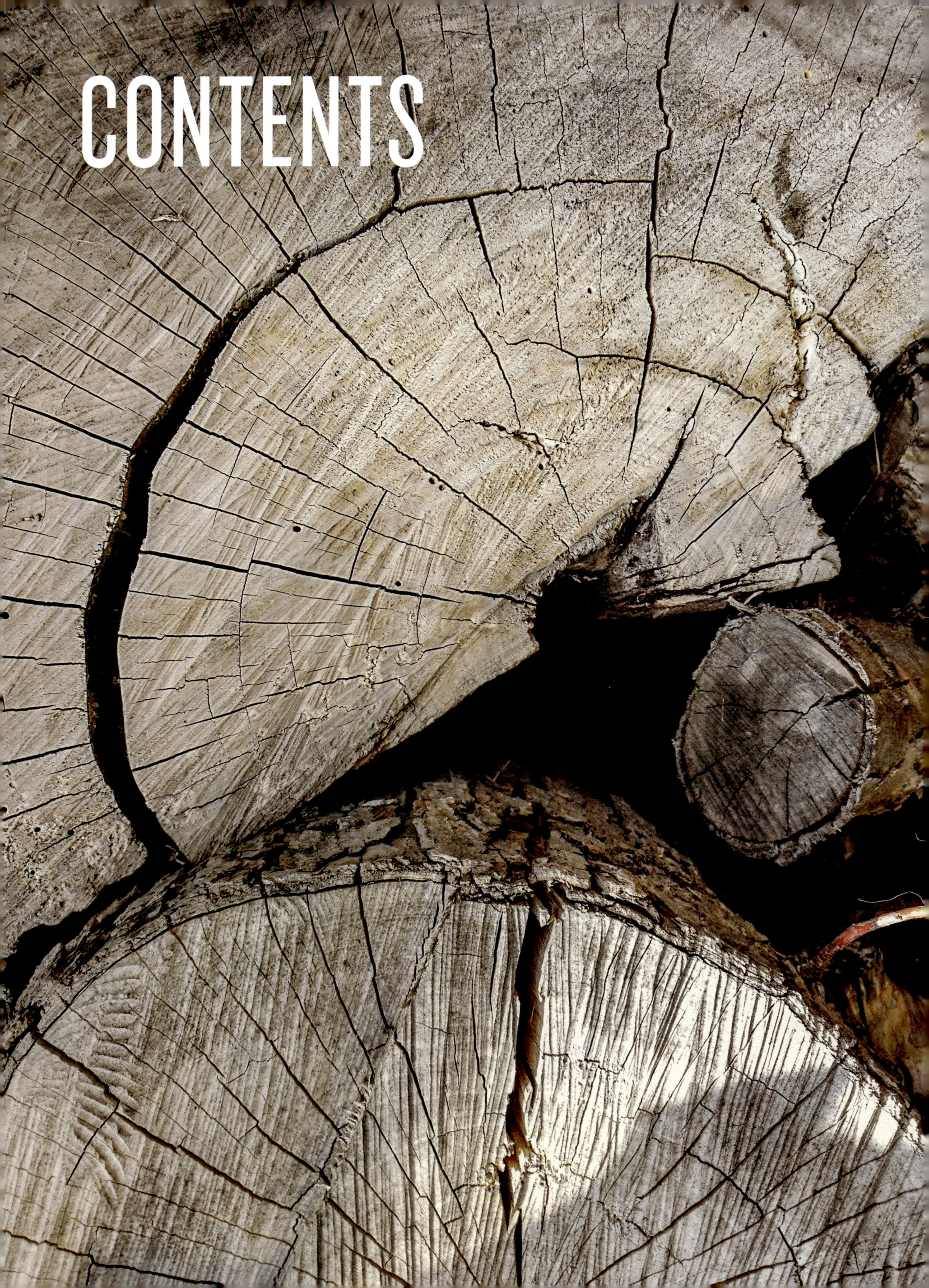

FOREWORD

DAN L. MONROE AND LYNDA ROSCOE HARTIGAN

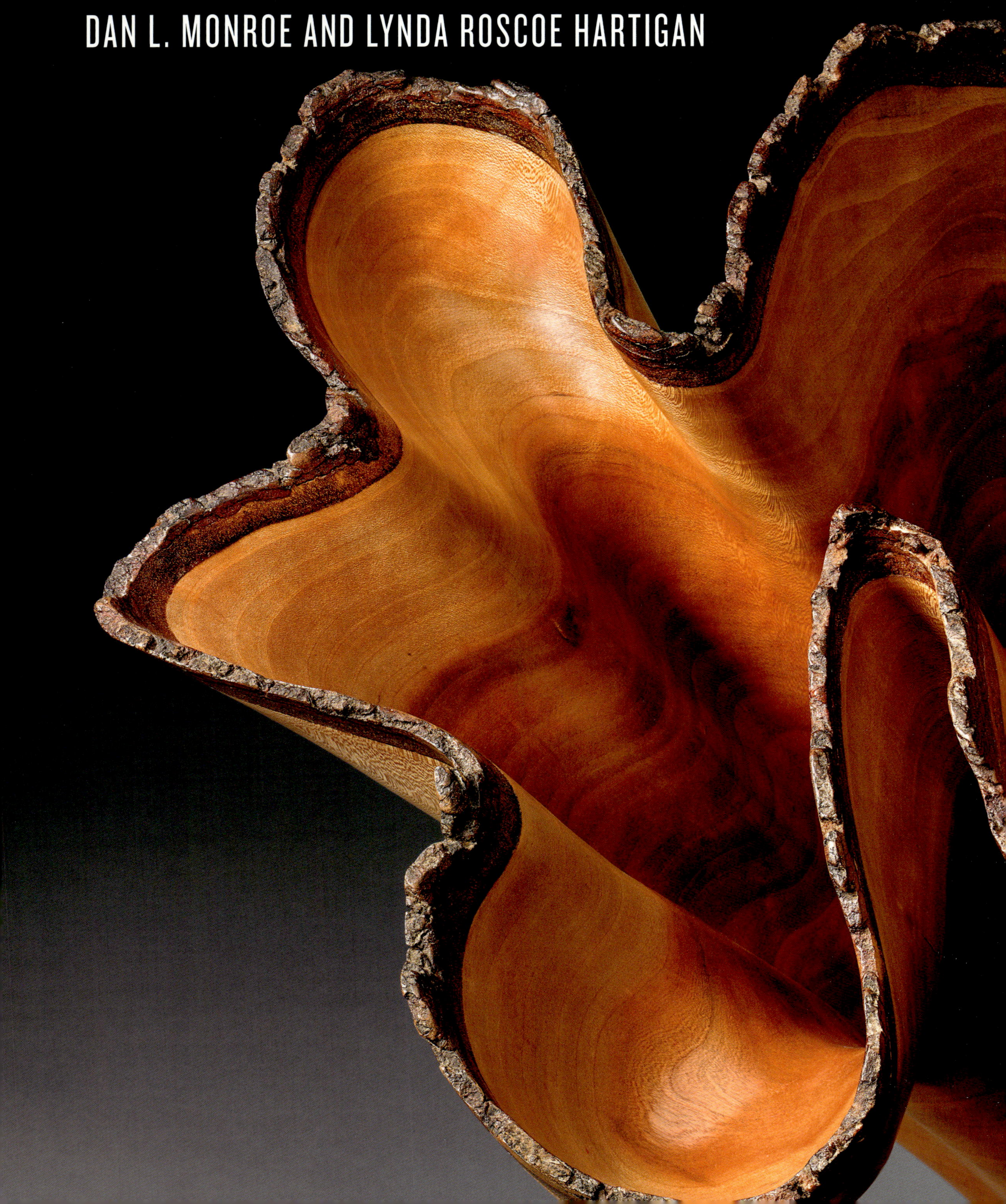

Wood is the most humanly intimate of all materials. Man loves his association with it, likes to feel it under his hand, sympathetic to his touch and to his eyes. Wood is universally beautiful to man.

–Frank Lloyd Wright

Silk, marble, leather, and even feathers and butterfly specimens–these materials and the preponderance of wood, from flooring to art, quickly announce that Bob and Lillian Montalto Bohlen have built a domestic environment that luxuriates in the textures, palette, multiplicity, and sensuality of nature. Similarly, antique rugs, historic African carvings and masks, contemporary Chinese ink paintings, paintings by modern and emerging American artists, and a global panoply of wood sculpture and objects attest to their immersion in the passionate and disciplined phenomenon of collecting. *Audacious: The Fine Art of Wood* honors the Bohlens' commitment to the marriage of nature and humanity, a marriage brokered through the hands of creativity.

Readily available, wood is flexible, durable, tactile, and symbolic. These properties have underwritten this material's logic and potential as a functional and artistic medium for centuries. Features like bark, grain, checks, burls, whorls, roots, and scale, as well as conditions like the degree of seasoning or growth stimuli caused by vines, rocks, or insects all determine what can be accomplished with a particular species or piece of wood. Any of these elements influence the ease or difficulty in turning, carving, or bending wood in order to create overall form and individual detail. An artist, artisan, or architect understands that these natural properties are not haphazard, and therefore often selects wood for these very features, working them to advantage. This holds true whether the object envisioned is to be a sculpture, a piece of furniture, a bowl, a building, or a column. Viewers, consumers, and collectors benefit from the same understanding because it provides the means to distinguish feats of nature from those of the maker.

The latter point quickly brings us to the matter of technical skill associated with those who work with wood. Proficiency is a mark of talent and esteem for many engaged in this practice or comparable endeavors. However, proficiency is not usually considered a positive or pertinent measure in more contemporary artistic quarters associated with assessment, interpretation, and criticism. Why? The ability to create visual and tactile effects by mastering the knowledge of wood's grains and properties, the use of specialized tools, and the coordination of hand, body, and eye suggest a predominantly physical realm of activity. Inherently, we are inclined to believe that something more physical can neither affect the higher cognitive functions of understanding and association nor create a truly aesthetic experience.

This inclination disregards an irrefutable fact: our sense of touch, which develops before our other senses, is an important tool of perception. Touch filters texture, shape, and temperature

Detail, Brad Sells, *Whirl*, 2003, (page 77). Peabody Essex Museum, Gift of Lillian Montalto Bohlen

to learn about our environment and to influence our behavior accordingly. These three properties—texture, shape, and temperature—carry diverse, elaborate messages and interpretations that stretch well beyond physical characteristics and activities into the realms of ideas and emotions. In short, our sense of touch is exploratory and inquisitive as it helps us create meaning, whether in cerebral, emotional, concrete, or creative form.

Picture the act of woodturning: the artist moves a piece of wood while a stationary tool, a lathe, cuts and shapes it. Understanding haptic perception, the process of discovering objects through touch, plays an important role in readjusting our estimation of the relationship between technical skill and aesthetic achievement. Thanks to our omnipresent skin, tactile sensory information enters our nervous system from every single part of the body. Haptics owes its effectiveness to the unique ability of the sense of touch to encode and decipher many different object properties simultaneously. We do this most efficiently by enveloping and manipulating an object with our whole hand and integrating information across our fingers. The more often someone experiences a type of touch, the better able that person's brain becomes in interpreting that information because new and more complex neural pathways and communication are being developed. With extended experience, for example, a tool or material held in the hand can become encoded as if it is an extension of the limb.

Many of our everyday interactions with the world involve coordinated visual-haptic perceptions, for we see not just with our eyes but also with our hands. By handling an object or material as well as looking at it, we access a much larger, richer pool of information and insights, while also strengthening the ability to create memories and long-term knowledge of what an object is, how it operates, or how to make it. Our hands have multiple touch points, which means that the fingers and palm collaborate as a 3-D "shape gauge." Our eyes have a single viewpoint, so visual exploration does not involve a similar encompassing mechanism for gauging shape, but instead contributes acuity for detecting and resolving, or unifying, details. Spatial visualization, which is at the heart of creating three-dimensional objects and architecture, is an ability that varies depending on how individuals can combine visual and haptic cues.

In this context, we can expand our understanding of how significant the connection between an artist and his or her artwork is because of the need to touch it in order to create it. This is particularly relevant for appreciating those who materialize the aesthetic fundamentals of rhythm, design, balance, and proportion in three-dimensional objects. A sculptural attitude also elevates contrast as a design principle: high and low relief, positive and negative space, fine and broad rendering, smooth and crunchy texture, repetition and variation of motifs, lights and darks afforded by stain, paint, and ink. An encounter with the unabashed sensuality, elegance, intricacy, or boldness of artists who turn wood to their creative intent ensures that their command of the tactile and sculptural will excite us viscerally and visually as fellow creatures of touch and sight.

Experiencing a private collection is a privilege and a treat. It is also a crossroads of intimacy and connection, providing access to the achievements of artists, as well as revealing the sensibility, thought processes, and aspirations of a collector. The dynamism of Bob and Lillian Montalto Bohlen as a collecting duo is easily matched by the avidity with which they have shared their collection with the public for the past two decades. Again and again, the Bohlens have opened their house, their collection, and their knowledge and story banks to the small army of our staff who have worked on this project, and we thank Bob and Lillian for the professional and personal camaraderie that we have developed together. We are honored that they have given forty-seven key works from their collection to the museum, an acquisition unveiled in this exhibition and publication. As we build out the Peabody Essex Museum's commitment to the creativity of our time, we are moving far beyond the usual territory described by the term contemporary art. Instead, we are embracing a wider and deeper pool of creative expression, from the handmade to the digital, the local to the global, and the visual to the multisensory and multidisciplinary.

Dean Lahikainen, our Carolyn and Peter Lynch Curator of American Decorative Art, has organized this project with imagination, diligence, and aplomb. Dean's discerning eye and skilled negotiations are evident in the Bohlens' generous gift of works to the museum, which in no small measure reflects their admiration for our transformation-oriented mission as well as his individual talent. Dean has graciously acknowledged our staff's interpretive, design, publishing, planning, and outreach contributions, and we applaud the collaborative commitment and energy that this represents. To the East India Marine Associates of the Peabody Essex Museum, we extend our appreciation for their support of this project and for their annual generosity to our overall exhibition program.

Finally, let us join in celebrating the ninety-seven artists featured here for the audacity of their creativity. Their works touch us precisely because they embody the urge to embellish the natural with evidence of the human presence.

Dan L. Monroe
The Rose-Marie and Eijk van Otterloo Director and CEO

and

Lynda Roscoe Hartigan
The James B. and Mary Lou Hawkes Chief Curator

ACKNOWLEDGMENTS

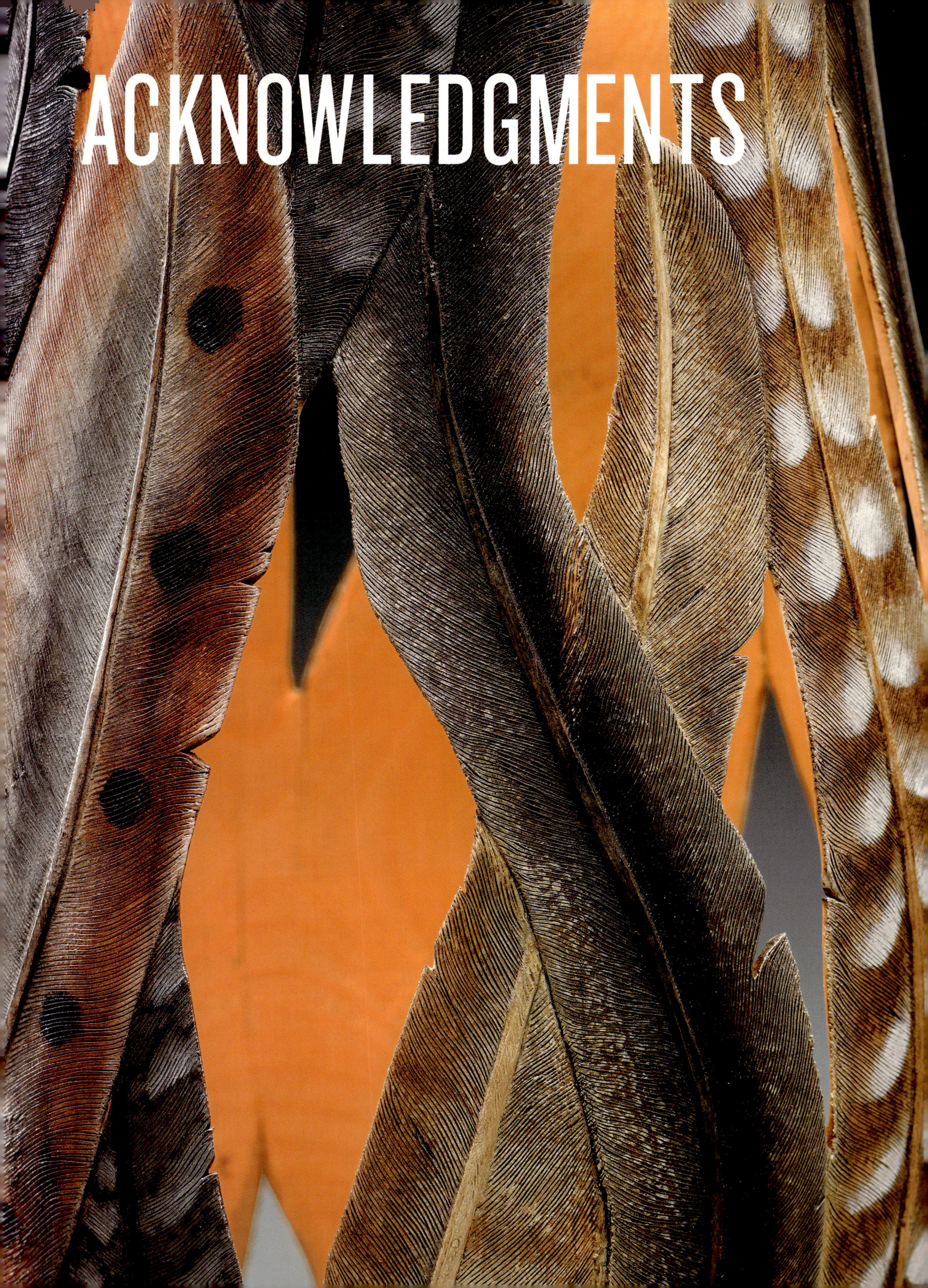

One of the greatest pleasures of being a museum curator is the opportunity to work with passionate collectors who are willing to share their vision, knowledge, and collection. This has certainly been the case with Bob and Lillian Montalto Bohlen, who have enthusiastically embraced all aspects of this project. They gave us great freedom in organizing the exhibition and publication and graciously accommodated all of the disruptive requests from our staff who needed access to their home. We also thank them for coordinating the photography by Terry Martin. But most of all, we are grateful for their very generous donation of forty-seven works from their collection to help us develop a comprehensive contemporary wood art collection at PEM.

Kathy Fredrickson, Director of Exhibition Research and Publishing, and her team consisting of Exhibition and Research Curator Paula Richter, Assistant Curator Catrina Hill, Editor Gail Spilsbury, and Digital Asset Manager Claire Blechman, produced this stunning volume working with freelance designer Jena Sher. Senior Photographer Walter Silver handled additional photography, and his dedication to excellence brings to life many of the works on the following pages.

Many people throughout the wood art world gladly provided helpful information, including: Sasha Ali, Craft & Folk Art Museum; Betty Bothereau, L'Attitude Gallery; Katlie Bowles and Mark Lindquist, Lindquist Studios; Dennis Eggemeyer, Spirits of the Wind Gallery; Rusty Freeman, Cedarhurst Center for the Arts; Giles Gilson, Woodturner; Rima Girnius, Figge Art Museum; Becky Hart and Terry Segal, The Detroit Institute of Arts; Julia Konkell, Bellevue Art Museum; Albert LeCoff, Center for Art in Wood; Raymond Leier, del Mano Gallery; Carr McCuiston, The Signature Shop and Gallery; Tib Shaw, AAW Gallery of Wood Art; Greg S. Smith, Woodturner; Freya Cooper Kiddie, Sarah Meyerscough Gallery; Ann-Marie White, The Suter Art Gallery Te Aratoi o Whakatu; William Zimmer, William Zimmer Gallery.

I want to personally thank the artists who generously shared their observations about the Bohlens and their legacy, including David Ellsworth, Ron Gerton, Binh Pho, and Betty Scarpino. Each of these artists also kindly wrote about their personal perspectives for the book, along with two others, Alain Mailland and Michael Mode. I also want to thank Hugh McKay for sharing his stories about the Bohlens, and Kevin Wallace, who has written so much about the history of the movement, for his informed comments. Verlyn Klinkenborg's essay provides a thoughtful and provocative way to think about contemporary wood art and we are grateful that he was willing to take on the task.

In the early stages of planning the exhibition, the museum's Curator of The Present Tense Trevor Smith and the New York-based artist and designer Sebastian Errazuriz provided useful insights into the unique nature of this collection and offered suggestions for its installation as an exhibition. This task ultimately fell to the museum's Director of Exhibition Design David Seibert, Exhibition Project Manager Kurt Weidman, and Graphic Designer Jackie Traynor, who together produced an exciting design, working with the Director of Exhibition Planning Priscilla Danforth and Exhibition Projects Coordinator Annie Lundsten. Gavin Andrews, Assistant Director for Family, Student, and Teacher Programs, capably handled the interpretation, working under the leadership of the Chief of Education and Interpretation Juliette Fritsch. Gavin worked closely with Integrated Media Director and Assistant Director, Jim Olson and Ed Rodley, to produce the interactive components.

All of this activity has been accomplished under the watchful eye of the museum's Chief Curator Lynda Roscoe Hartigan and Director Dan L. Monroe, who have enthusiastically embraced contemporary wood art as an exciting and viable new collecting area for PEM. Finally, I want to thank my wife Elizabeth, who again proved to be a useful sounding board for ideas and problem solving, providing the kind of support that always leads to success.

Dean Lahikainen
The Carolyn and Peter Lynch Curator of American Decorative Art

Detail, Frank Sudol and Cam Merkle, *Hawks & Owls*, 2000 (page 164)

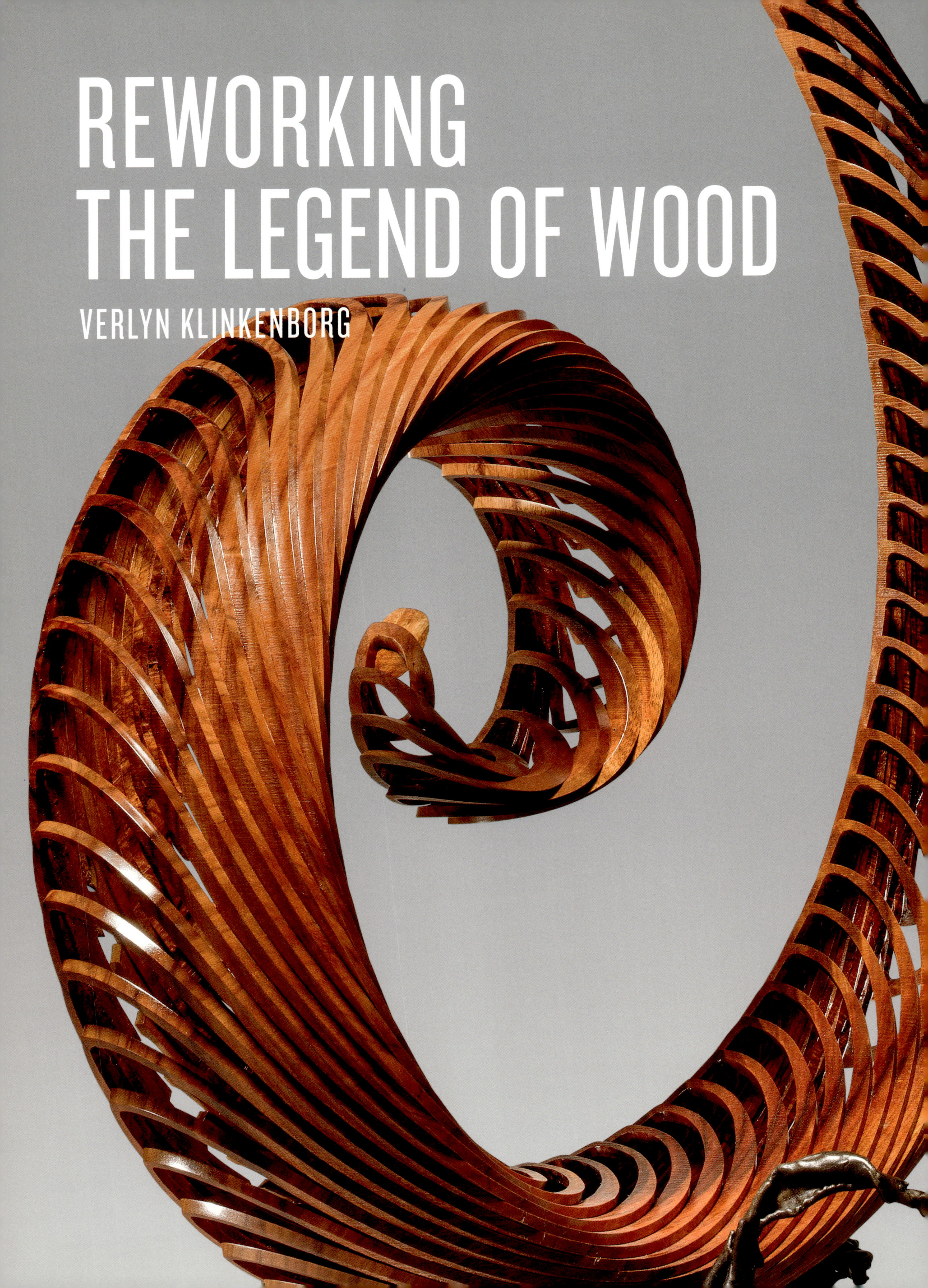
REWORKING
THE LEGEND OF WOOD
VERLYN KLINKENBORG

The eye is easily fooled, which is why we have a familiar phrase–trompe l'oeil–for fooling the eye. But the sense of touch is not so easily tromped. It's a keen judge of reality, and it incorporates an inner scale of weights and balances with which we intuitively weigh the things around us. We know from long experience just how heavy the world is. The surprise caused by fooling our inner scale is greater, I think, than the surprise of fooling the eye. It toys with our innate sense of gravity, which is the constant of constants in our lives. And, after all, we so rarely get to be surprised in that way. One of the fundamental lessons of childhood is "Don't touch!"–a lesson not easily set aside.

Suppose you're at the Museum of Modern Art contemplating Brancusi's *Bird in Space*–or one of Houdon's marble busts of Voltaire in the National Gallery, or perhaps a scrimshaw whale tooth in the Peabody Essex Museum (figs. 1, 2, and 3). Everything you know about the heft, the feel, the density of these objects is an inference–sight filling in for touch, which is the sense that goes to the museum only by proxy. According to the official record, the Brancusi sculpture has age and height and depth and width, but we are never told its weight. It's as though that datum were immaterial. "Bronze," the catalogue record says, and indeed Brancusi's sculpture looks like highly polished bronze. But the only sense that could put its materiality to the test–does it feel like bronze? Is it as heavy as bronze?–is the very one we're prohibited from using.

I mention these things because I happen to have picked up and held several of the remarkable works in the Montalto Bohlen Collection. One by one, the collector, Bob Bohlen, handed them to me with a look of anticipation. I knew what to expect–grams instead of kilograms, weightlessness not weight–but my brain somehow couldn't warn my hands in time. My eyes told them how heavy Eucled Moore's untitled urn (page 116) should be, and yet it wasn't. *Trompe la main,* I suppose. It's a trick that for some reason works just as well the second time and the time after that. It never gets old. The balance between eye and hand–the sense of proportion linking what we see and what we expect to feel–is so deeply rooted in us that it's almost inviolable.

Weightlessness is an example of the legerdemain that lies behind many of the works you'll see in the coming pages. They're all works in wood, but their real medium is the viewer's expectations, expectations aroused not so much by the shapes, geometric or organic, but by wood itself. This is a planet of many densities, and it seems somehow miraculous that the finest, most ubiquitous materials of medium density–soft enough to be easily worked, hard enough to endure–simply grow up naturally among us in the form of trees. There's a global forest to be found in the works of these artists, though it's a grove that would unsettle any naturalist who found these species growing together. Here, tropic and temperate forests merge, though the tropics prevail. There are blue mahoe, white ash, white pine, pink ivory, purpleheart, yellowheart, black walnut, red maple, and Osage orange. There are boxwood and cottonwood and rosewood and redwood; bloodwood, satinwood, kingwood, basswood. There are spaltings and quiltings and all the torturous involutions that show up in the burls of madrone and bimblebox and thuya and maple. There are branches, trunks, roots, knees, and crotches, all of them suggesting an analogical kinship with the human body.

Detail, Ron Gerton, *Revolution Evolution,* 2012
(page 85)

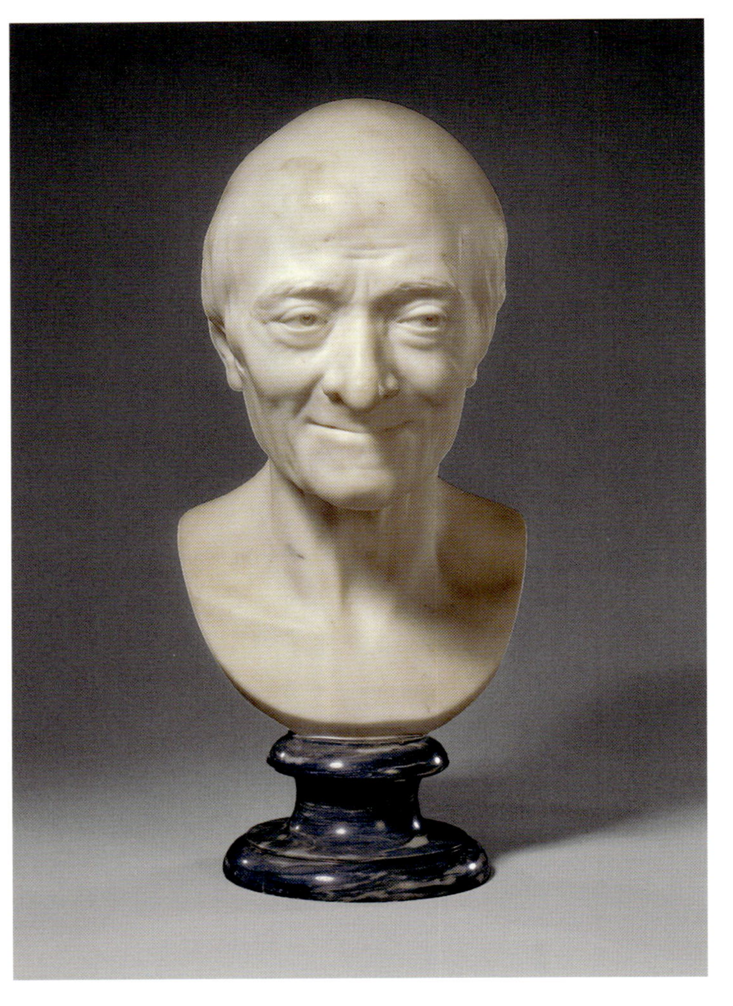

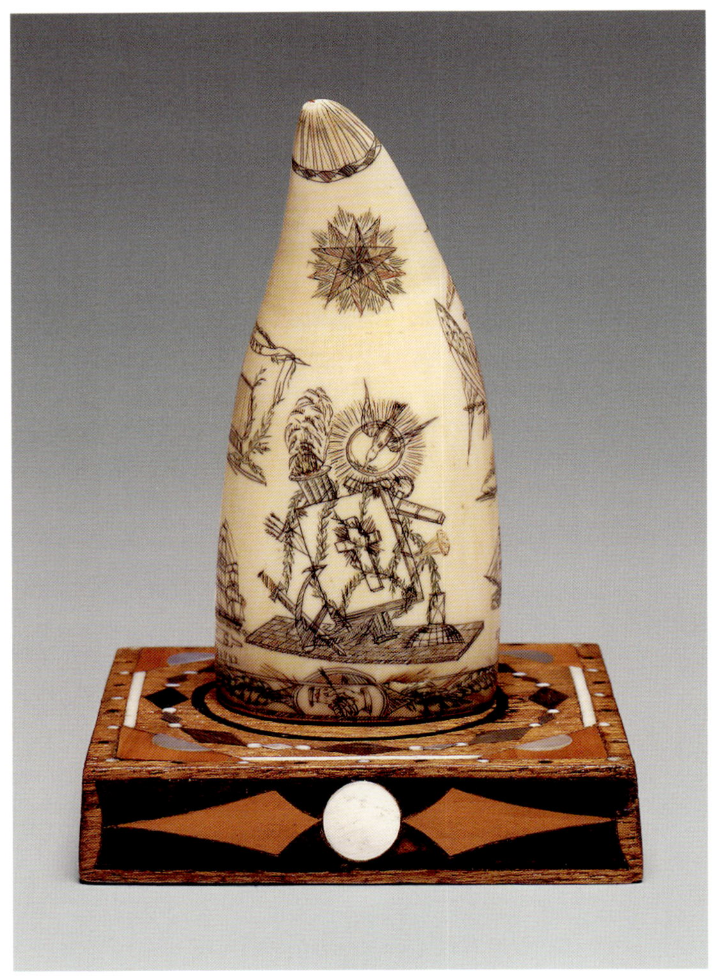

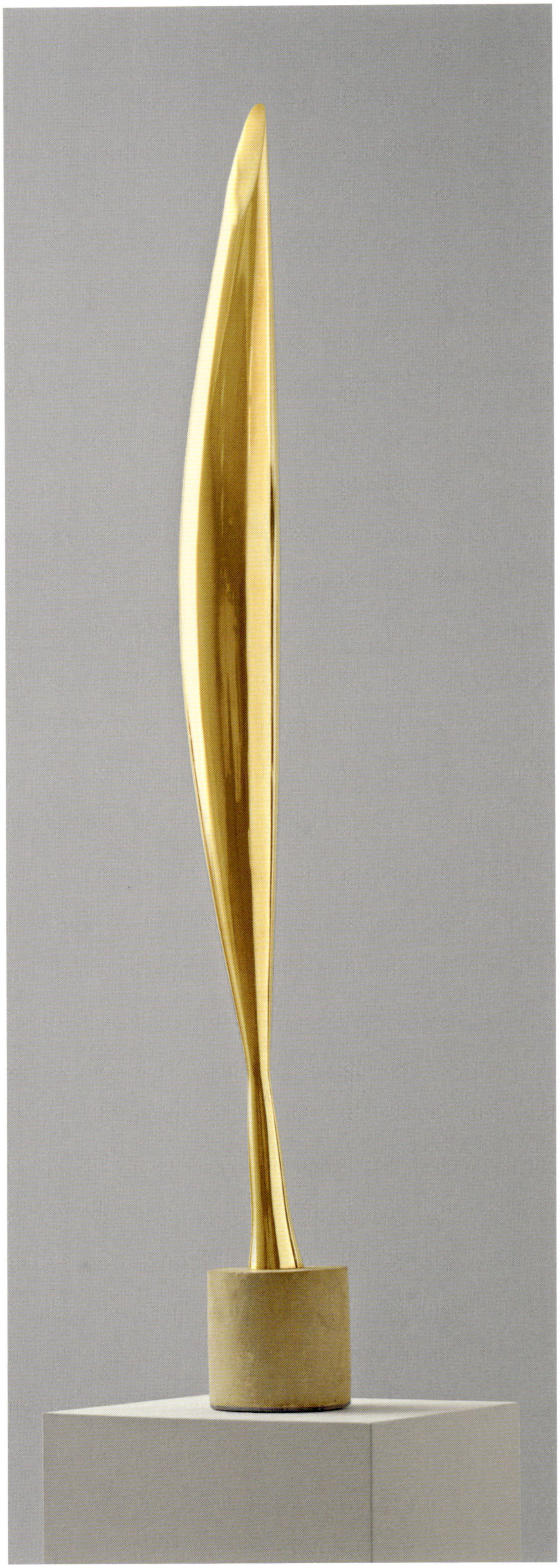

But what there is *not,* overwhelmingly, is the massiveness of wood. The technique that underlies most of these works is woodturning, which is essentially the art of removing material from a spinning blank of solid wood. That may sound a little paradoxical or reductive, like calling classical sculpture the art of removing marble. But an expert woodturner—a woodturning artist—is above all an expert at creating voids: shapely voids, intricate voids, regular and irregular voids, but voids nonetheless. And this is where the material properties of wood are so serviceable. Even reduced to its thinnest skin—devoid of most of its substance and now nearly weightless—it is the trick of wood and its cells, its rays, its grain, still to suggest the massive organism from which it comes. These works are all made of wood, and yet the wood in these works winks back at us, a gossamer kind of wood that merely alludes to its former state, when it was still standing, still timber.

Somehow that makes these works—the majority of them—more essentially wooden than they seem at first—wooden not in the sense of being static or, perhaps, un-balletic, but in the sense of celebrating their organic origins, no matter how far from the organism they may have strayed. It's easier to see this if you imagine these turnings and artifices and objects in an artistic continuum that includes the extraordinary sculptures of Tilman Riemenschneider (fig. 4), who worked in Bavaria between 1483 and 1531, and the plywood boxes of Donald Judd, made mostly in the 1970s (fig. 5).

Though the visible grain of the wood survives in the works of both Riemenschneider and Judd, it is, in some sense, really meant to disappear. Riemenschneider worked mainly in limewood, which was chosen for its even, light grain, qualities that essentially allowed it to vanish when painted in pure colors. Judd's boxes were manufactured (for him) of marine-grade Douglas fir plywood, and they too were meant, in a way, to dissolve and to banish the notion of the artist's personal craftsmanship. The difference? Judd's plywood was meant to be absorbed into theory, to embody the mental tracings he had worked out in his pathfinding essay, "Specific Objects," which was published in 1964. They were meant to become pure form, works in which three dimensions conquered the two dimensions of traditional painting.

And where do the works in the Montalto Bohlen Collection fit? They are neither sacred nor, for the most part, representational, unlike Riemenschneider's sculptures. Nor are they industrial in spirit or purely abstract, like Judd's boxes. What they share with Riemenschneider and Judd, besides the use of wood, is a character that is all too easy to call obsession, an absolute insistence on perfection. They remind us that an artist's job is finding the power, the wherewithal to cause the work to be made, to transcend the imagining of it. For some artists—the greatest ones, I think—the reality of the finished work is so forceful that it allows the question of technique to subside almost completely. When we wonder how works of that caliber came to be made, the answer seems to lie in the nature of the artist, not in the conquest of the artist's materials.

Opposite, clockwise:

Figure 1 Jean-Antoine Houdon, *Voltaire,* 1778, marble, 14 3/8 x 8 3/8 x 8 3/8 in. (36.5 x 21.3 x 21.3 cm). Chester Dale Collection. National Gallery of Art, Washington, D.C., 1963.10.240

Figure 2 Constantin Brancusi (1876–1957), *Bird in Space,* 1928, bronze (unique cast), 54 x 8 1/2 x 6 1/2 in. (137.2 x 21.6 x 16.5 cm). The Museum of Modern Art, New York, NY. Given anonymously. Artists Rights Society (ARS), NY. Digital Image © The Museum of Modern Art/Licensed by SCALA/Art Resource, NY

Figure 3 J. B. Walton, *Scrimshaw,* 1848 (reverse), tooth, wood, mother of pearl, ivory, 5 1/2 x 4 x 4 in. (13.97 x 10.16 x 10.16 cm). Peabody Essex Museum, Salem, Massachusetts, M1834

But the objects in the Bohlen Collection are different. They insist, each in its own way, on the technical achievement that produced them. They are virtuoso pieces, which means that the sense of their virtuosity—their technical mastery—never really goes away. No matter what else we're meant to see in them, we're meant to go on seeing the skill, the mastery that went into their making. The grain of the wood may disappear under a finish that looks like porcelain or glass. All trace of "wood"—an organic legend of sorts—may disappear beneath the layering of symbolic narrative, as in the works of Binh Pho. But nearly every work on display here makes us wonder how it was made, whether we're wondering at the skill of the artist, the unbelievable punctilio of his performance, or the windswept concentration of mind and purpose. The work stands between the viewer and the artist, not just an object to be contemplated but also a sign of the difference between the viewer and the artist. Many artists, these days, construct what you might call a narrative of process, a kind of self-annotation of the work in progress, meant to be considered right alongside the work itself. That kind of narrative keeps us close to the artist's intention, while usually saying little about the province of skill or technical mastery. Many of the works in the Montalto Bohlen Collection do something similar. But no account of them would be complete without acknowledging a technical mastery that goes far beyond explanation. In its own way, each of these works embodies an almost feverish discipline—days and months and years of relentless practice.

What binds the works in the collection together, besides the things I've already mentioned, is their lavish discarding of function. You could put some of these works to use—some of them look like familiar vessels, like urns and bowls and vases—but the use would be trivial, a misappropriation. They are almost entirely antithetical to Judd's work in plywood, most of which was fabricated for him, not by him. Much of Judd's work seems to shimmer within two realities at once. Chair? Stool? Sculpture? It makes no difference. Judd manages to preserve the utility of the crafts tradition while completely discarding what you might call the vanity of the craftsman who must make the work himself. The objects in the Montalto Bohlen Collection do just the opposite. They discard the utility of the crafts tradition—they discard the very idea of "craft"—while revering the personal labors of the craftsman.

This helps explain, I think, some of the uneasiness it's possible to feel in the presence of these objects. They are stunning but often, it seems, slightly out of register, as if we had trouble bringing them into focus. Again, this is a matter of the viewer's expectations. The aspiration in these objects is obvious, but what is being aspired to? The technical mastery is evident, but it can seem like an end in itself, the solving of a set of obliquely elaborate problems. The narrative or symbolic meaning of many of these objects is inscribed into their surface or form (or materials) with a deliberateness we simply don't expect to see in "pure" works of art. And, as I've suggested, many of them contain a kind of tricksterism that can't be felt simply by looking at them. They must be handled to be believed.

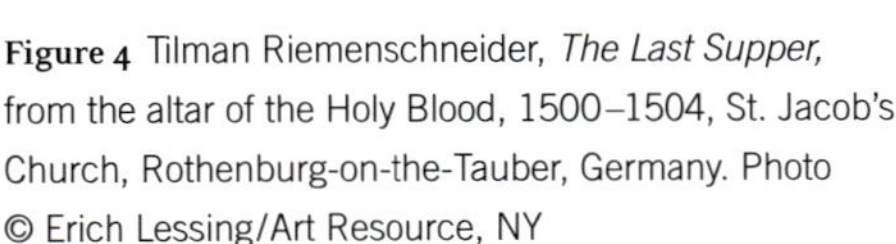

Figure 4 Tilman Riemenschneider, *The Last Supper,* from the altar of the Holy Blood, 1500–1504, St. Jacob's Church, Rothenburg-on-the-Tauber, Germany. Photo © Erich Lessing/Art Resource, NY

Figure 5 Donald Judd, *Untitled,* 1976. Dia Art Foundation, gift of the Brown Foundation. Photo by Bill Jacobson

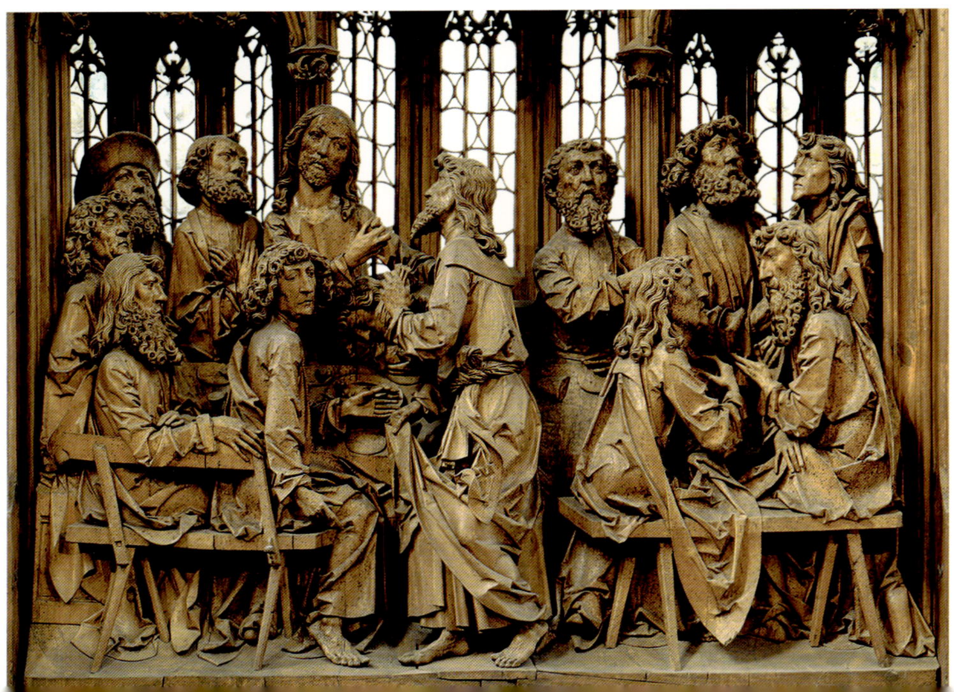

Gathered together like this, the wooden objects in the Montalto Bohlen Collection look, at one moment, like a gathering of technical solipsisms and, at another, like a coherent body of work produced by artists working along similar lines. They are both. There's certainly something personally driven about creating an urn from 13,400 pieces of mahogany, maple, Padauk, and wenge, (page 116) or turning a nearly enclosed globe from a kind of synthesized wood that once took the form of comic books (page 156). Yet what you see here is also the result of a kind of technical sharing and teaching that seems to arise more naturally from the tradition of apprenticeship within the crafts tradition than it does from the solitary zeal of the high artist. Look at these works closely enough, and you will see the lineages that branch among them. Among objects that can often look miserly–by which I mean having the self-secluding focus of the miser–you can also usually find a spirit of deep generosity, the feeling of collaborating in a wide-reaching exploration of the woodturner's art.

The idea of the "outsider" artist–a figure like Simon Rodia or Henry Darger, for instance–has almost lost its usefulness. These days, it seems, many artists would like to be able to add the word "outsider" to their curriculum vitae, though the oblivion or unawareness the word implies is hard to come by. An artist may be an outsider socially or culturally, but the art world shows a sometimes lopsided eagerness to bring outsider art inside. The very qualities that once characterized outsider art–unrelenting focus on a personal vision without concern for conventional cultural boundaries (or perhaps even awareness of them)–seem, these days, like the basic terms of artistic heroism.

The artists represented in the Montalto Bohlen Collection are not outsider artists. And yet the uneasiness of their work sometimes arouses a peculiar, fleeting kinship with the effects caused by outsider art. What do we notice in outsider art? It's easy to feel that you're looking into worlds within worlds. It's easy to become almost painfully aware of the artist's absorption in the technical task at hand. It's easy to find yourself thinking in terms of "activity" rather than "object," to find yourself looking through the work to the artist at work and wondering about the psychological forces that keep him there. It's easy to detect a repurposing of conventional materials. This may sound like it describes Joseph Cornell or William Blake and his angels. But it also describes, say, Dale Nish and his work in wormy ash (page 66).

You, the viewer, have some work to do here. These objects do not fall easily into a togetherness. The names that have been used to group them–wood art, for instance–are makeshift at best. They share a bond–the use of woodturning, the use of wood–but they share no single aesthetic or psychological bond. They come at you from all directions, and you will have to welcome them or fend them off, one by one, as you see fit. The tools you already have for understanding art or craftsmanship may not fit the task these objects propose merely by existing. Suffice it to say that they do exist, and here they are, and hence the curious, fascinating challenge of meeting them one by one.

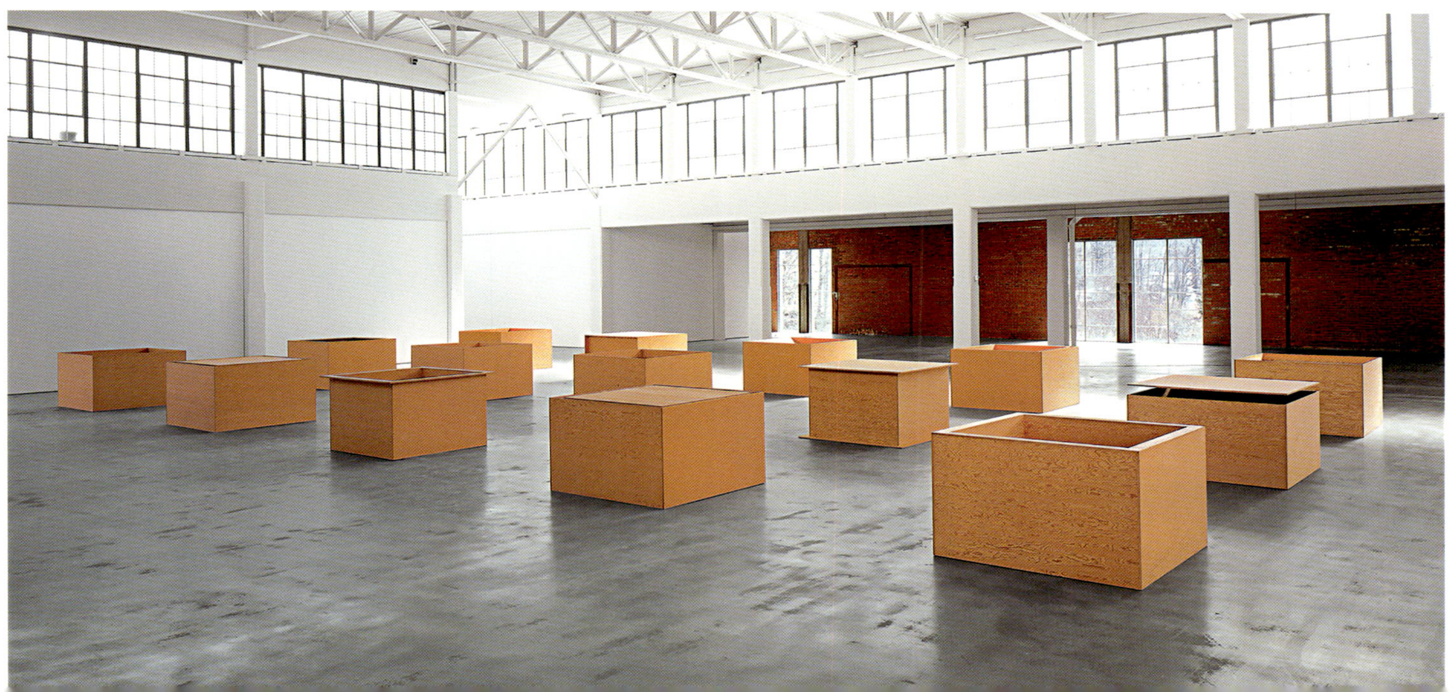

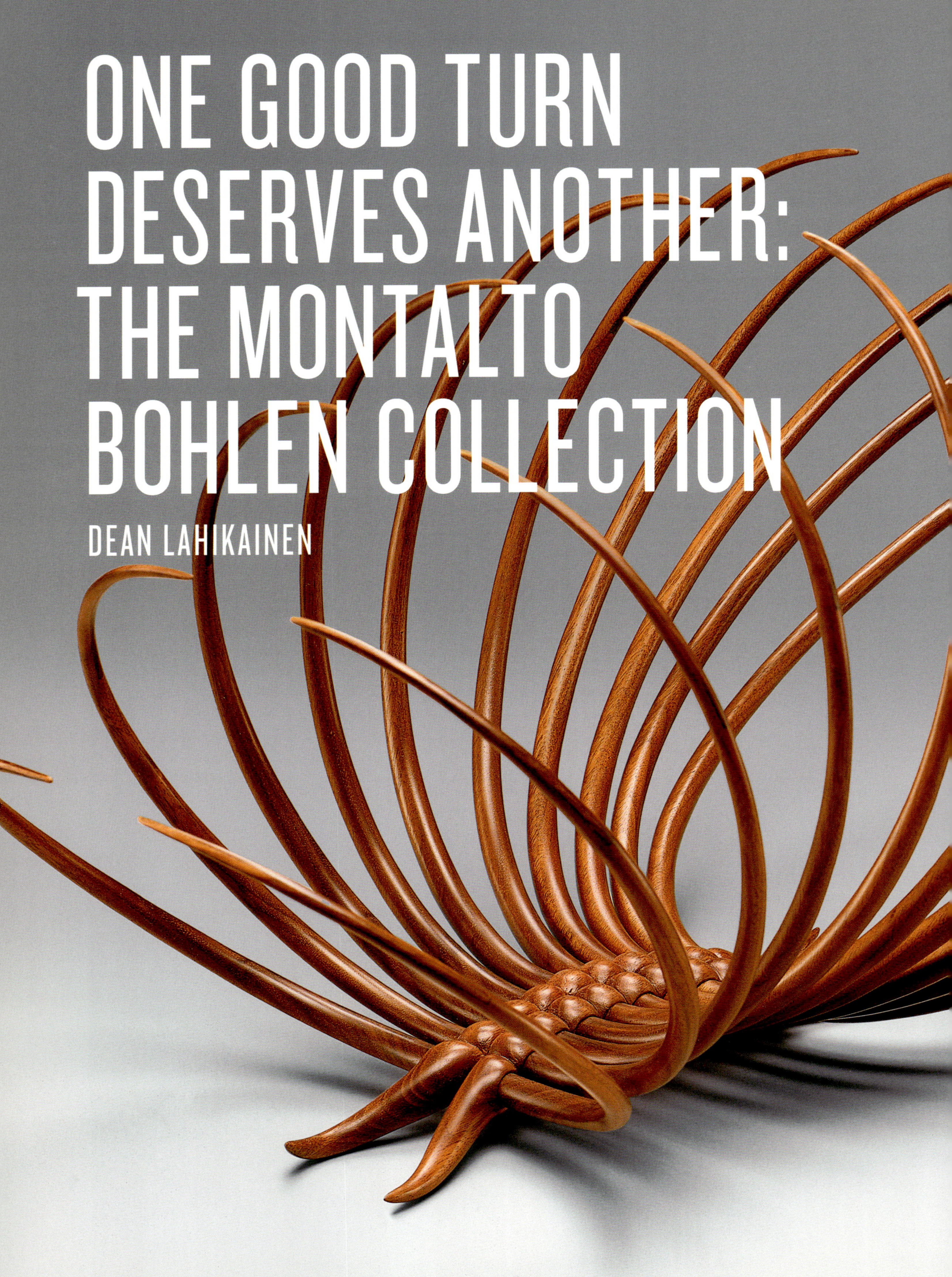

ONE GOOD TURN DESERVES ANOTHER: THE MONTALTO BOHLEN COLLECTION

DEAN LAHIKAINEN

Bob Bohlen and his wife Lillian Montalto Bohlen have played a significant role in promoting the field of artistic woodturning, often referred to as wood art. When the Bohlens started collecting contemporary wood art in 1997, many of the artists who used the lathe as their primary tool were still exploring "the boundaries of the vessel aesthetic to find a new freedom of expression long enjoyed by ceramists and glass artists."[1] Artists, such as Betty Woodman and Dale Chihuly, reimagined the artistic possibilities of their respective mediums—ceramics and glass—by producing exciting new sculptural forms that challenged long-held beliefs about the distinctions between art, craft, and design. While wood has been used to create sculptural forms in many cultures for centuries, its long association with folk art and the production of common utilitarian objects, including furniture, tablewares, and architectural details, prejudiced some people's perceptions of its appropriateness to create fine art. Historically, most sculptors have chosen more permanent materials, such as marble, bronze, and other metals. Yet, a number of sculptors successfully empowered wood as a medium during the twentieth century, among them Constantin Brancusi, Isamu Noguchi, Louise Nevelson, and Martin Puryear. More recently, wood has been embraced by a much wider array of artists and designers worldwide, further challenging traditional classifications and cultural meaning.[2]

Bob Bohlen had been involved in several fine art galleries in Los Angeles, Chicago, Ann Arbor, and Washington, Connecticut, in the 1980s and knew the discrepancy in the marketplace between what was considered fine art or craft. He saw the difference between the number of people who collected ceramic and glass works and those who collected wood art. Seeing growth potential in the wood art movement, he and Lillian enthusiastically joined the ranks of other collectors, gallery owners, and museum curators to promote turned wood as fine art.

Bob had also been successful in numerous business ventures, including cattle breeding and, with Lillian, real estate, so that they naturally took an entrepreneurial approach to collecting. Initially they hired four museum curators as consultants to determine the most important artists working with wood worldwide, a logical first step in building a collection. Early on Bob and Lillian displayed their independence. "As with all areas of study," noted Kevin Wallace, a historian of the movement, "a 'common knowledge' developed about which artists have been central to the growth of the field and which artists have created the most significant work. When Bob Bohlen entered the field, he did so with the spirit of an iconoclast, trusting his own eye and instincts, rather than this common knowledge. Having collected in other areas, including painting, furniture, and African art, he was well aware that he had entered into a field that was still undergoing the pains of adolescence. Like a coach or recruiter from a progressive university, he set about selecting artists based on a highly individual criteria and trusted those artists he saw talent in to suggest players who were similarly showing potential under the radar."[3]

As a mentor to business people throughout the world and as coauthor with artist Terry Martin of *Clarity: A 30 Day Foolproof Plan for Increasing Your Performance, Productivity and Profit* (2010),

Detail, Arthur Jones, *Exhibitionist*, 2001 (page 86)

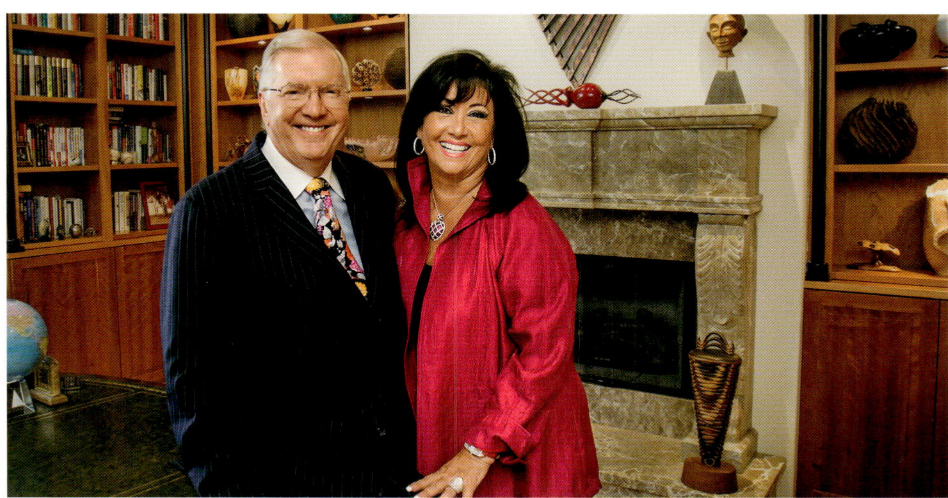

Robert and Lillian Montalto Bohlen in their library, Andover, Massachusetts, 2014

Bob early on saw the need to elevate the field by helping emerging artists become better businesspeople in terms of how they produced and sold their work. To jump-start this process, the Bohlens put eighteen artists on their payroll for a year or more to give them time and freedom to develop their artistry, without the worries of making a living in other ways. In return, Bob and Lillian had the first opportunity to acquire the best examples of the artists' works at lower prices. This Renaissance model of patronage generated some controversy within the wood art movement, especially from gallery owners and other collectors, but the Bohlens believed the arrangement was the best way to nurture raw talent and foster creativity. Binh Pho, now a leading figure in the field, recalled how early in his career he hoped to meet the Bohlens because he had heard that they "helped many emerging woodturners, inspiring their growth as artists." Frank Sudol once told Pho that Bob "had elevated his confidence, leading him to be a much better artist than he ever thought he would be."[4] Sudol produced the monumental ribbon vessels for the Bohlens in 2002 (fig. 2), in direct response to Bob's challenge to create larger and thinner forms with a more expressive use of color and texture. These are Sudol's largest works and among the most striking and colorful pieces in the Montalto Bohlen Collection.

The Bohlens' arrangement with certain artists also facilitated the purchase of works intended for donation to art museums. Bob and Lillian firmly believed a museum presence was the most effective way to affirm the work's artistic quality and elevate the standing of the individual artist, as well as wood art in general, within the fine art world. Just three years after becoming wood art collectors, the Bohlens donated 130 works to the Detroit Institute of Arts, a gift celebrated in the museum's exhibition and publication *The Fine Art of Wood* (2000). Four years later, the exhibition *Nature Transformed* marked the donation of a significant body of works to the University of Michigan Museum of Art. In all, the Bohlens have donated some 820 pieces to museums, including the Montreal Museum of Fine Arts, Saginaw Art Museum in Michigan, Mobile Museum of Art in Alabama, and the Museum of Arts and Design in New York. The recent donation of forty-seven works to the Peabody Essex Museum continues this generous legacy.

The Bohlens' approach to collecting has fostered deep personal relationships with many of the artists featured in this volume. Initially the Bohlens "didn't want to meet the artists," Binh Pho has commented. "They didn't want the relationship with the artists to affect their buying, but later they realized the importance of these relationships. [Lillian] explained that knowing the artists, and being aware of the positive change they brought to their lives and careers, was one of the greatest pleasures of their experience as collectors." Pho also remarked that unlike many collectors of his work, "Bob and Lillian know the story behind every piece that I have created."[5] The Bohlens understand the rich, complex imagery and symbolic meaning of the motifs Pho uses, such as the poppy (mystery) and dragonfly (military helicopters), to tell the story of his life (fig. 1). This level of personal interest enhances the collectors' enjoyment and strong attachment to each and every wood piece.

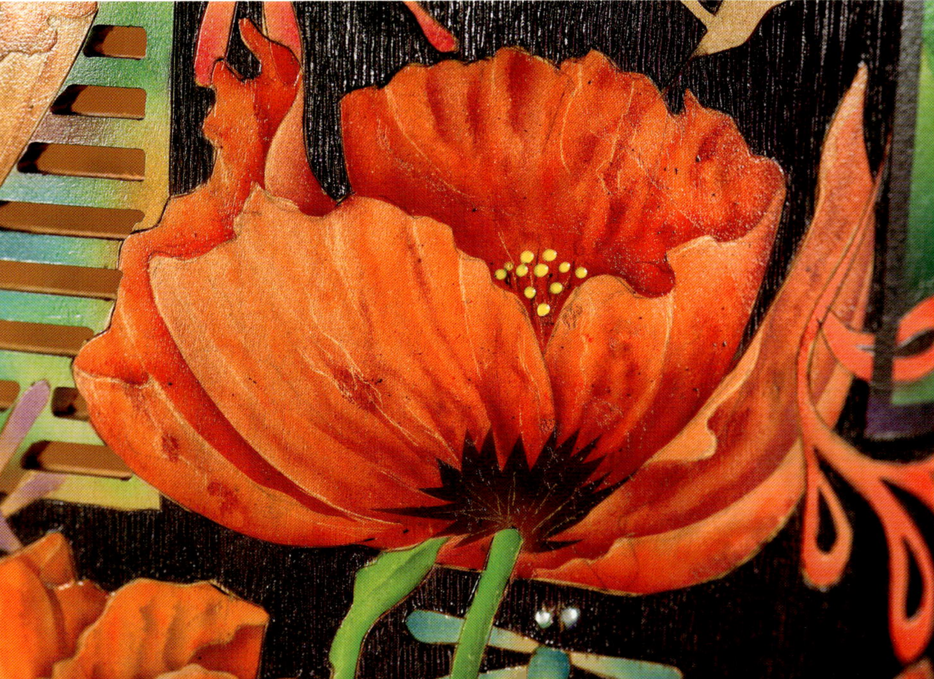

Figure 1 Detail, Binh Pho, *Seven Poppies,* 2009 (page 173)

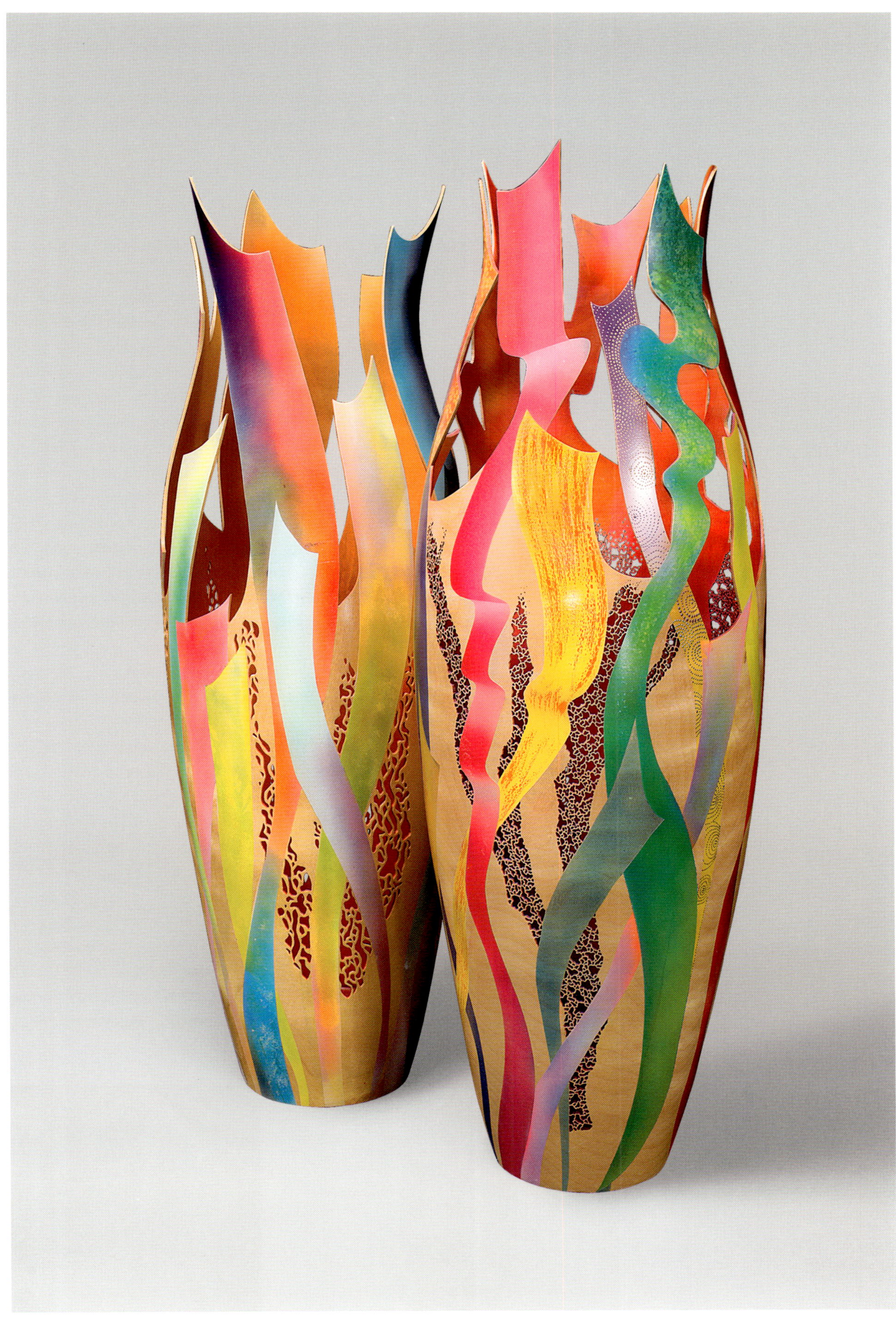

Figure 2 Frank Sudol, *Giant Ribbons #1* and *#2*, 2002 (page 138)

Artist Ron Gerton once observed that "Bob and Lillian collect with a passion based on their love of art pieces, love of makers, and love of material. . . . Bob does not follow the trends of what to collect, but collects what he finds a deep connection with."[6] Before making a purchase, the Bohlens consider the work three times to make sure it has "positive energy." They have filled their home and real-estate offices with art, because, as Bob notes in *Clarity,* the art has "a very positive influence on people's creativity and their life, once they begin to understand it and focus on it. . . . If you surround people with art in the place where they work, it encourages a more creative psyche."[7]

It is difficult to apply a traditional art historical lens to fully evaluate the Montalto Bohlen Collection, because the definition of what constitutes wood art today is changing as artists continue to explore new techniques and materials in search of their own distinct voices and styles. One can point to the handful of early, classic works in the Montalto Bohlen Collection by some of the pioneers of the movement—Bob Stocksdale, Melvin Lindquist, Dale Nish, and David Ellsworth—and assume that Bob and Lillian set out to build a comprehensive historical collection, as they acquired many of these early works long after they were made. Some works were purchased from Dr. Irving Lipton, one of the pioneer collectors of wood art, just before his death in 2001. But the idea of comprehensiveness is quickly challenged when you consider the number of accomplished wood artists represented in other recently published private collections, including those formed by David and Ruth Woodbury, Fleur and Charles Bresler, Jane and Arthur Mason, and Dr. Irving Lipton, who are not found in the Montalto Bohlen Collection and vice versa. Kevin Wallace, curator of the Lipton collection, noted that while many collectors feature "the usual suspects," the Bohlens "have developed a collection that surprises and informs. It is a collection that indeed questions the common knowledge . . . something history has a way of reinterpreting due to the impact of individuals who change the game."[8]

The approximately three hundred works currently in the Montalto Bohlen Collection reflect the personal tastes of the owners and their entrepreneurial approach to collecting during the past seventeen years. One hundred and seven artists from eight different countries are represented. The majority are from the United States, where the wood art movement began, but the collection also includes artists from other countries who have settled here to work, such as Souphom and Souphong Manikhong from Laos and Binh Pho from Vietnam. Many of the artists supported by the Bohlens are represented by multiple works in their collection, including Binh Pho, Mark Bressler, Donald Derry, Ron Gerton, Giles Gilson, Matt Hatala, John Morris, Brad Sells, and Frank Sudol.

In her review of the exhibition of the Montalto Bohlen Collection at the Museum of Arts and Design in 2006, *New York Times* critic Grace Glueck found that the "range of techniques is dazzling as is the variety of woods," and that collectively these "splendid examples of the wood turner's art . . . [hold their] own as an aesthetic domain." But she also found some of

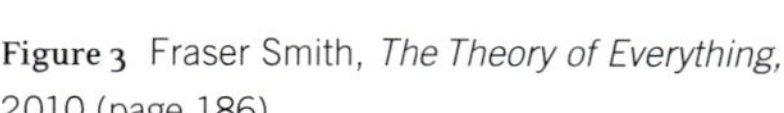

Figure 3 Fraser Smith, *The Theory of Everything,* 2010 (page 186)

Figure 4 Raphaelle Peale, *Venus Rising from the Sea—A Deception,* about 1822, oil on canvas, 29 1/8 x 24 1/8 in. (73.98 x 61.28 cm). The Nelson-Atkins Museum of Art, Kansas City, Missouri, William Rockhill Nelson Trust, 34–147

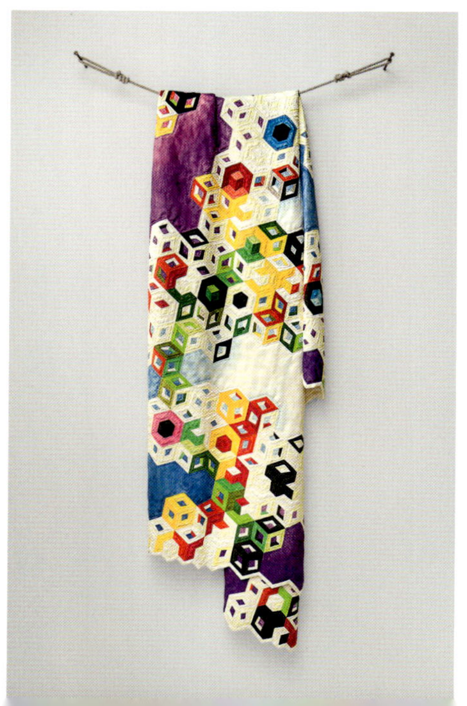

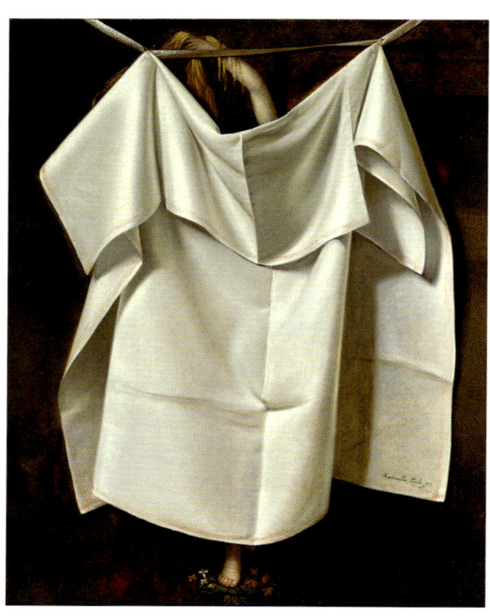

the works to be "cutesy, over fancy, dull, derivative, or kooky," suggesting that the collectors have been willing to push the boundaries of what constitutes wood art or good taste to encompass a much wider spectrum of artistic expression that goes beyond the sanctioned "usual suspects" found in other collections.[9] And indeed, the Bohlens have collected works that have nothing to do with a lathe, such as the trompe-l'oeil, three-dimensional quilt by Fraser Smith, carved entirely from wood (fig. 3). Suspended on a piece of real rope attached to the wall, it challenges easy classification but also clearly relates to the long tradition of trompe-l'oeil art by such American masters of realism as Raphael Peale, whose 1822 painting *Venus Rising from the Sea—A Deception* (fig. 4) creates an equally successful deception of hanging fabric. It also relates to the more recent work of Tom Eckert, who also carves hyperrealistic sculptures of draped cloth.

In a dynamic, changing field, historians will need to navigate through the politics of taste and competition to evaluate the array of abstract and realistic works dubbed wood art from a number of perspectives to determine which artists will stand the test of time and be seen as important to the development of the wood art movement. This has already been done to a large extent for the first generation of wood artists who have been celebrated in exhibitions and publications since the late 1970s.[10] The Bohlens have acquired a few iconic works from this first generation, works that shifted the boundaries of wood art in their day, such as Dale Nish's worm-eaten ash vessel of 1984 (page 66). Nish was one of the first artists to embrace the aesthetic beauty of the natural defects in wood and to link them to a concern for the environment. David Ellsworth, with his vessel of 1991 from his groundbreaking *Solstice Series* (page 127), was among the first artists to explore altering the natural characteristics of the wood surface using paint and a blow torch.

"As in any art," Glueck noted in her review, "the best works [in the Montalto Bohlen Collection] reflect a deep consideration of the medium's special possibilities and innovative attempts to explore them."[11] This philosophy has guided the Bohlens' search for new talent around the world, most recently evident in the acquisition of large-scale works by Brad Sells and Hunt Clark (pages 75 and 58, respectively). Each artist displays a new level of technical prowess and sense of volumetric form on a more monumental scale. Clark has also explored using a video projection to enliven the surface of one piece, taking wood art in an entirely new and exciting direction.[12]

Innovation, exploration, and collaboration are also evident in the work of Hugh McKay, who started his career carving wooden molds for a local aluminum manufacturer. McKay recalls being fascinated by the transformation that took place when his mold was cast in another material. After turning to more artistic woodworking in the early 1980s, he began incorporating bits of glass into his sculptures. He liked the effect of combining various textures and found that light passing through the glass added a striking new dimension to his work. In 1998 the Bohlens purchased a kiln for him, so that he could experiment with casting glass.

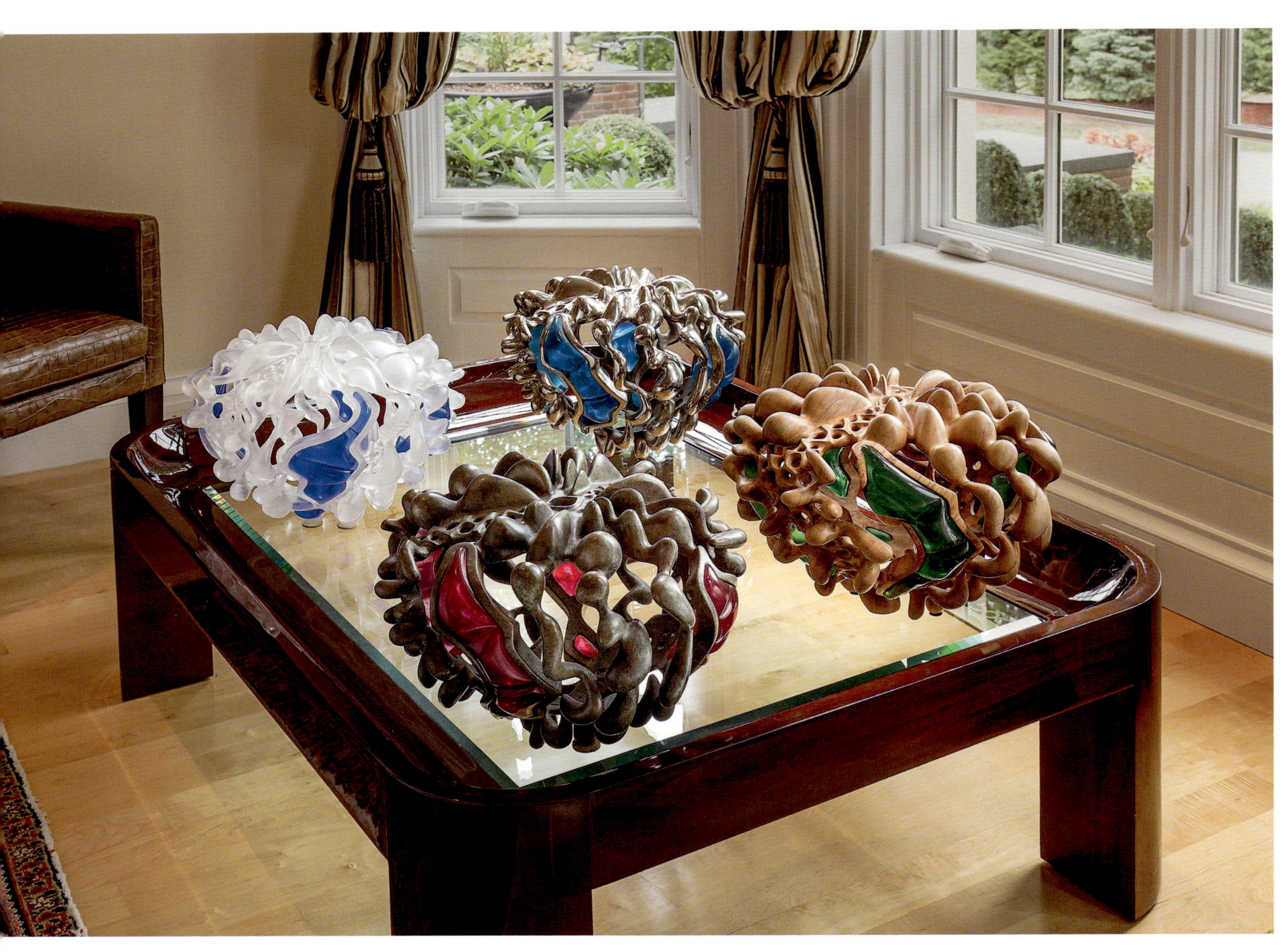

Figure 5 Hugh McKay, *Ruach*, 1998 (pages 96–97), displayed in the library of the Bohlen home, Andover, Massachusetts

This direction eventually led to attempts to cast some of his wood sculptures entirely in glass and, after establishing a relationship with a local foundry, in bronze or other metals.

This innovative exploration produced the three mixed-media works in the collection cast from his original wood sculpture. When grouped together (fig. 5), the four works create an exciting visual dialogue that changes the viewer's perception of each work, not only because of each material's difference in visual characteristics, be it shiny, dull, warm, or cold, but also because of our cultural perceptions of the value of each medium. Bronze is perceived as eternal, permanent, monumental, and classical; glass as ethereal and fragile because of the effects of transient light, most often associated with the stained glass windows in great cathedrals; and nickel as glamorous, celebratory, and expensive.

McKay mastered the casting process after many trials and errors using two additional kilns purchased by the Bohlens. He now casts glass works for other artists, including the glass version of the wood teapot by Binh Pho in the Montalto Bohlen Collection (page 171). In the Echoes of Place section of this book, Binh Pho comments that "Glass has the opposite characteristics of wood—it is flashy, brilliant, reflects color, and is rigid but fragile." When his two teapots are displayed together, they create a balance. The Bohlens recently added a bronze version of the teapot to the collection (page 171).

By sharing their business knowledge and wealth with emerging artists, the Bohlens have transformed many lives. When asked about the future of the wood art movement, Bob characteristically takes a business stance first, saying it all depends on income and sales and the ability of an artist to make a decent living selling his art. But he is also quick to note that the medium's future depends on artists creating superior works of art that move people, generate excitement, and have positive energy. Collectors and museum curators play a critical role in advancing the wood art movement by continuing to acquire works of exceptional quality. In any emerging field, new talent will always need to be nurtured and artistic exploration encouraged. Similarly, the wood art movement will continue to grow and possess a bright and dynamic future because of proactive patrons like Bob and Lillian Montalto Bohlen.

Notes

1 Bonita Fike with Michael Mendelson, *The Fine Art of Wood: The Bohlen Collection* (Detroit Institute of Arts, 2000), 6.

2 For recent exploration of wood see the Museum of Arts and Design, *Against the Grain: Wood in Contemporary Art, Craft and Design* (New York: Monacelli Press and the Museum of Arts and Design, 2012) and Barbara Glasner and Stephen Ott's *Wonder Wood: A Favorite Material for Design, Architecture and Art* (Basel: Birkhäuser, 2013).

3 Kevin Wallace to Dean Lahikainen, email, July 7, 2014, Peabody Essex Museum.

4 Binh Pho to Dean Lahikainen, email, July 1, 2014, Peabody Essex Museum.

5 Ibid.

6 Ron Gerton to Dean Lahikainen, email, July 10, 2014, Peabody Essex Museum.

7 Bob Bohlen and Terry Martin, *Clarity: A 30 Day Foolproof Plan for Increasing Your Performance, Productivity and Profit* (Wichita: Prime Concepts Group Publishing, 2010), 97.

8 Kevin Wallace to Dean Lahikainen, email, July 7, 2014, Peabody Essex Museum.

9 Grace Glueck, "Wood Art from the Bohlen Collection at Museum of Arts and Design," *New York Times*, June 2, 2006.

10 For historical surveys of the movement see *Wood Turning in North America Since 1930* (Wood Turning Center and Yale University Art Gallery, 2001) and *Conversations with Wood: The Collection of Ruth and David Waterbury* (Minneapolis Institute of Art, 2011).

11 Glueck, "Wood Art," June 2, 2006.

12 Museum of Arts and Design, *Against the Grain*, 92.

PERFECTED FORM

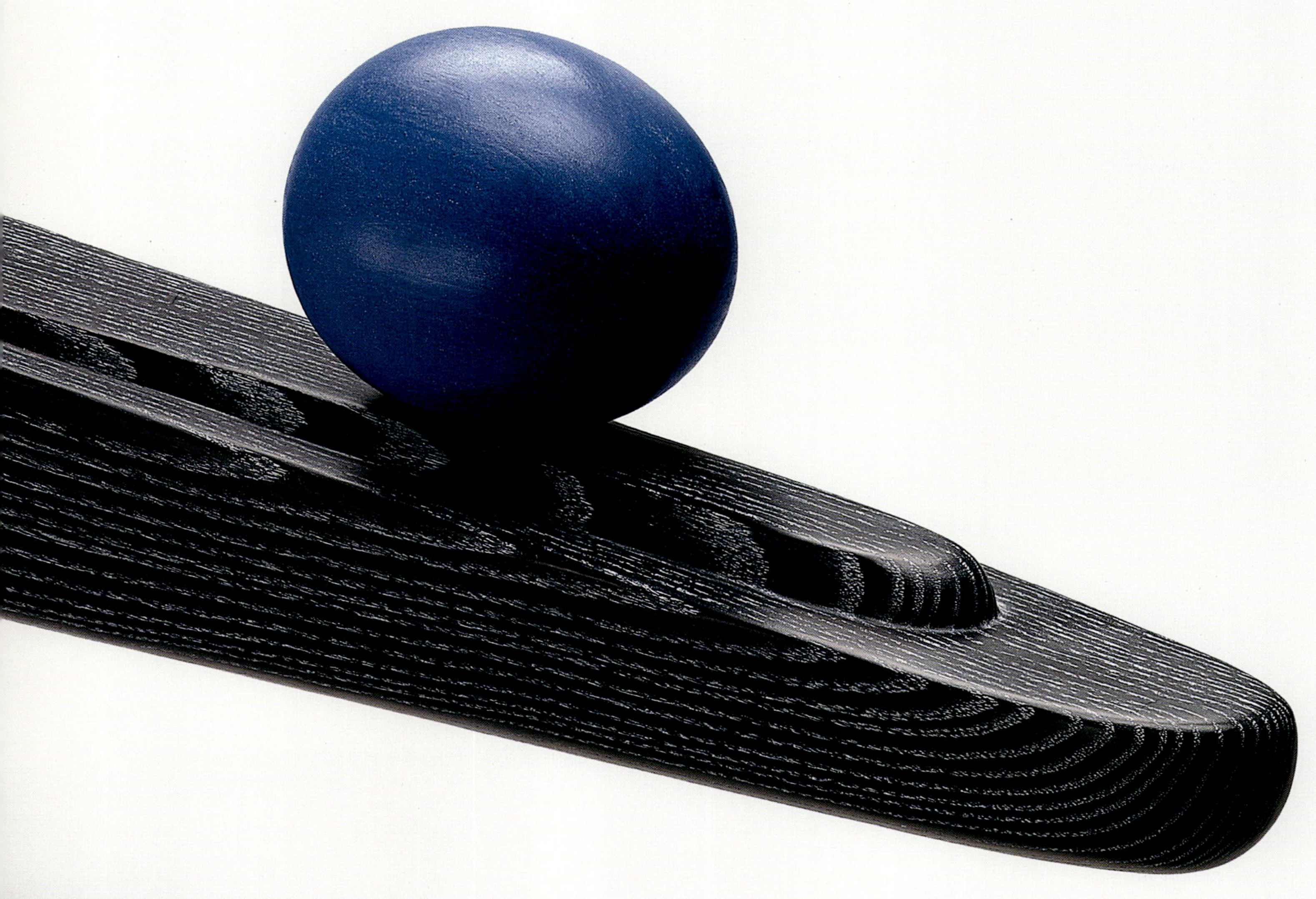

Traditional lathe turning produces smooth circular forms that honor the natural grain of the wood. The founders of the wood art movement perfected classically inspired utilitarian bowls and vessels that celebrate the beauty of simplicity. Small-scale puzzle turnings and exquisite, thin-covered goblets recall the exacting work produced by master turners in the royal workshops of Europe in the sixteenth and seventeenth centuries. With the development of multi-access turning, artists have been able to create larger and more complex forms with obsessively smooth surfaces.

BETTY SCARPINO: DISTINCTIVE SHAPE

The grain of the wood within the Bohlen collection is varied, and each artist's expression in maple, ash, or walnut can be distinctive, even when sharing a collective starting point. The lathe is just the machine to render an egg—or a vessel—perfectly formed. The ability to individually create distinctly shaped vessels is strongly expressed in the turned objects of Bob Stocksdale, David Ellsworth, Gael Montgomerie, and Donald Derry. Flowing beyond pure woodturning is the work of Grant Vaughan.

Launched: A perfectly turned egg perched on a precipice, my son graduating from high school ready to explore the world. Reflecting on the objects I make, what do I learn about my life? Was the foundation for a successful launch sufficiently solid? What do I reveal? Insecurity, joy?

Many objects in this collection tell a story, perhaps interpreted differently from my own musings. Words tagged onto *Launched* can help inform, but I sense them somewhat devoid of the feelings involved in the making. I recollect strong emotions as I carved and cut, leaving just the right expanse of wood to gloriously send off a young man.

Regard one lone item selected for inclusion in a museum exhibition, a slice of a life on display; follow its intricate grain pattern back to the maker. What was her intention? Does the sculpture evoke enough interest to find out more? Is there a connection to be made, one that could enrich your life? Almost all of the artists represented in the Montalto Bohlen Collection are living. That says much about the emerging field of wood art: It is as though the trees themselves still live.

Detail, Betty J. Scarpino, *Launched,* 2002 (pages 44–45)

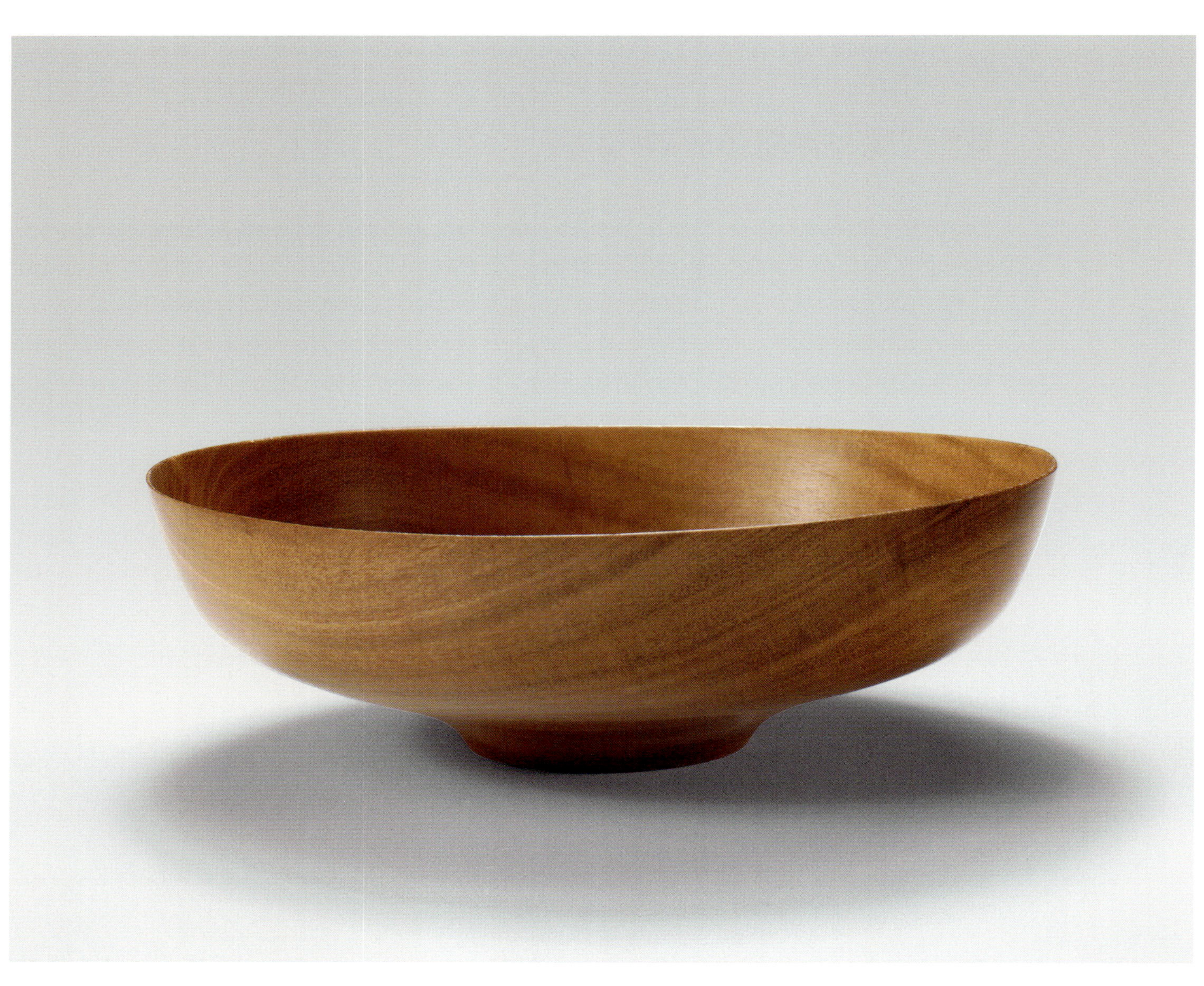

BOB STOCKSDALE 1913–2003, worked Berkeley, California
MAHOE FROM KEY WEST 1996, blue mahoe, 1 $^{3}/_{4}$ x 5 $^{1}/_{2}$ in. (4.5 x 14 cm), Peabody Essex Museum, Gift of Lillian Montalto Bohlen

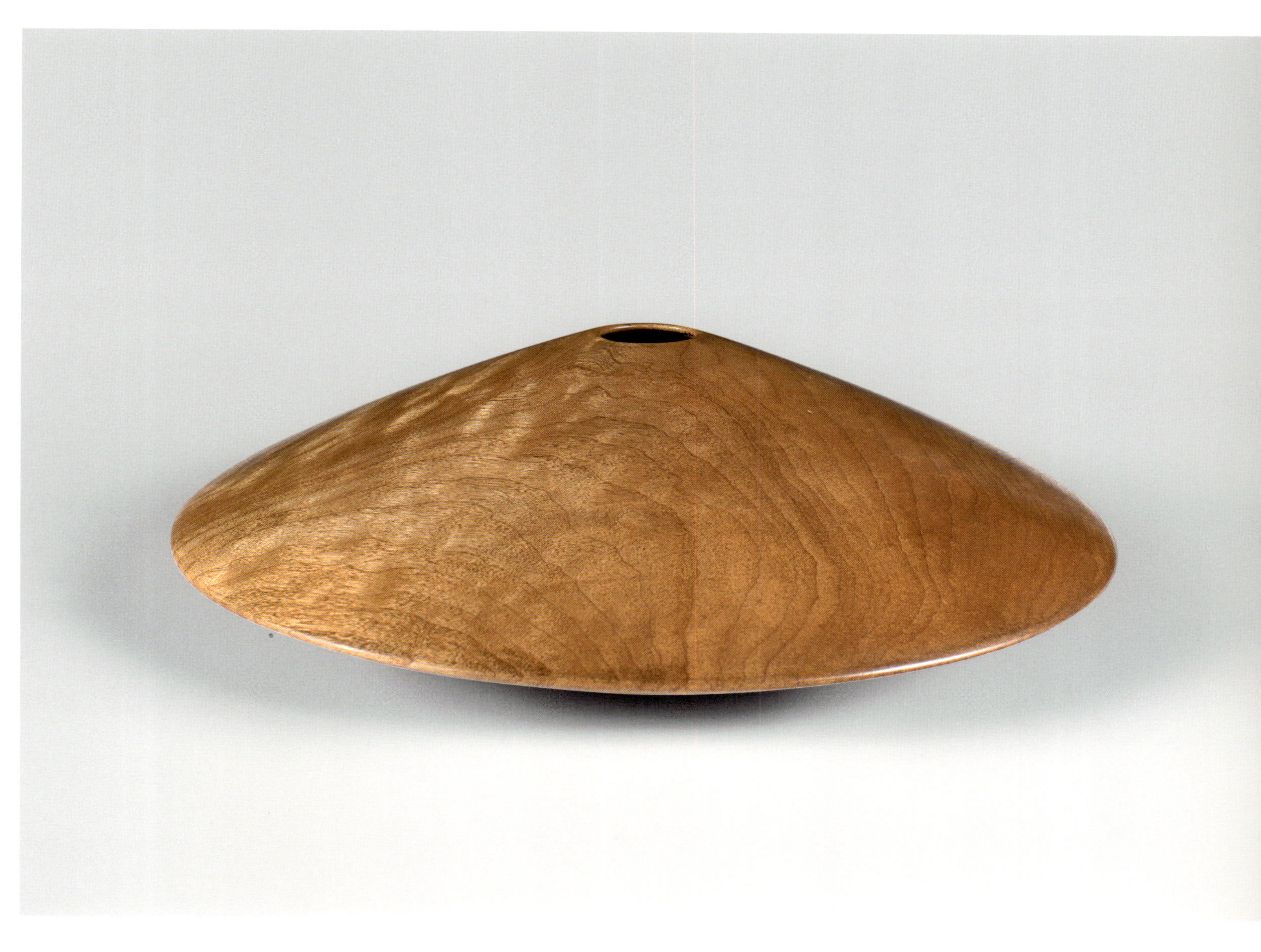

DAVID ELLSWORTH born 1944, works Quakertown, Pennsylvania
VESSEL 1979, quilted maple, 2 3/4 x 9 in. (7 x 23 cm), Peabody Essex Museum, Gift of Lillian Montalto Bohlen

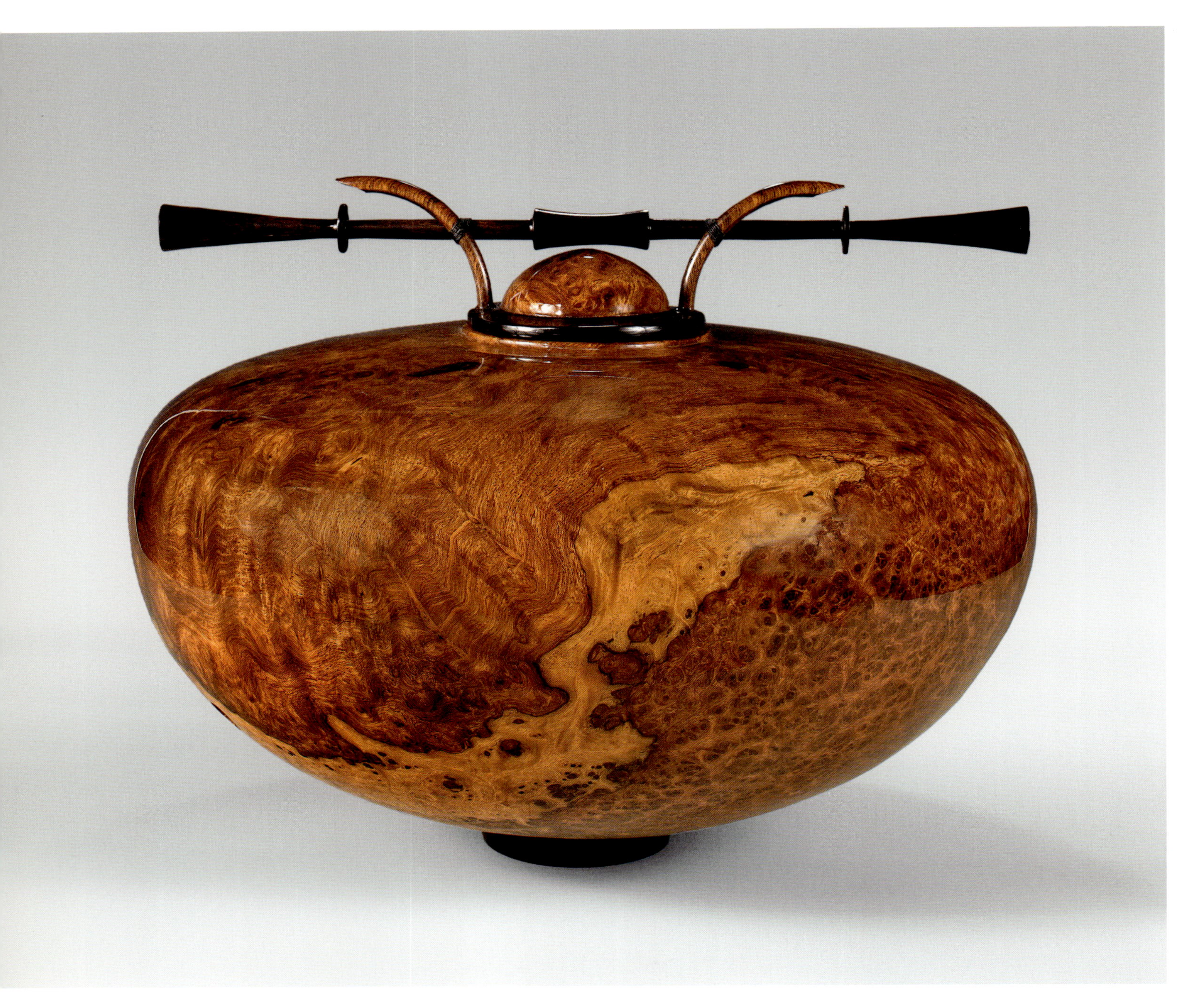

MATT HATALA born 1952, works Danielsville, Georgia
AMBOYNA BURL HOLLOW FORM 2003, rosewood, amboyna burl, blackwood, 12 x 16 in. (30.5 x 40.6 cm)

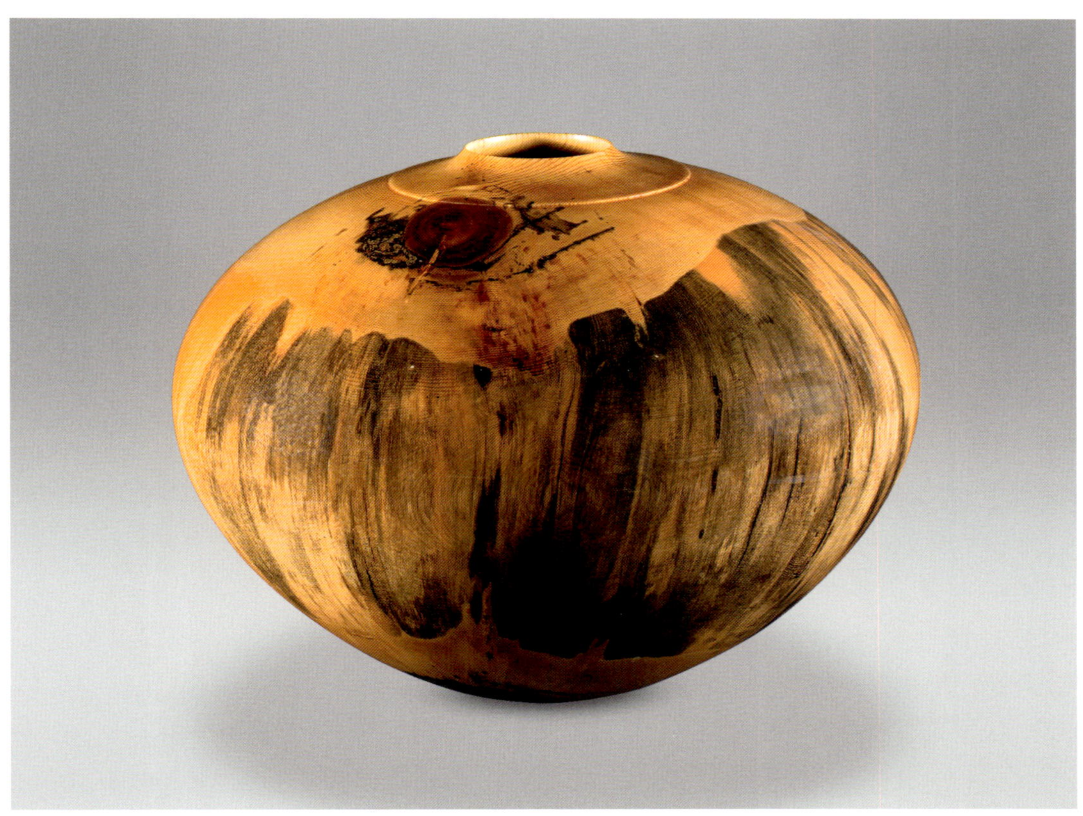

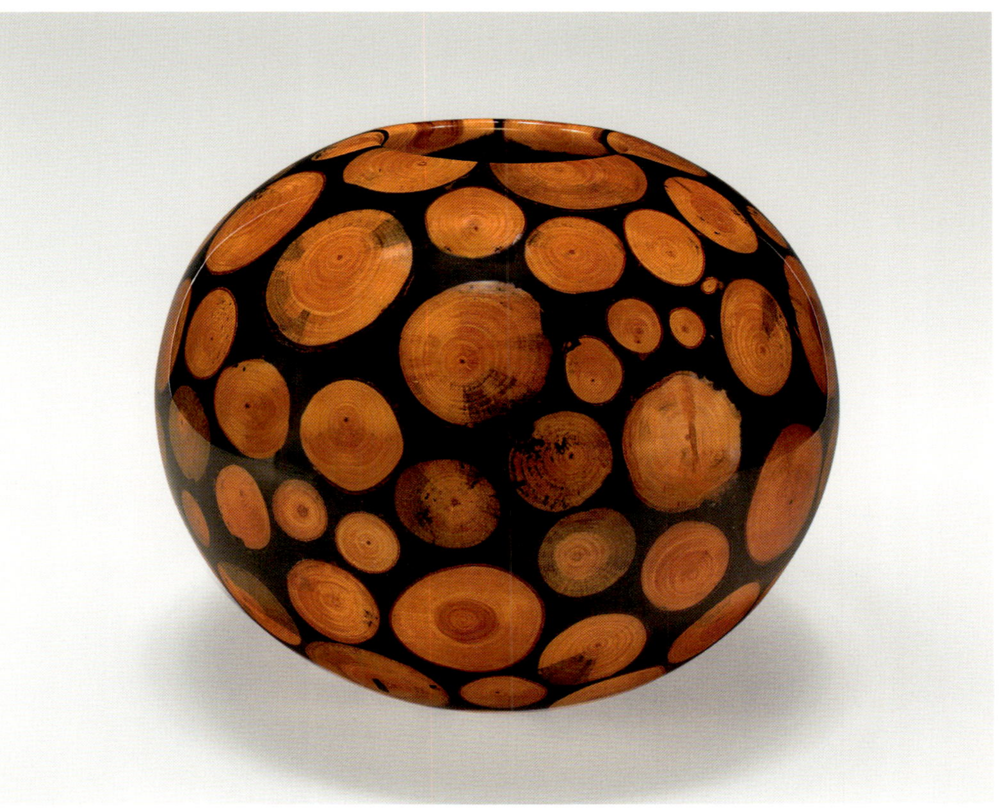

Top: **TED KNIGHT** born 1947, works Dallas, Texas
UNTITLED 1998, ponderosa pine, 20 x 25 1/2 in. (50.8 x 64.8 cm)

Bottom: **PHILIP MOULTHROP** born 1947, works Marietta, Georgia
WHITE PINE MOSAIC BOWL #8940 1996, white pine, resin, carbon black, 8 1/2 x 10 1/2 in. (21.6 x 26.7 cm)

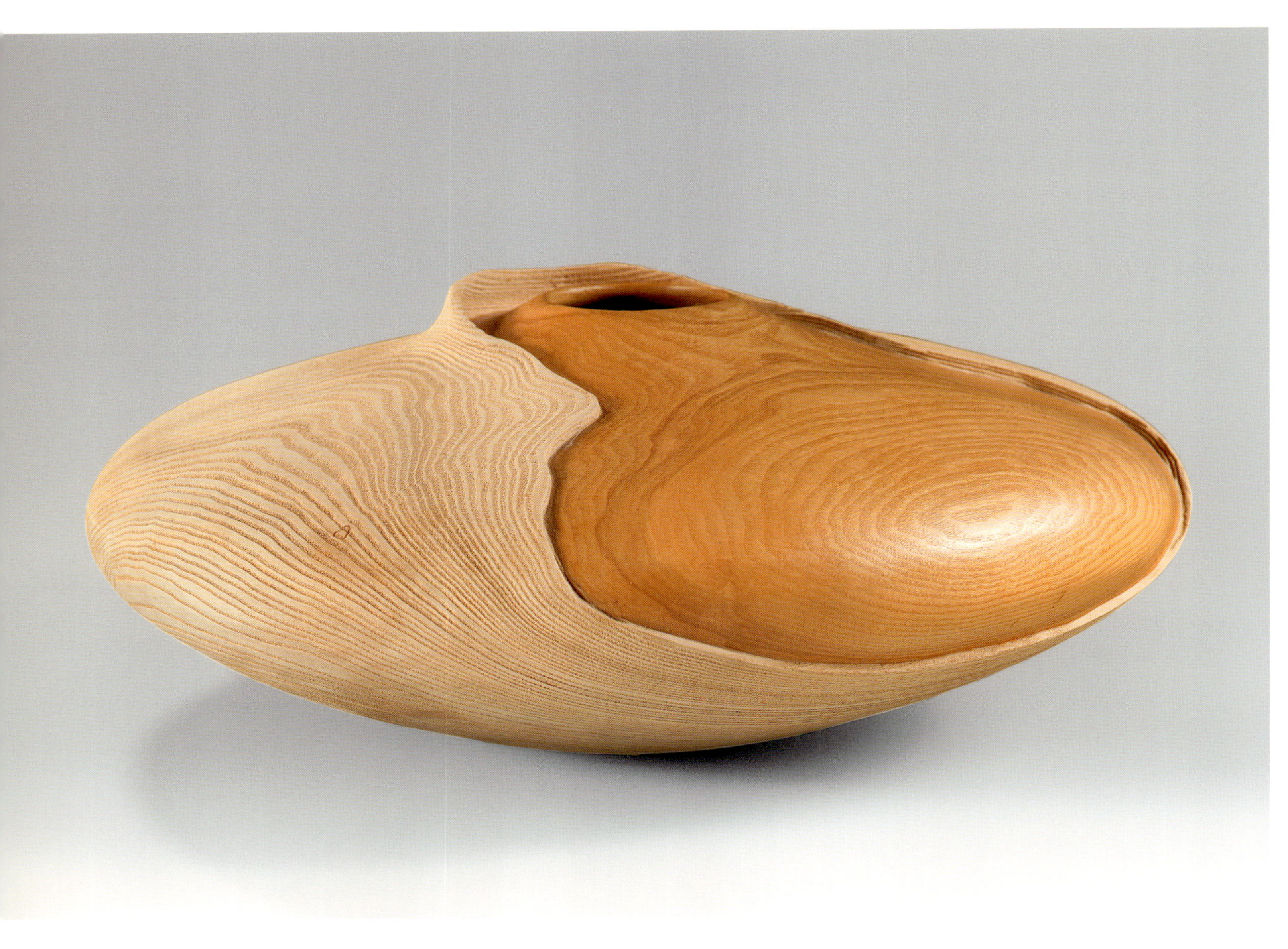

TRENT BOSCH born 1970, works Fort Collins, Colorado
SIENNA SERIES 1999, white ash, 5 3/4 x 15 in. (14.6 x 38.1 cm)

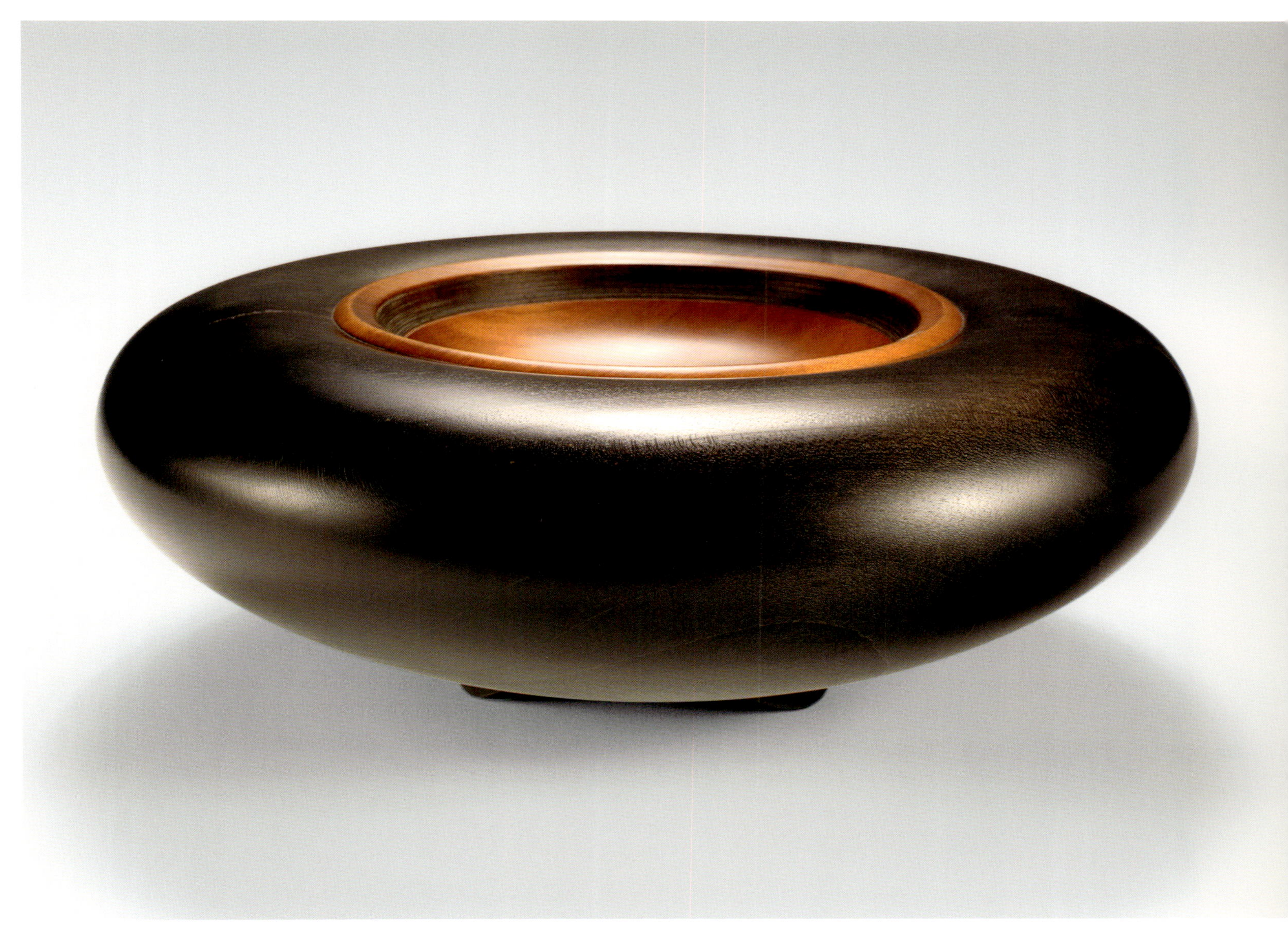

GAEL MONTGOMERIE born 1949, works Nelson, South Island, New Zealand
UNTITLED 1997, sycamore totora, 4 x 10 1/2 in. (10.2 x 26.7 cm), Peabody Essex Museum, Gift of Lillian Montalto Bohlen

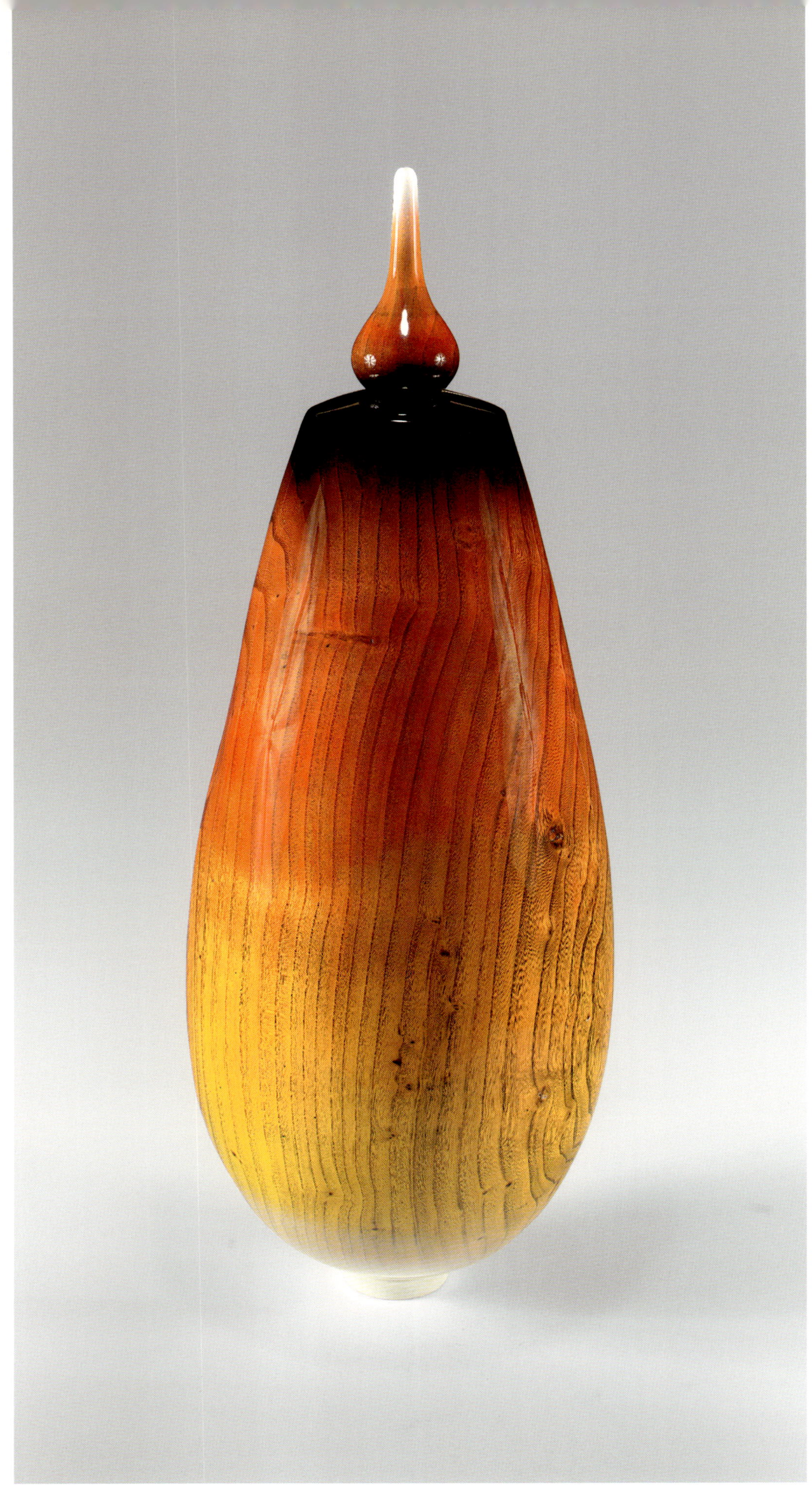

DONALD DERRY born 1956, works Ellensburg, Washington
UNTITLED #4 1999, Chinese elm, industrial paint, lacquer, 23 x 8 $^{1}/_{2}$ in. (58.4 x 21.6 cm)

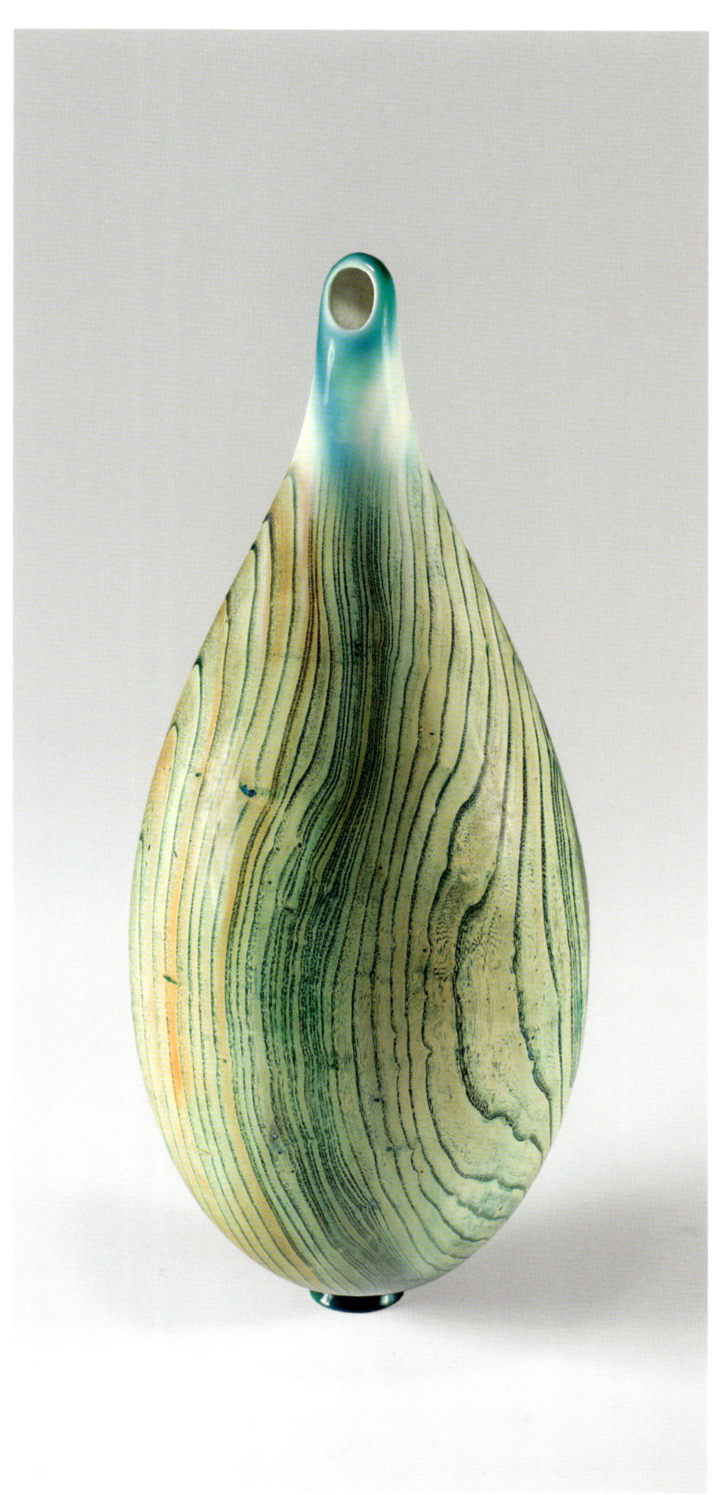

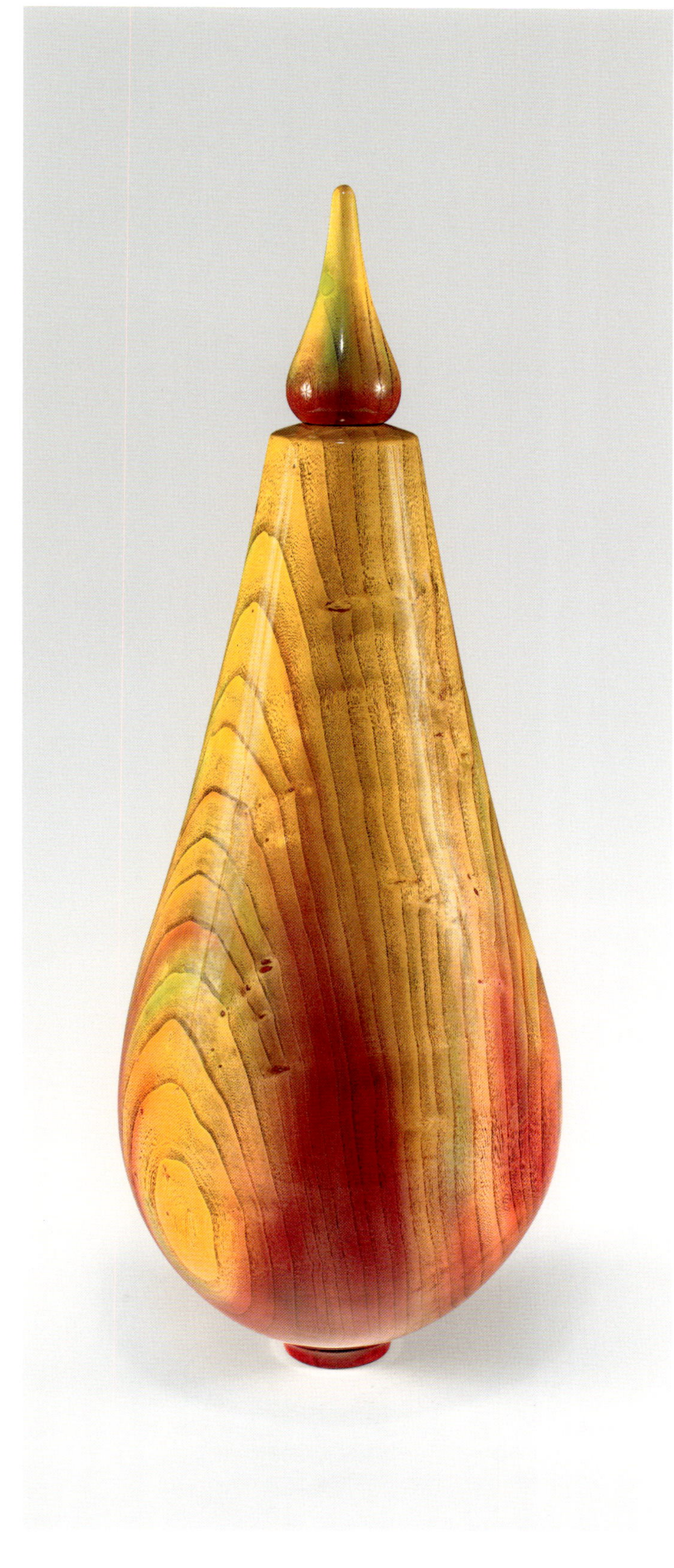

Left to right: **DONALD DERRY** born 1956, works Ellensburg, Washington
UNTITLED #1 1999, Chinese elm, industrial paint, lacquer, 23 x 9 ½ in. (58.4 x 24.1 cm)
UNTITLED #2 1999, Chinese elm, industrial paint, lacquer, 26 x 8 in. (66 x 20.3 cm)

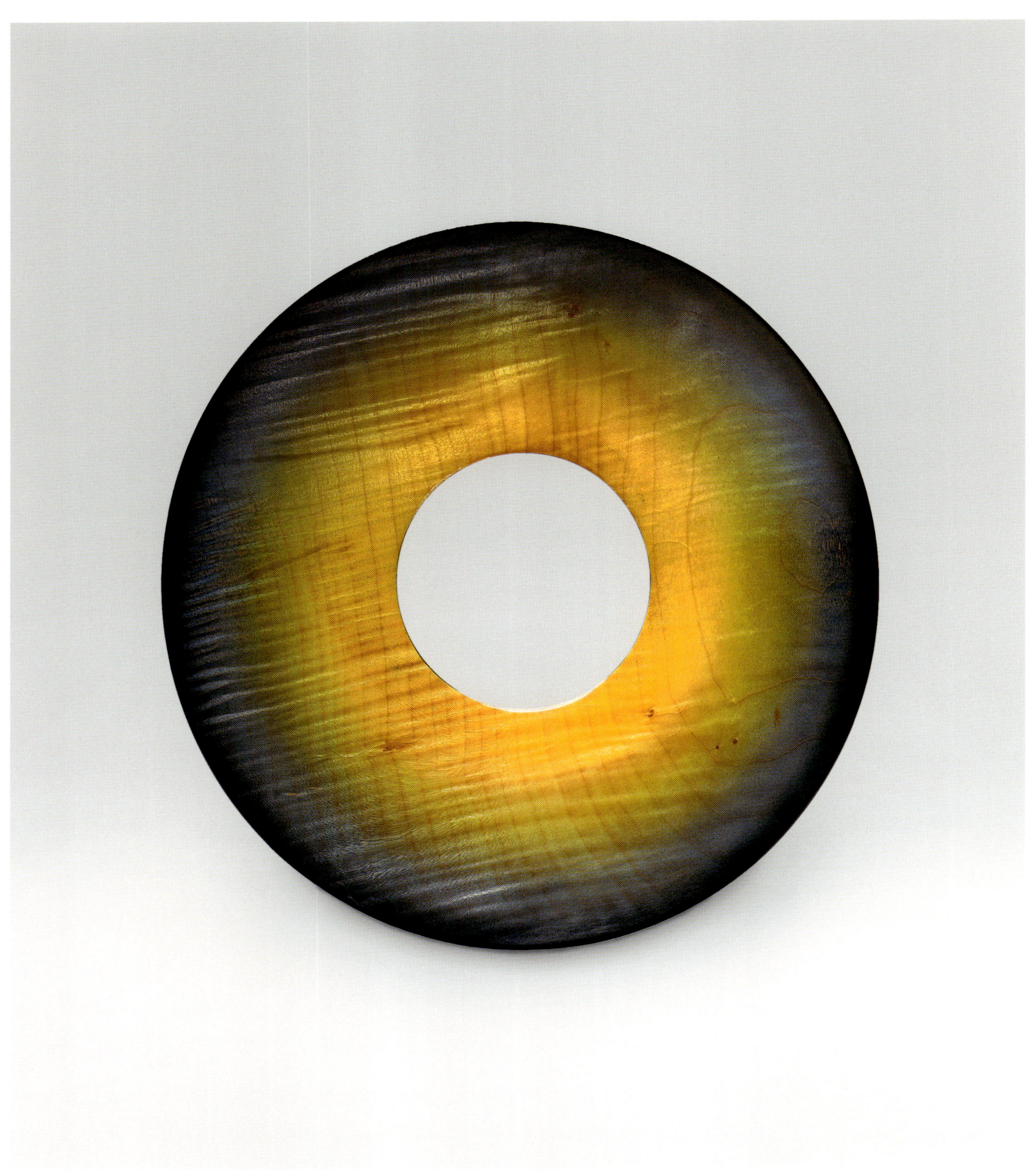

GREG S. SMITH born 1941, works Troy, Michigan

FULL MOON II 2010, figured maple, metal-complex dyes, high-gloss lacquer, 10 ¾ x 2 in. (27.3 x 5.1 cm), Peabody Essex Museum, Gift of Lillian Montalto Bohlen

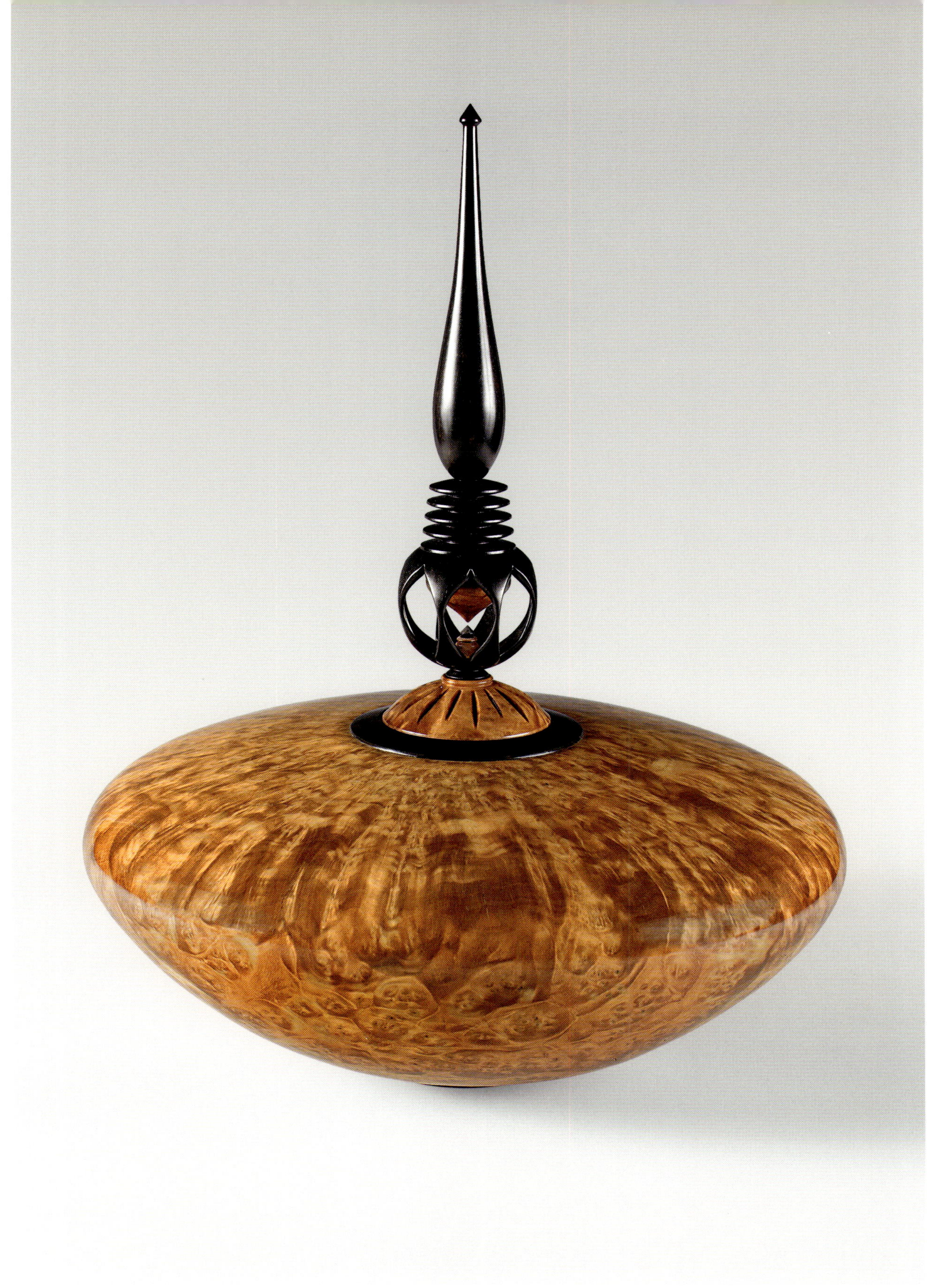

BARRY MACDONALD born 1954, works Grosse Pointe, Michigan
UNTITLED BOTTLE about 1997, paela burl, Gabon ebony, 15 x 12 in. (38.1 x 30.5 cm)

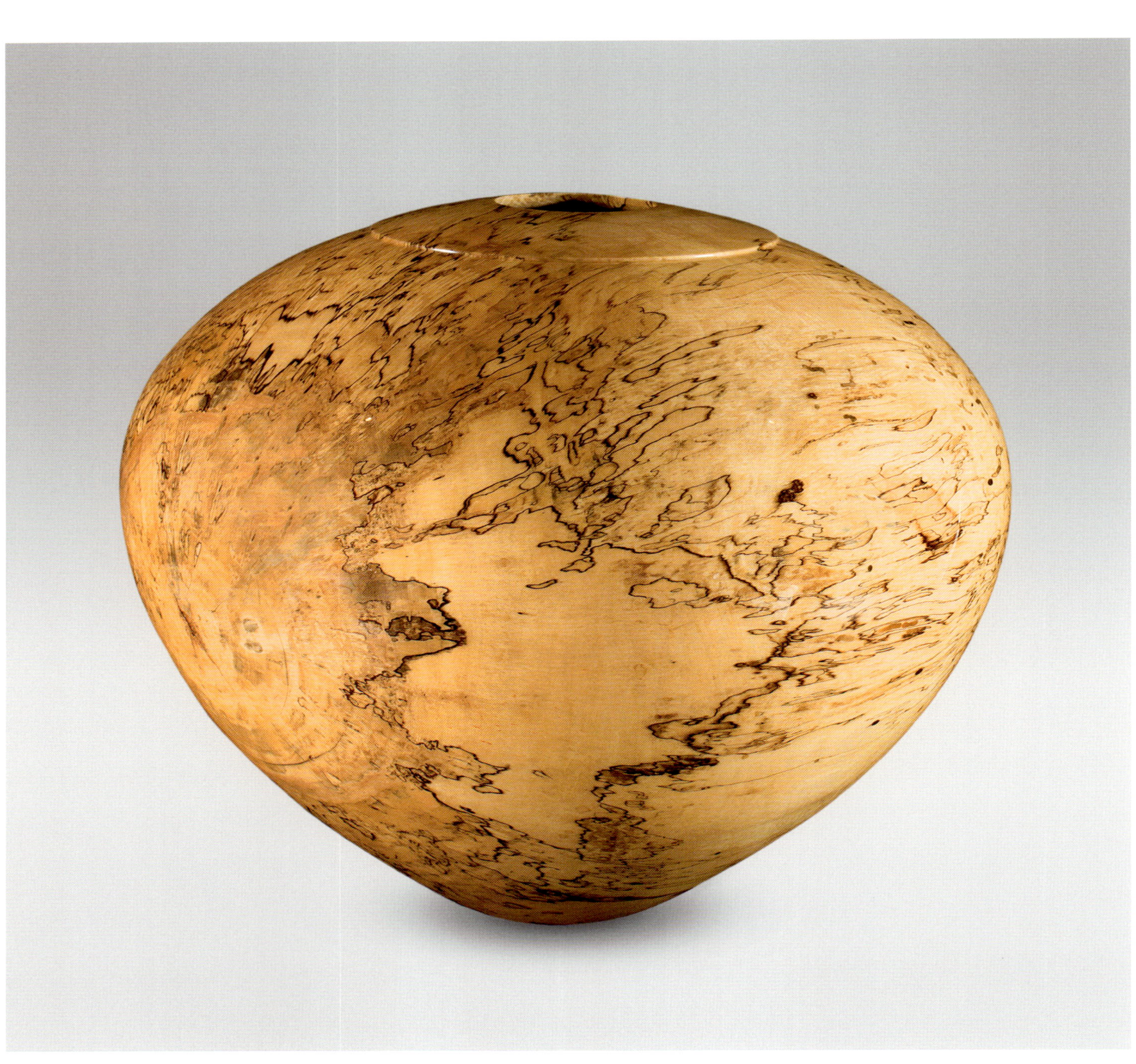

TED KNIGHT born 1947, works Dallas, Texas
MY TRUE LOVE 2009, spalted silver-leaf maple, 19 x 16 in. (48.3 x 40.6 cm)

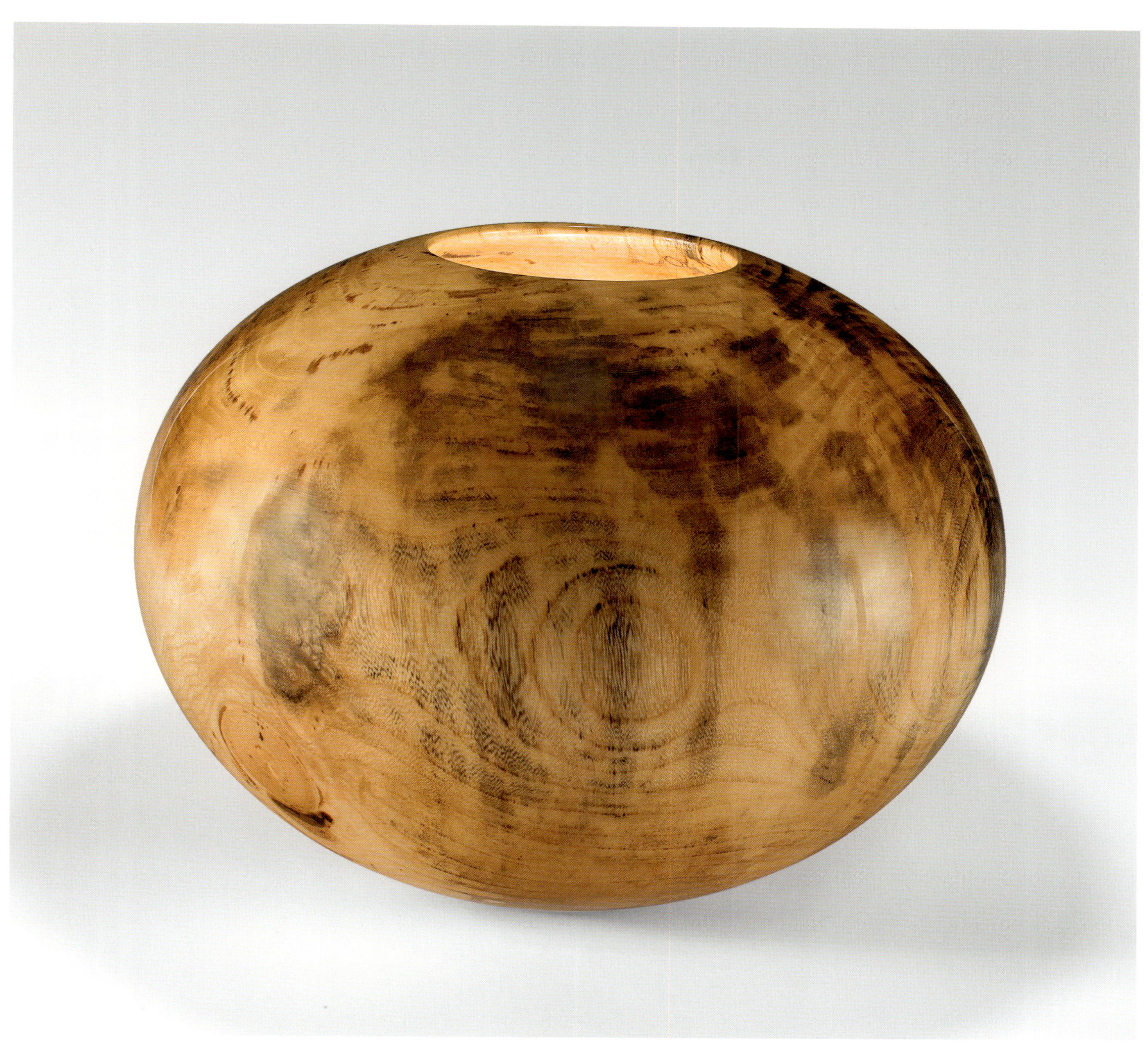

PHILIP MOULTHROP born 1947, works Marietta, Georgia
CELTIC OCCIDENTALIS 1999, spalted harkberry, 8 1/2 x 10 1/2 in. (21.7 x 26.7 cm), Peabody Essex Museum, Gift of Lillian Montalto Bohlen

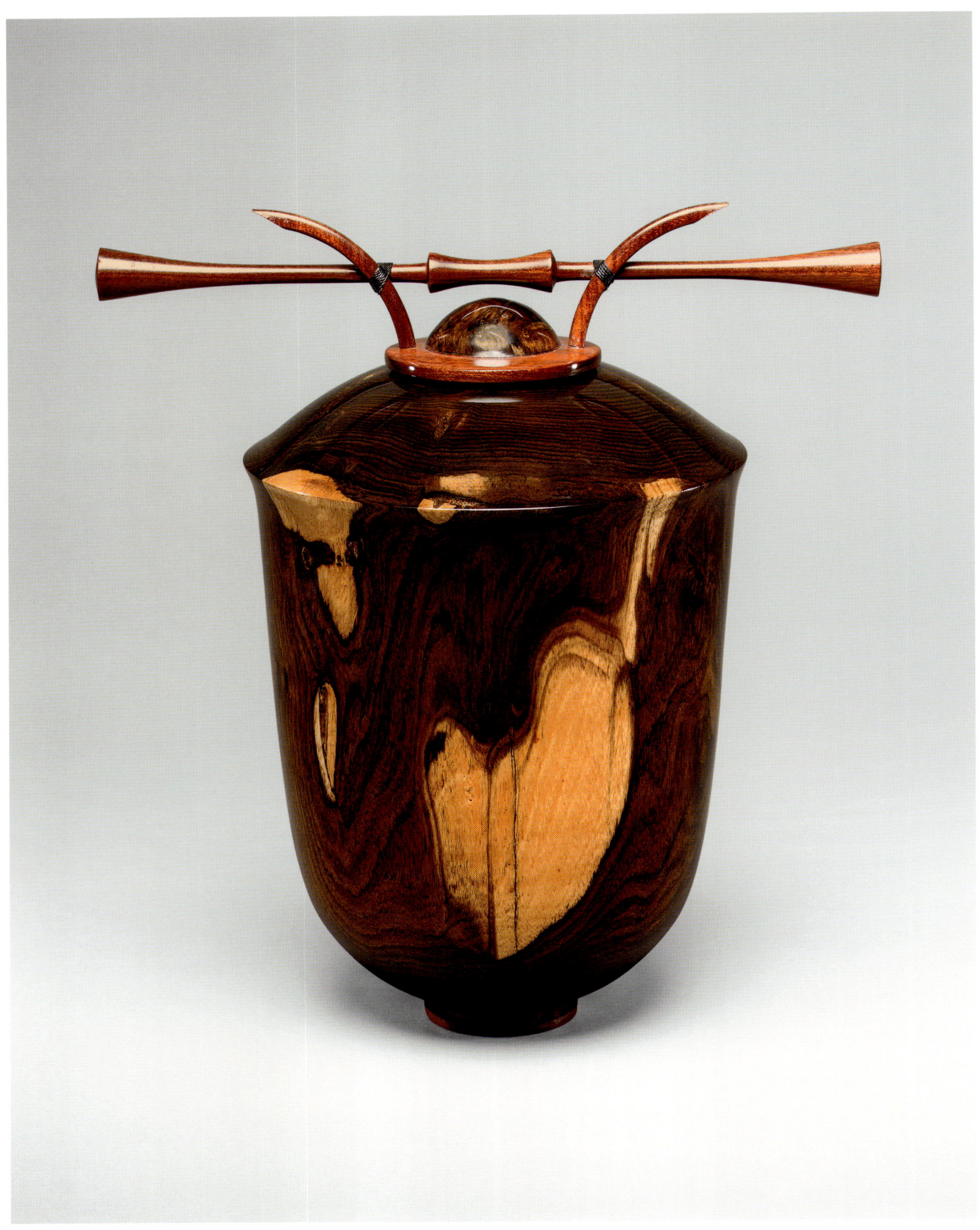

MATT HATALA born 1952, works Danielsville, Georgia
AFRICAN BLACKWOOD VESSEL 2002, blackwood, 12 x 12 x 10 $^1/_2$ in. (30.5 x 30.5 x 26.7 cm), Peabody Essex Museum, Gift of Lillian Montalto Bohlen

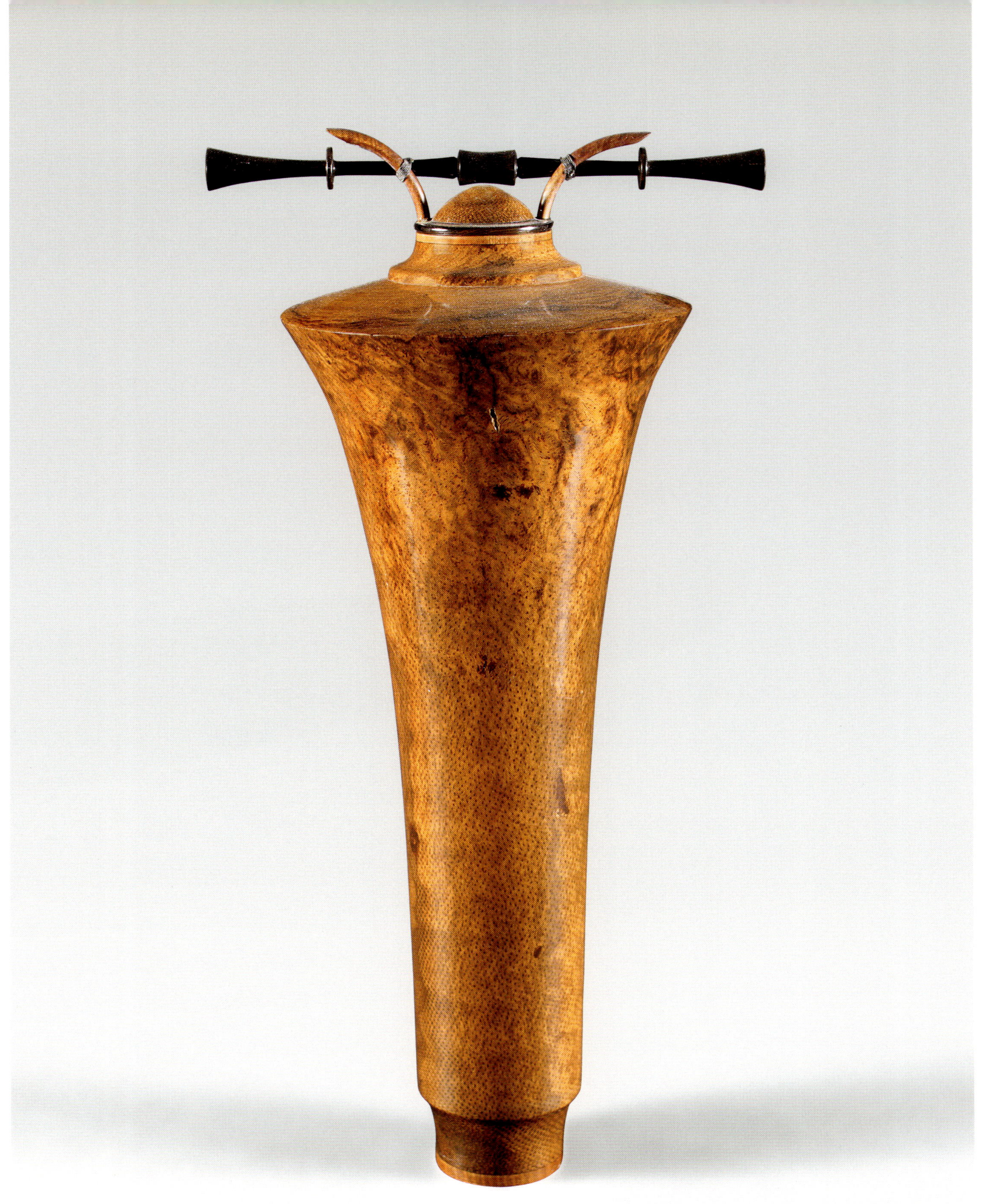

MATT HATALA born 1952, works Danielsville, Georgia
SENTINEL IN THE SHADOW OF ULURU 2003, Australian grass tree, 23 3/4 x 11 1/2 x 8 1/4 in. (60.3 x 29.2 x 21 cm)

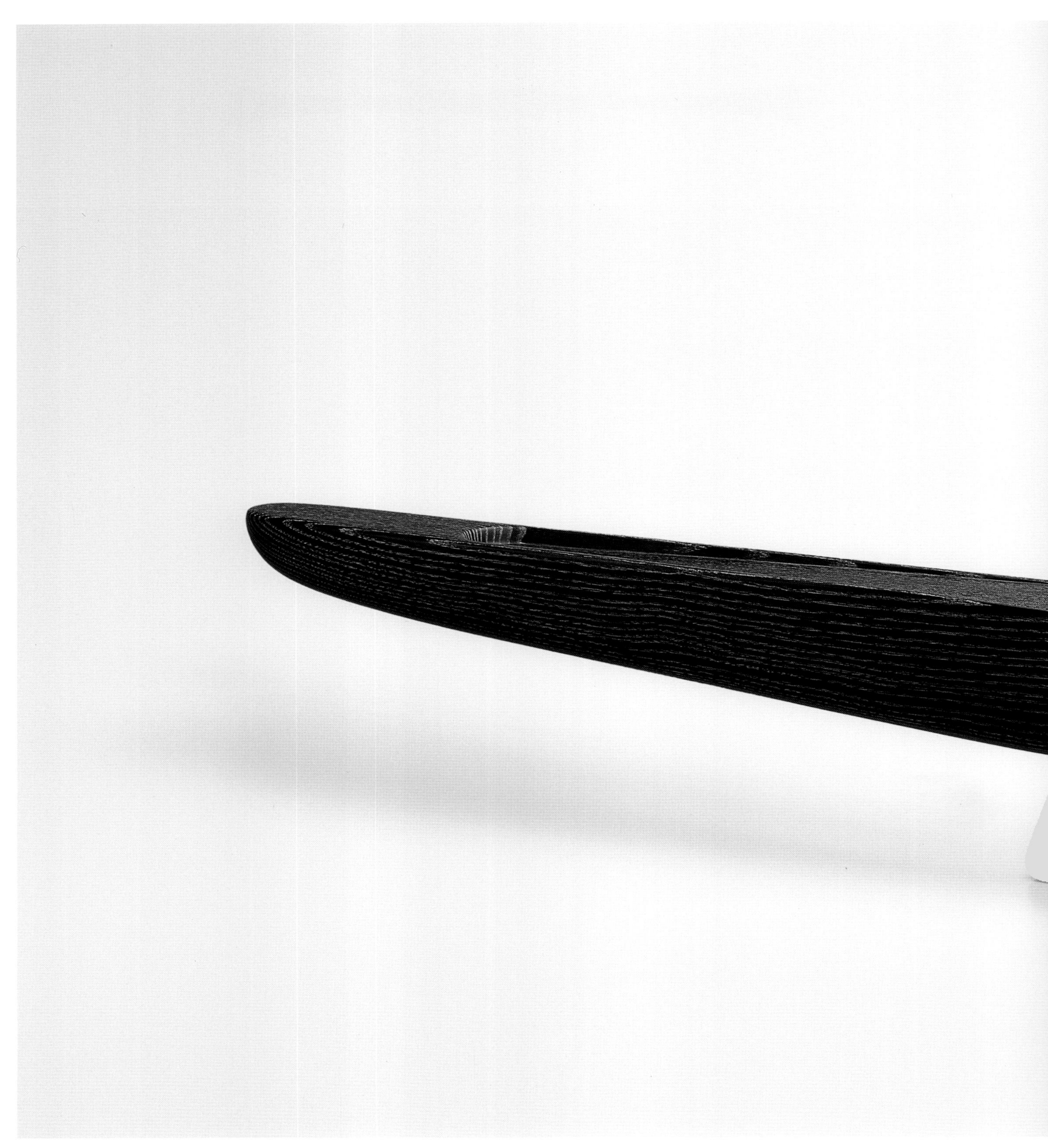

BETTY J. SCARPINO born 1949, works Indianapolis, Indiana
LAUNCHED 2002, ash, stained, filled with liming wax; egg: poplar, milk paint, 8 3/4 x 44 x 3 in. (22.2 x 111.8 x 7.6 cm)

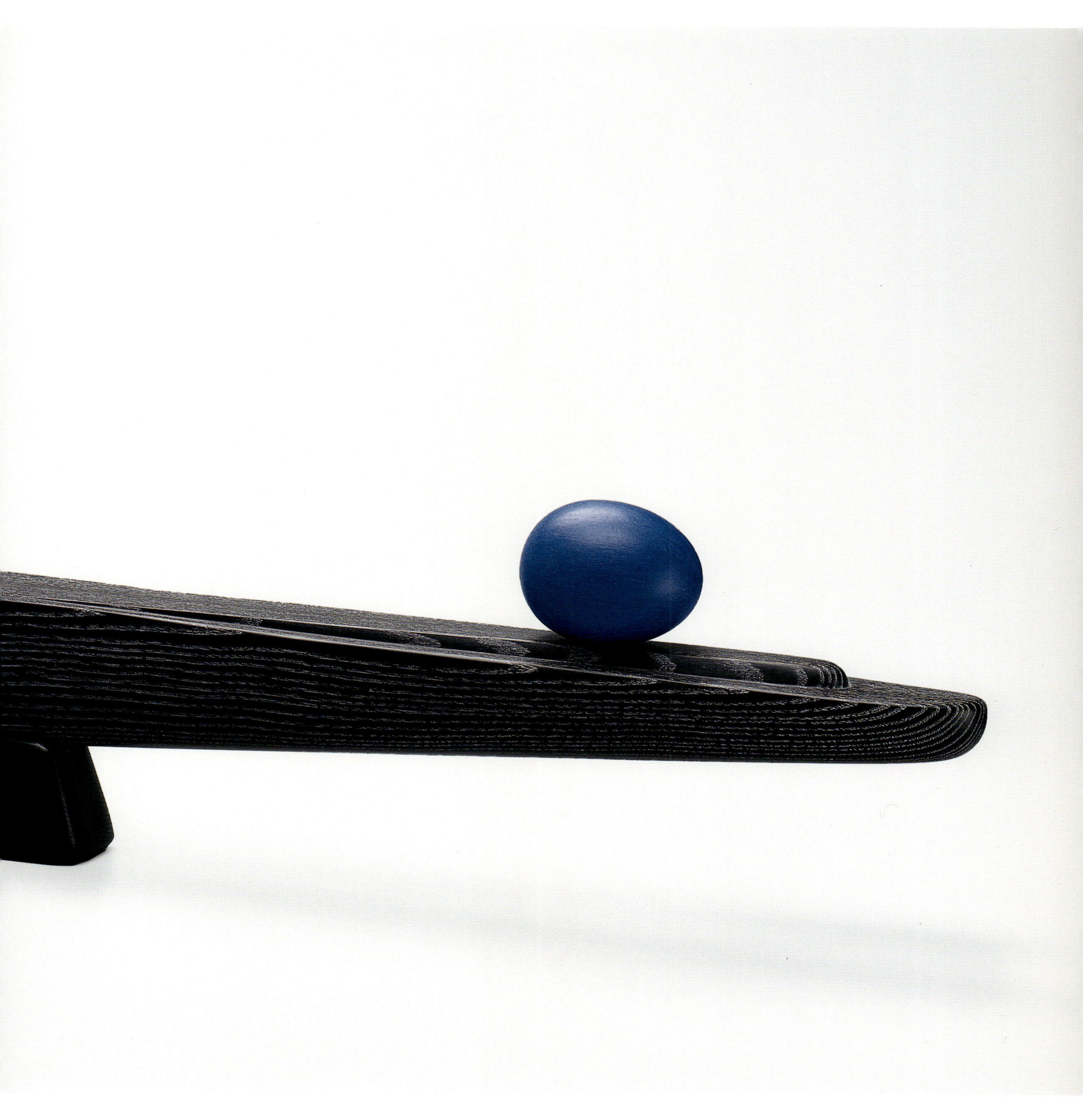

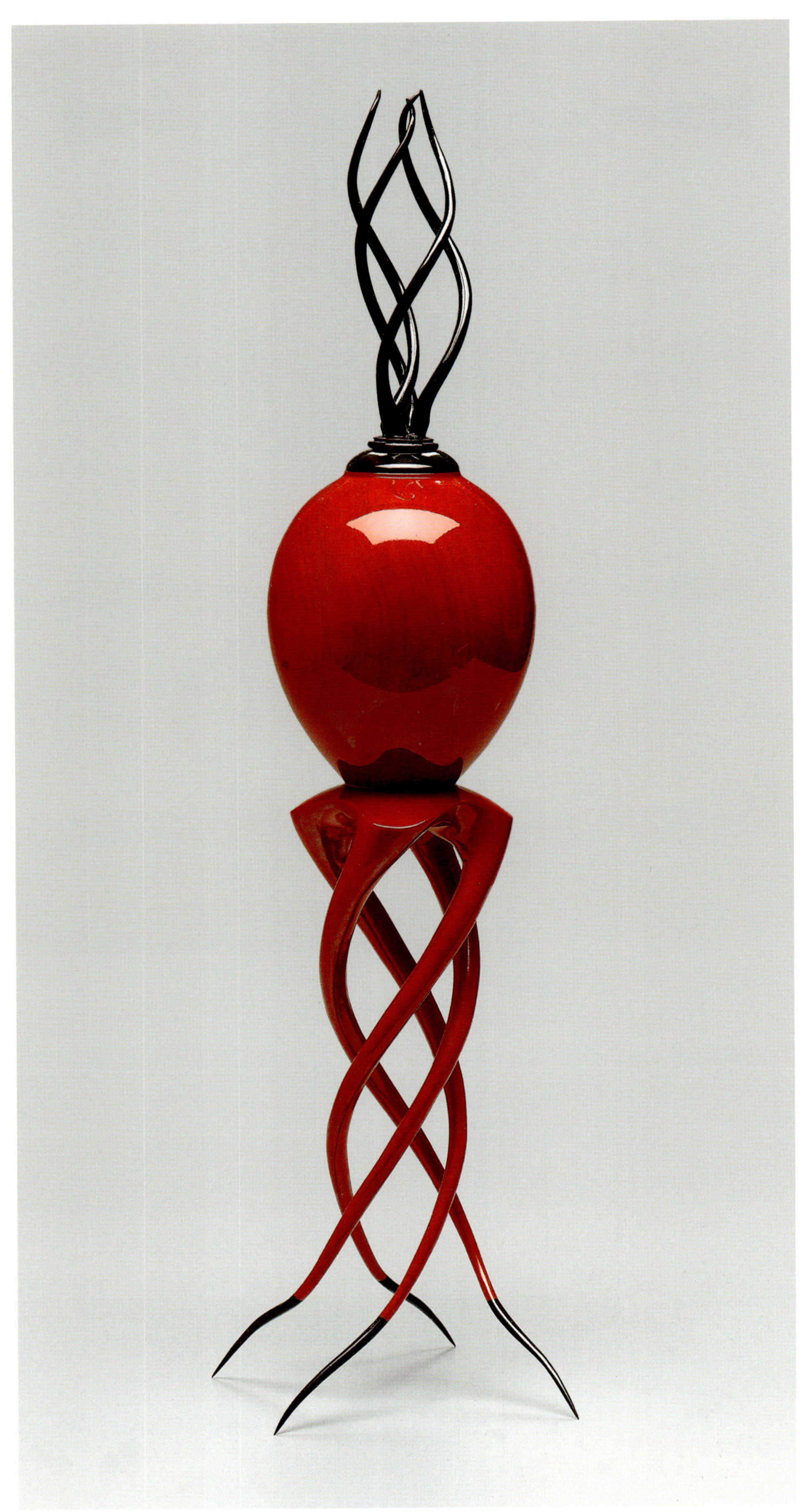

STUART MORTIMER born 1942, works Grateley, Hampshire, England
SQUID SERIES #2 2002, pink ivory, ebony, 22 $^{1}/_{2}$ x 7 x 7 $^{1}/_{4}$ in. (57.2 x 17.8 x 18.4 cm)

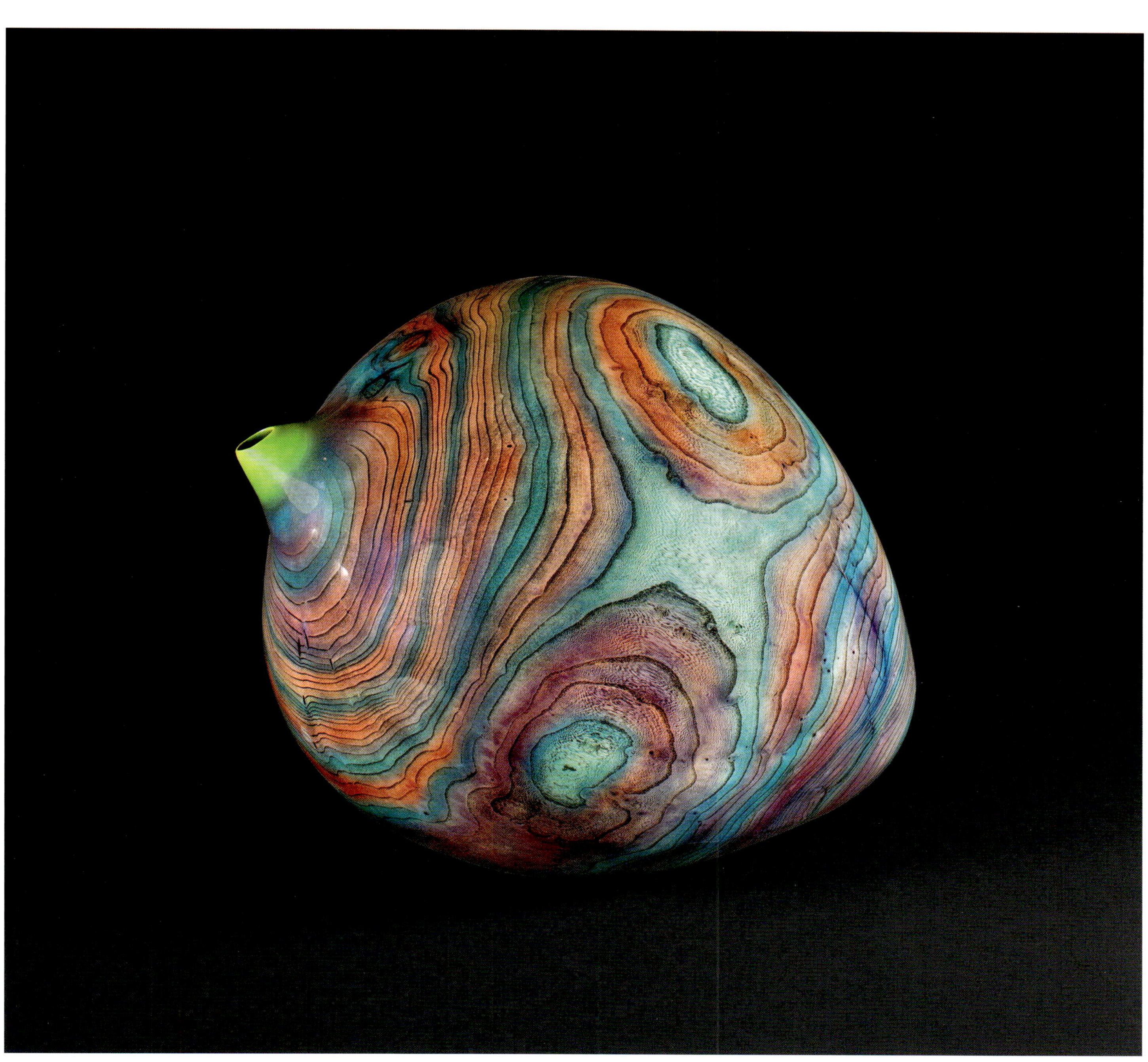

DONALD DERRY born 1956, works Ellensburg, Washington
OF THE RAINFOREST 2006, Chinese elm, 19 x 18 x 21 in. (48.3 x 45.7 x 53.3 cm)

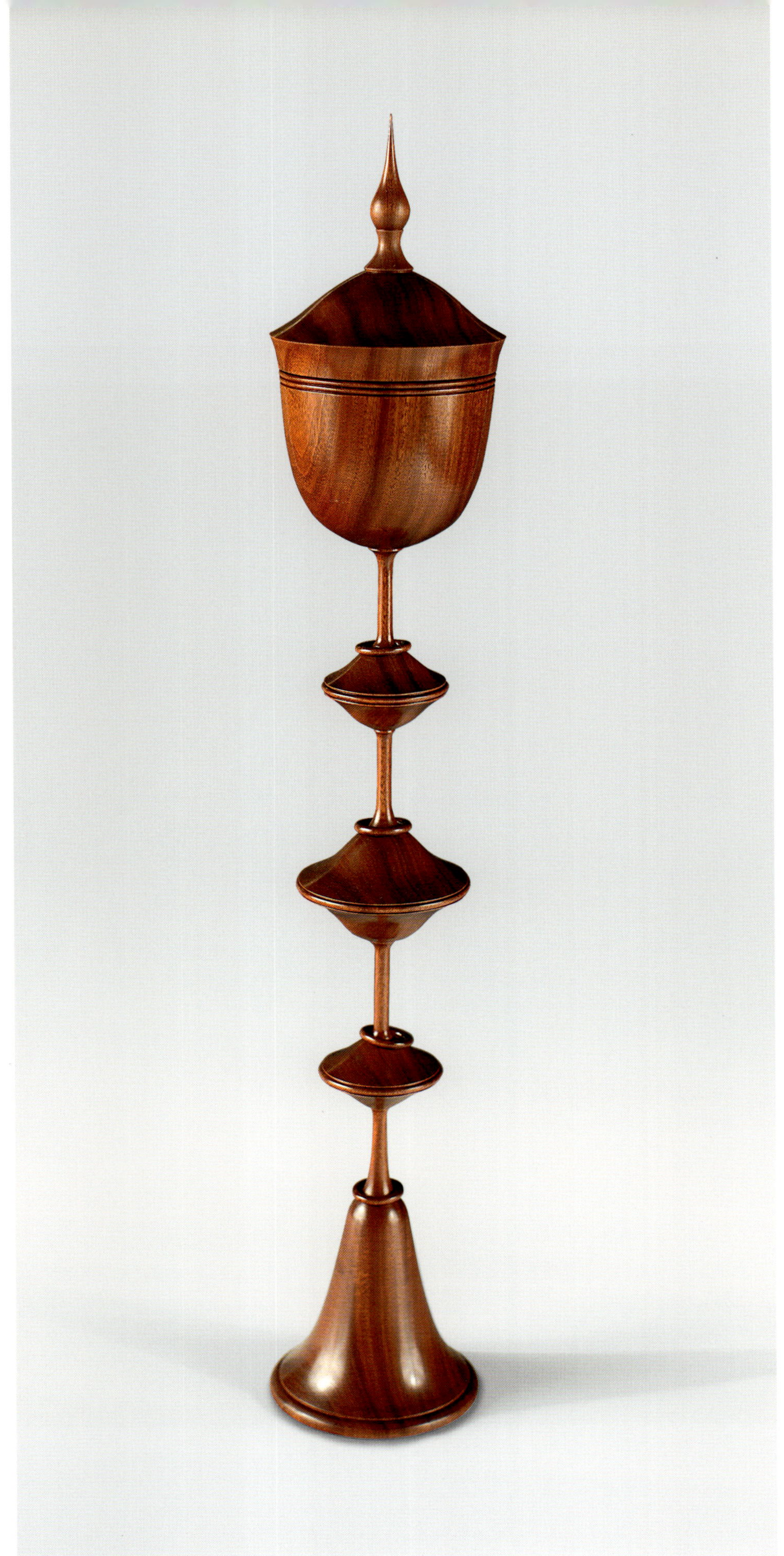

MARK NADEAU born 1970, works Portsmouth, Rhode Island
TREMBLEUR BOX #001 (THE MATHEMATICIAN) 2010, balsamo, 17 1/4 x 3 in. (43.8 x 7.6 cm), Peabody Essex Museum, Gift of Lillian Montalto Bohlen

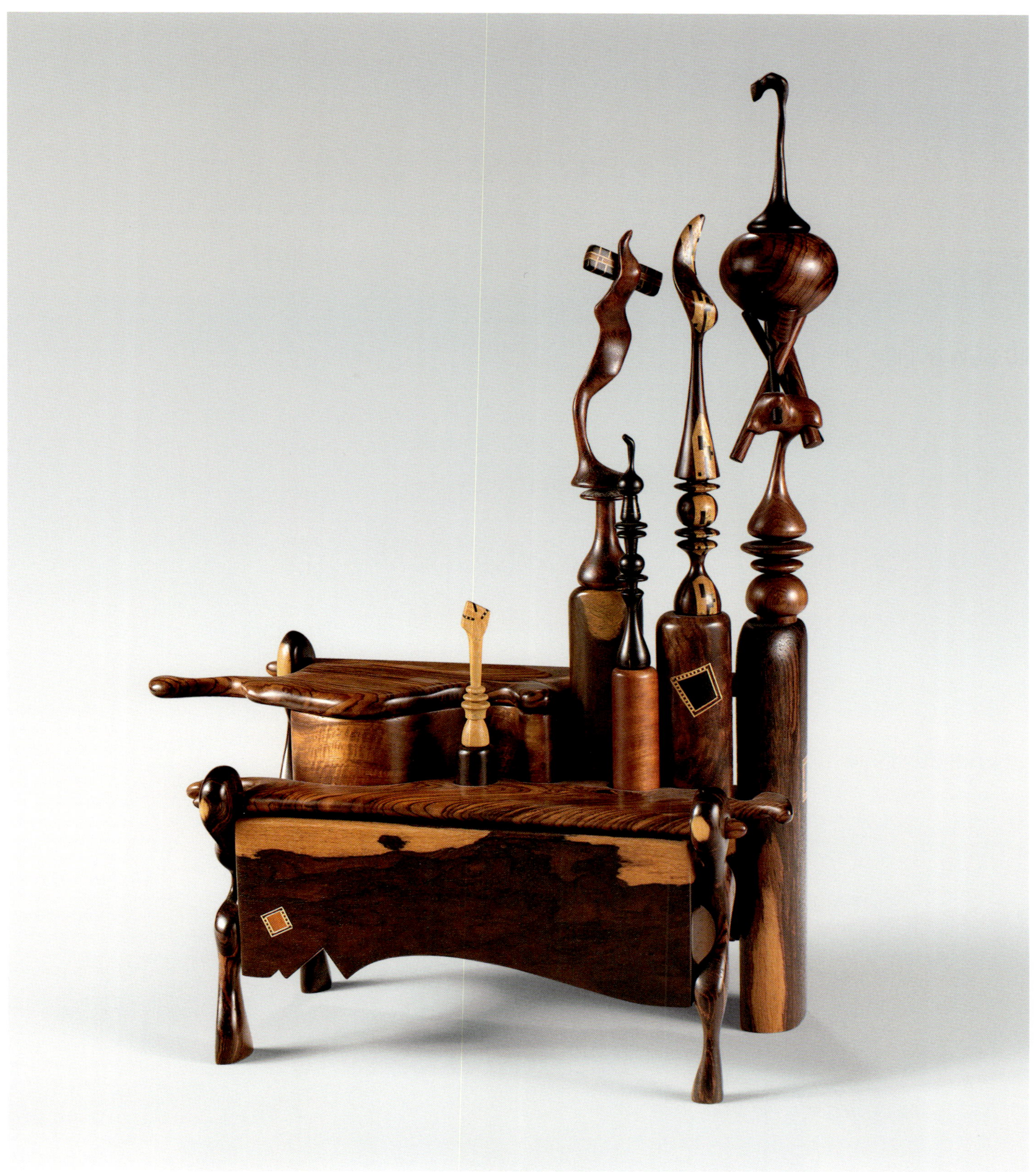

CHRISTOPHER CANTWELL born 1960, works Oakhurst, California
WONDERLAND A.K.A. IMAGINATION BOX 1996, ziricote, cocobolo, curly narra, bocote, Mexican kingwood, Honduran rosewood, walnut, granadillo, ligum vitae, pink ivorywood, ebony, satinwood, Brazilian kingwood, maple, koa, Osage orange, chakte kok, purpleheart, gold leaf, 14 3/4 x 10 1/2 x 5 1/4 in. (37.5 x 26.7 x 13.3 cm)

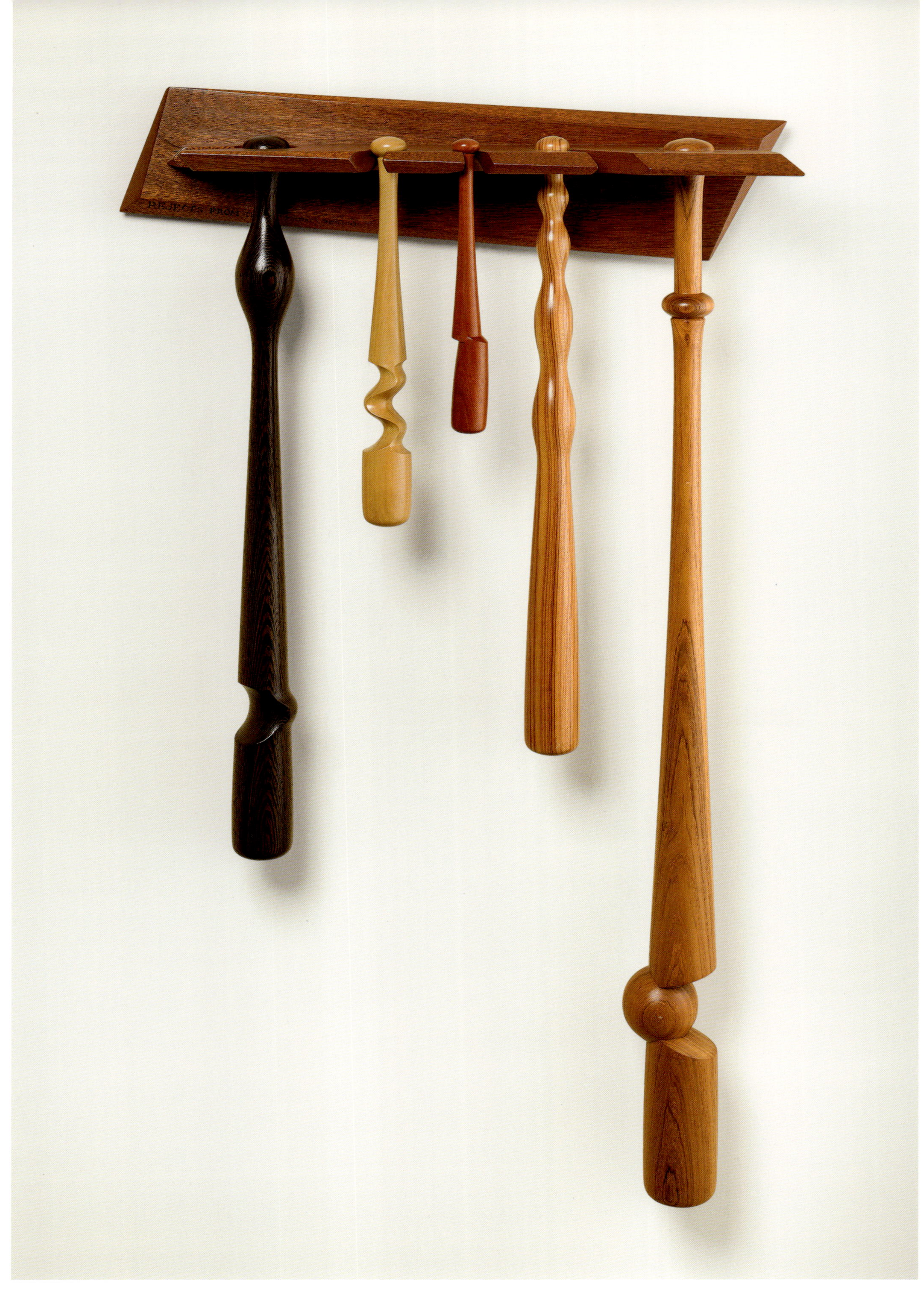

MARK SFIRRI born 1952, works New Hope, Pennsylvania
REJECTS FROM THE BAT FACTORY 2011, wenge, boxwood, pink ivory, tulipwood, teak, mahogany, 40 x 26 x 7 in. (101.6 x 66 x 17.8 cm)

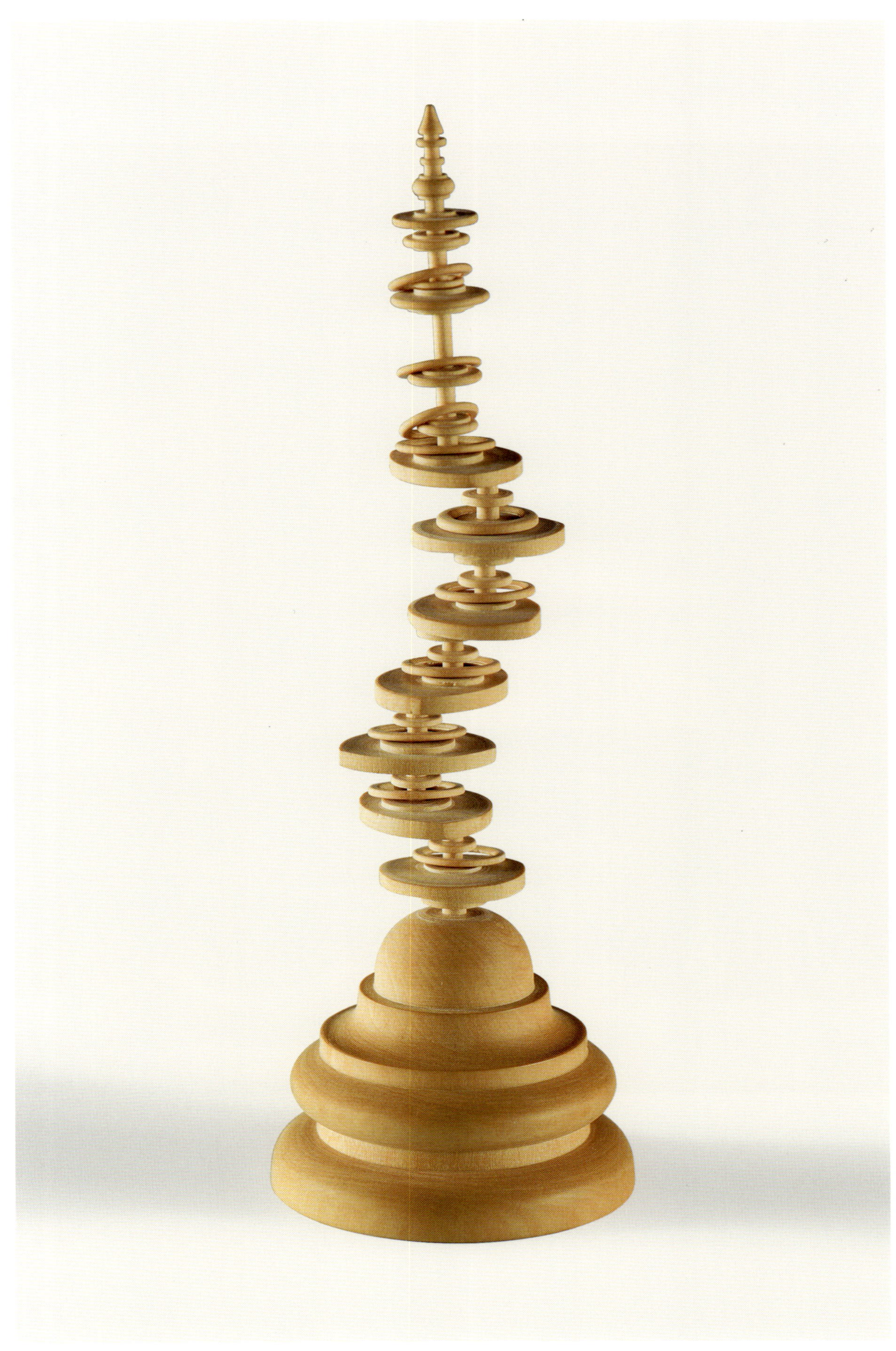

HANS WEISSFLOG born 1954, works Hildesheim, Germany
CLASSICAL PIECE 1996, European boxwood, 5 1/4 x 2 in. (13.3 x 5.1 cm)

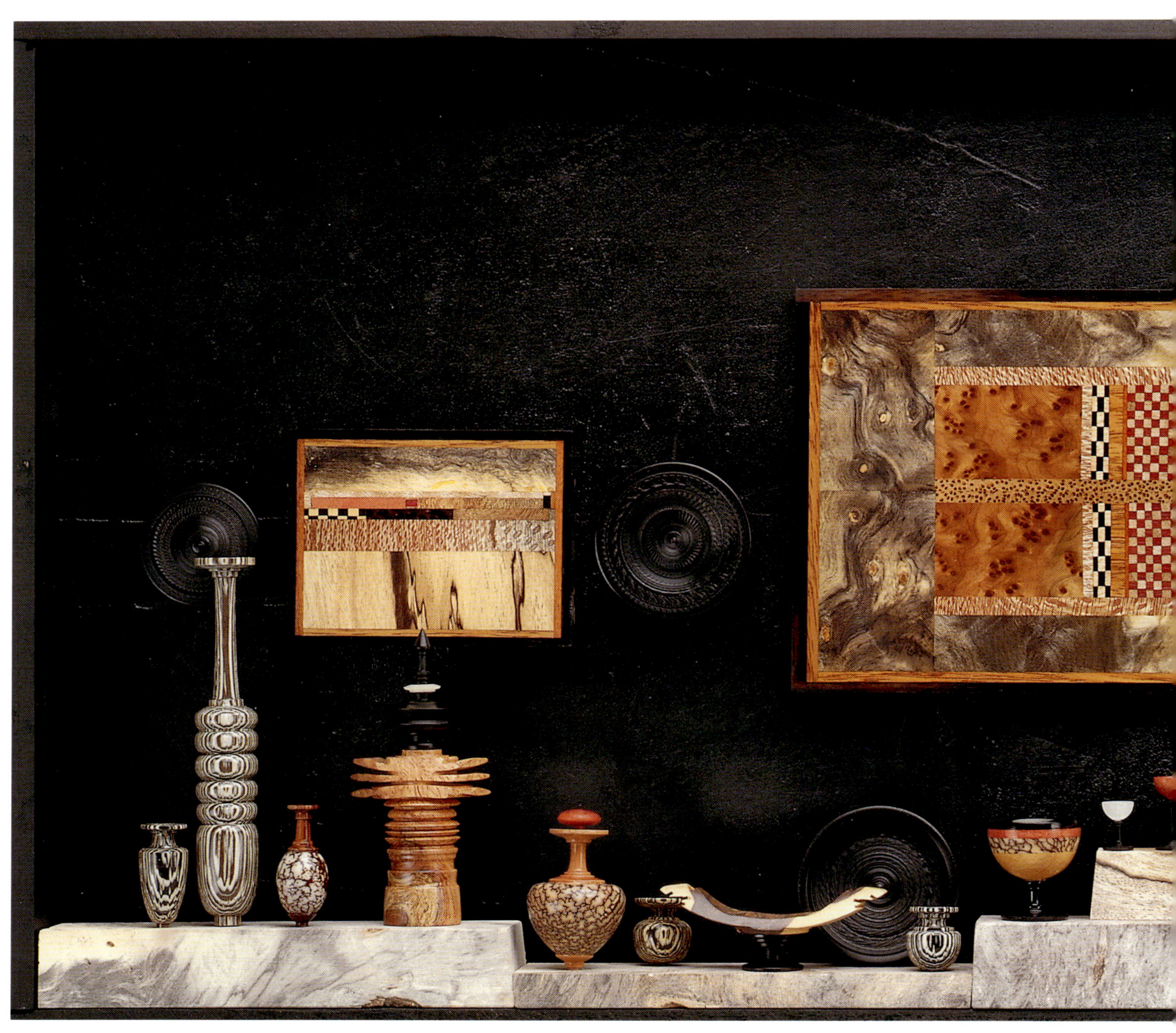

STEPHEN PAULSEN born 1947, works Glen Ellen, California
THE MOST RECENTLY EXPOSED ANNEX TO DR. MARQUARD'S NOTORIOUS CLANDESTINE MUSEUM ON THE THIRD PLANET, WITH TWO LANDSCAPES, A CLASSIC SKY QUILT AND THIRTY-THREE ARTIFACTS ILLEGALLY IMPORTED BY MARQUARD AND CREW FROM THE VOID, IN CLEAR VIOLATION OF THE COMPACT 1999, arariba, bimblebox burl, boxwood, buckeye burl, canary wood, cercocarpus, coconut palm, ebony, jacaranda, kingwood, lauan, leopard palm, lyonothaminus, makamong burl, maple, oreocallis, oysterwood, pernambuco, pink ivory, poinciana, purpleheart, royal palm, satinwood, thuya burl, vegetable ivory, wenge, wild lilac burl, 17 1/2 x 31 1/8 x 2 in., includes the black shadowbox frame (44.5 x 79.1 x 5.1 cm)

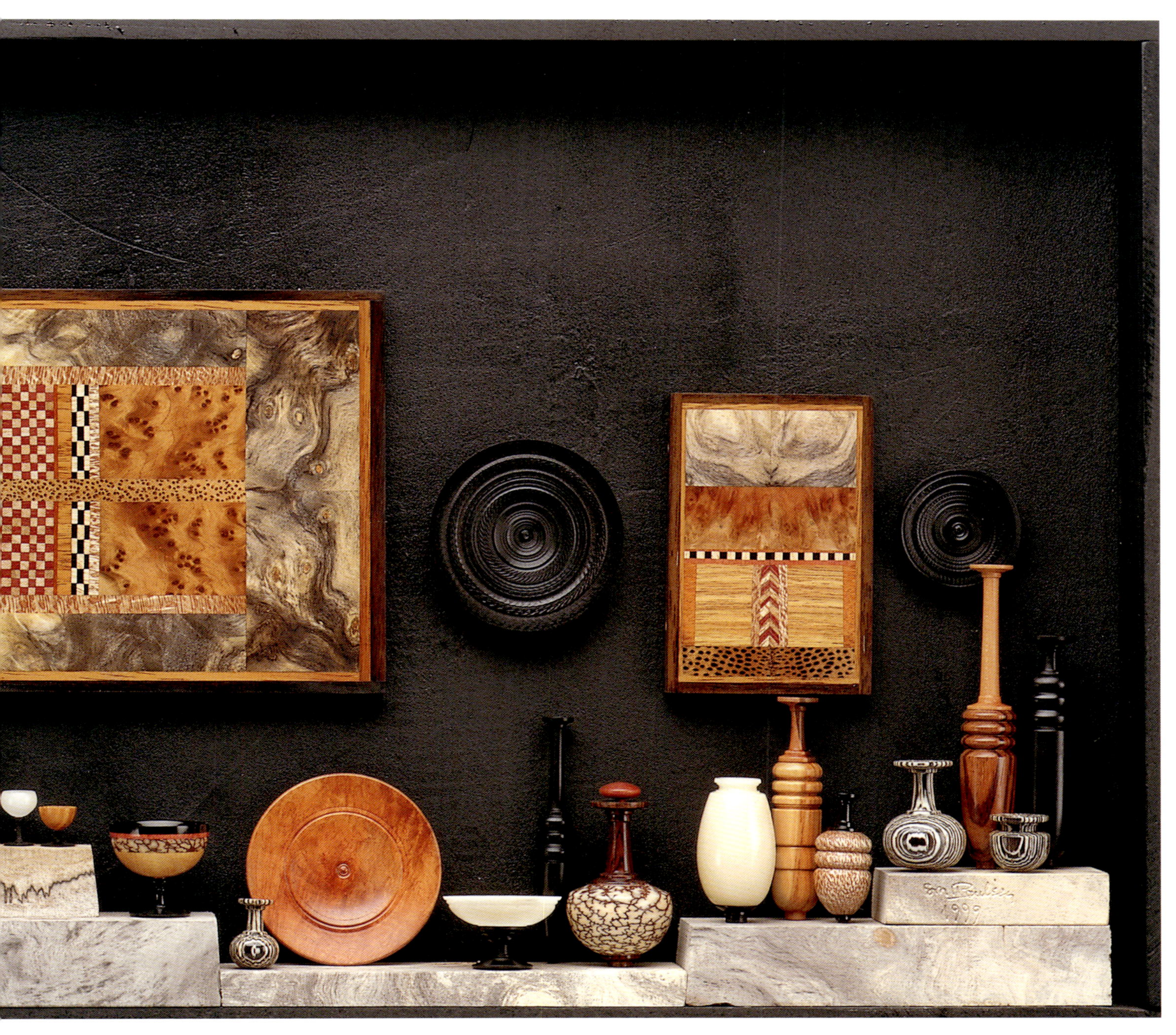

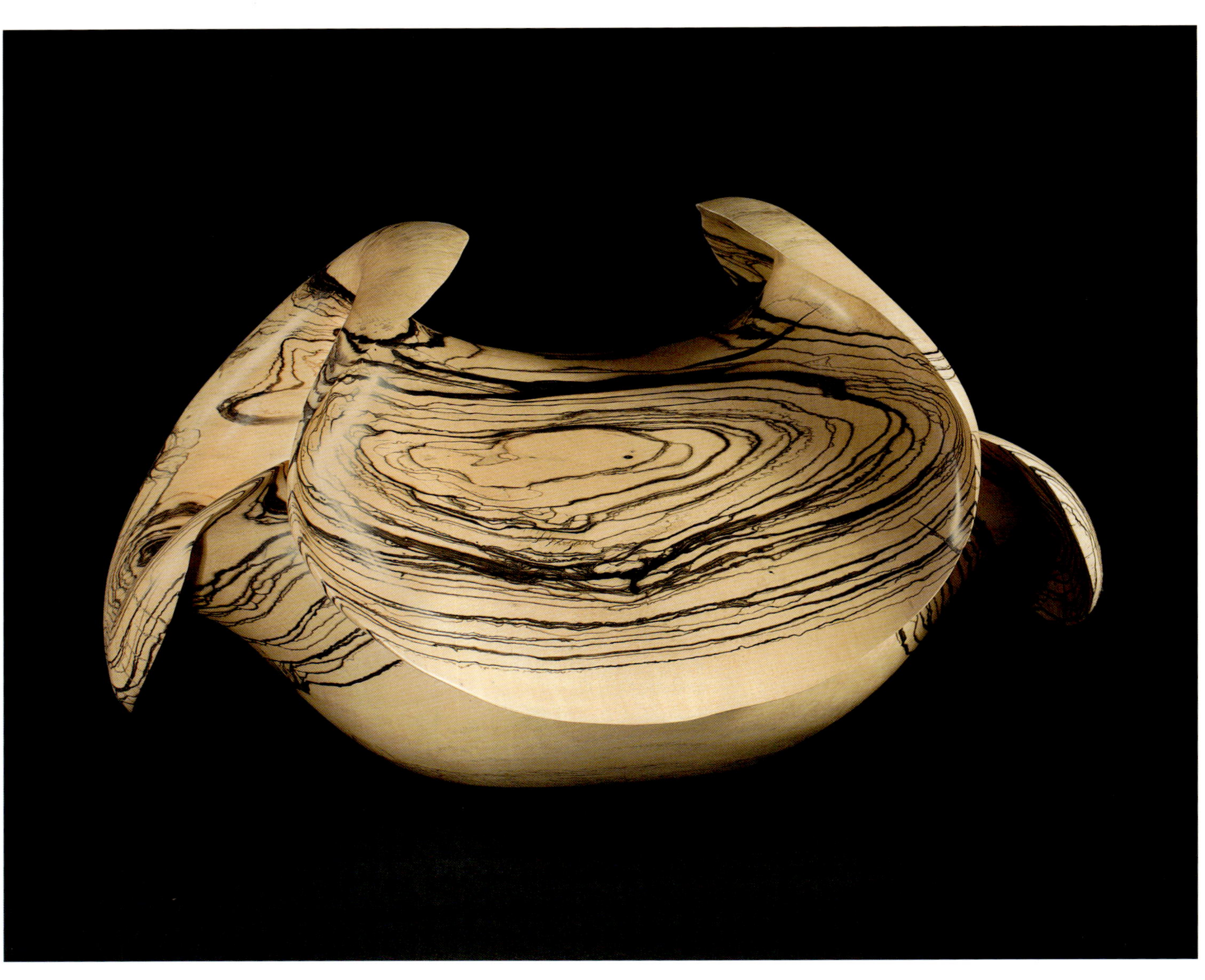

SOUPHOM & SOUPHONG MANIKHONG born 1957, born 1961, work Sacramento, California
MARBLED POD 2009, black and white ebony crotch, 17 x 28 x 15 $^{1}/_{2}$ in. (43.1 x 71.1 x 39.4 cm)

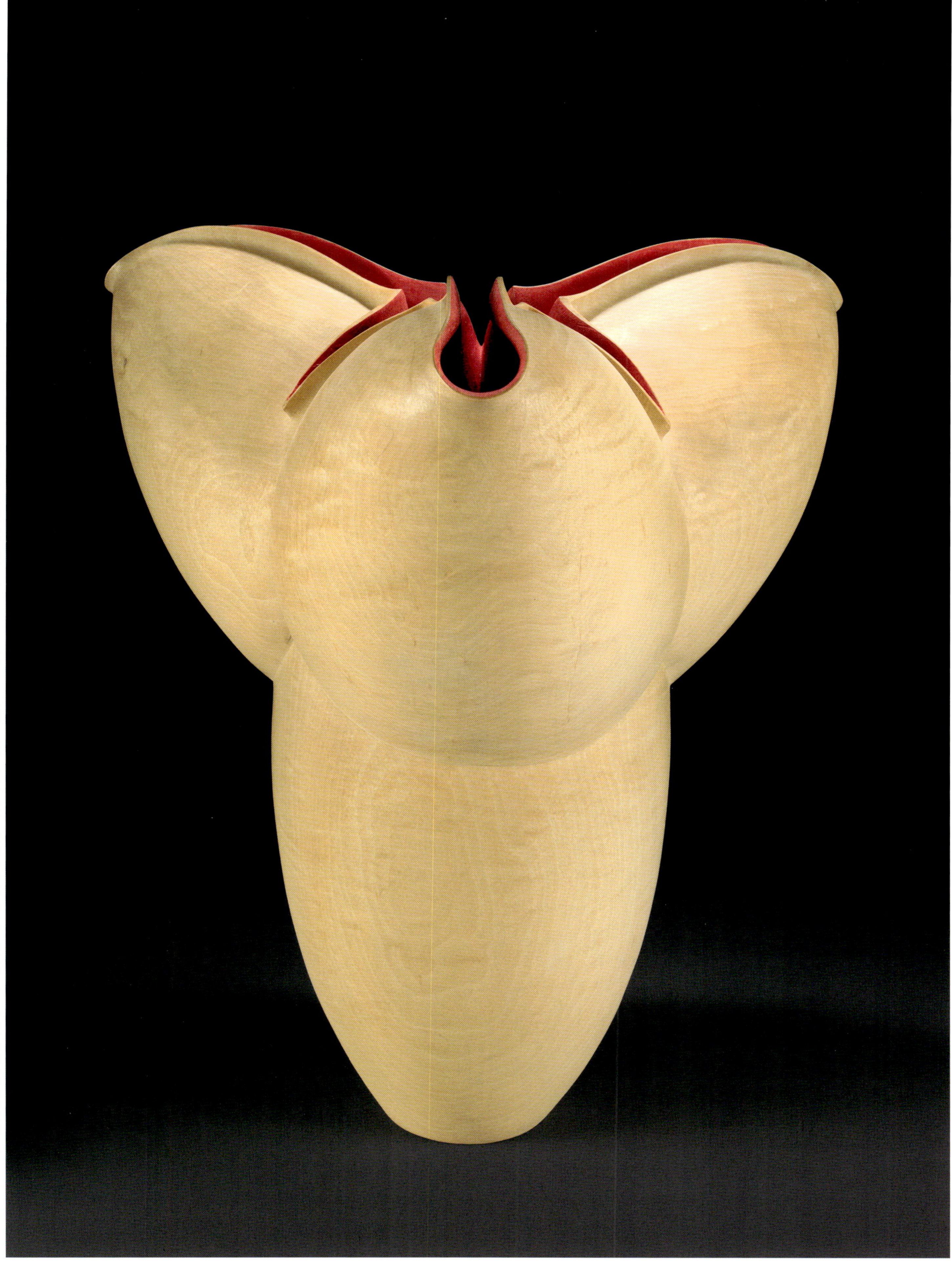

PETER HROMEK born 1947, works Sinntal-Schwarzenfels, Germany
PARADISE 2008, bleached maple, 13 1/4 x 11 1/2 x 11 1/2 in. (13.7 x 29.2 x 29.2 cm)

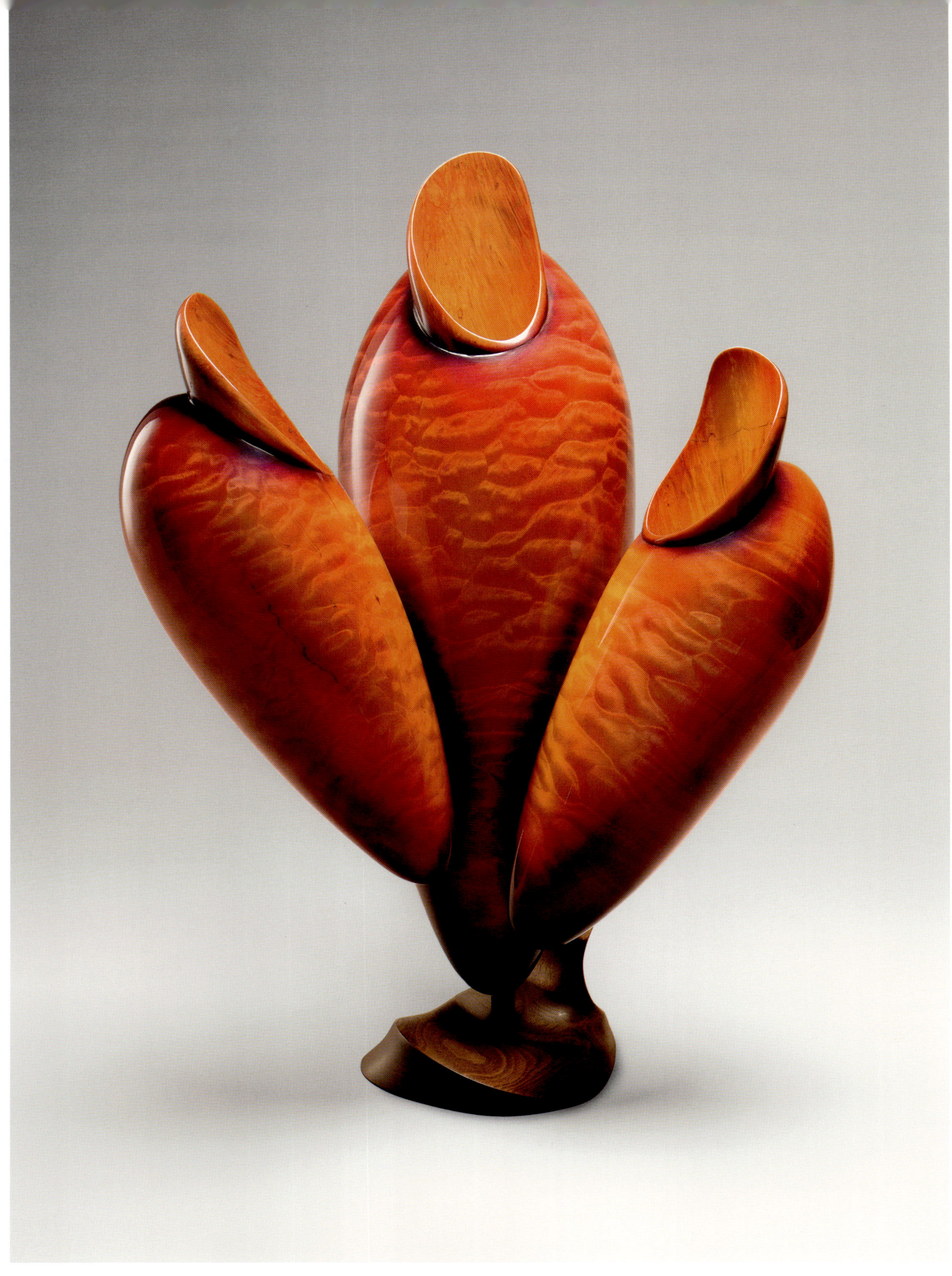

DONALD DERRY born 1956, works Ellensburg, Washington
MOTHER AND DAUGHTERS 2002, Western big-leaf maple, dye, lacquer, 17 x 12 x 7 in. (43.2 x 30.5 x 17.8 cm), Peabody Essex Museum, Gift of Lillian Montalto Bohlen

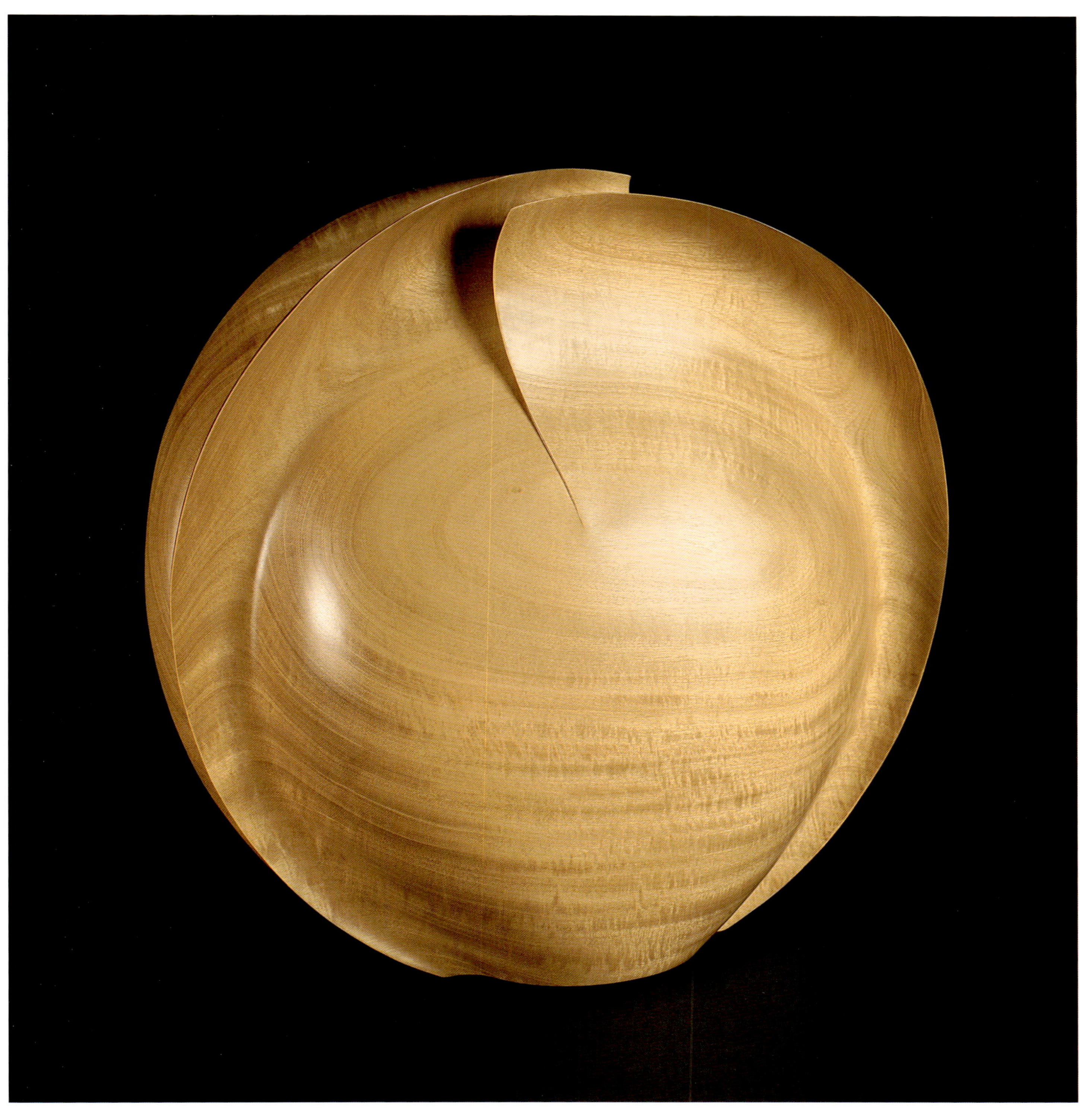

GRANT VAUGHAN born 1954, works Rock Valley, New South Wales, Australia
SPLIT FORM #5 2009, Australian white beech, 17 x 16 x 7 in. (43.2 x 40.6 x 17.8 cm)

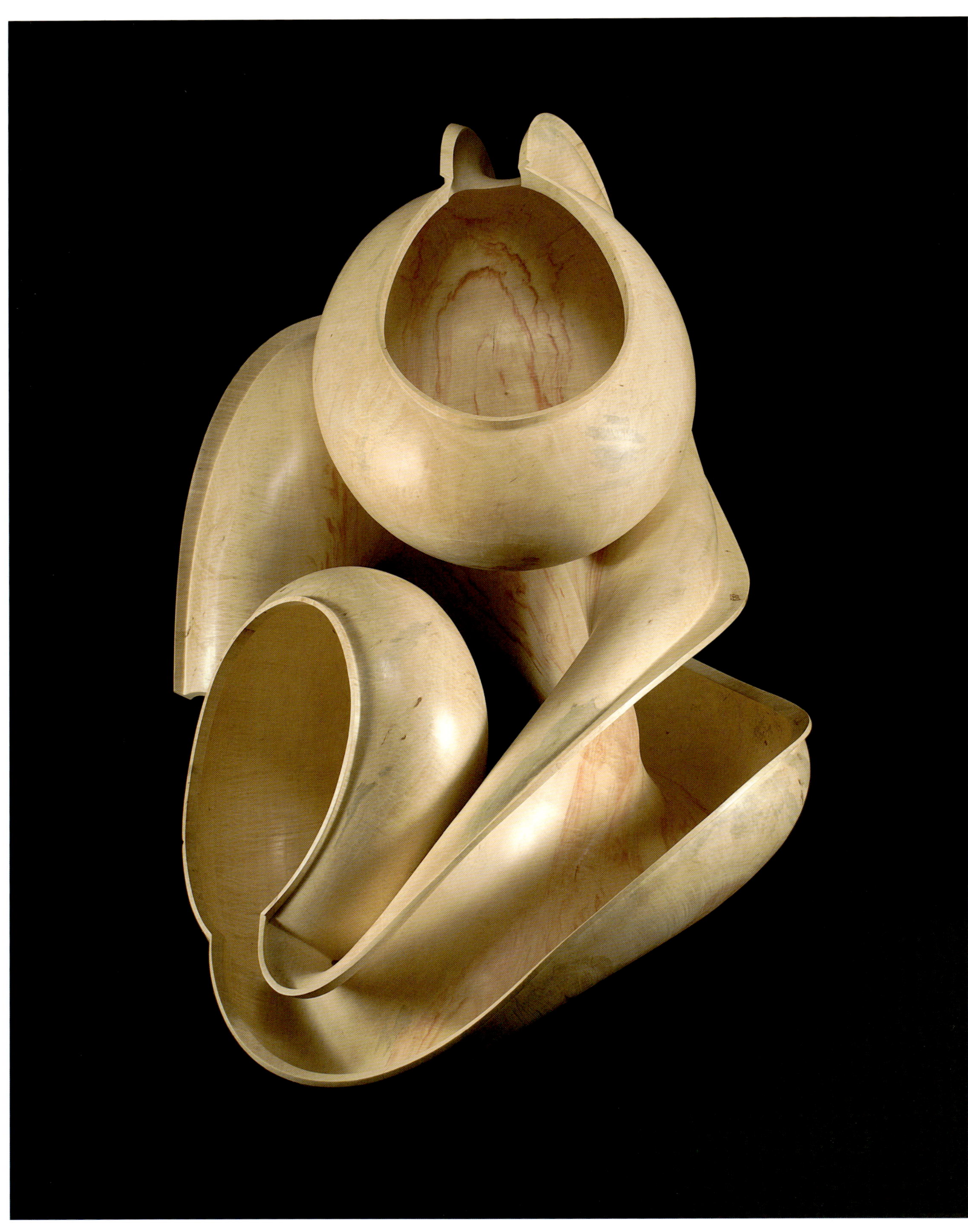

HUNT CLARK born 1969, works Sparta, Tennessee
UNTITLED 2010, ash leaf maple, 31 x 46 x 26 in. (78.7 x 116.8 x 66 cm)

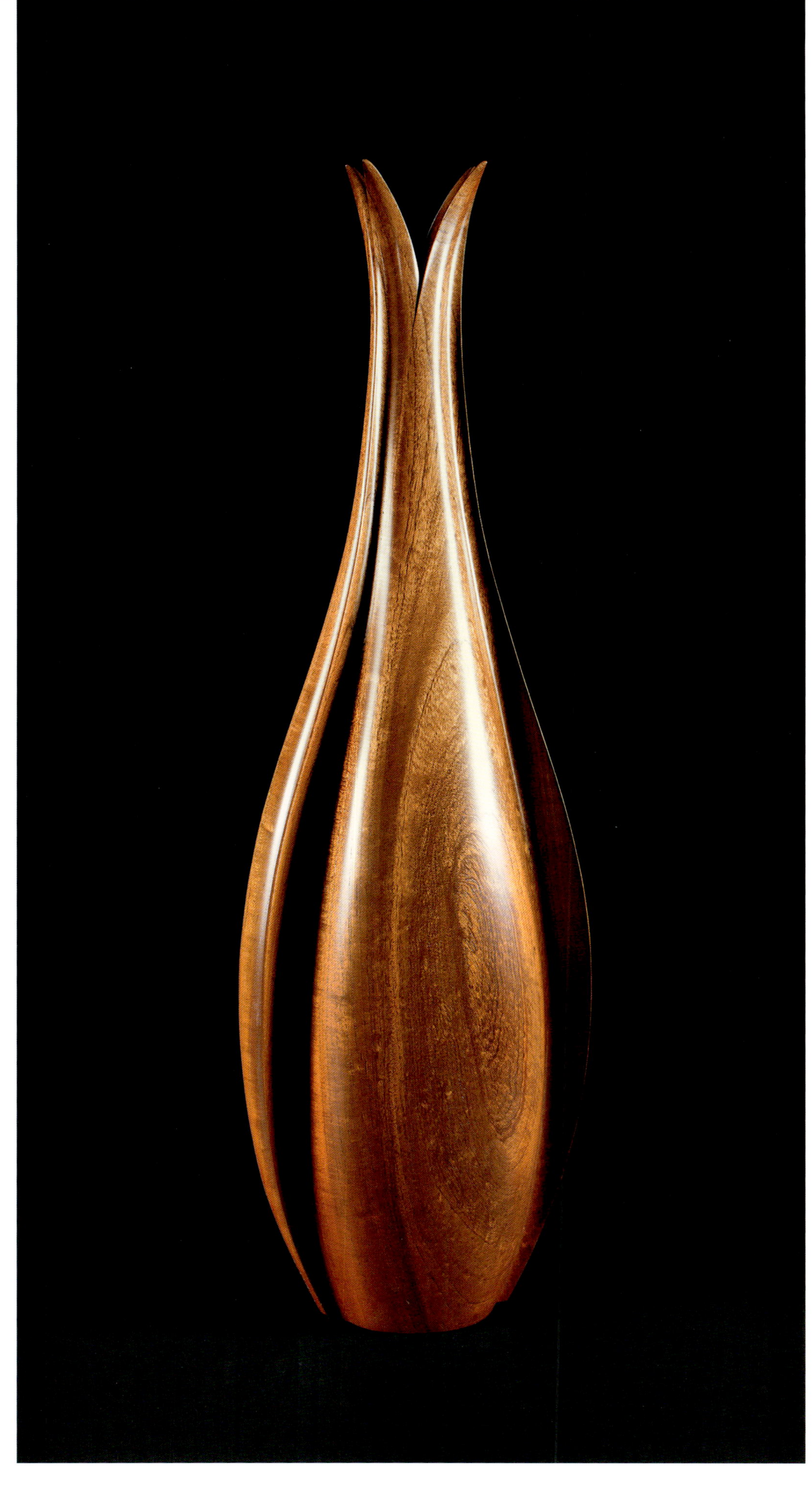

GRANT VAUGHAN born 1954, works Rock Valley, New South Wales, Australia
SPLIT FORM #7 2009, Australian red cedar, 38 x 12 x 7 in. (96.5 x 30.5 x 17.8 cm)

THE NATURAL EDGE

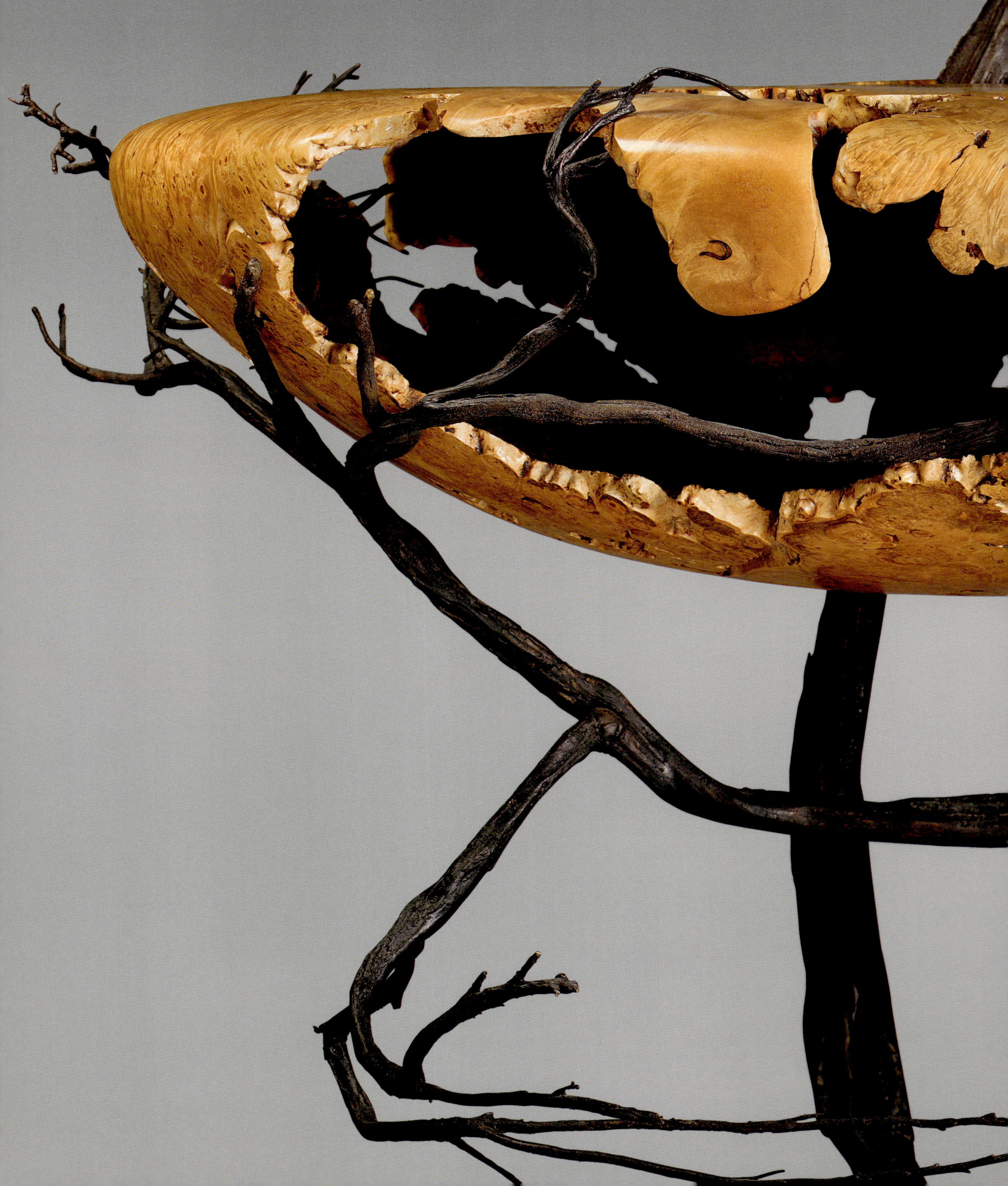

In the beginning, woodturners removed the defects and flaws in a piece of wood. But some artists see beauty in these natural characteristics and incorporate them into their design, making nature a partner in the creative process. The texture of a burl, the irregularities of tree bark, or the holes made by insects, all form natural edges that define contours, add texture, or create negative space.

RON GERTON: DEFECTIVE BEAUTY

The term "natural edge" is used to describe a feature of some wood art pieces. But what is a "natural edge"? It can be argued that any edge surface that the artist has created in working the wood is "unnatural," for the artist has had his way with the wood—chain sawing, woodturning, carving, piercing, sanding, hammering, or burning it.

But if an edge exists that has not had any human involvement, then it is a "natural edge." The rim of a wood bowl or the opening at the top of a hollow vessel are obvious edges. A void or an imperfection on the side of a bowl or a hollow vessel also contain an edge. If the edges have some feature not created by a human, such as bark being present, or insect damage, then this is a natural edge. The wood art piece "edge" may also include the actual surface of the object.

Almost the entire surface of Dale Nish's wormy ash vase is riddled with insect holes. Even though the entire vase was shaped and hollowed out by the skilled master's hands, the surface of the vase is still considered a natural edge. Had the artist carved or pierced the holes, it would not be a natural-edge art piece.

Brad Sells often leaves the rough bark on the edges of his carvings, which seems to enhance the beautiful, smooth, and sensual polished wood below the bark. It is easy to see how his breathtaking piece, *Traveler's Bridge,* was created from the trunk of a large tree. Yet it is almost impossible to understand how he made it.

The wonderful, bumpy side surface of Bob Womack's *Capital Reef* vase is a natural feature that exists on some burl woods when the bark is removed. This same natural edge appears in Terry Martin's *Temple* piece, where the entire top has the bumpy burl surface.

Many times the most impressive color and patterns occur where the tree has had to grow over or around an injury or defect, or insects and decay have created unique features. For many artists it is a challenge to make a treasure from wood that might appear as detritus to others.

Detail, Ron Gerton, *A Tree Runs Through It,* 1998 (page 64)

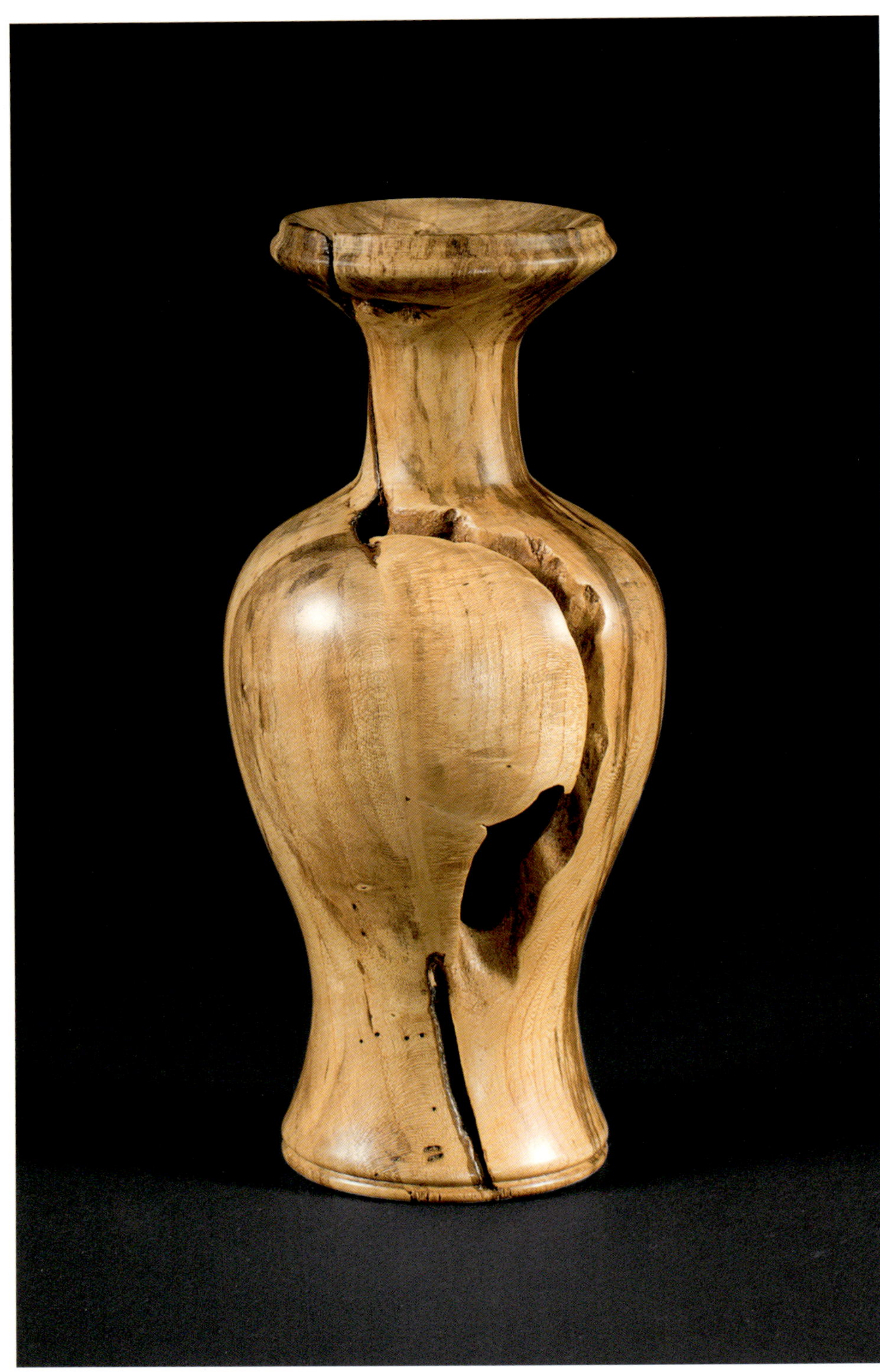

MELVIN LINDQUIST 1911–2000, worked Quincy, Florida
VASE 1996, hackberry, 11 x 5 in. (28 x 12.7 cm), Peabody Essex Museum, Gift of Lillian Montalto Bohlen

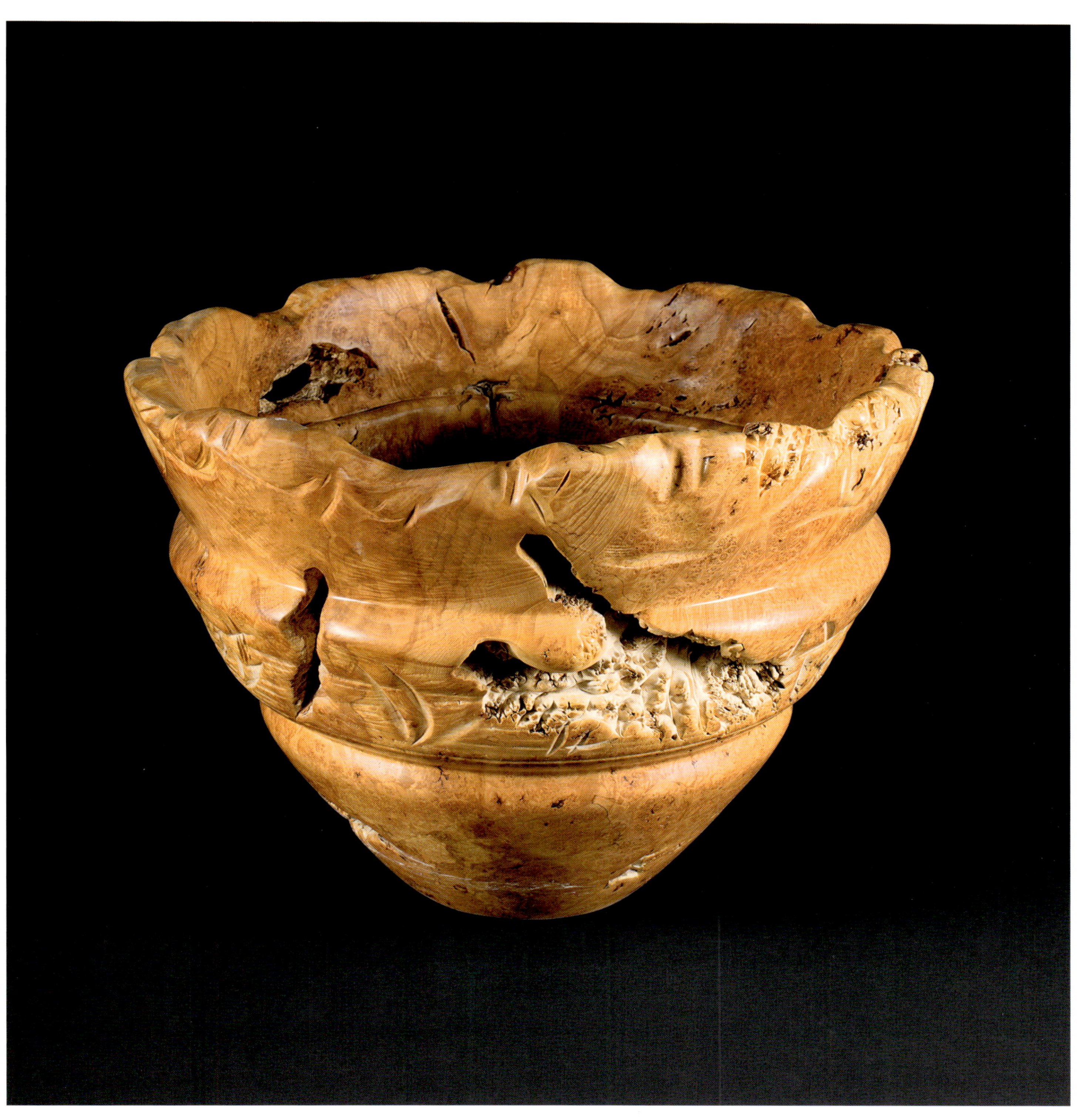

DENNIS ELLIOTT born 1950, works Fort Myers, Florida
B2116 PERIGREE II 1999, big-leaf maple burl, 16 1/2 x 23 3/4 x 23 in. (42 x 60.3 x 58.4 cm)

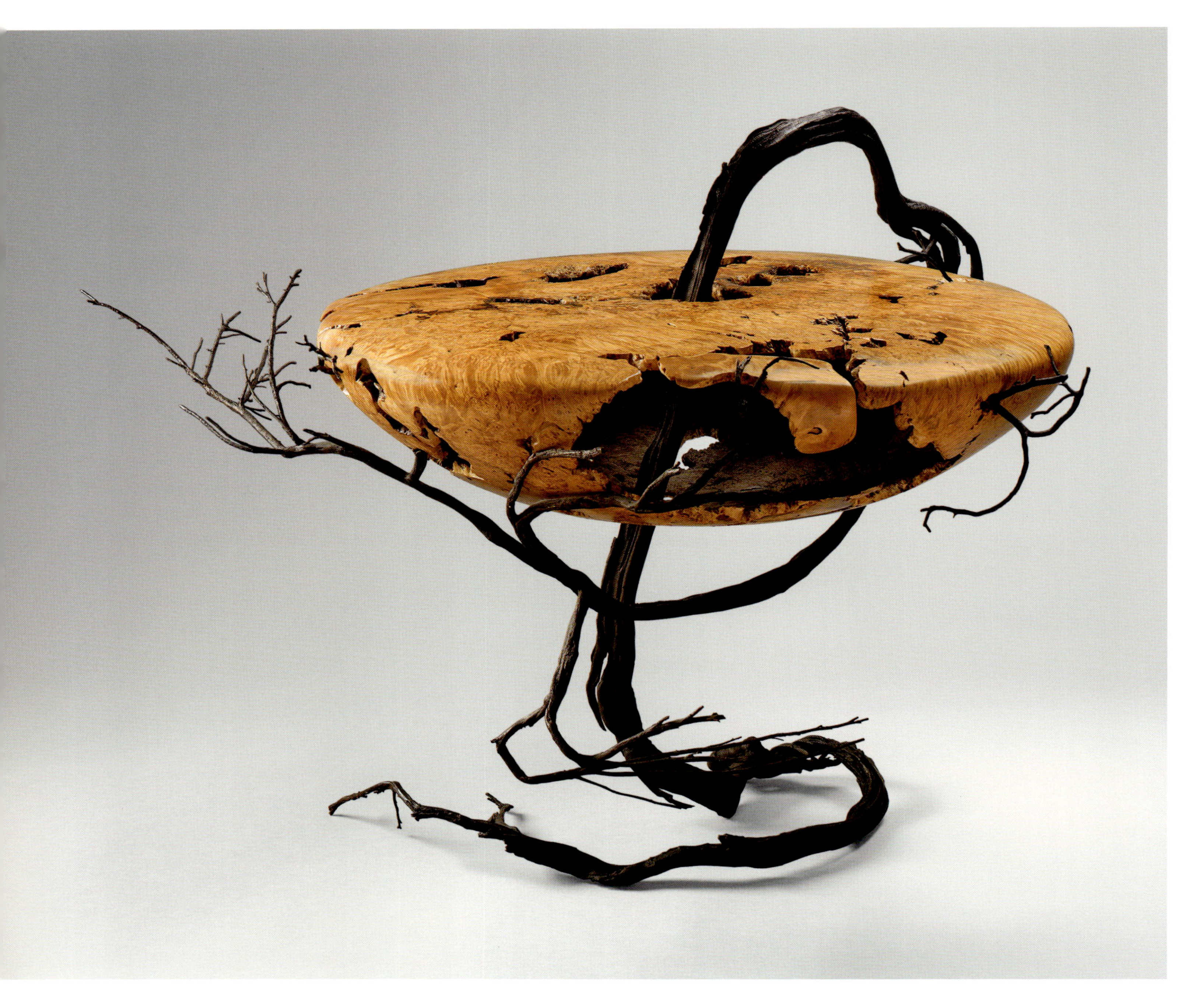

RON GERTON born 1946, works Richland, Washington
A TREE RUNS THROUGH IT 1998, spalted maple burl, bronze, 28 x 40 x 30 in. (71.1 x 101.6 x 76.2 cm)

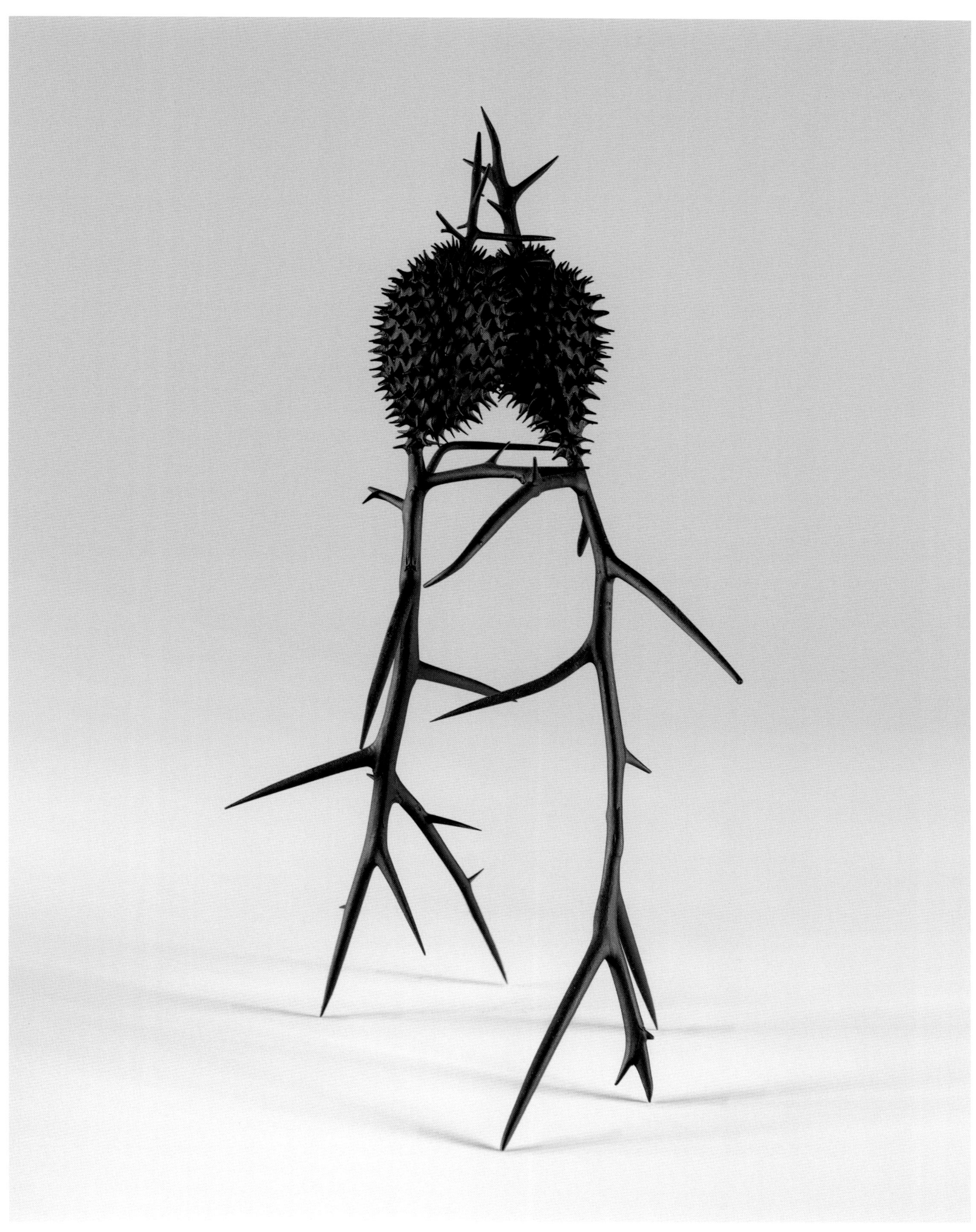

DAVID SENGEL born 1951, works Boone, North Carolina
THE KISS 2000, pear wood, locust, rose thorns, dye, 10 x 6 x 6 in. (25.4 x 15.2 x 15.2 cm)

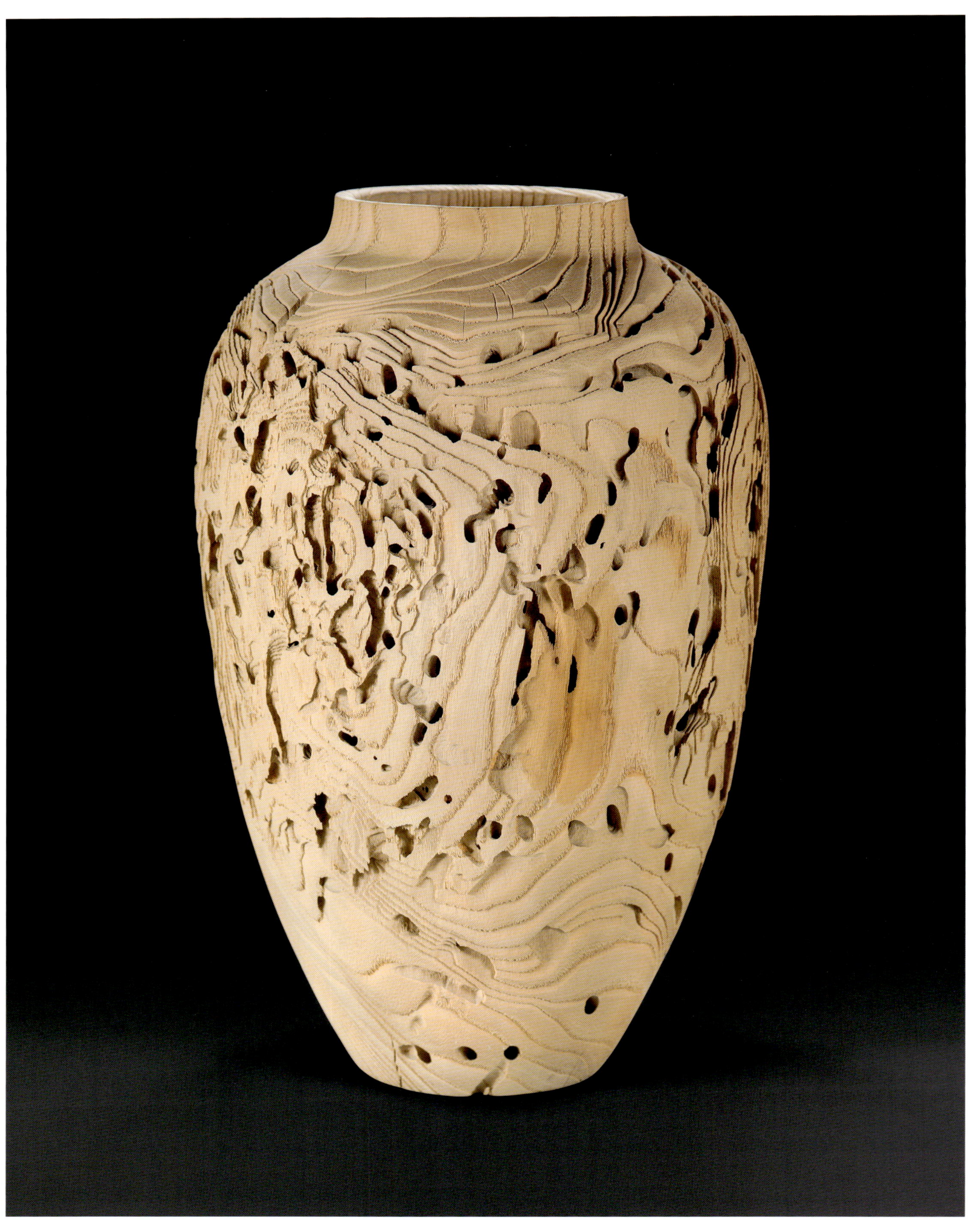

DALE NISH 1932–2013, worked Provo, Utah
UNTITLED 1984, wormy ash, 12 $^{1}/_{2}$ x 7 $^{1}/_{2}$ x 7 in. (31.8 x 19 x 17.8 cm), Peabody Essex Museum, Gift of Lillian Montalto Bohlen

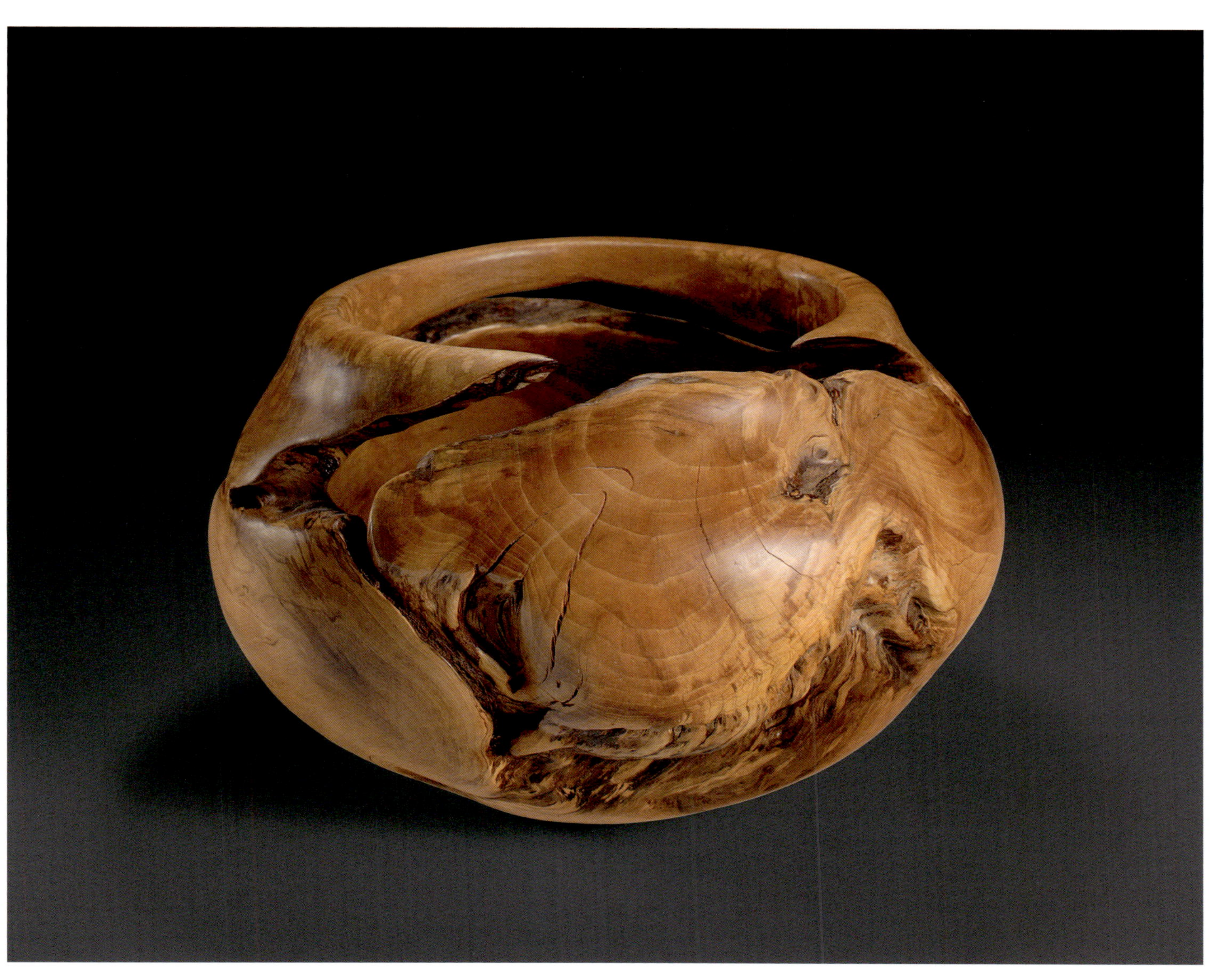

MELVIN LINDQUIST 1911–2000, worked Quincy, Florida
BOWL 1996, sugar maple burl, 5 $^{1}/_{2}$ x 8 in. (14 x 20.3 cm), Peabody Essex Museum, Gift of Lillian Montalto Bohlen

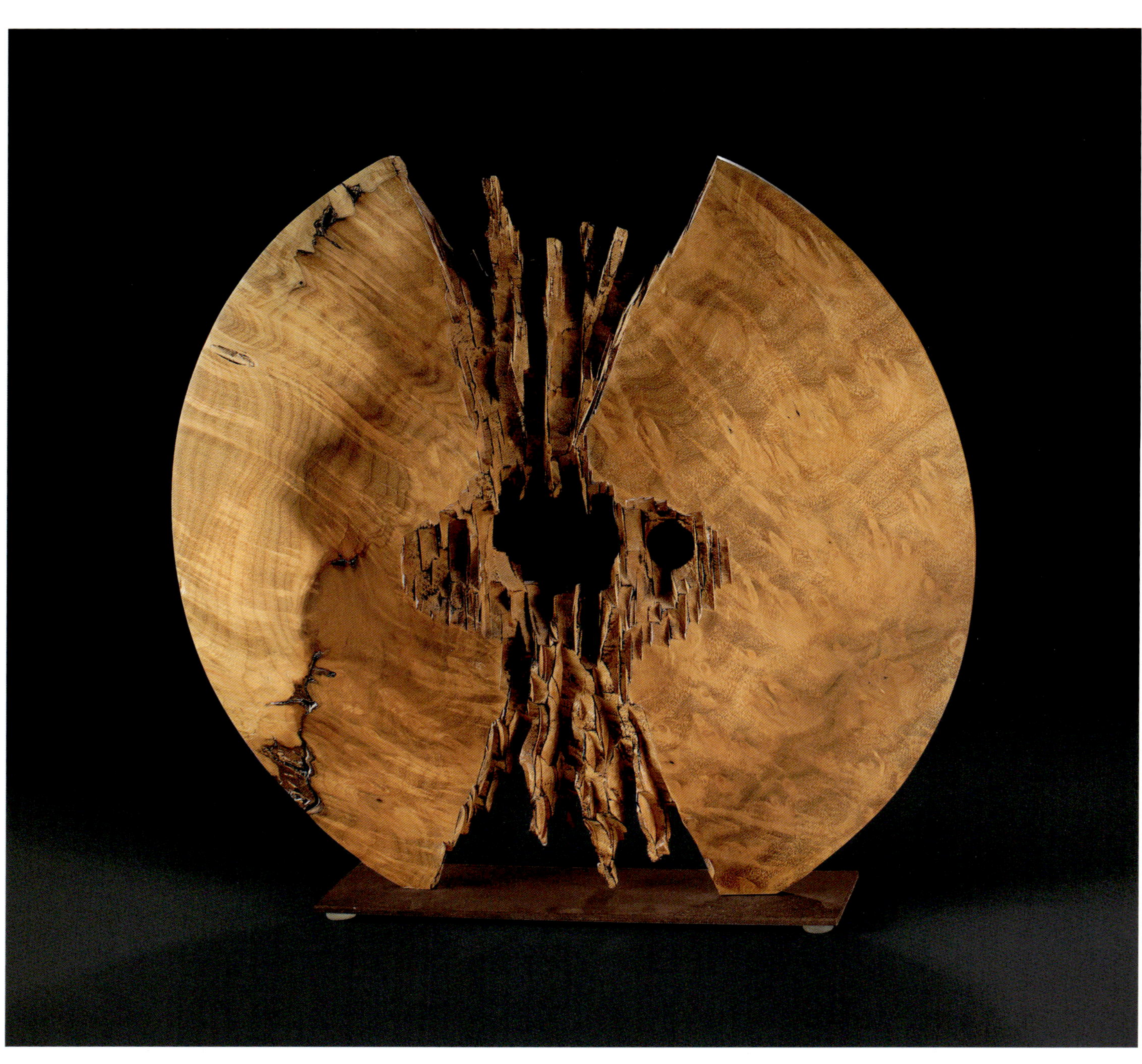

JACK SLENTZ born 1963, works Santa Fe, New Mexico
DEGENERATING DISK 2004, steel and bay laurel burl, 11 x 11 $^{1}/_{2}$ x 2 in. (28 x 29.2 x 5.1 cm)

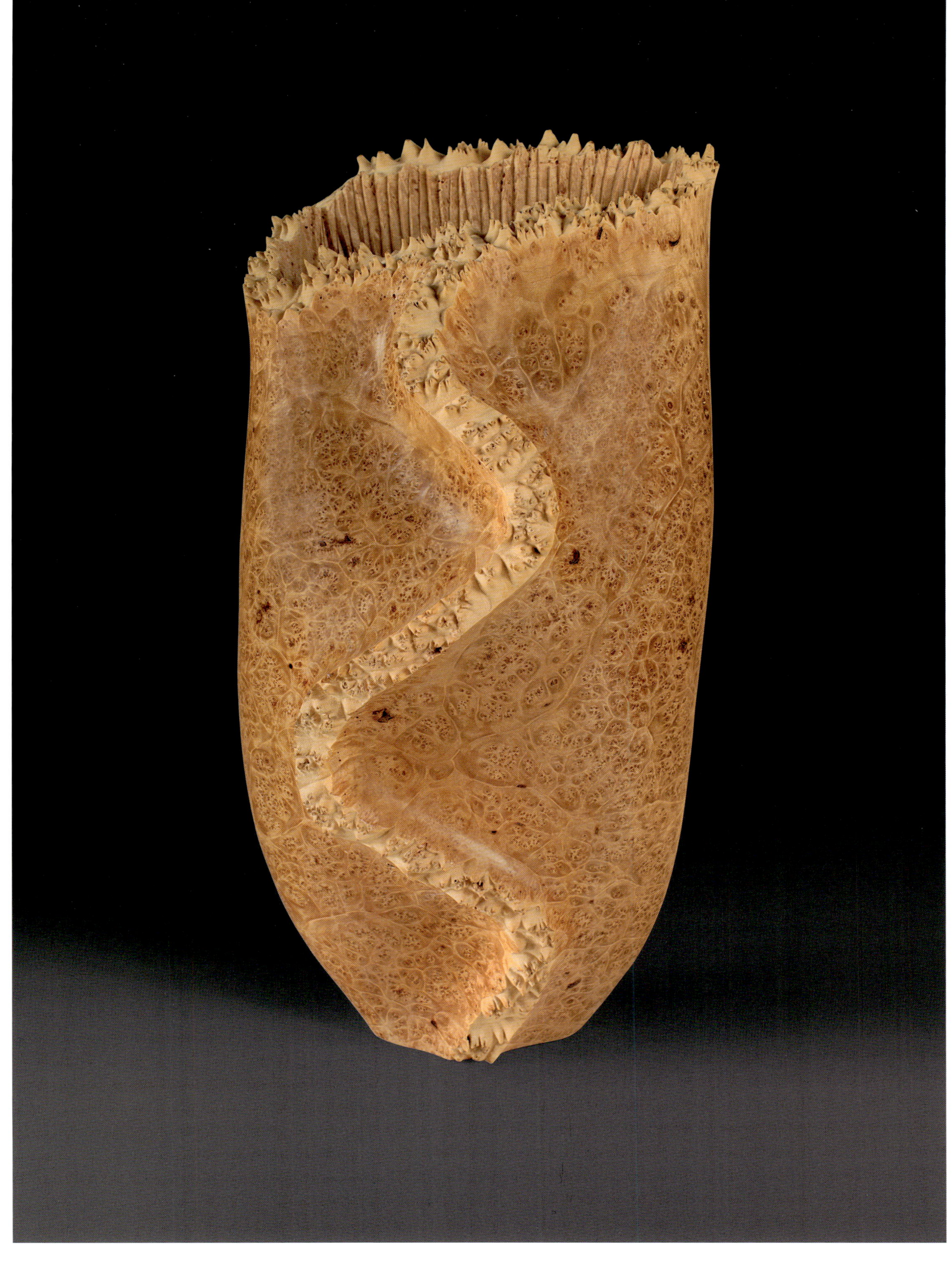

BOB WOMACK born 1947, works Cortez, Colorado
CAPITAL REEF 1998, big-leaf maple burl, 14 1/2 x 7 1/2 x 5 1/2 in. (36.8 x 19.1 x 14 cm)

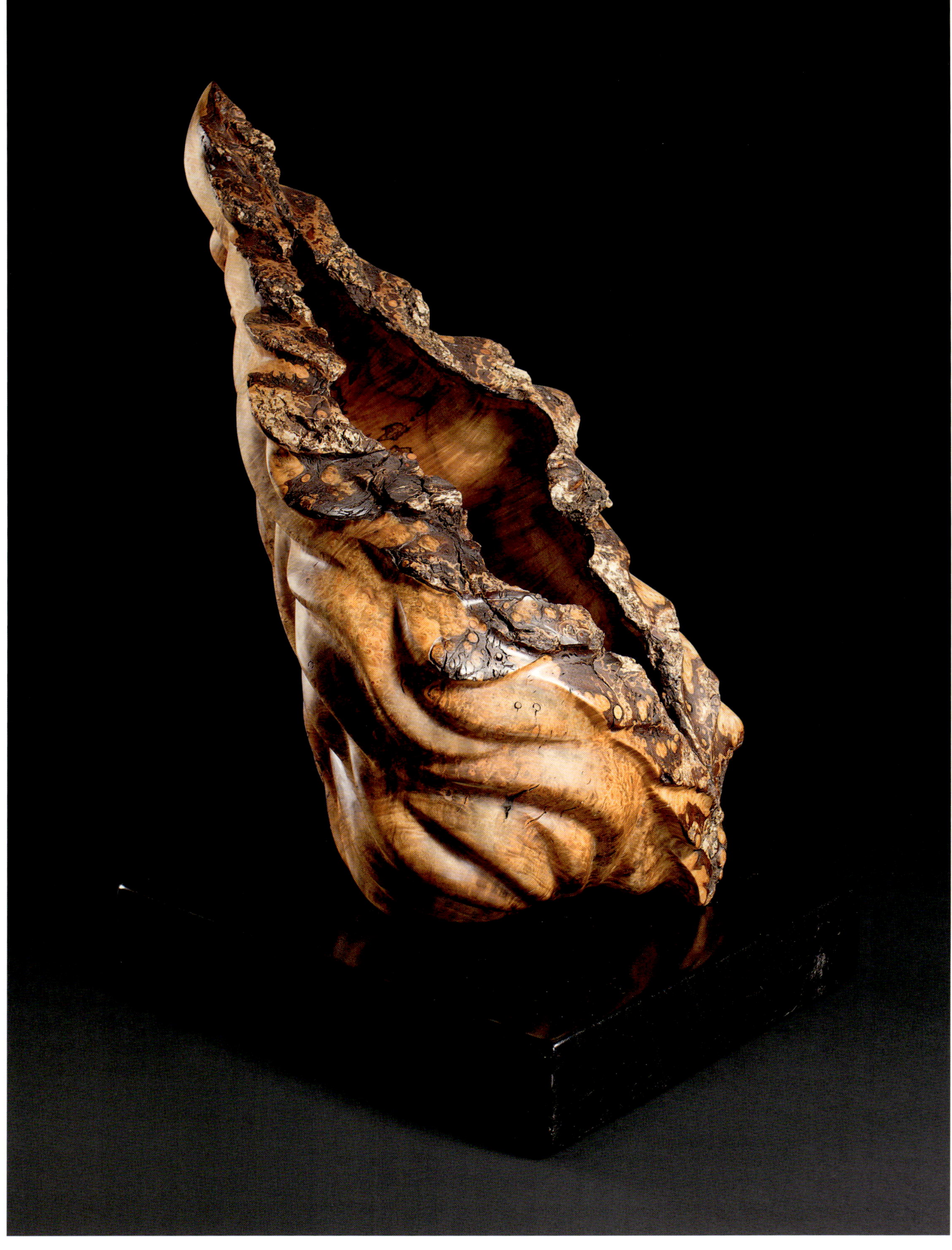

MARK BRESSLER 1951–2010, worked Santa Fe, New Mexico
GLACIER 2008, oak burl, 30 x 20 x 16 in. (76.2 x 50.8 x 40.6 cm), Peabody Essex Museum, Gift of Lillian Montalto Bohlen

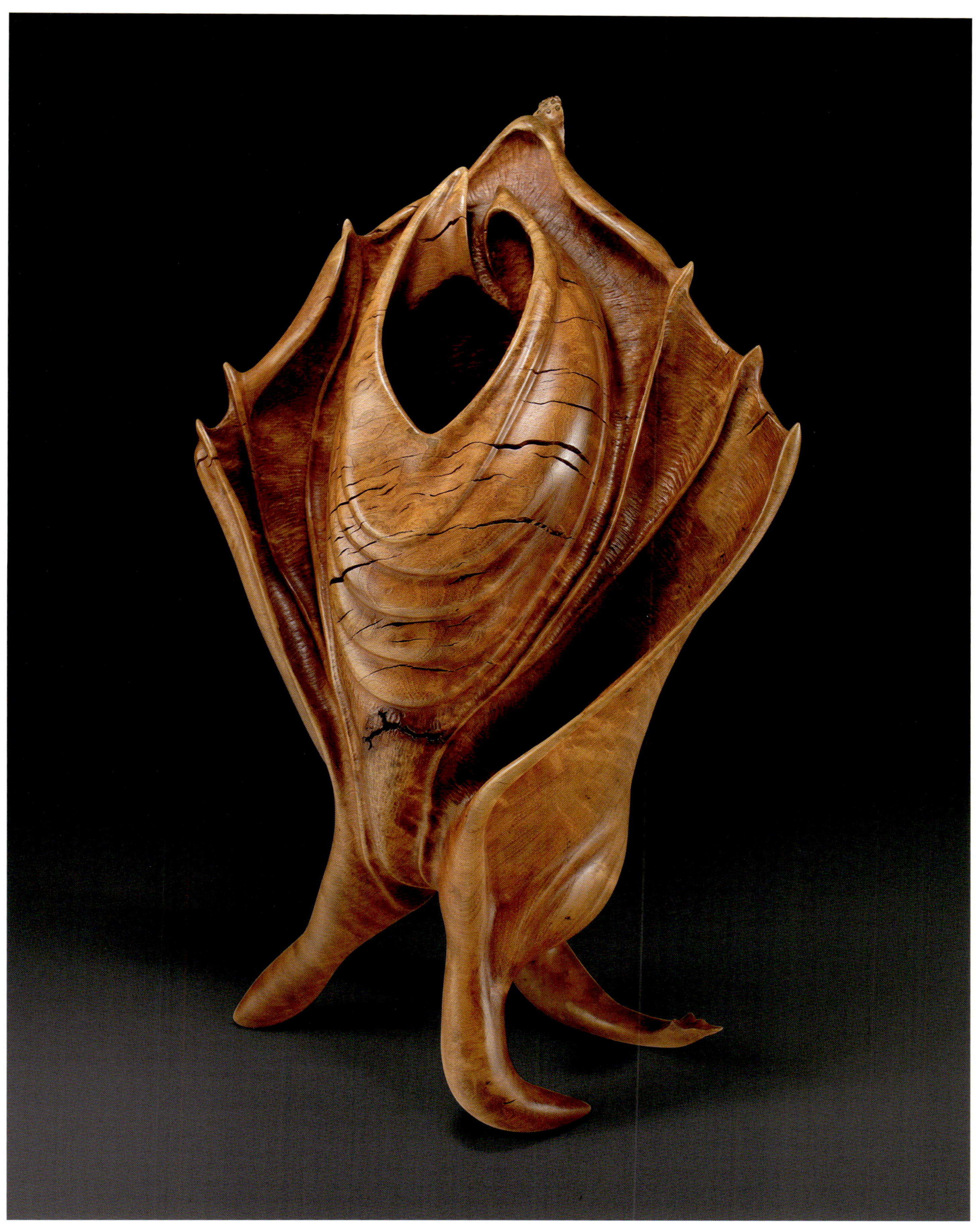

MICHAEL LEE born 1960, works in Kapolei, Hawai'i
PTEROSAUR 1994, madrone burl, 15 x 9 x 6 in. (38.1 x 22.9 x 15.2 cm)

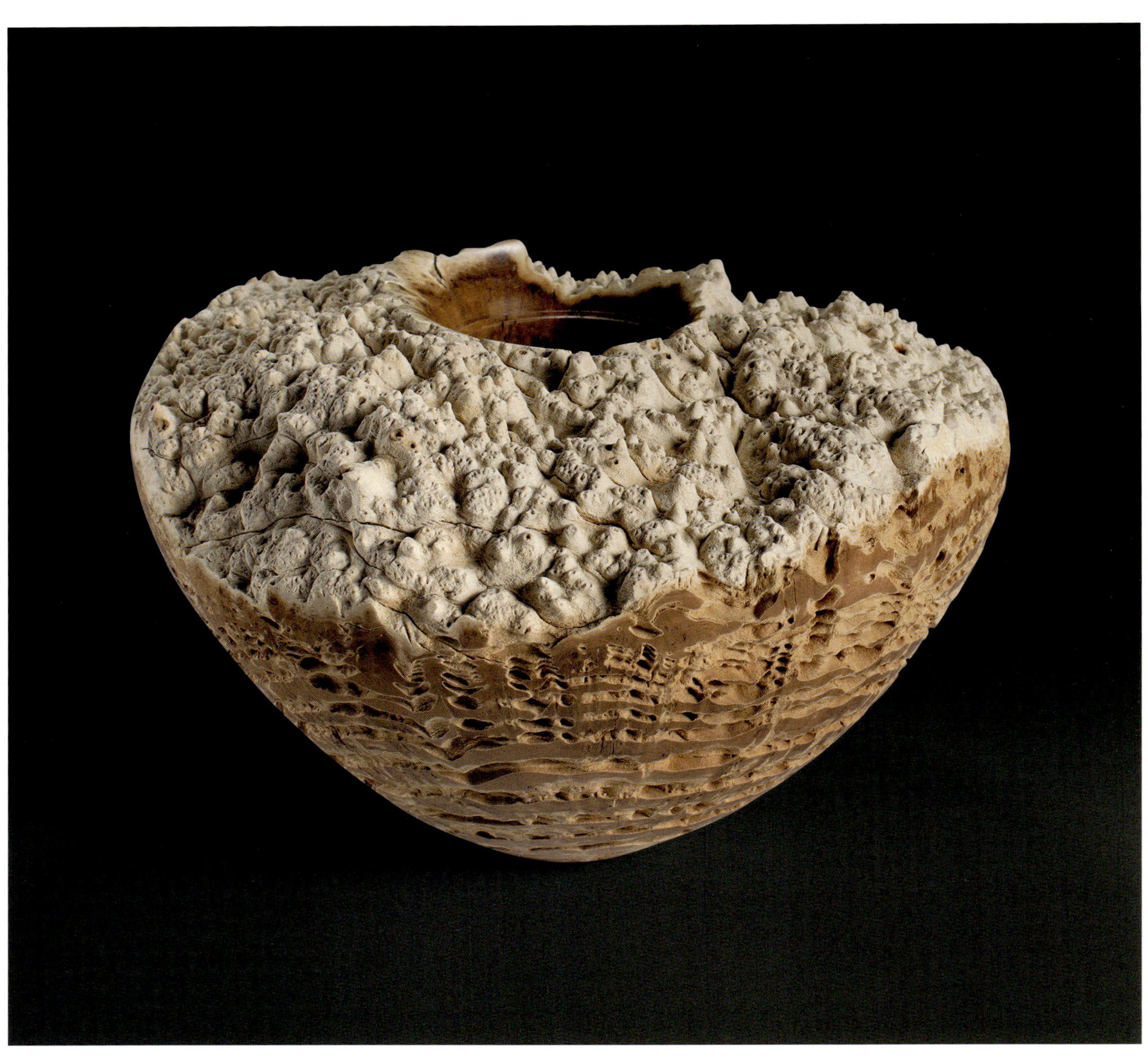

KIP CHRISTENSEN born 1955, works Springville, Utah
WHITED SEPULCHER SERIES 2002, Russian olive burl, 4 1/4 x 7 1/2 x 8 in. (10.8 x 19 x 20.3 cm), Peabody Essex Museum, Gift of Lillian Montalto Bohlen

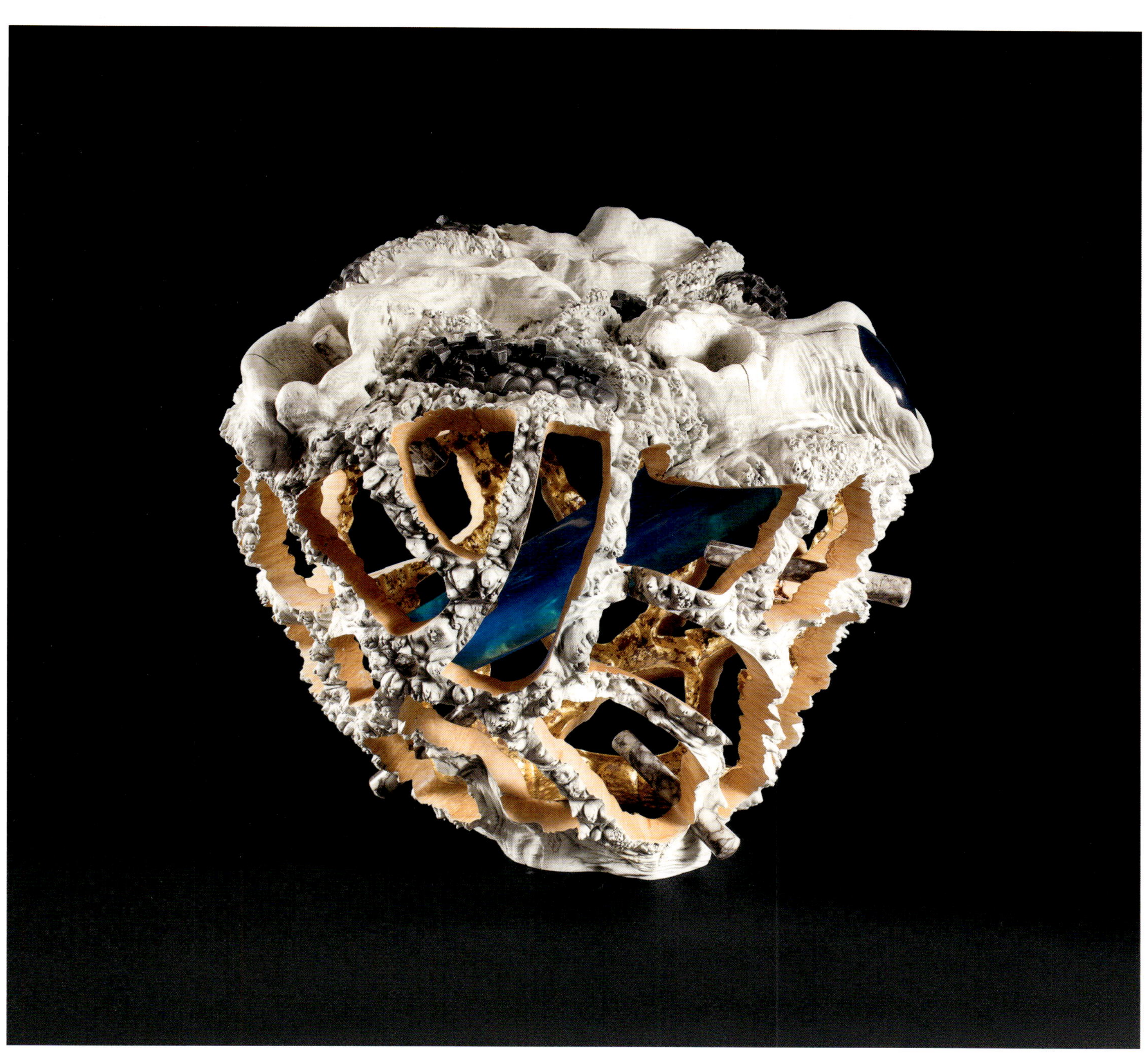

HUGH MCKAY born 1951, works Spencer, Iowa
BURL CULT 2002, maple burl, cast glass, cast lead, stone on alabaster, gold leaf, paint, 30 x 32 x 30 in. (76.2 x 81.3 x 76.2 cm)

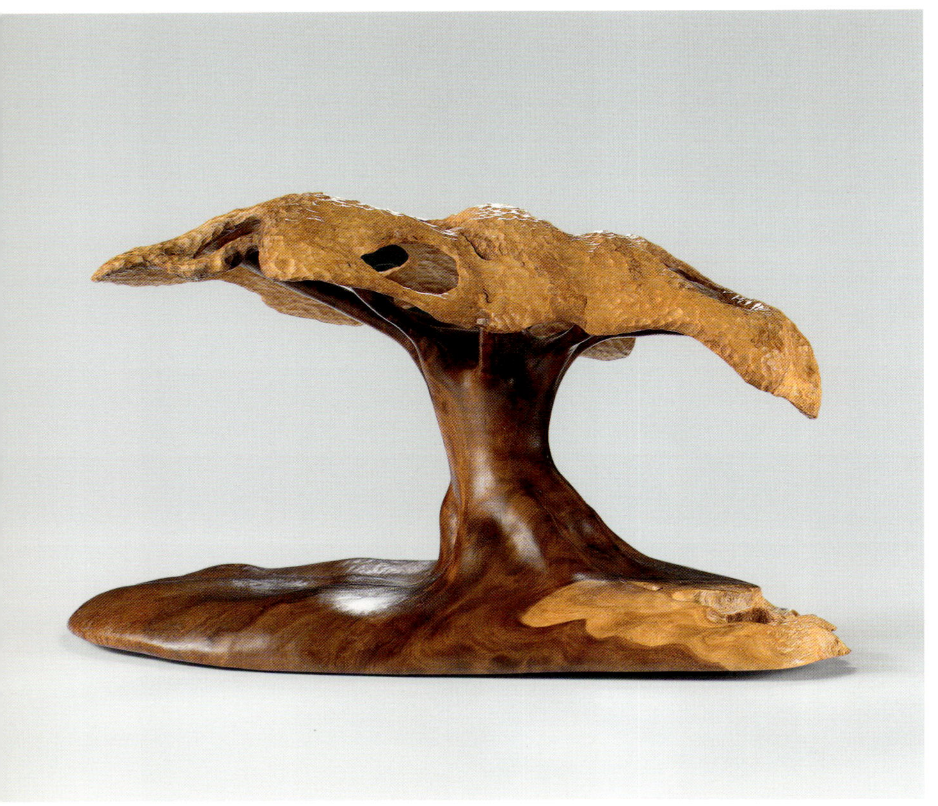

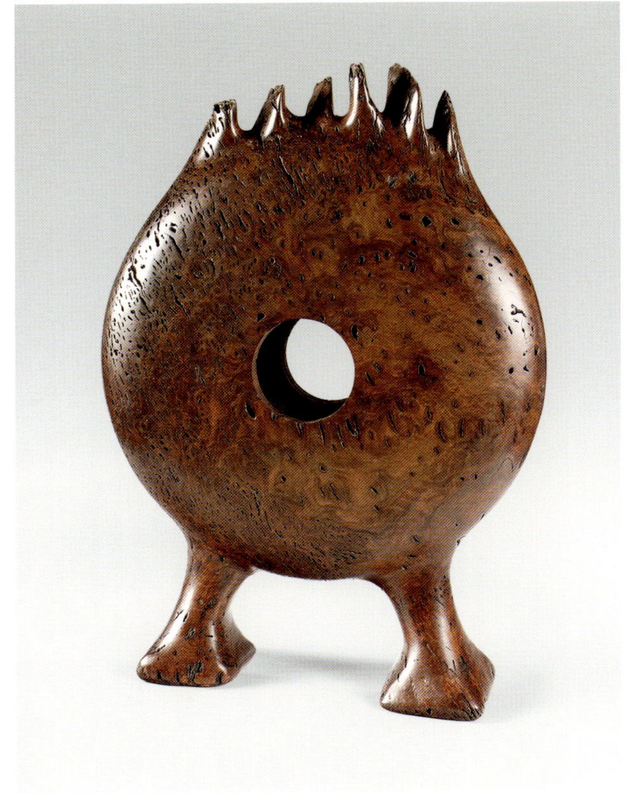

Left to right: **TERRY MARTIN** born 1947, works Toowong, Queensland, Australia

BONSAI 2002, jarrah burl, 4 1/2 x 8 x 5 3/4 in. (11.4 x 20.3 x 14.6 cm), Peabody Essex Museum, Gift of Lillian Montalto Bohlen

BIGCLOPS 2000, jarrah burl, 23 1/2 x 16 1/2 x 5 1/2 in. (59.7 x 41.9 x 14 cm)

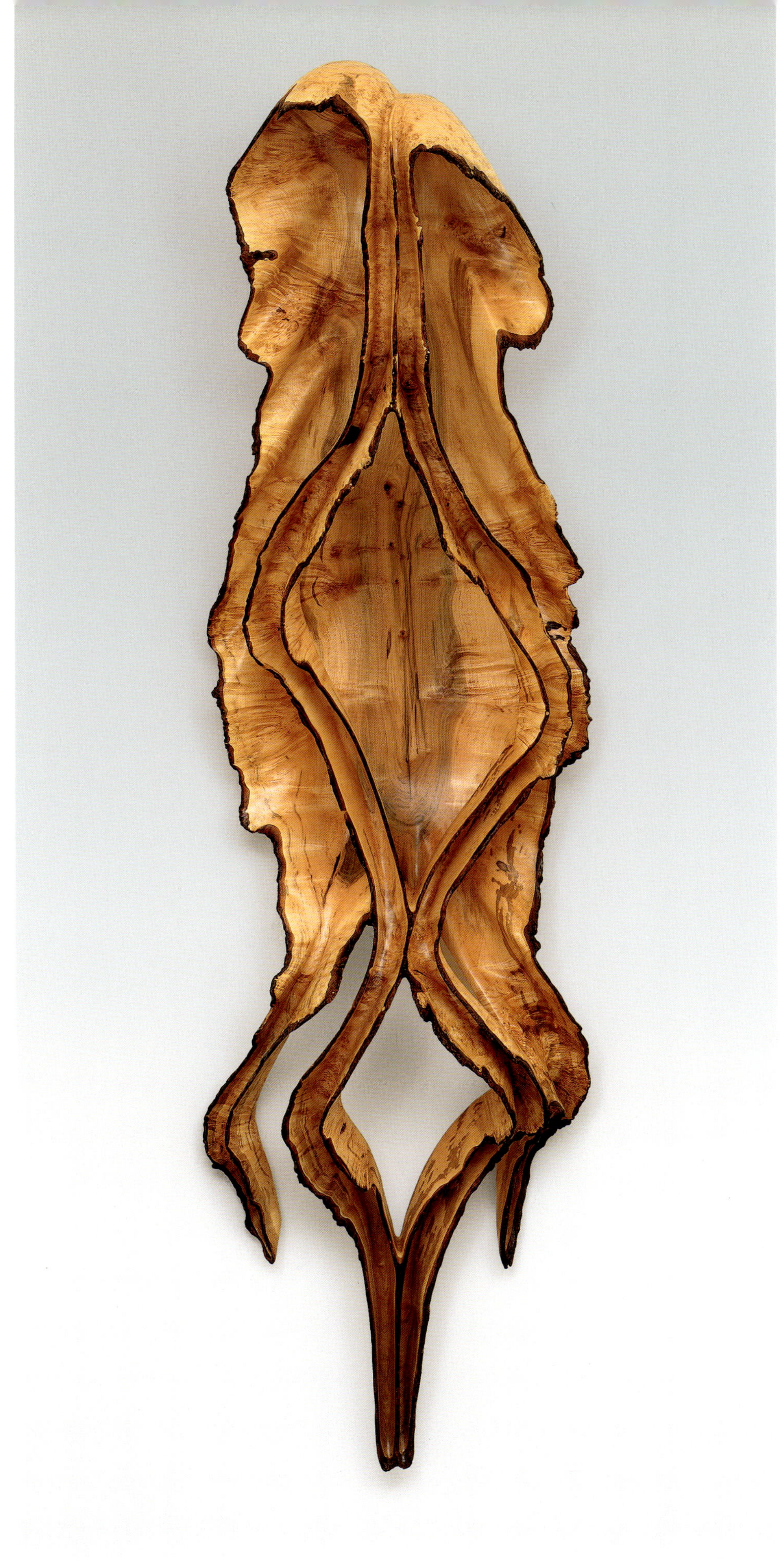

BRAD SELLS born 1969, works Cookeville, Tennessee
TRAVELER'S BRIDGE 2001, maple burl, 96 x 24 x 16 in. (243.8 x 61 x 40.6 cm)

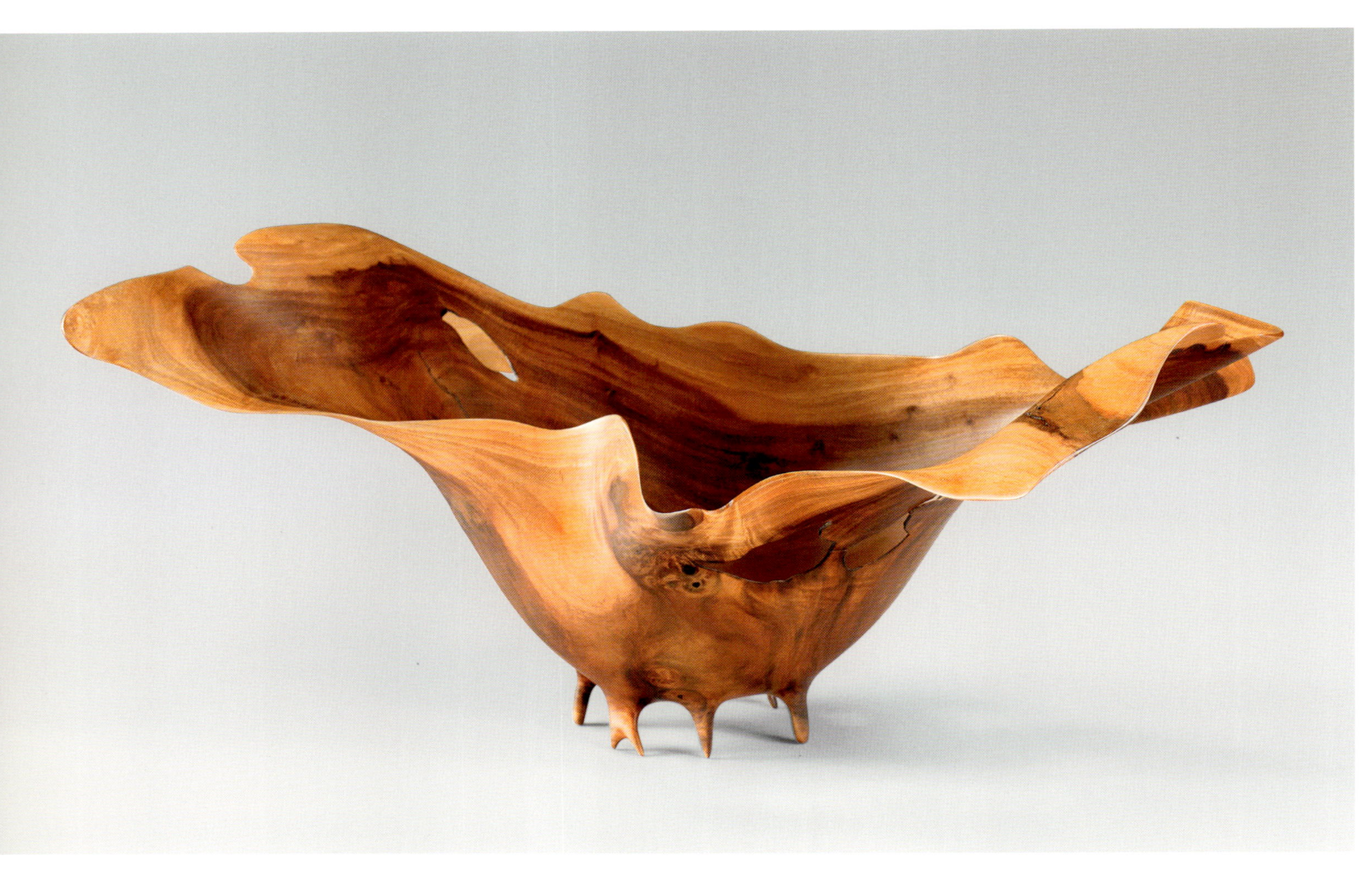

DEREK BENCOMO born 1962, works Wailuku, Hawai'i
PAIA VALLEY 1997, Maui milo wood, 11 $^{3}/_{4}$ x 26 x 13 in. (29.8 x 66 x 33 cm)

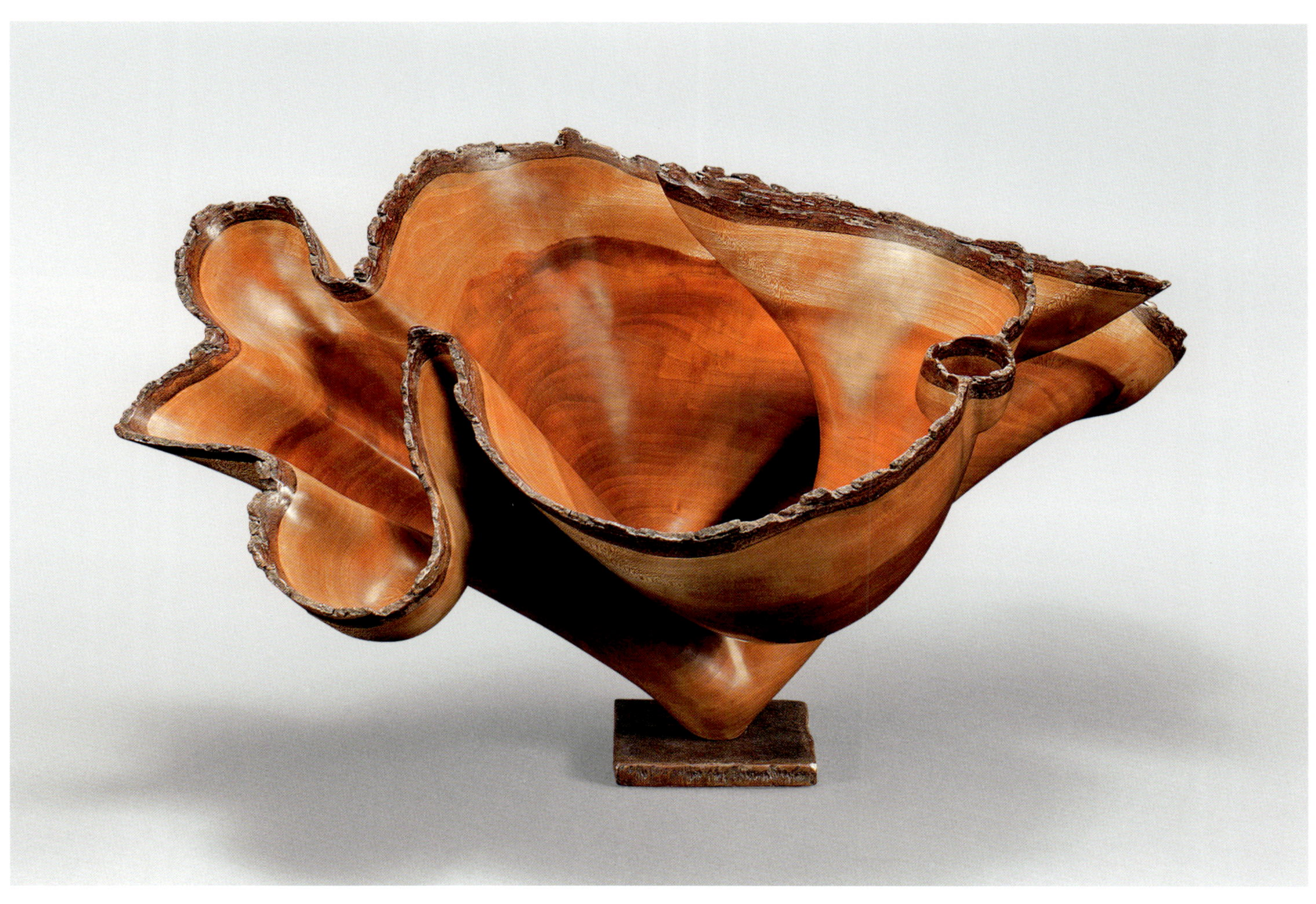

BRAD SELLS born 1969, works Cookeville, Tennessee
WHIRL 2003, cherry, 19 x 30 x 18 in. (48.2 x 76.2 x 45.7 cm), Peabody Essex Museum, Gift of Lillian Montalto Bohlen

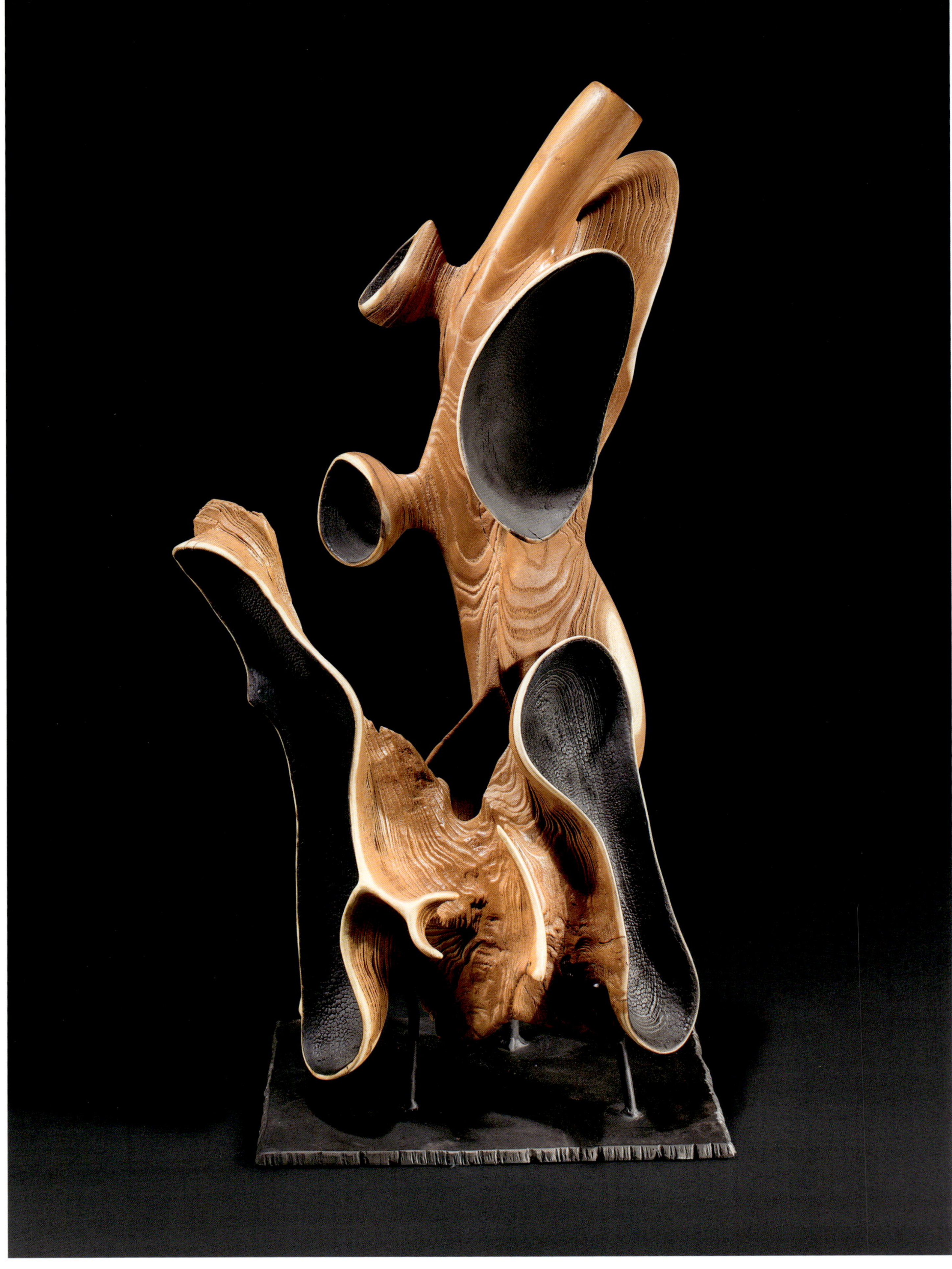

BRAD SELLS born 1969, works Cookeville, Tennessee
RAIN AND FIRE 2013, mulberry, 29 x 13 $^{1}/_{4}$ x 9 in. (73.7 x 33.7 x 22.9 cm)

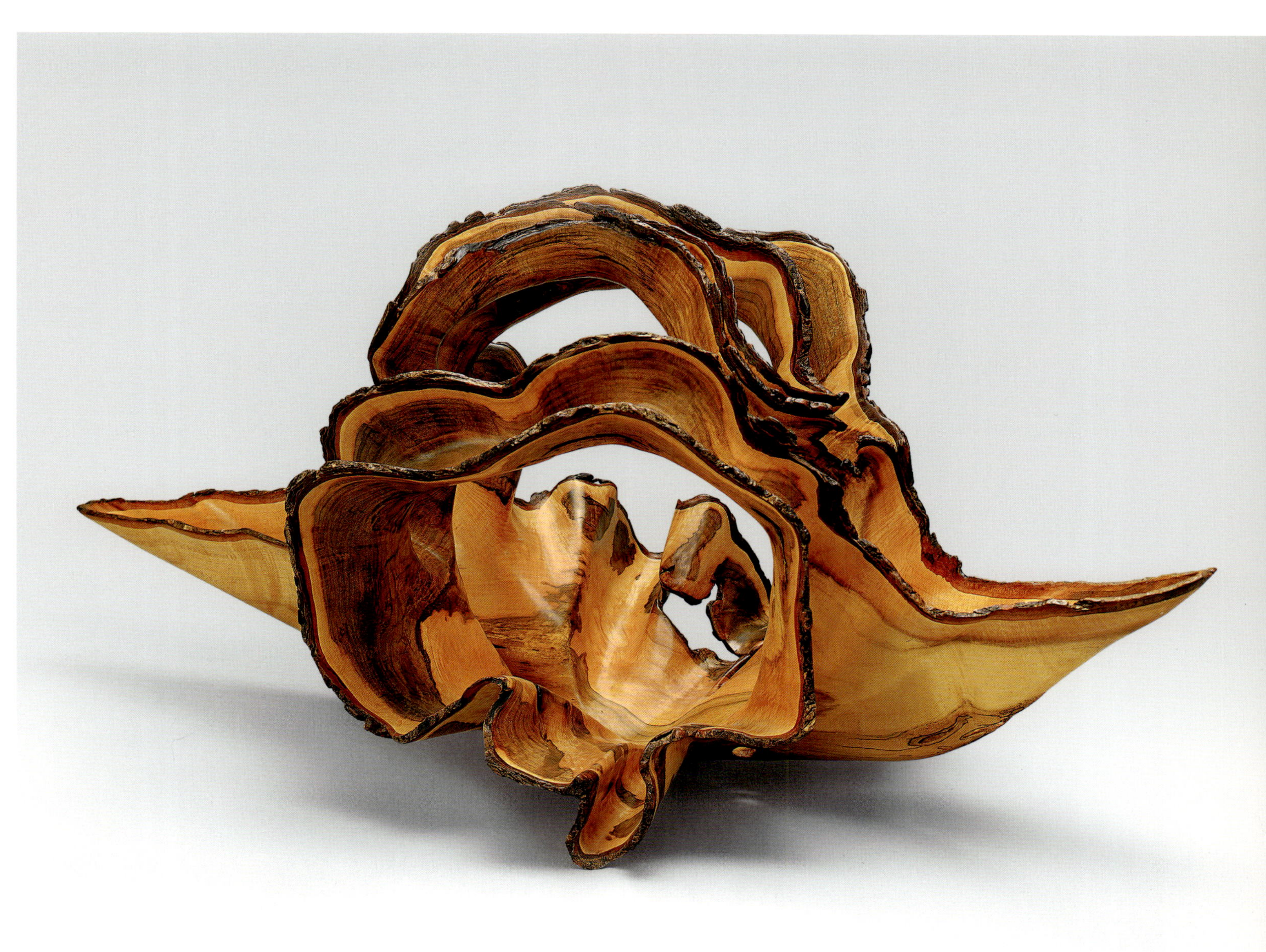

BRAD SELLS born 1969, works Cookeville, Tennessee
TRES BASTARDOS 2001, spalted maple burl, 15 x 39 $^{1}/_{2}$ x 17 in. (38.1 x 100.33 x 43.18 cm)

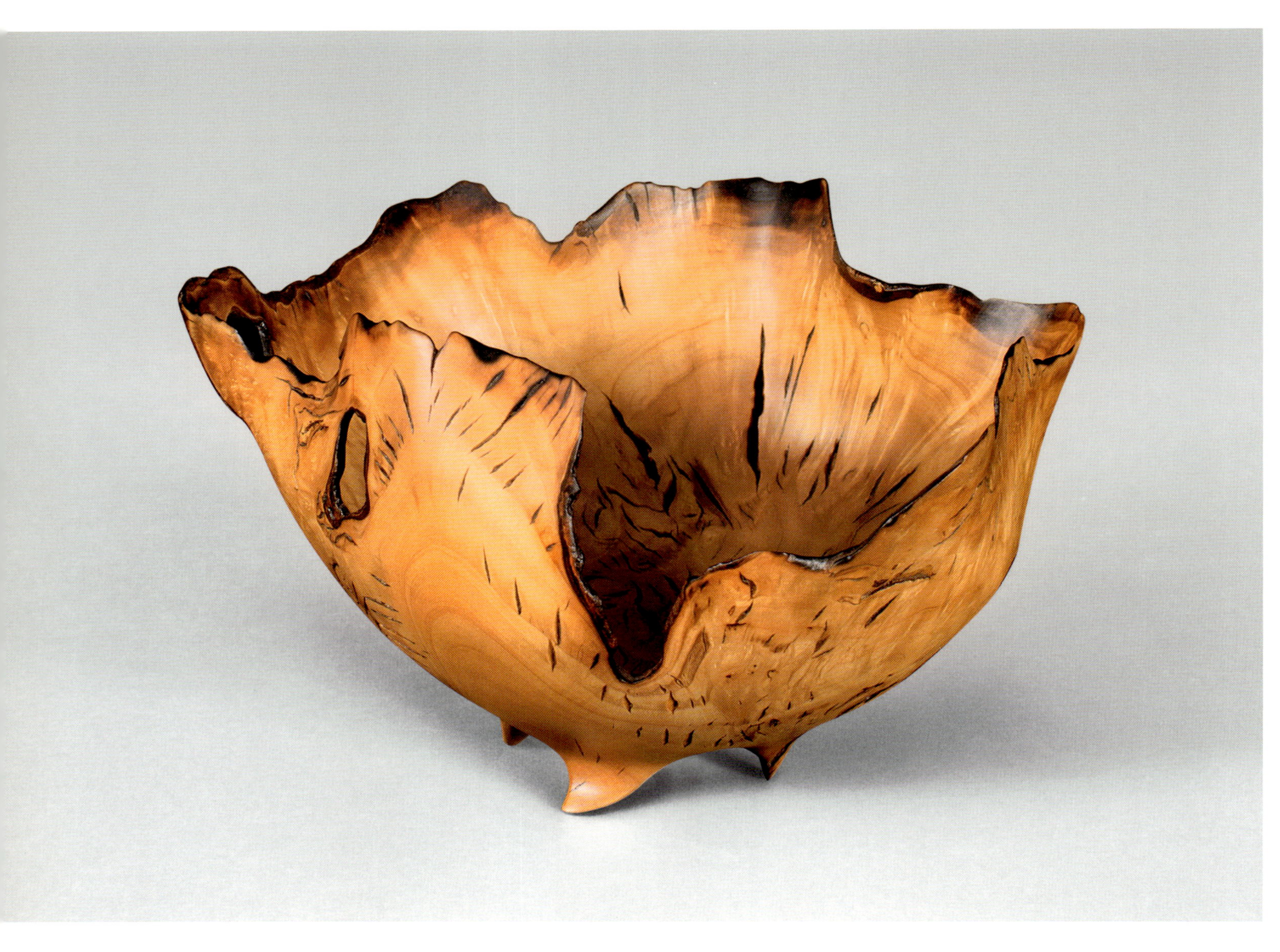

DEREK BENCOMO born 1962, works Wailuku, Hawai'i
SMALL BOWL 1997, olive burl, 6 $^{1}/_{2}$ x 7 in. (16.5 x 17.8 cm), Peabody Essex Museum, Gift of Lillian Montalto Bohlen

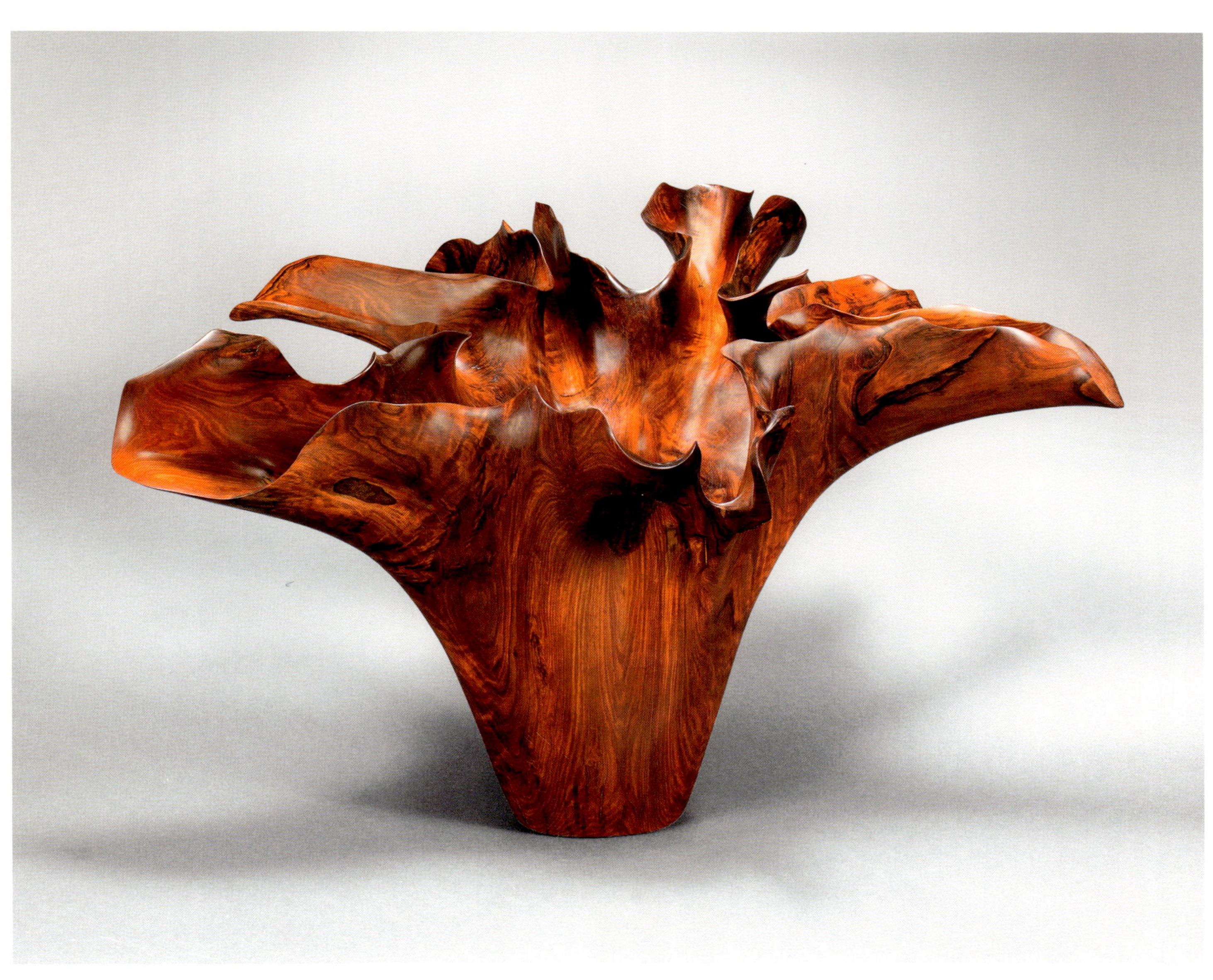

SOUPHOM AND SOUPHONG MANIKHONG born 1957, born 1961, work Sacramento, California
TREE ROOT 2008, Thai rosewood, 24 x 33 x 11 in. (61 x 83.8 x 28 cm)

CASTING SHADOWS

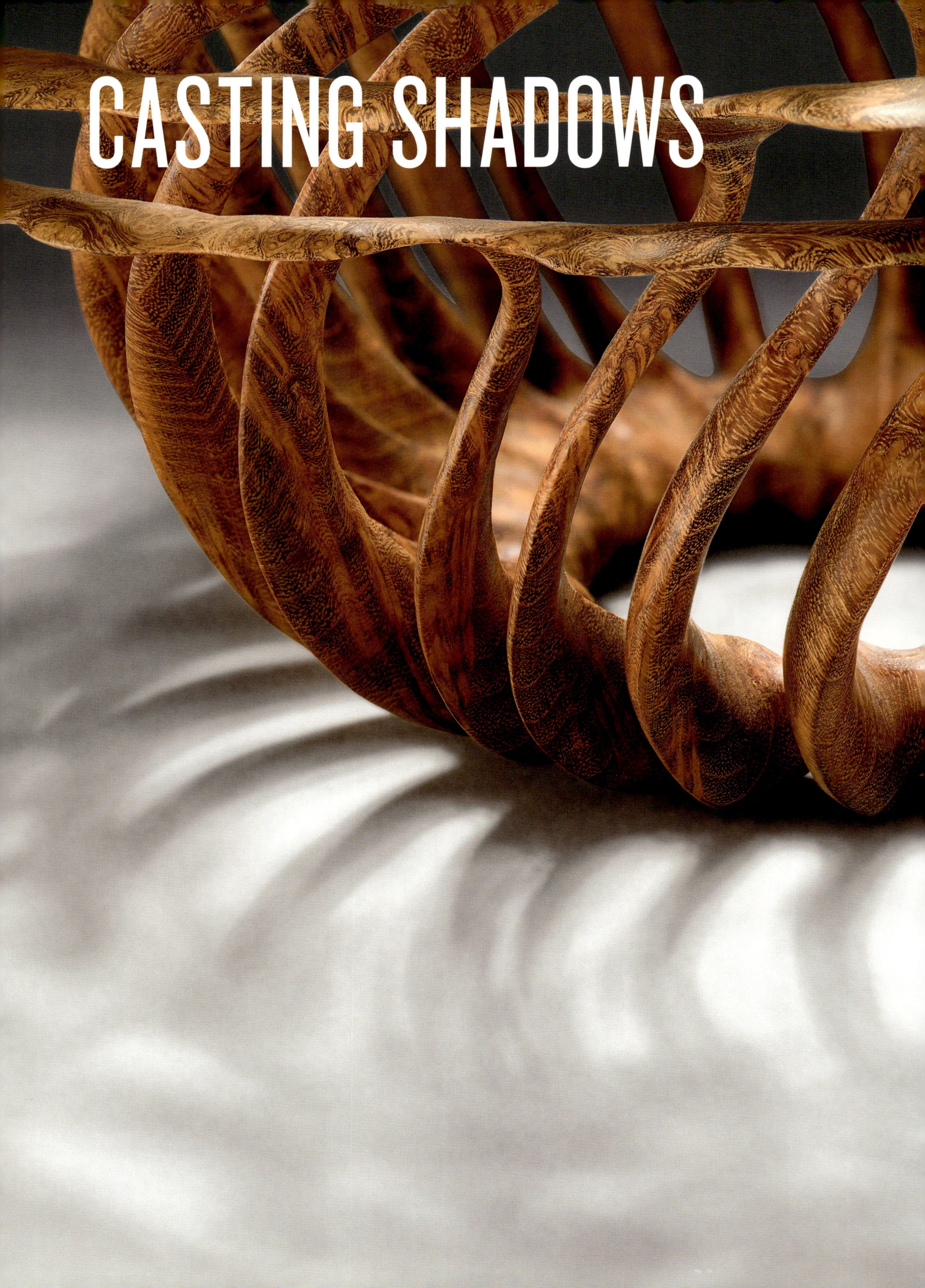

By selectively removing pieces of wood from the original block, artists create pure sculptural forms that accentuate the interplay of light and shadow as well as the geometric patterns of intersecting circles and lines. Sometimes the wood's natural characteristics guide the carving process, resulting in open organic forms that highlight the natural color of the wood.

ALAIN MAILLAND: SPACE AND ENERGY

Life is organized around emptiness, the structure of matter, the cosmos, space, and energy. When I create a piece, I do nothing but make space, remove the matter—a lot at the beginning—and then progressively less, until the last sandings and polishings allow me to approach a good shape. I have been studying the art of bonsaï with a Japanese master, and he taught me that when you look at a tree, you must be more careful of the space around the tree than of the tree itself. Emptiness gives energy, lets light come in, through a tree's leaves, around a bird's wings, or on the sea's surface. This is what I want: to give energy to my pieces, as if they were alive.

Detail, Alain Mailland, *Grace,* 2000 (page 91)

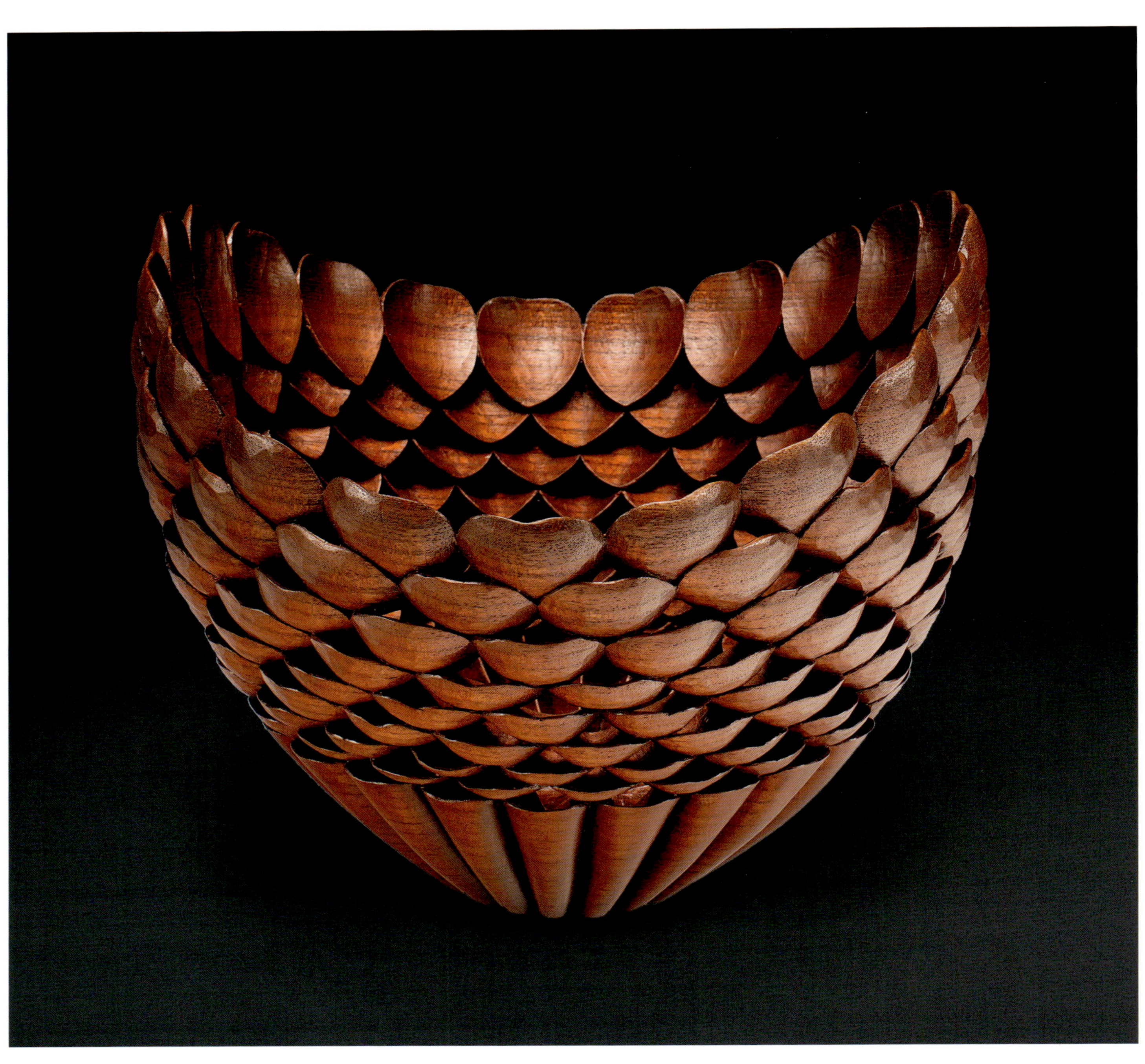

ROBERT HOWARD born 1949, works South Brisbane, Queensland, Australia
A SEARCH FOR ORDER 2007, Australian red cedar, 10 1/2 x 12 x 13 in. (26.7 x 30.5 x 33 cm)

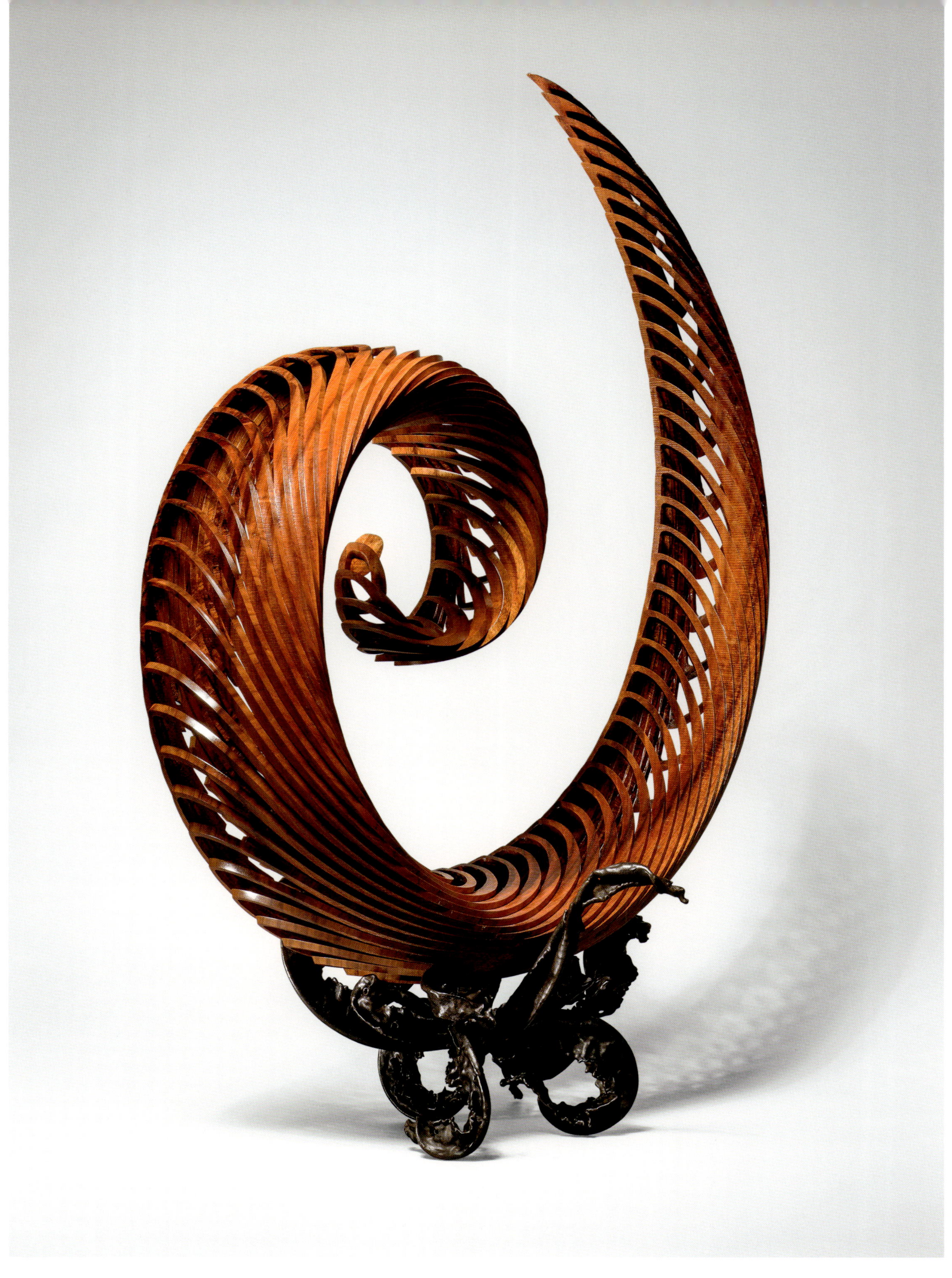

RON GERTON born 1946, works Richland, Washington
REVOLUTION EVOLUTION 2012, curly koa, bronze ore, 34 x 25 x 13 in. (86.4 x 63.5 x 33 cm)

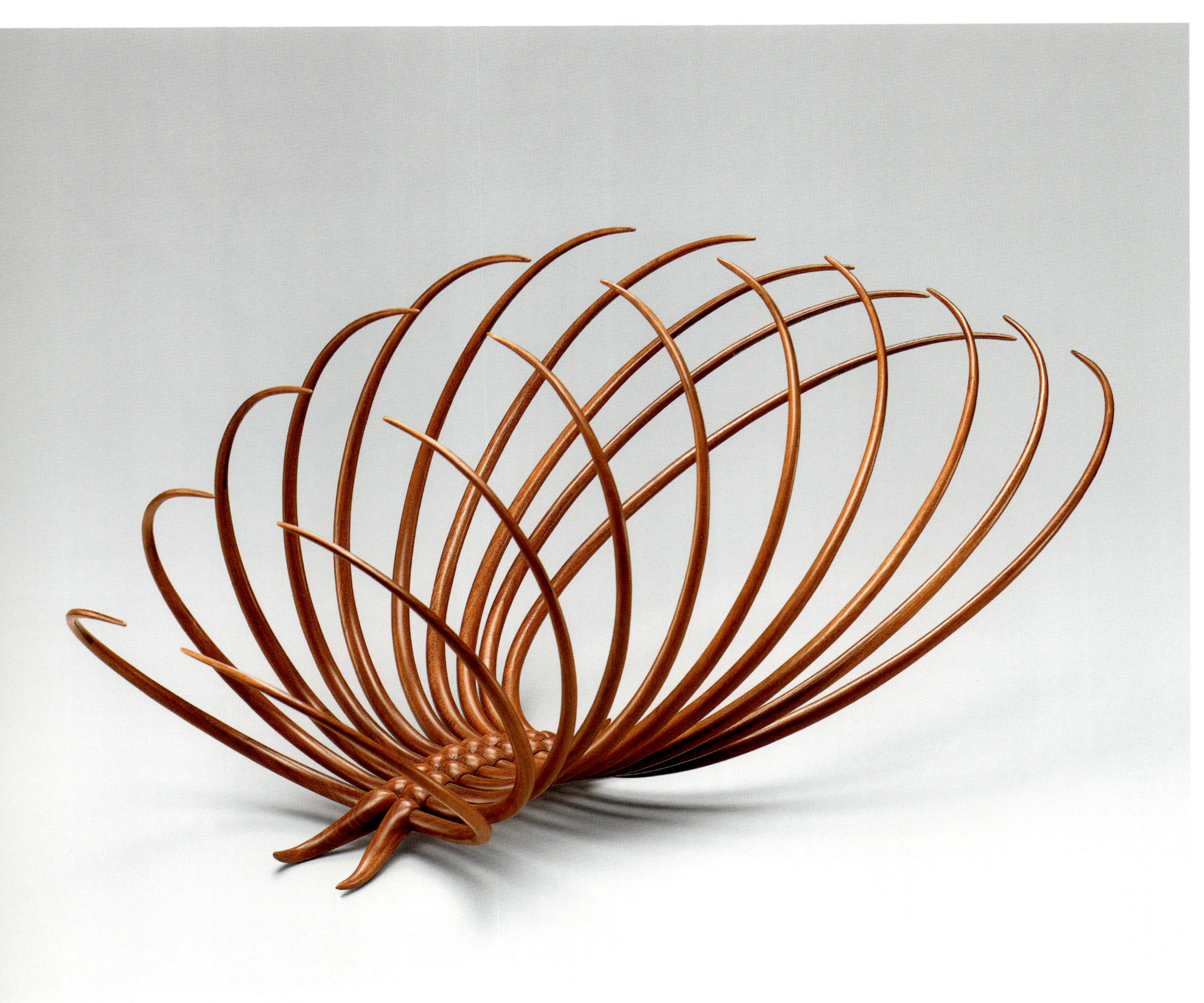

ARTHUR JONES born 1937, works Winter Park, Florida
EXHIBITIONIST 2001, walnut, 11 x 25 x 11 in. (28 x 63.5 x 28 cm)

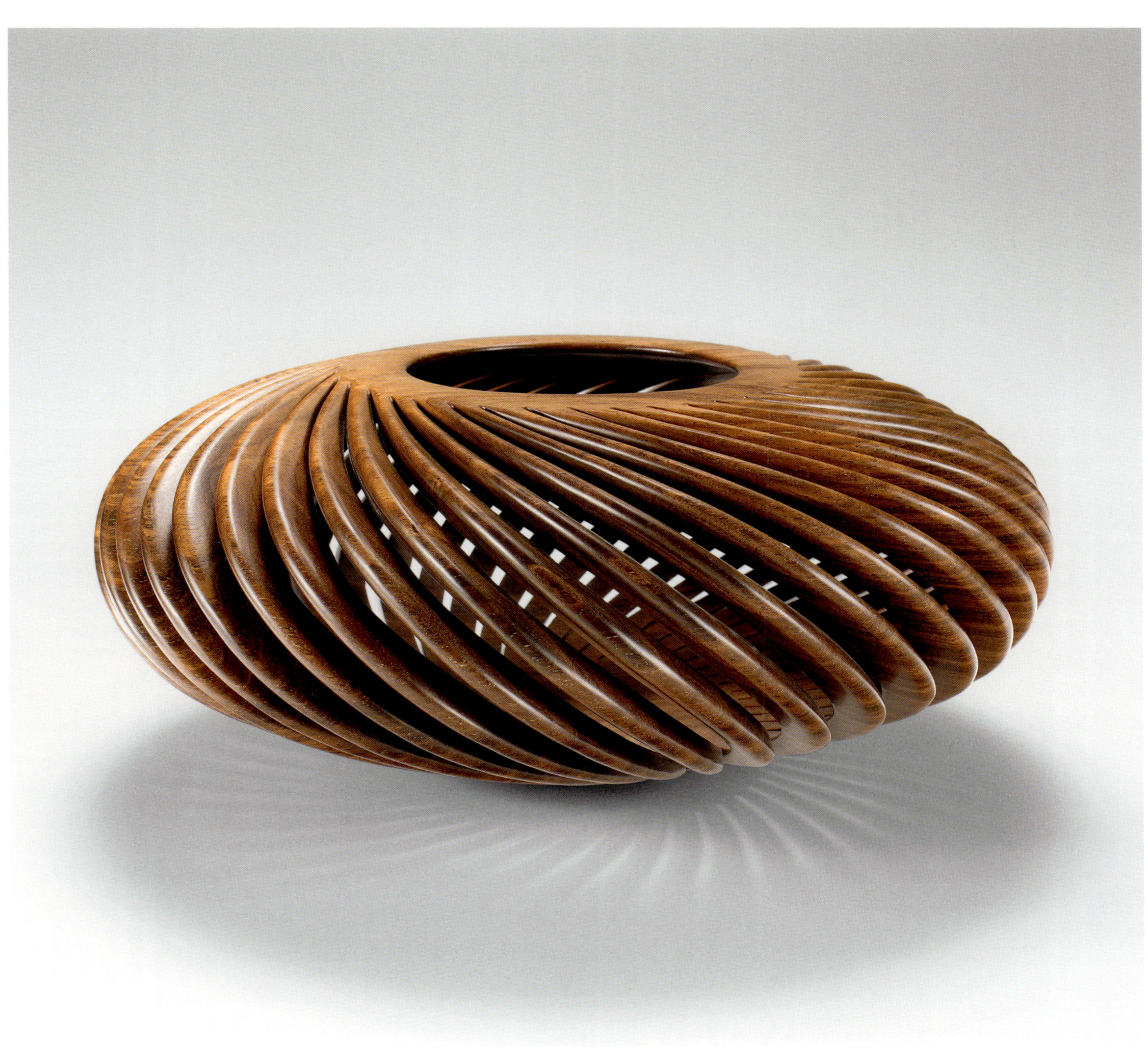

WILLIAM HUNTER born 1947, works Rancho Palos Verdes, California
CONTEMPLATING RHYTHMS 1998, cocobolo, 6 $^{3}/_{4}$ x 14 in. (17.1 x 35.6 cm)

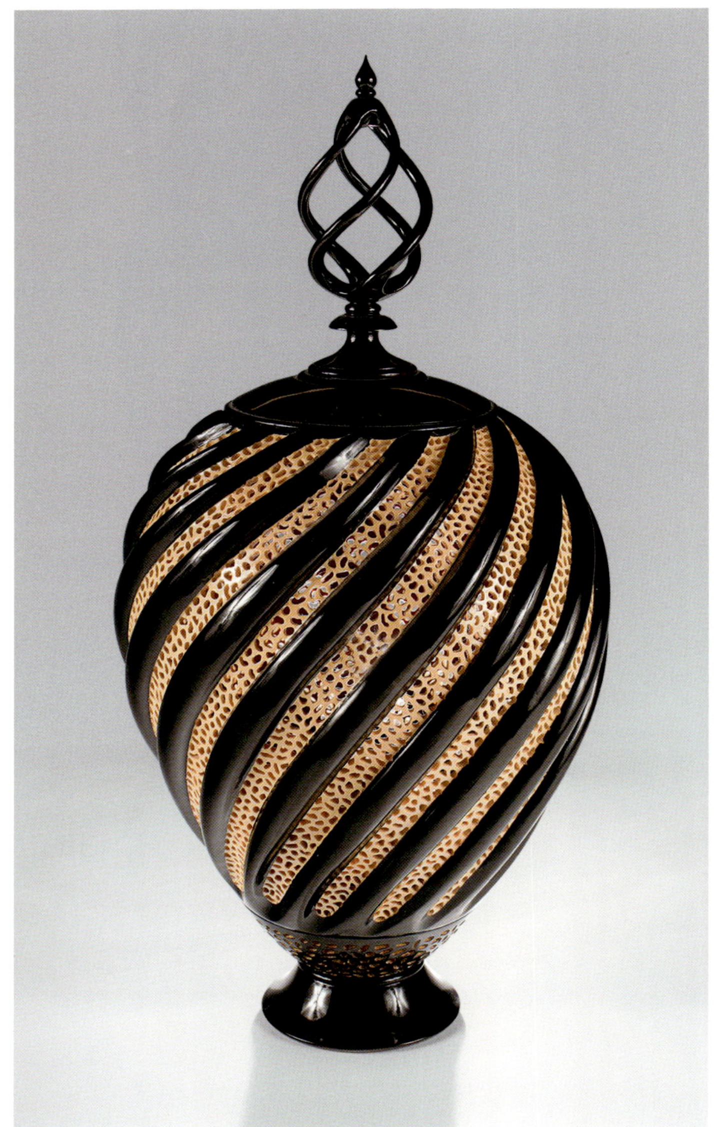

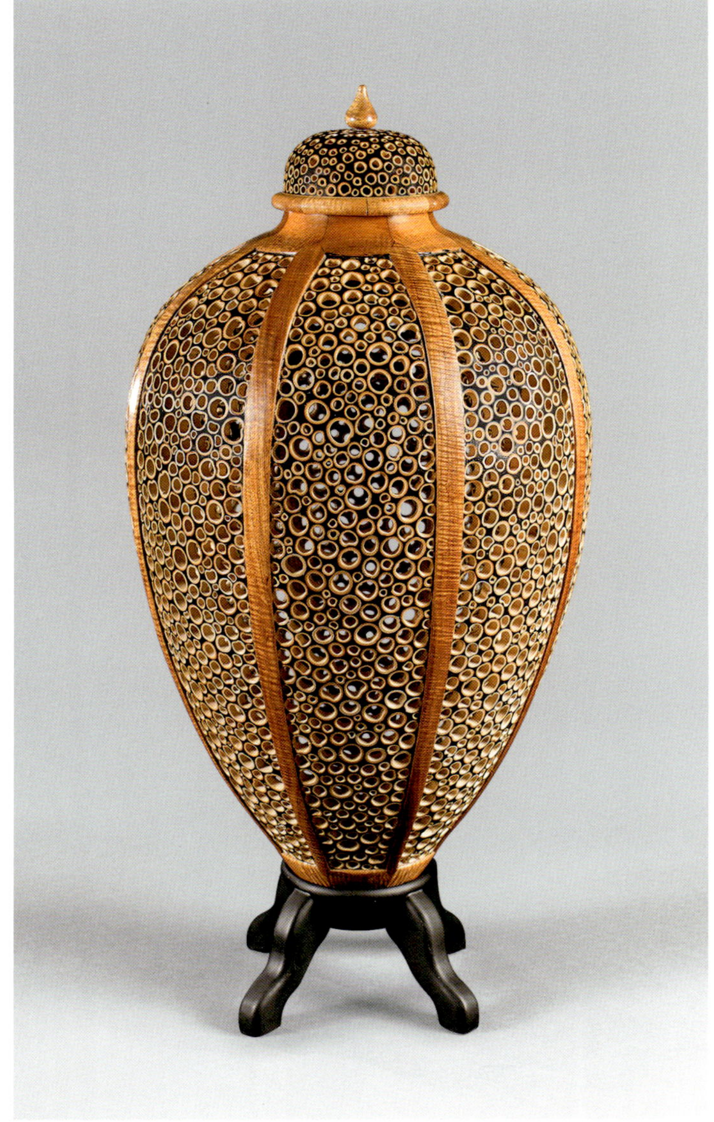

Left: **STUART MORTIMER** born 1942, works Grateley, Hampshire, England
UNTITLED 2002, sycamore, ebony, bronze flakes and dust, lacquer, 18 x 9 in. (45.7 x 22.9 cm)

Right: **R. W. BUTTS** born 1949, works Kan'ohe, Oahu, Hawai'i
BAMBOO TEMPLE VESSEL 2002, bamboo, curly koa, 36 x 15 in. (91.4 x 38.1 cm); stand: 3 1/2 in. (8.9 cm)

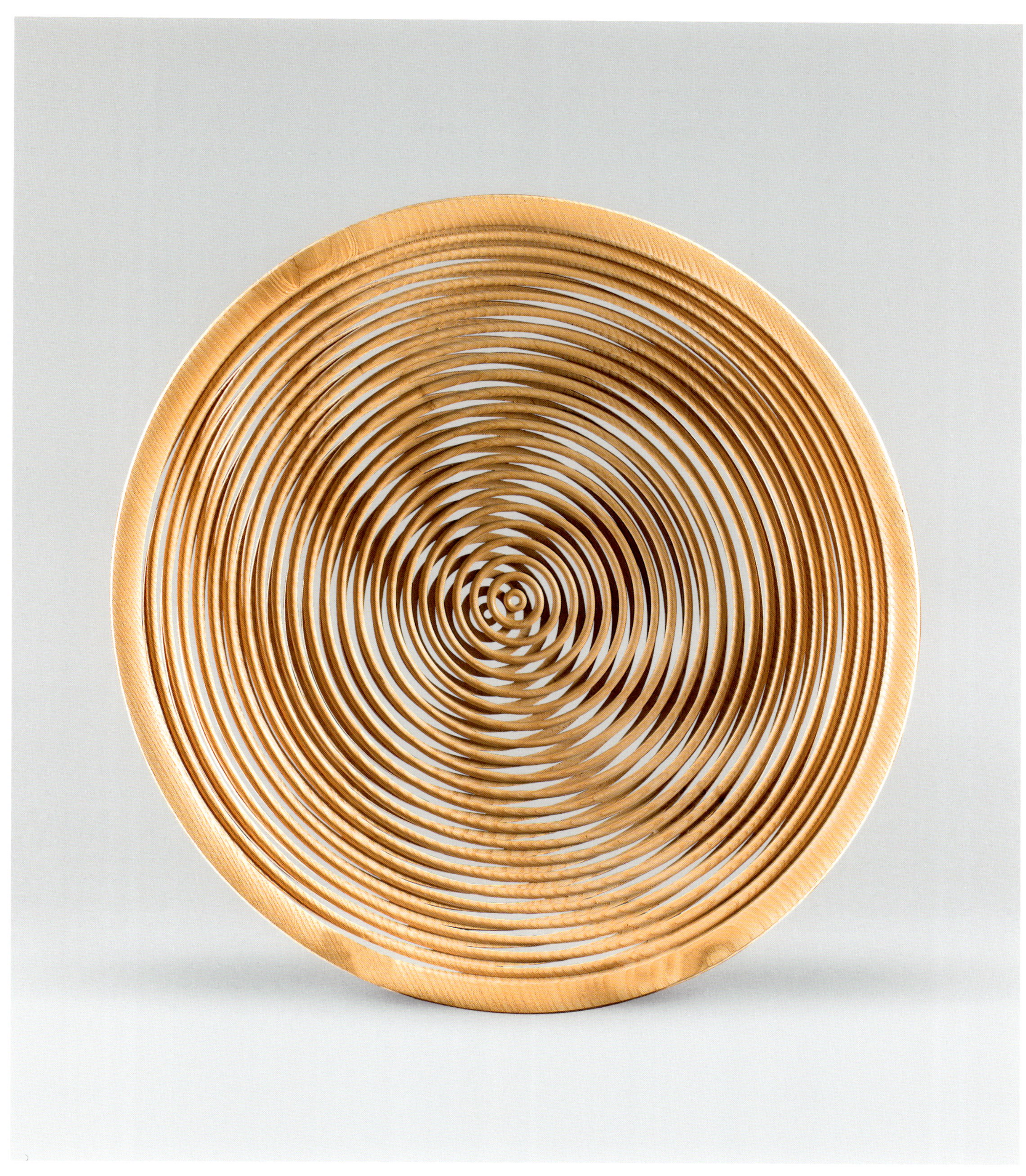

HANS WEISSFLOG born 1954, works Hildesheim, Germany
LARGE DISH 2000, ash, 17 x 17 x 3 in. (43.2 x 43.2 x 7.6 cm)

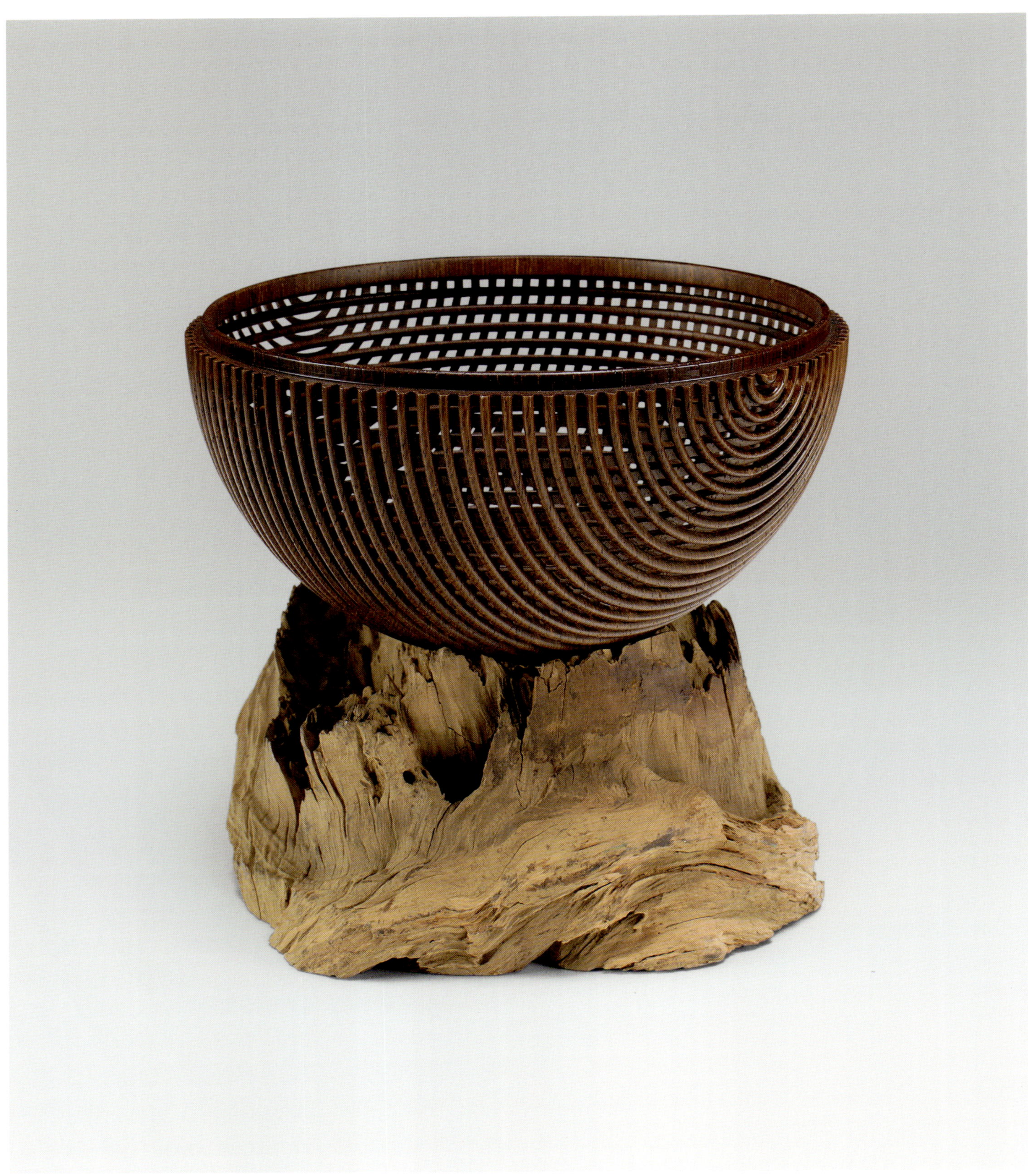

HANS WEISSFLOG born 1954, works Hildesheim, Germany
BALL BOX 2002, Amazon rosewood, monkey puzzle, 12 1/2 x 9 x 8 1/2 in. (31.8 x 22.9 x 21.6 cm), Peabody Essex Museum, Gift of Lillian Montalto Bohlen

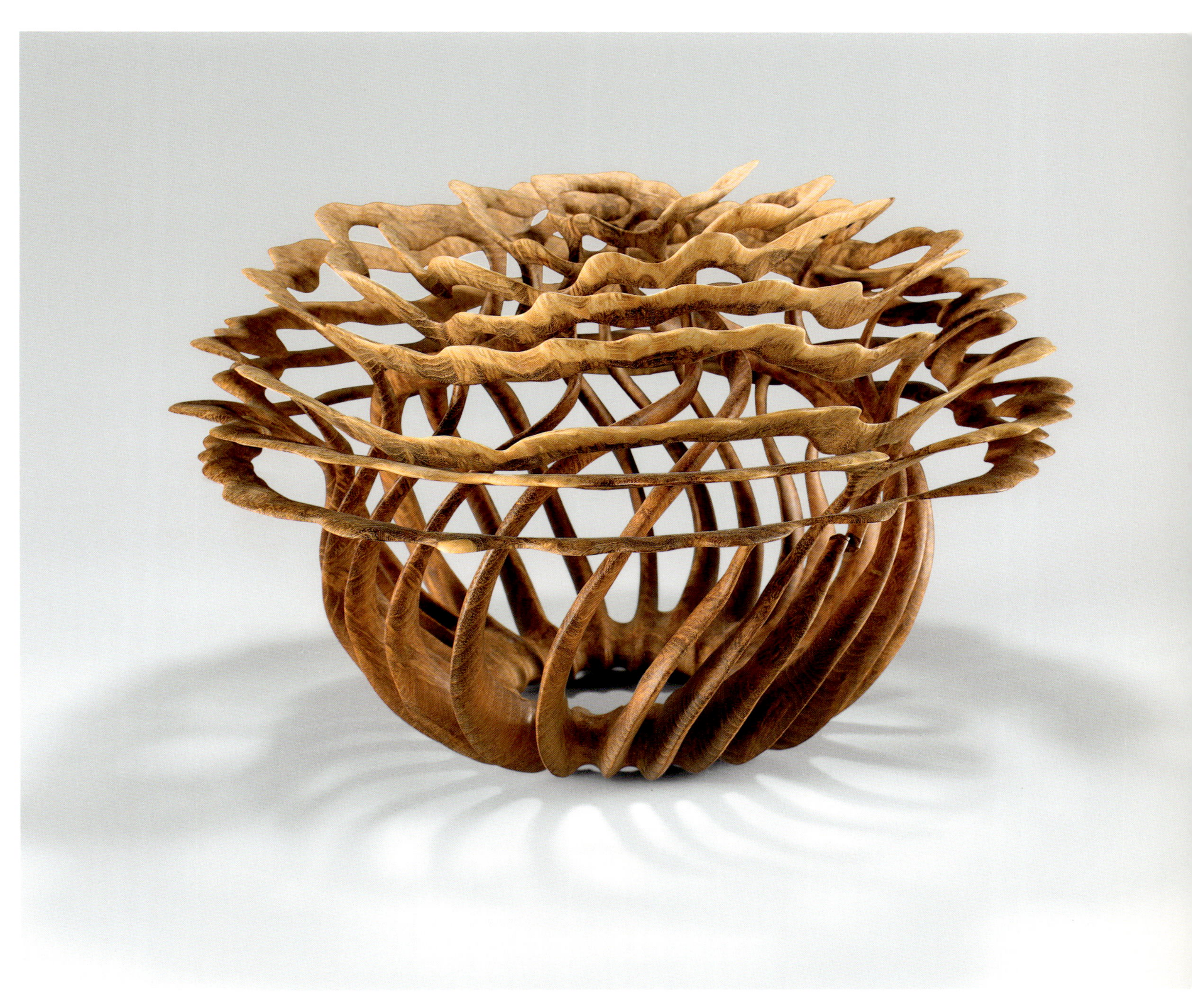

ALAIN MAILLAND born 1959, works Chamborigaud, France
GRACE 2000, locust burl, 7 1/4 x 10 1/2 in. (18.4 x 26.7 cm)

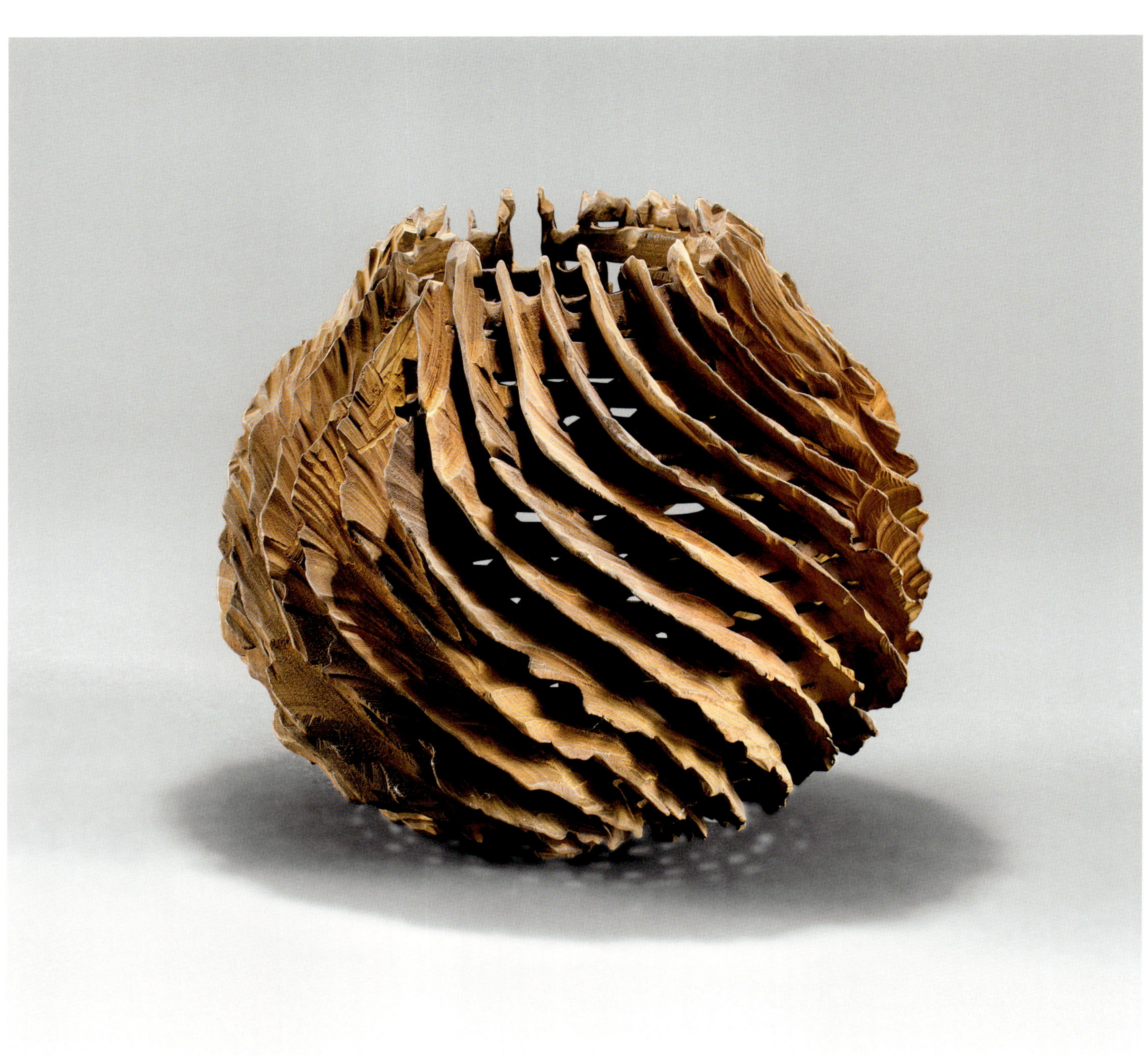

MARC RICOURT born 1963, works Vaux-Saules, France
UNTITLED 2010, pear wood and ferrous oxide, 10 1/2 x 10 in. (26.7 x 25.4 cm)

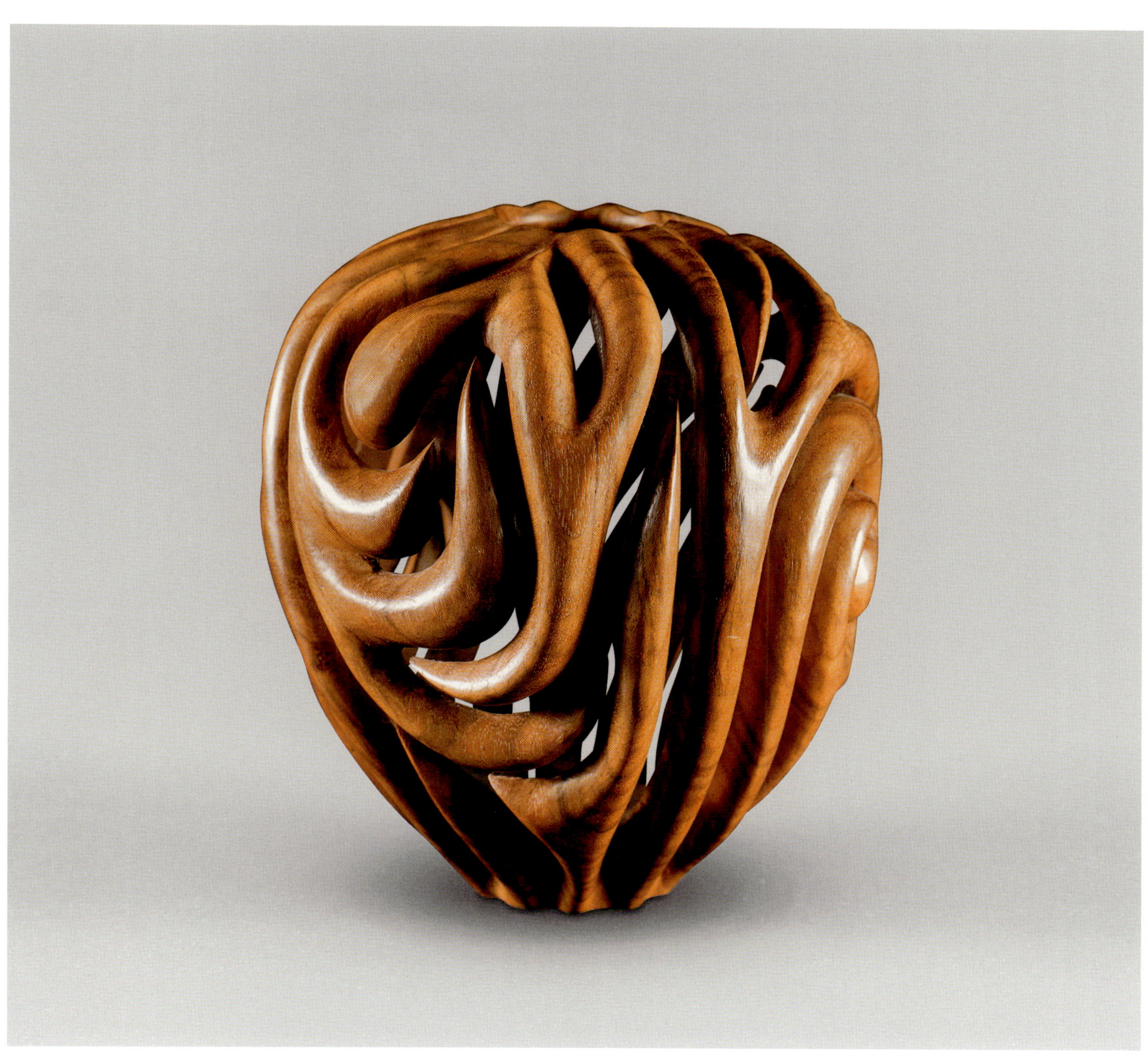

JACK WOHLSTADTER born 1932, works Rock Falls, Illinois
#623 1996, walnut, 7 1/2 x 6 in. (19 x 15.2 cm)

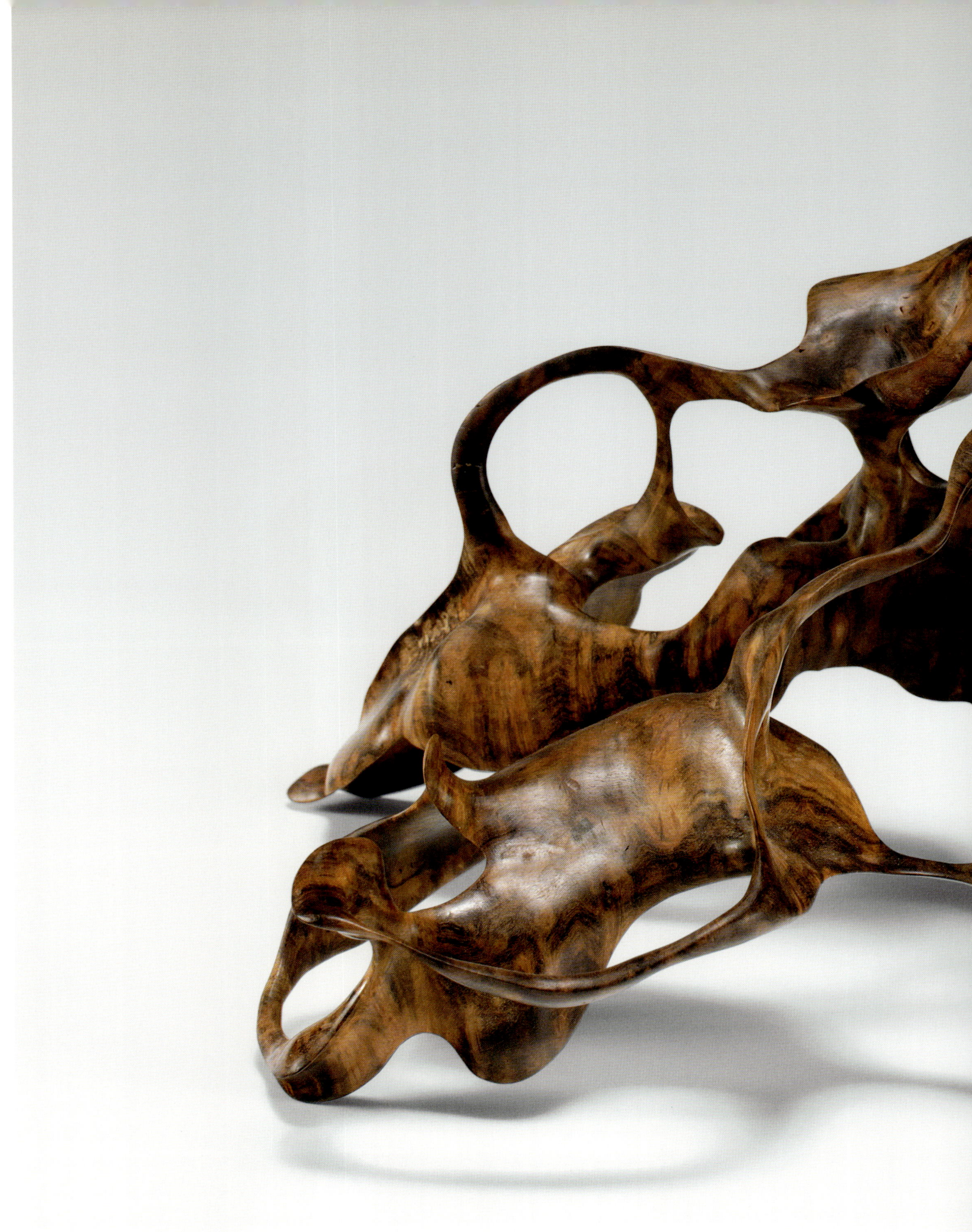

ELISABETH MEZIÈRES born 1963, works Chamborigaud, France
VEGETAL DREAM 2001, pistachio root, 7 x 12 $^5/_8$ x 10 in. (17.8 x 32.1 x 25.4 cm)

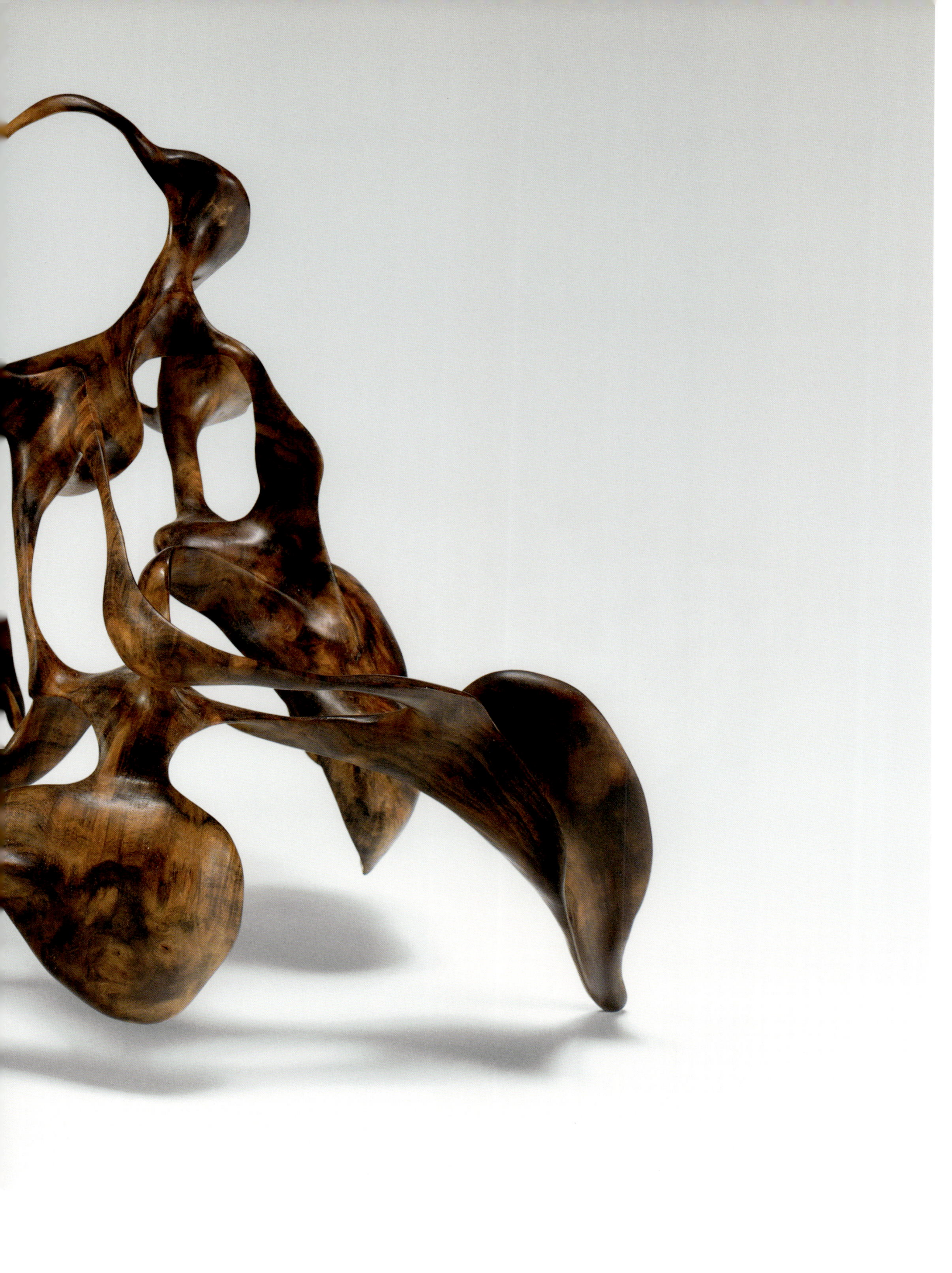

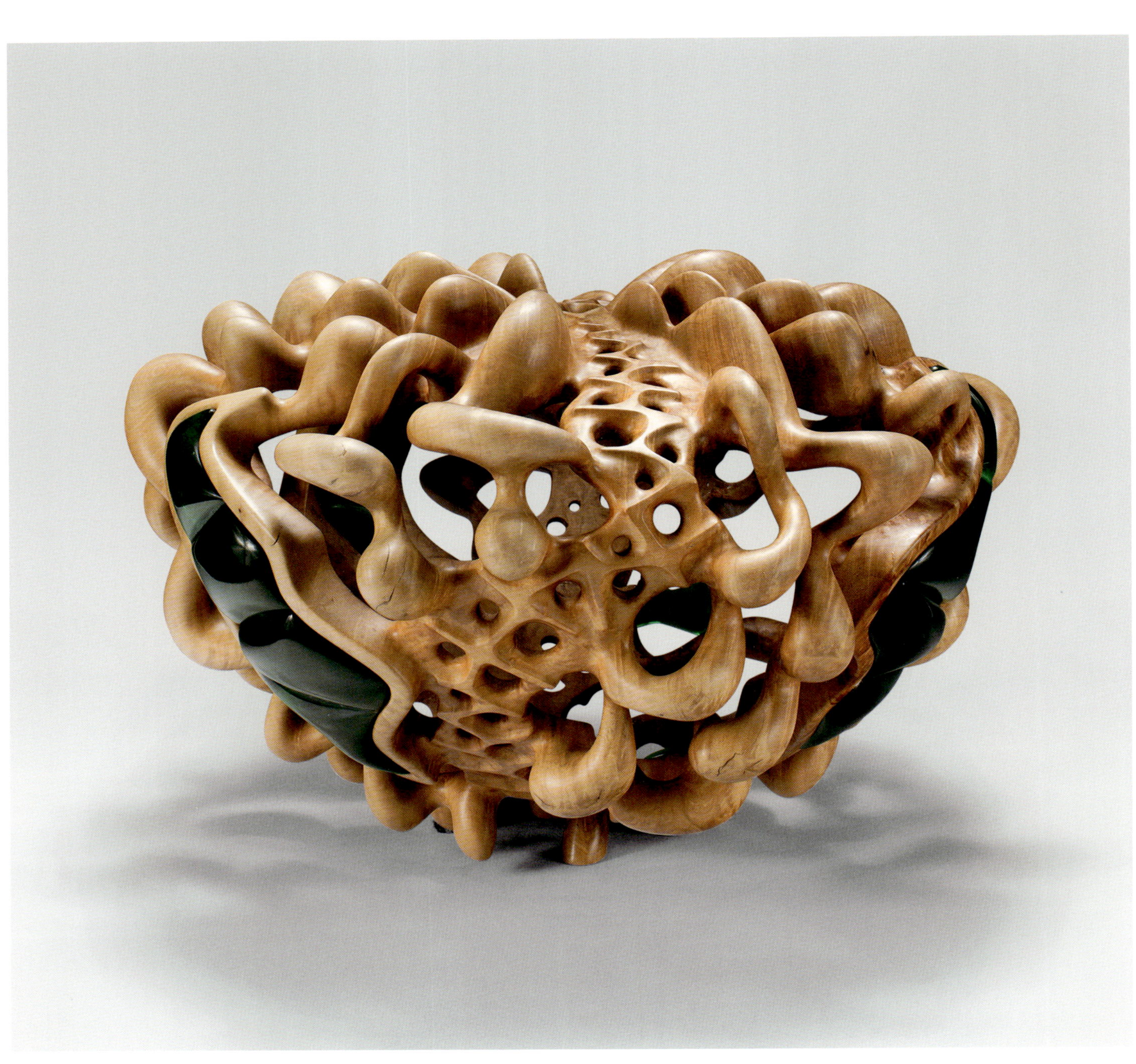

HUGH MCKAY born 1951, works Spencer, Iowa
RUACH 1998, madrone burl, cast glass, bronze, nickel, 12 x 18 in. each (30.5 x 45.8 cm)

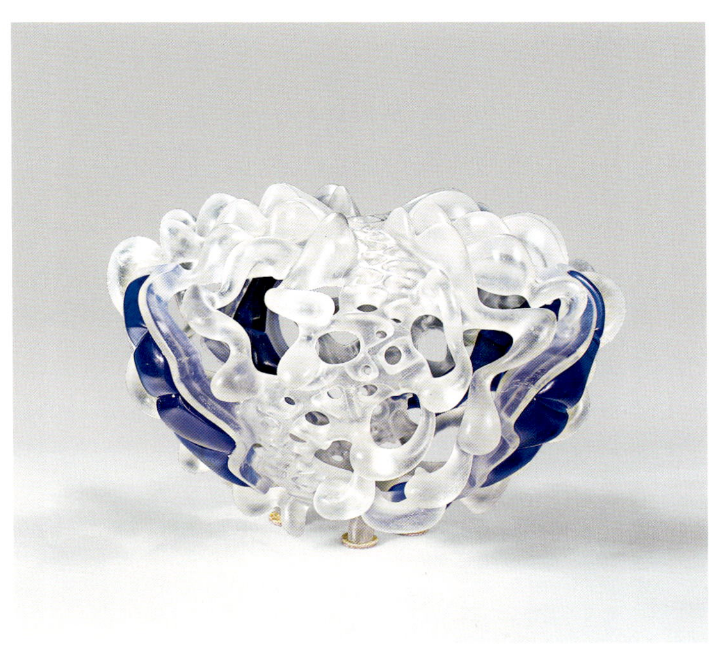

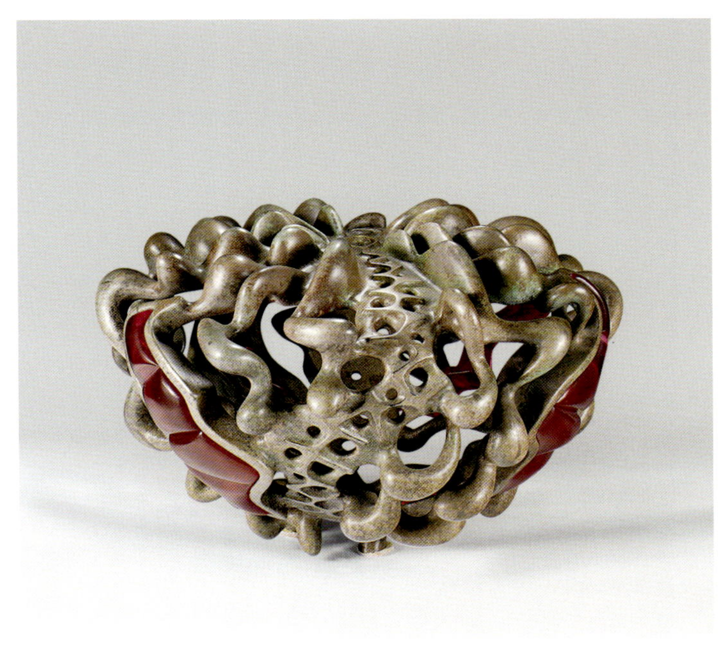

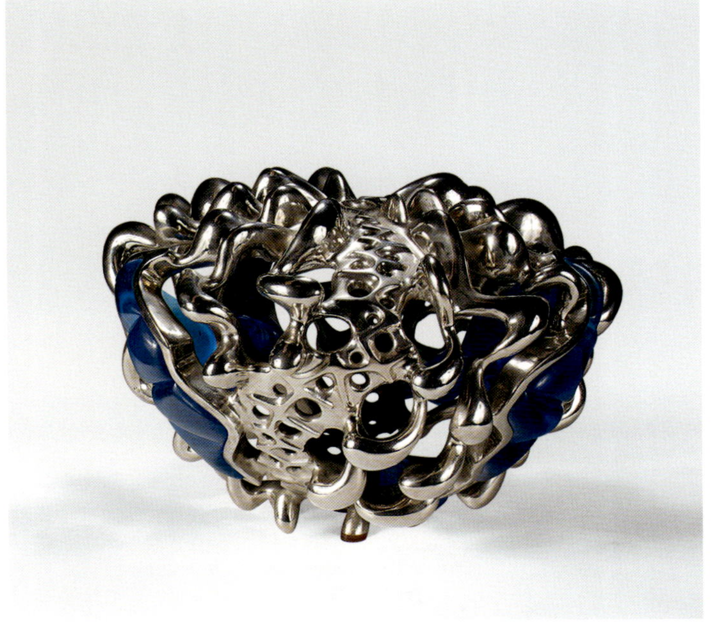

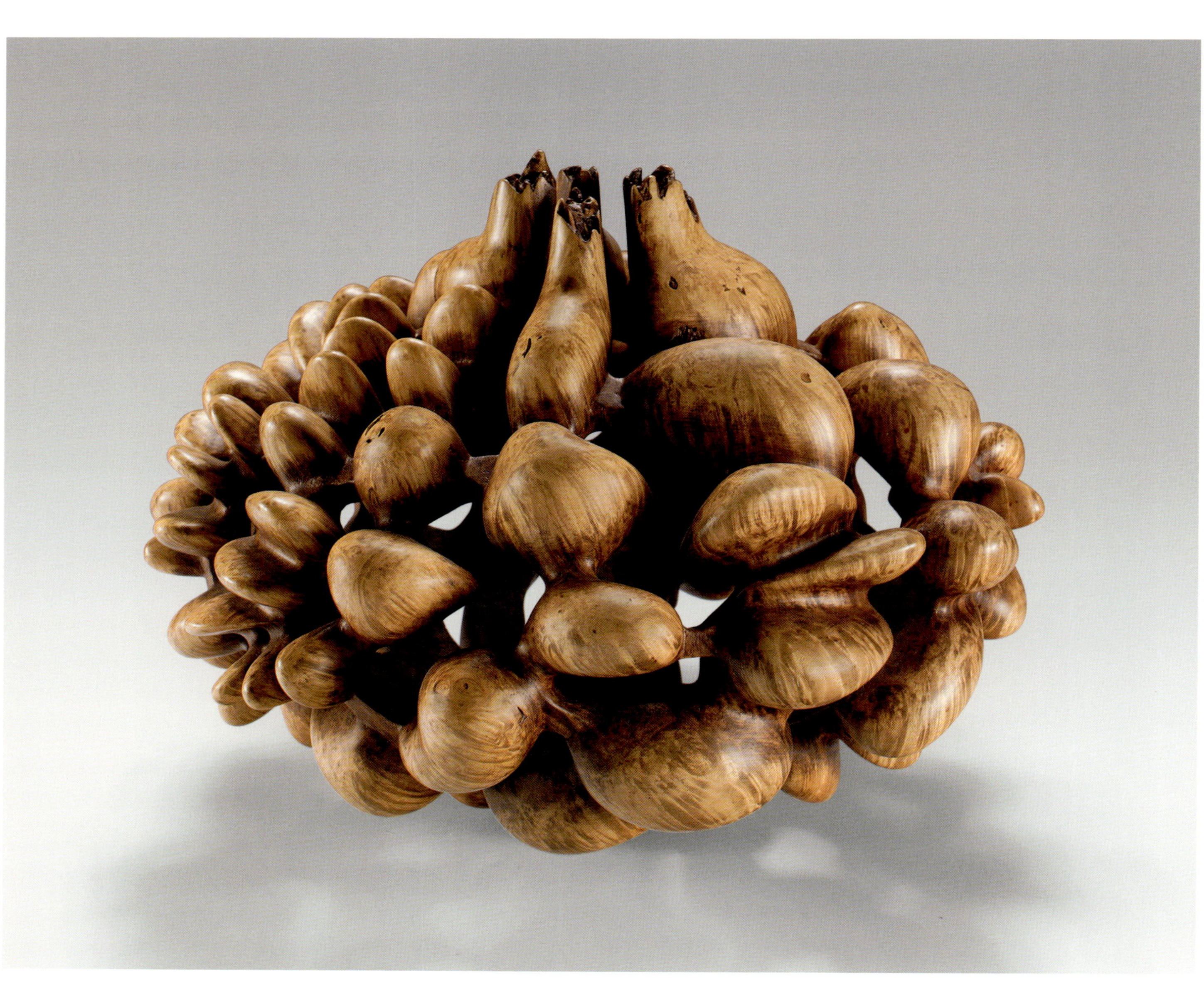

HUGH MCKAY born 1951, works Spencer, Iowa
TSAAR 2002, maple burl, 10 $^1/_4$ x 13 in. (26. x 33 cm)

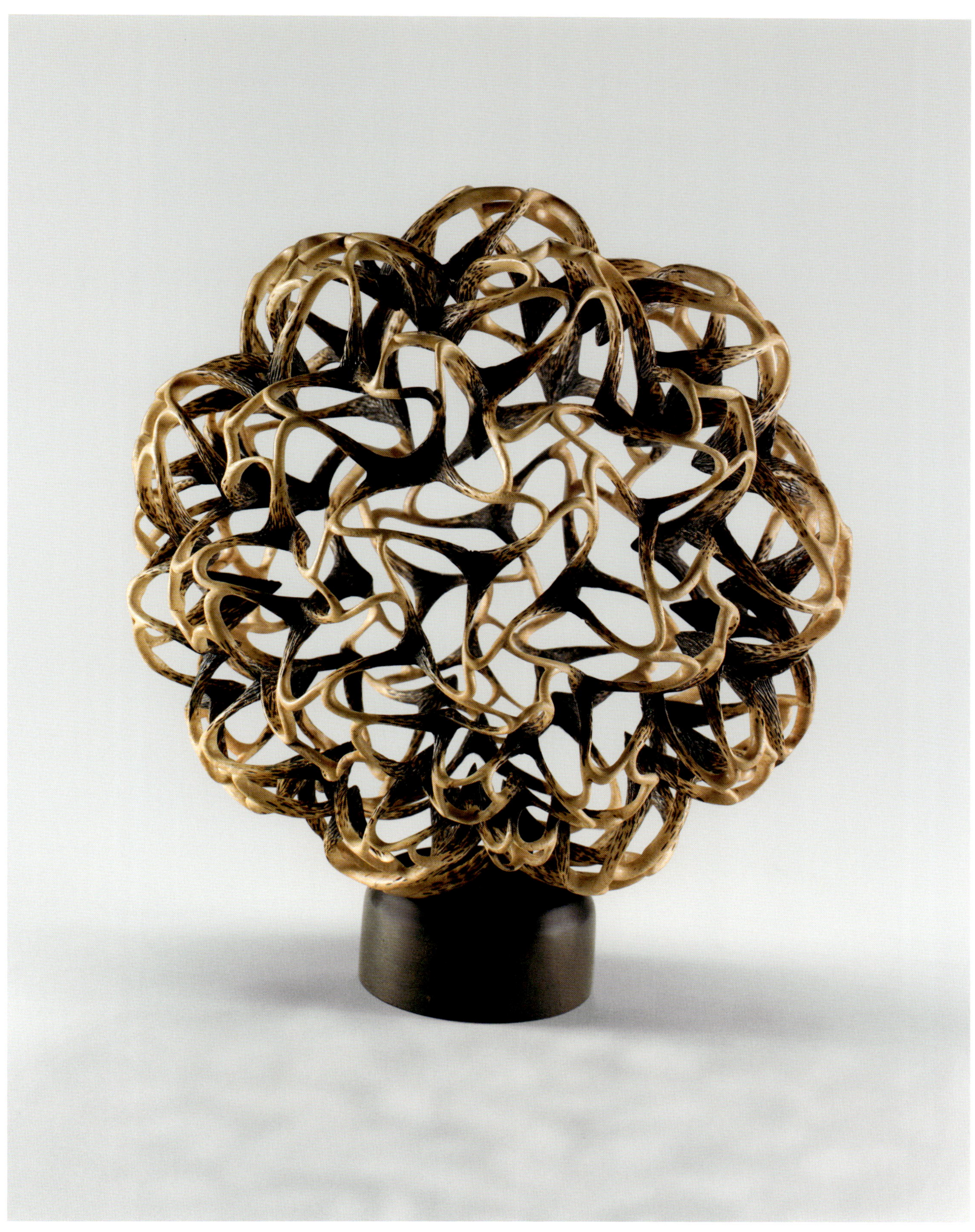

ALAIN MAILLAND born 1959, works Chamborigaud, France
COSMOS 2008, ash, pigments, 7 x 7 in. (17.8 x 17.8 cm)

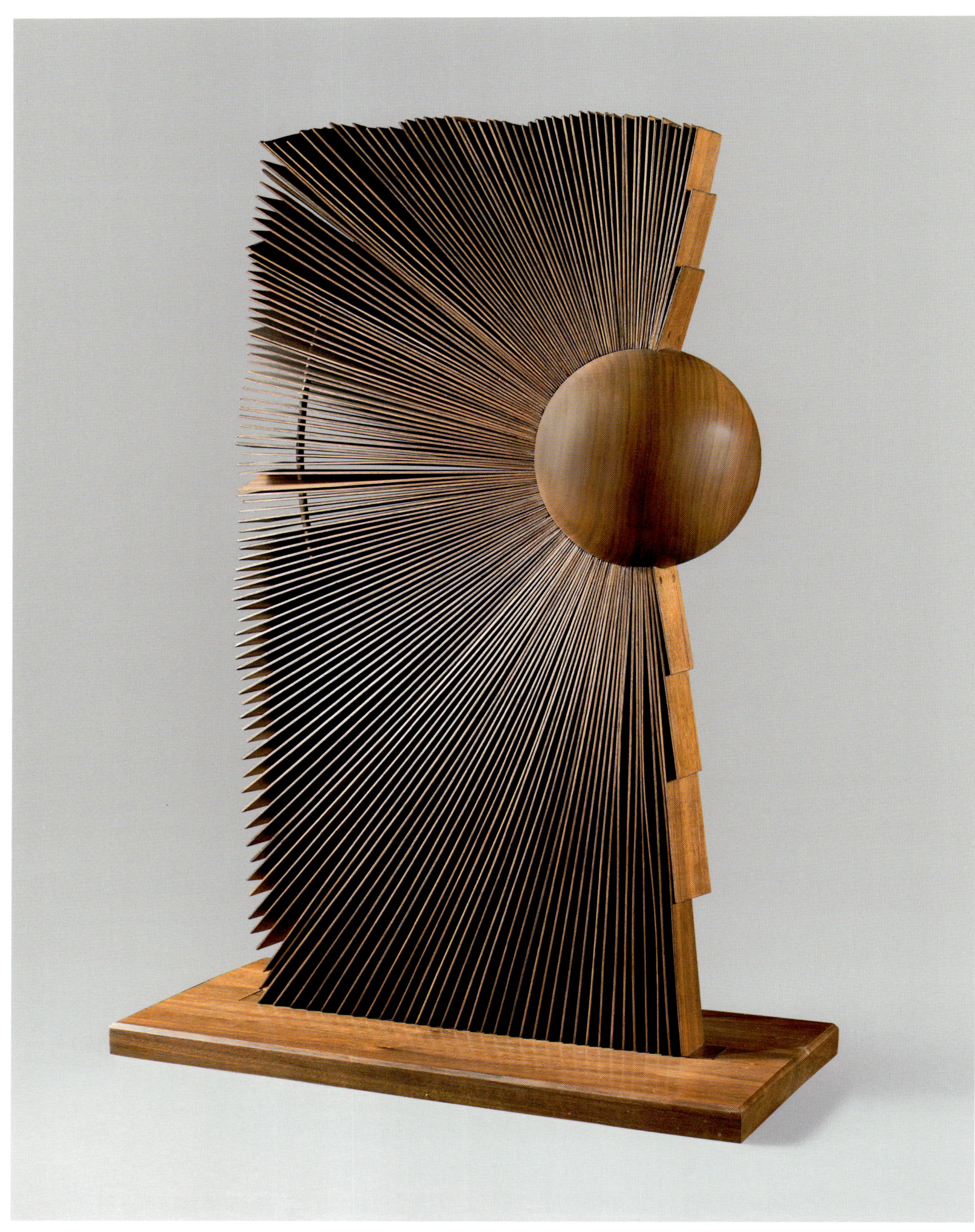

ARTHUR JONES born 1937, works Winter Park, Florida
DUSK STAR 2002, walnut, 30 $^{1}/_{2}$ x 22 x 10 $^{1}/_{2}$ in. (52.1 x 55.9 x 26.7 cm)

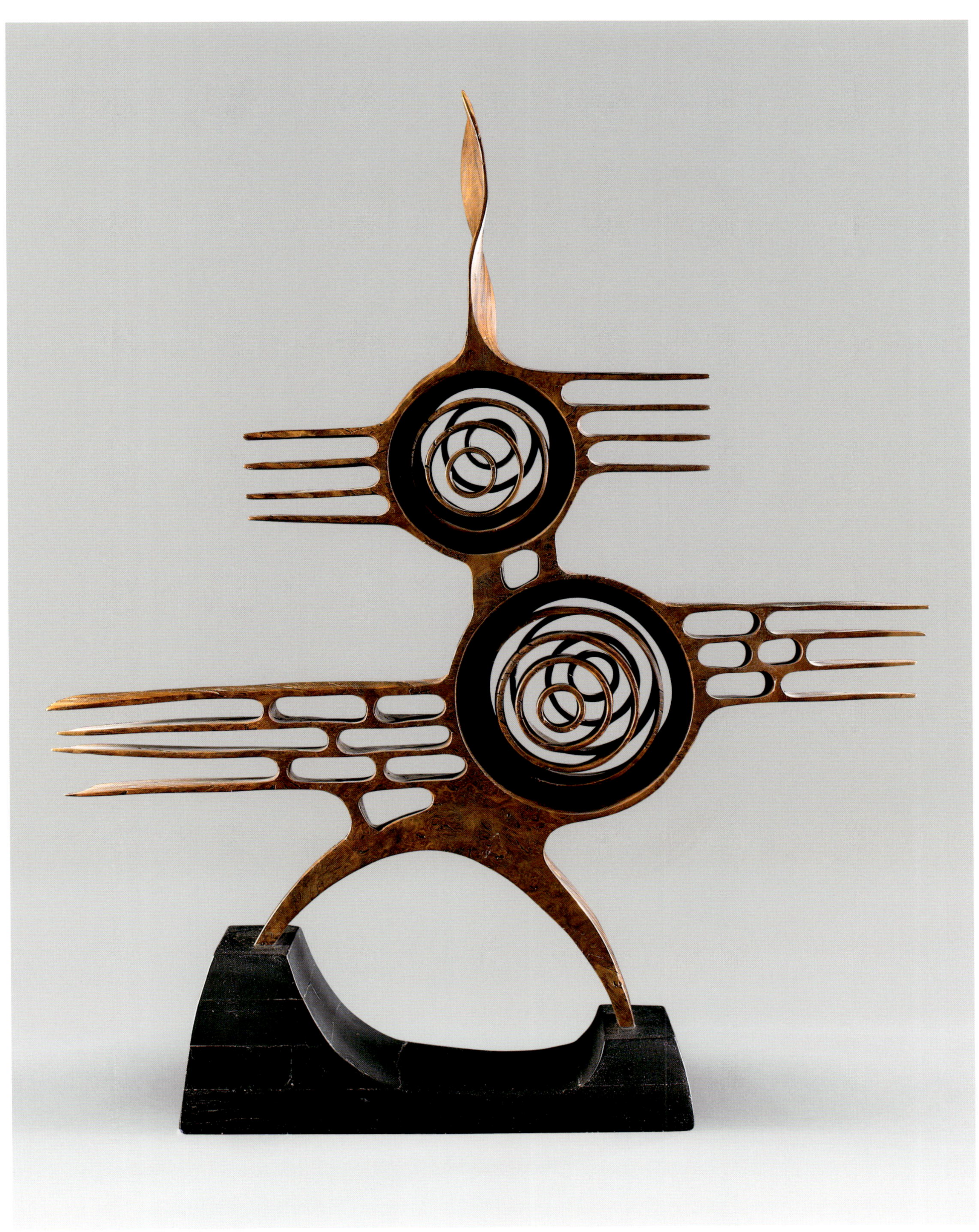

JOHN WOOLLER born 1939, works Foster, Victoria, Australia
IN MY INTRICATE IMAGE about 1993, jarrah burl, 32 $^{1}/_{2}$ x 28 x 7 in. (82.6 x 71.1 x 17.8 cm), Peabody Essex Museum, Gift of Lillian Montalto Bohlen

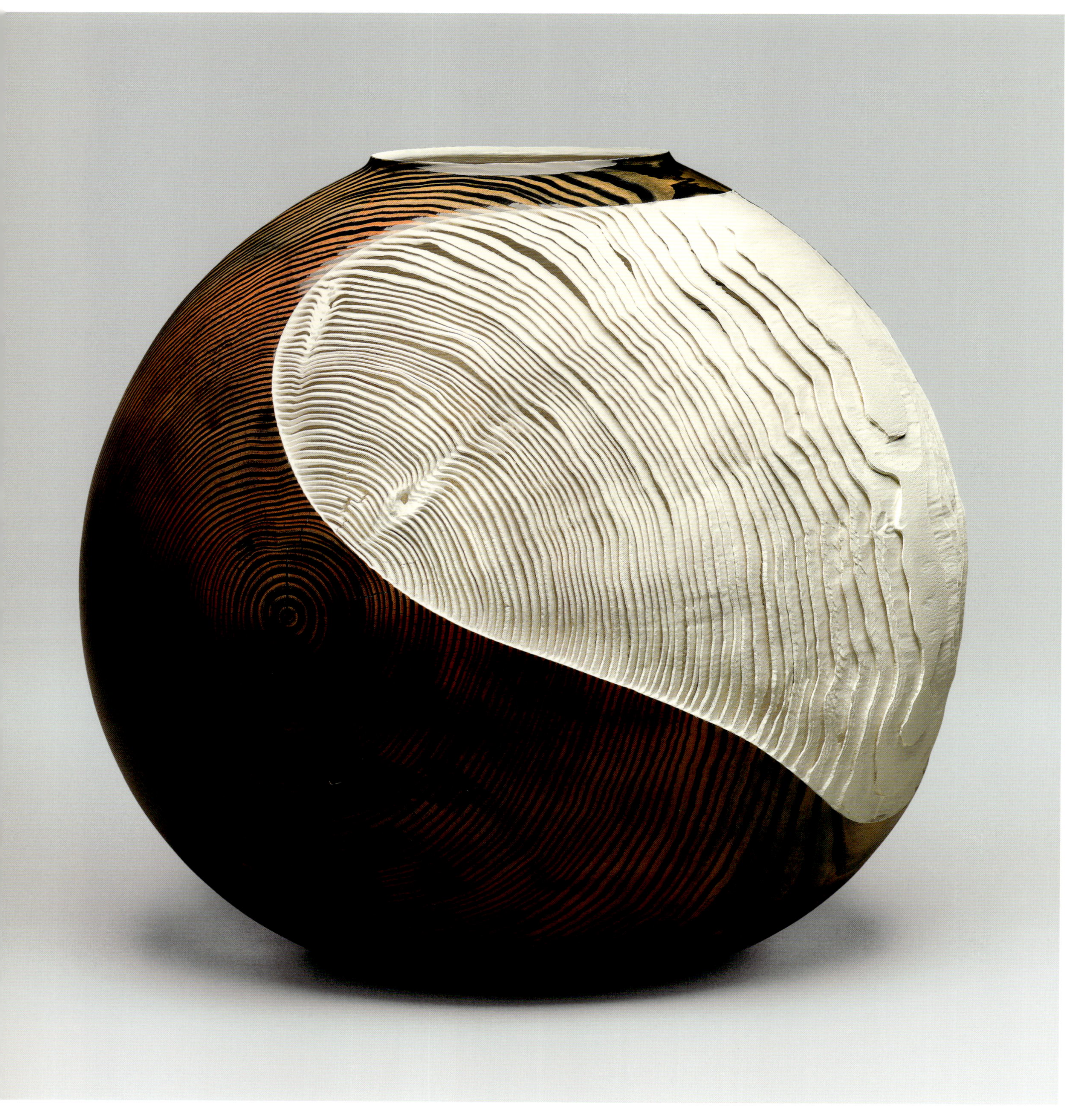

BENJAMIN PLANITZER born 1981, works Munich, Germany
SKELETTVESSEL 2013, douglas fir, lacquer, wax, 19 x 18 x 20 in. (48.3 x 45.7 x 50.8 cm)

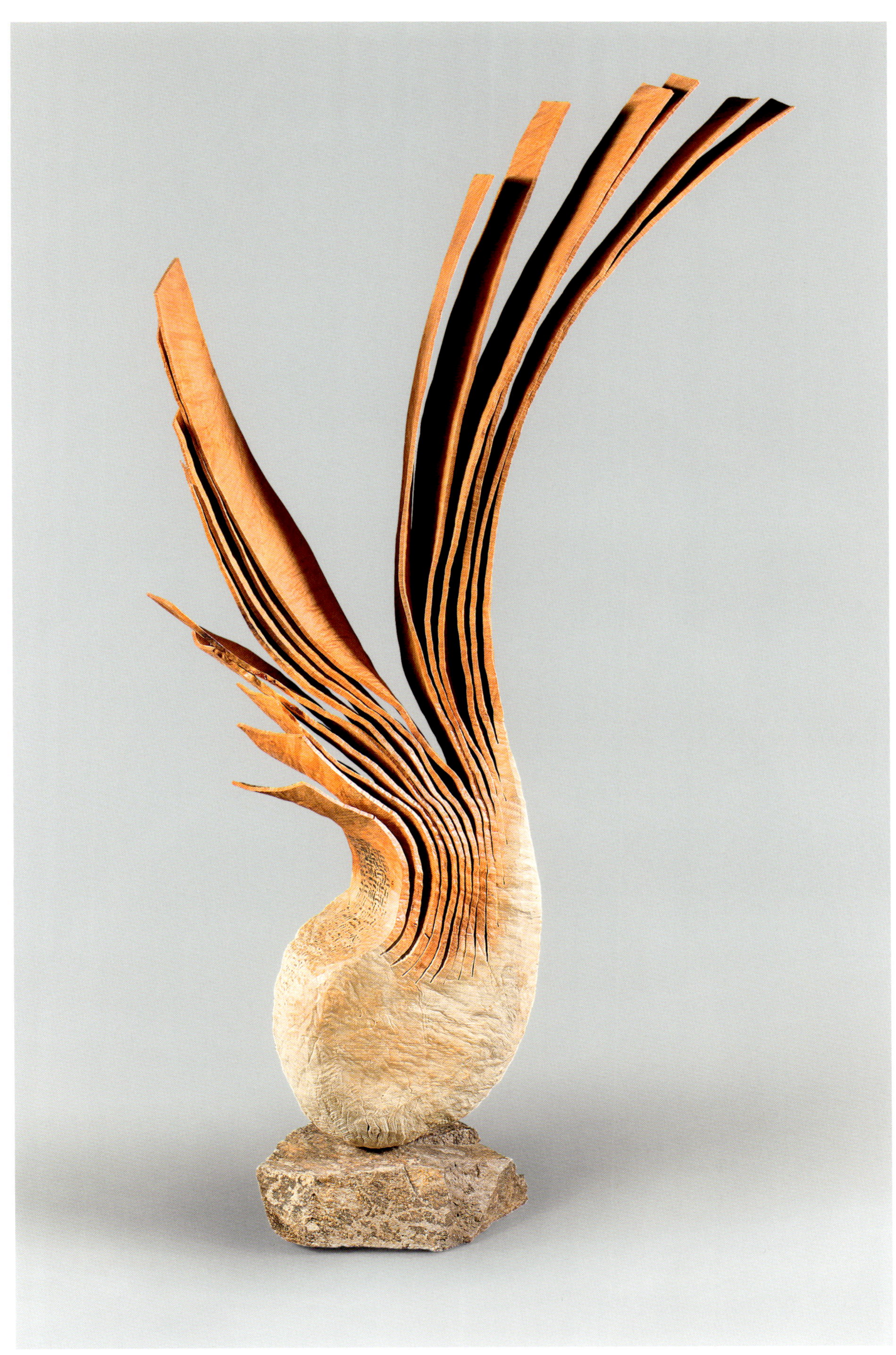

CHRISTIAN BURCHARD born 1955, works Ashland, Oregon
WRESTLING WITH THE RIDDLE #13 2010, madrone burl, Billy rock, 38 3/4 x 20 x 7 in. (98.4 x 50.8 x 17.8 cm)

GOING TO PIECES

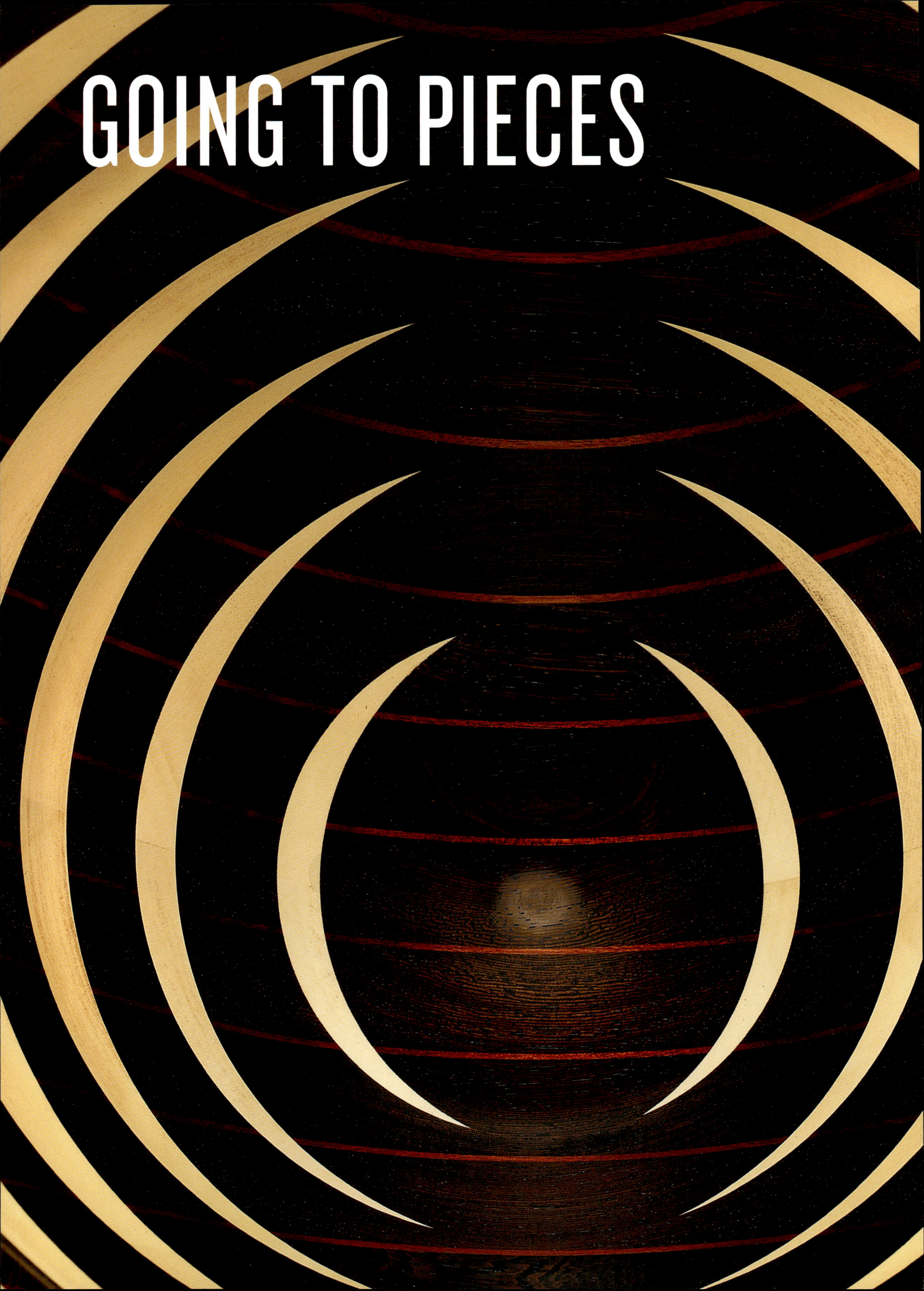

Pattern and movement result when the artist glues together hundreds or thousands of pieces of wood and then turns the block on a lathe. Mathematical calculations, extraordinary technical skills, precision, and a leap of faith that a striking design will emerge distinguish the art of segmented turning. Masters of this technique have produced dramatic and audacious pieces.

MICHAEL MODE: SOMETHING MAGICAL

I like intricate designs, symmetry, color, and the process of making things; and I like wood. I have patience, persistence, good hand skills, an innate sense of geometry, and a desire to create. Add to that the inspirations that strike me from time to time, and a certain inevitability occurs. My lack of a conscious intention to become an artist did not prevent the above factors from becoming an outpouring of finely crafted wooden objects. Many of these feature patterns composed of different species of colorful woods made visible in the well-finished surface of each piece.

Something magical happens in the process of segmentation: the lathe becomes a machine of revelation uncovering surprising relationships and unexpected designs in the carefully planned and visualized schemes of the artist, simply by carving a rectilinear form into a round one. A quick glance at the various segmented objects in this exhibition illustrates some of the variety flowing from this magician's trick.

Attempting to fully master this process, although probably futile, challenges me, as does the possibility of more fully expressing certain inspirations. For example, the art and architecture of Islam and its abstract design ethos continue to fascinate and encourage me. Segmentation techniques bring these abstractions to life in wood, and include its texture, color, and warmth in the designs.

Trees support the canopy of the forest over our heads and the roofs of our houses; they provide an undying beauty in our daily surroundings. All of us who work in or admire wood art benefit from the richness of the forest and the subtleties of a material that once lived and grew. We experience joy seeing wood's beauty combined with the designs and geometries of segmentation. For this reason I often say to a curious admirer or prospective client, "You can't put anything in that bowl; it's already full!"

Detail, Michael Mode, *Ask No Questions,* 2002 (page 108)

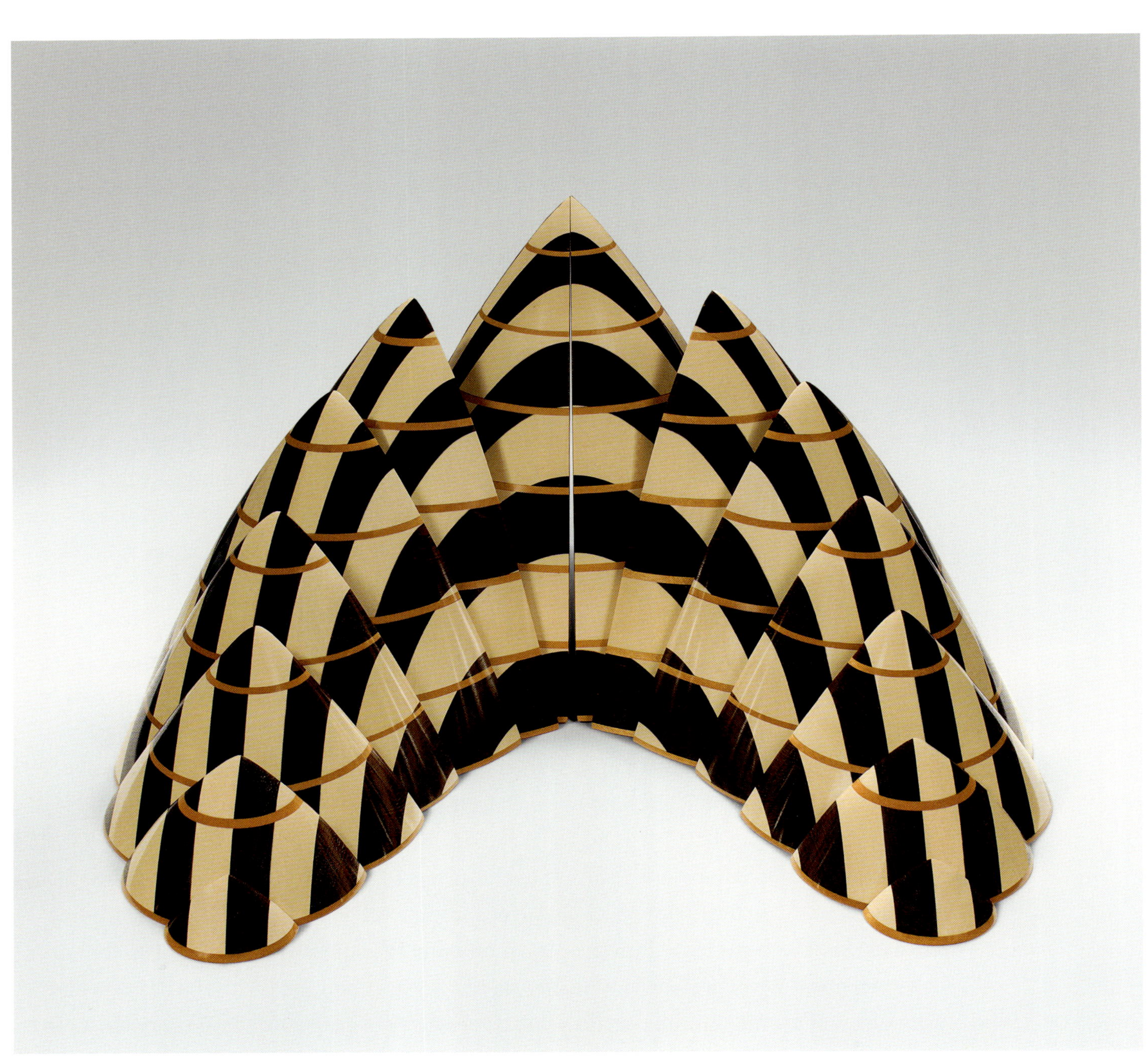

MICHAEL MODE born 1946, works New Haven, Vermont
CONJUNCTION ASCENDING 2007, holly, wenge, yellowheart (8 wood bowls), 12 x 20 x 22 in. (30.5 x 50.8 x 55.9 cm)

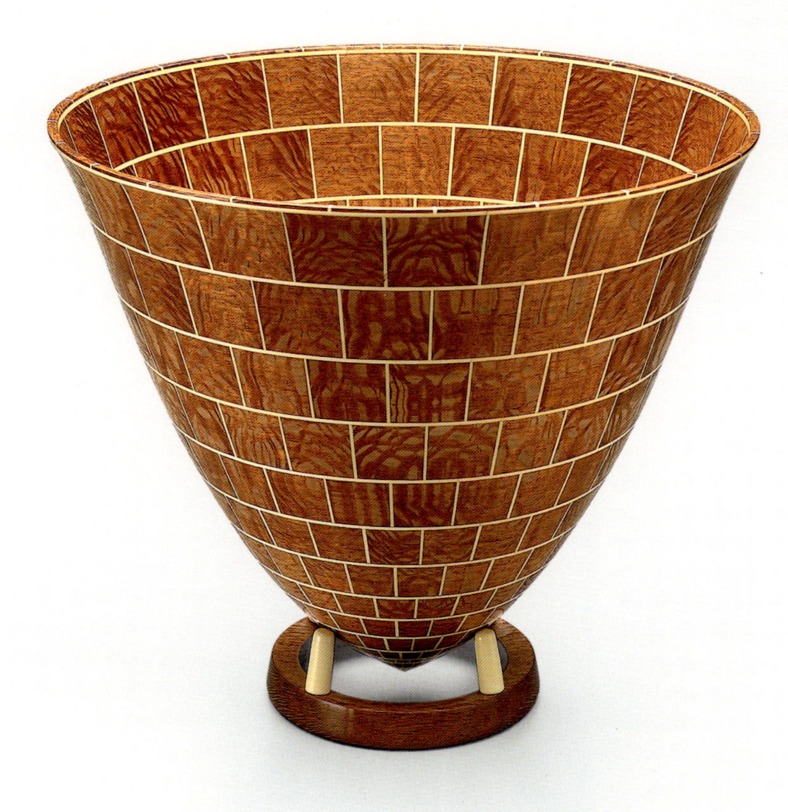

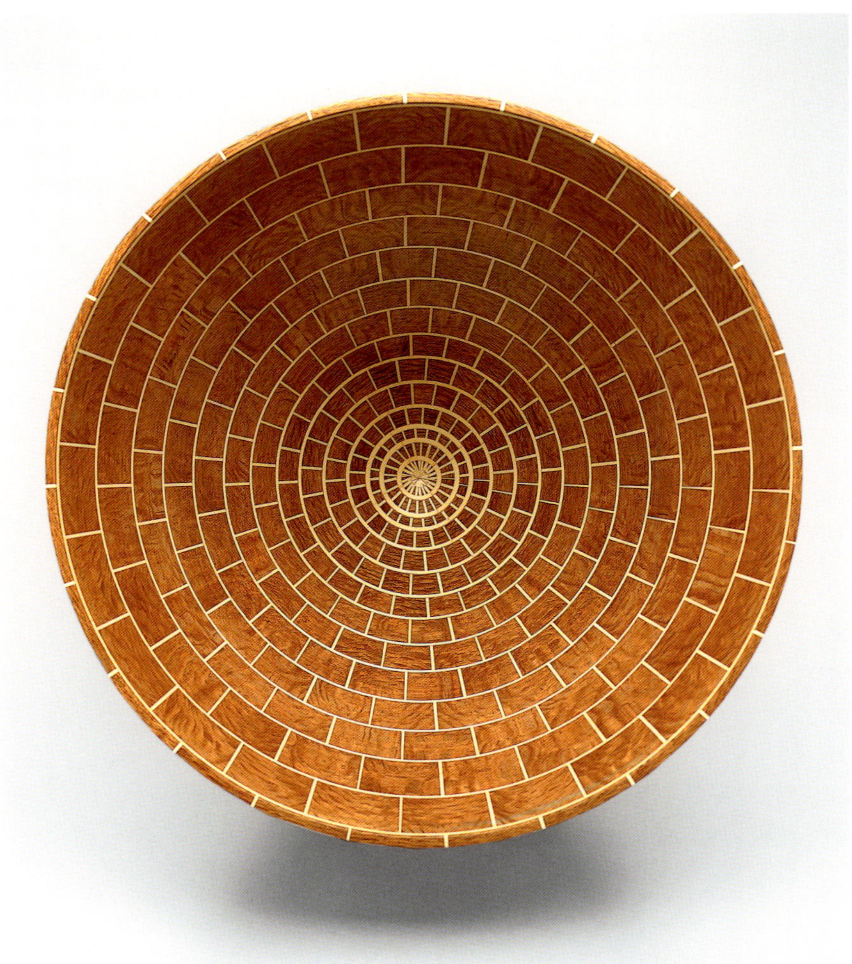

MICHAEL MODE born 1946, works New Haven, Vermont
HOLDING THE HONEY 2003, lacewood, holly, 16 1/2 x 15 1/4 x 14 1/2 in. (41.9 x 38.7 x 35.6 cm), Peabody Essex Museum, Gift of Lillian Montalto Bohlen

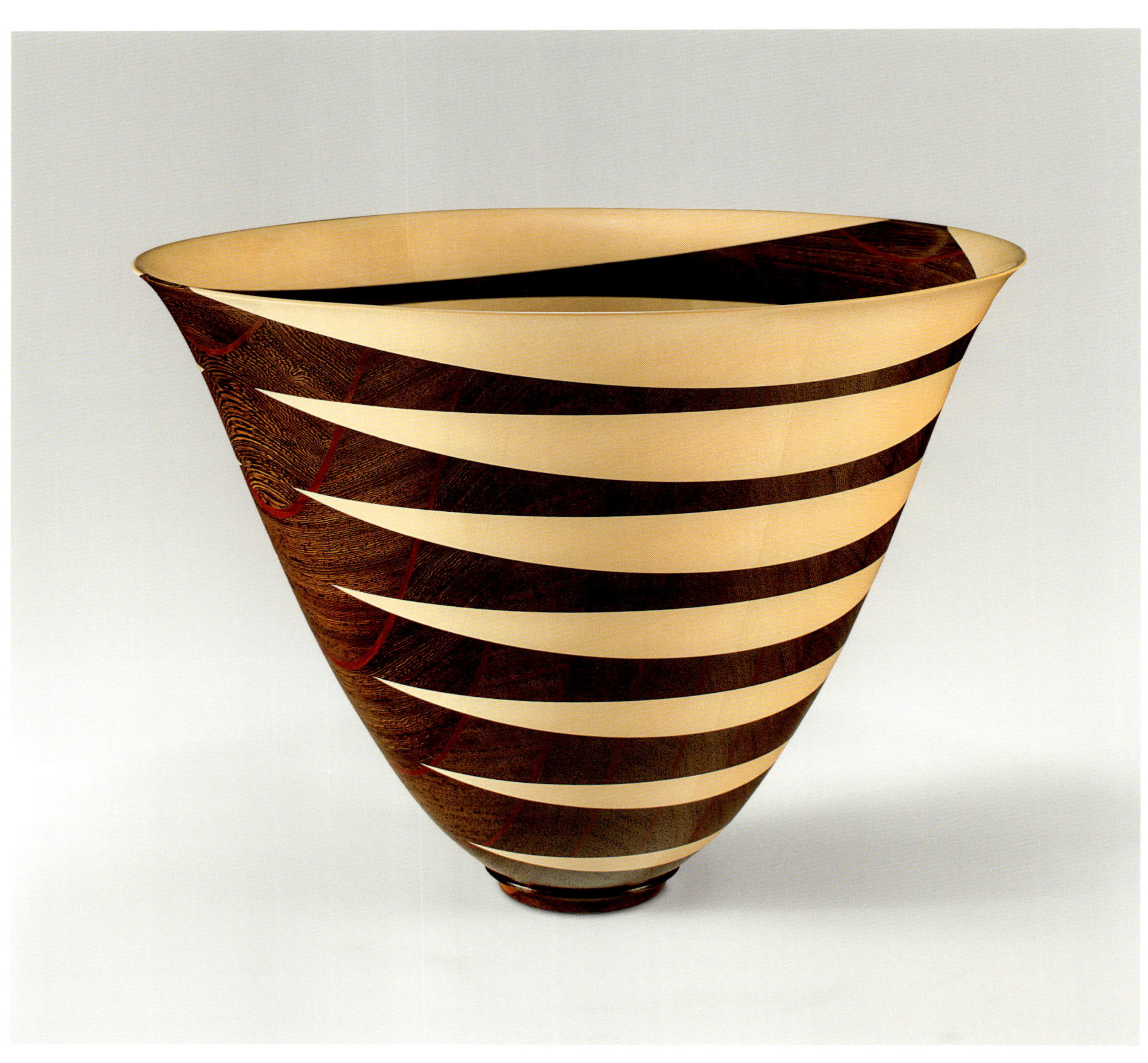

MICHAEL MODE born 1946, works New Haven, Vermont
ASK NO QUESTIONS 2002, wenge, holly, bloodwood, 11 x 14 in. (28 x 35.6 cm)

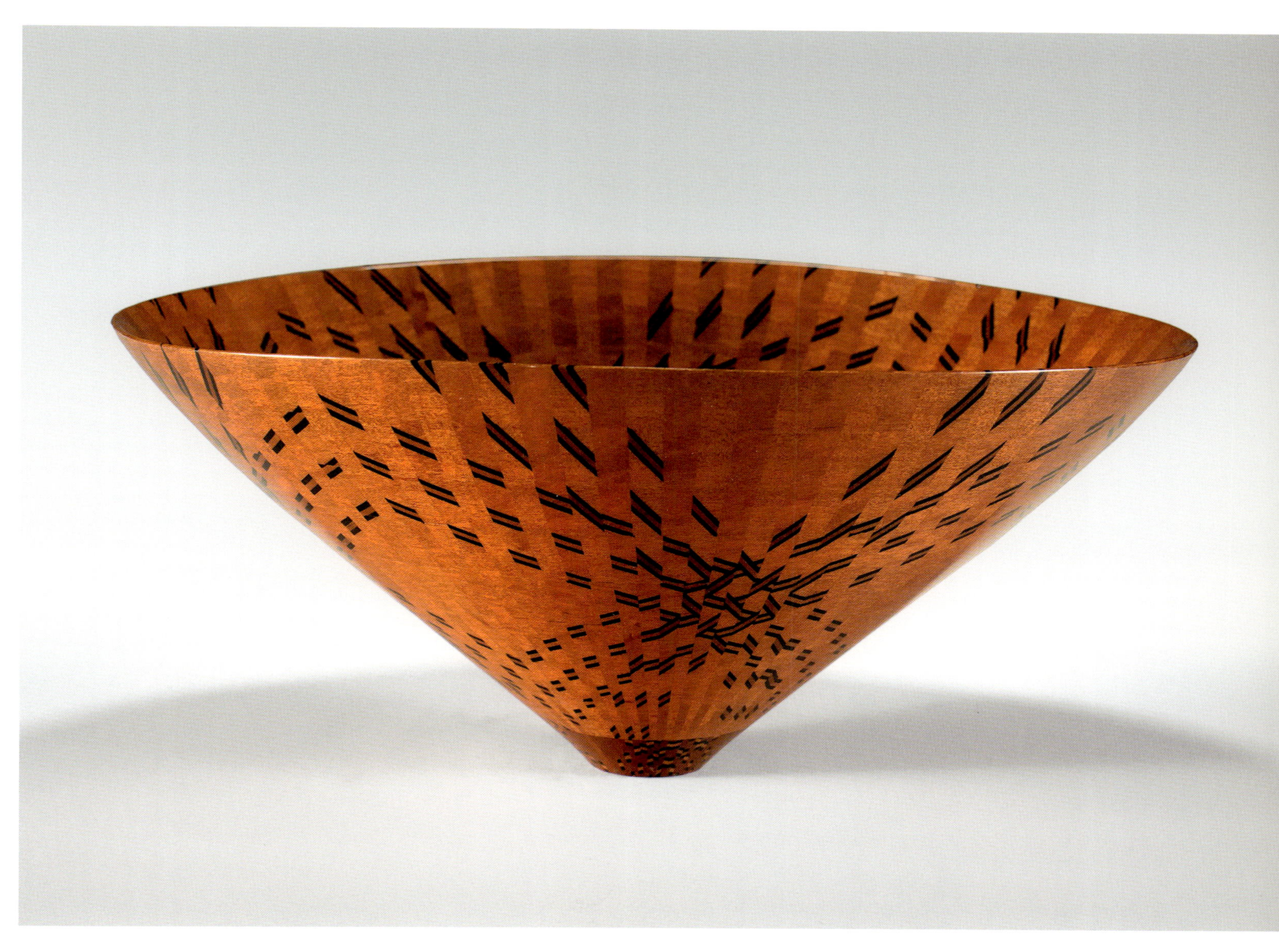

MICHAEL SHULER born 1950, works Santa Cruz, California
#729 1994, pink ivory, Gabon ebony, 5 $^1/_2$ x 12 in. (14 x 30.5 cm), Peabody Essex Museum, Gift of Lillian Montalto Bohlen

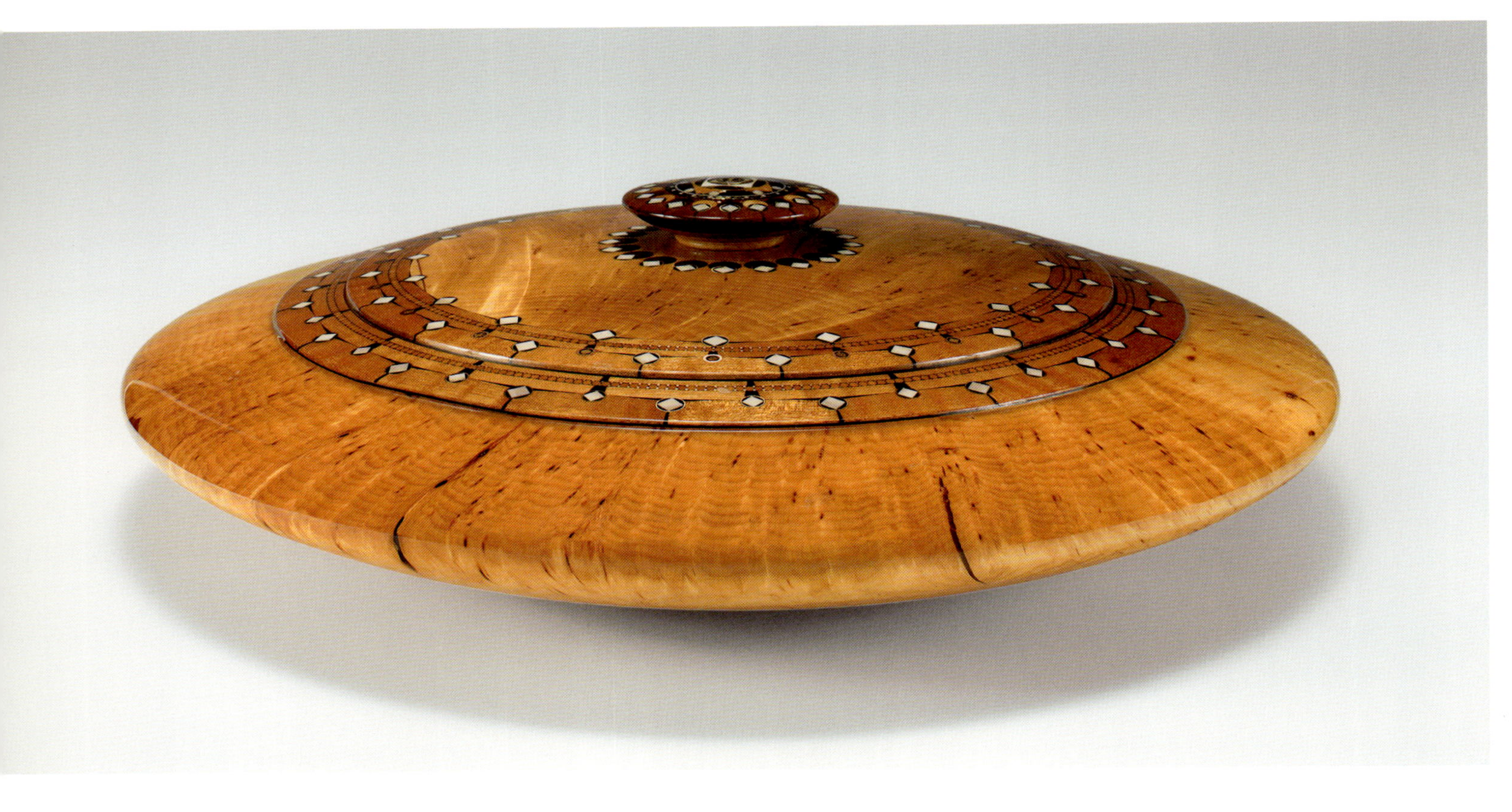

ROBERT CUTLER born 1944, works Kenai, Alaska

AURORA BOREALIS 1997, Alaskan masur birch burl, brass, copper, curly mahogany, fossil bone, fossil mammoth ivory, fossil walrus ivory, moose antler, silver, tagua nut, 4 $^{1}/_{2}$ x 19 in. (11.4 x 48.3 cm)

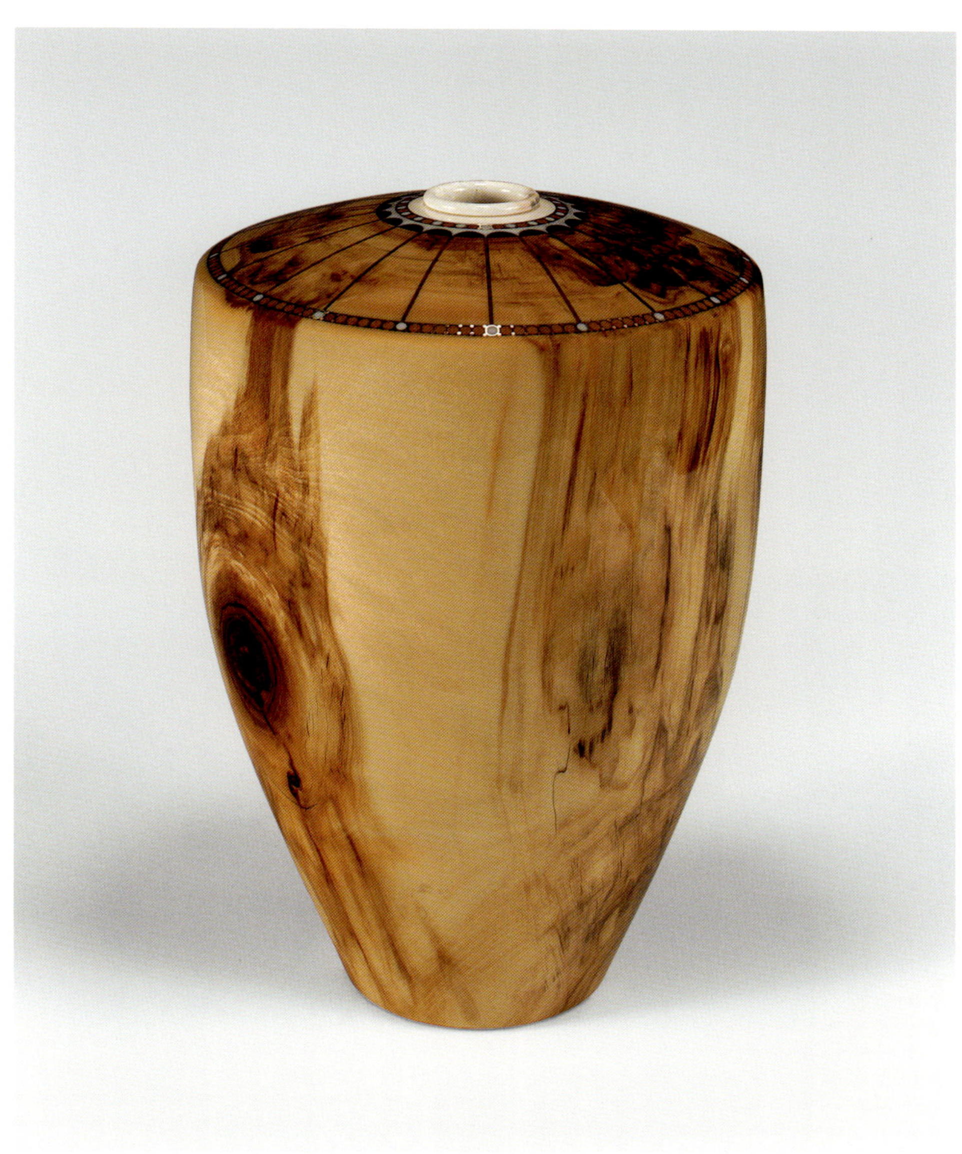

ROBERT CUTLER born 1944, works Kenai, Alaska
AND BULLET 1997, mahogany, Alaskan aspen, fossil mammoth ivory, fossil walrus ivory, copper, silver, 9 x 5 $^{1}/_{2}$ in. (22.9 x 14 cm)

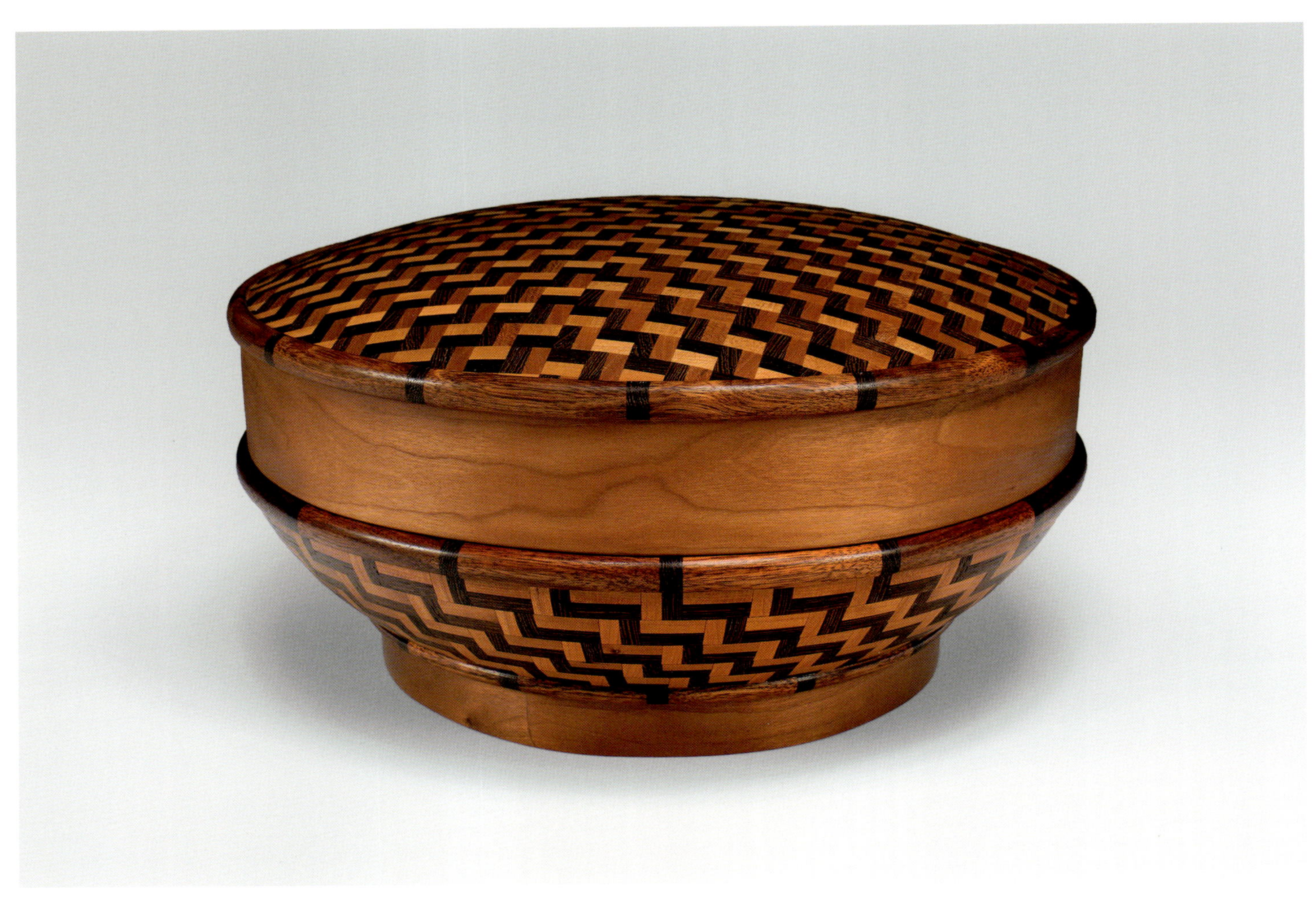

LINCOLN SEITZMAN born 1923, works Ocean, New Jersey
PETRIFIED SEWING BASKET 1992, cherry, wenge, imbuia, 6 $^{3}/_{4}$ x 13 in. (17.1 x 33 cm), Peabody Essex Museum, Gift of Lillian Montalto Bohlen

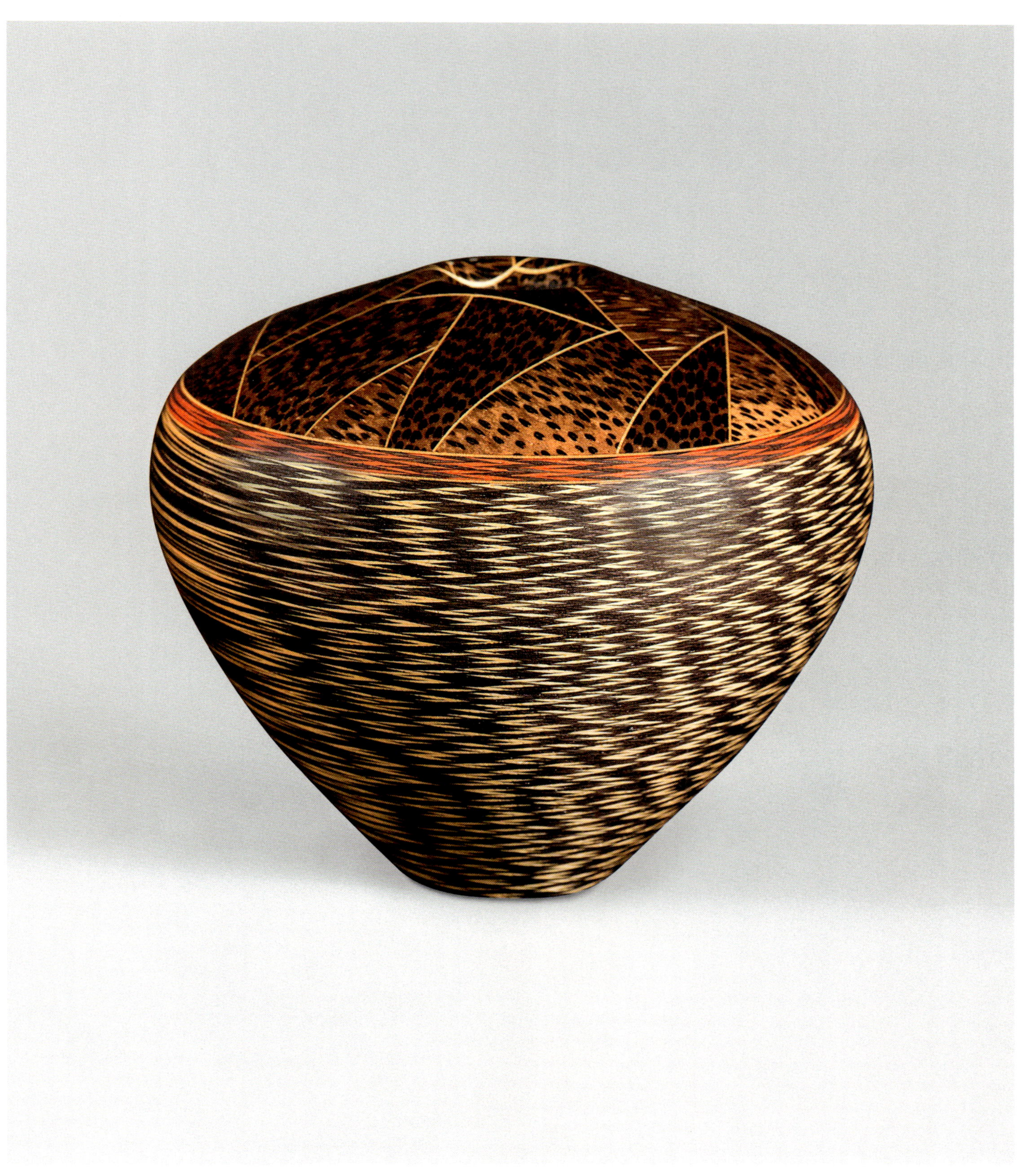

GALEN CARPENTER born 1946, works Sedona, Arizona
SEGMENTED VESSEL 2001, colorply, black palm, maple, antler, 6 x 6 in. (15.2 x 15.2 cm)

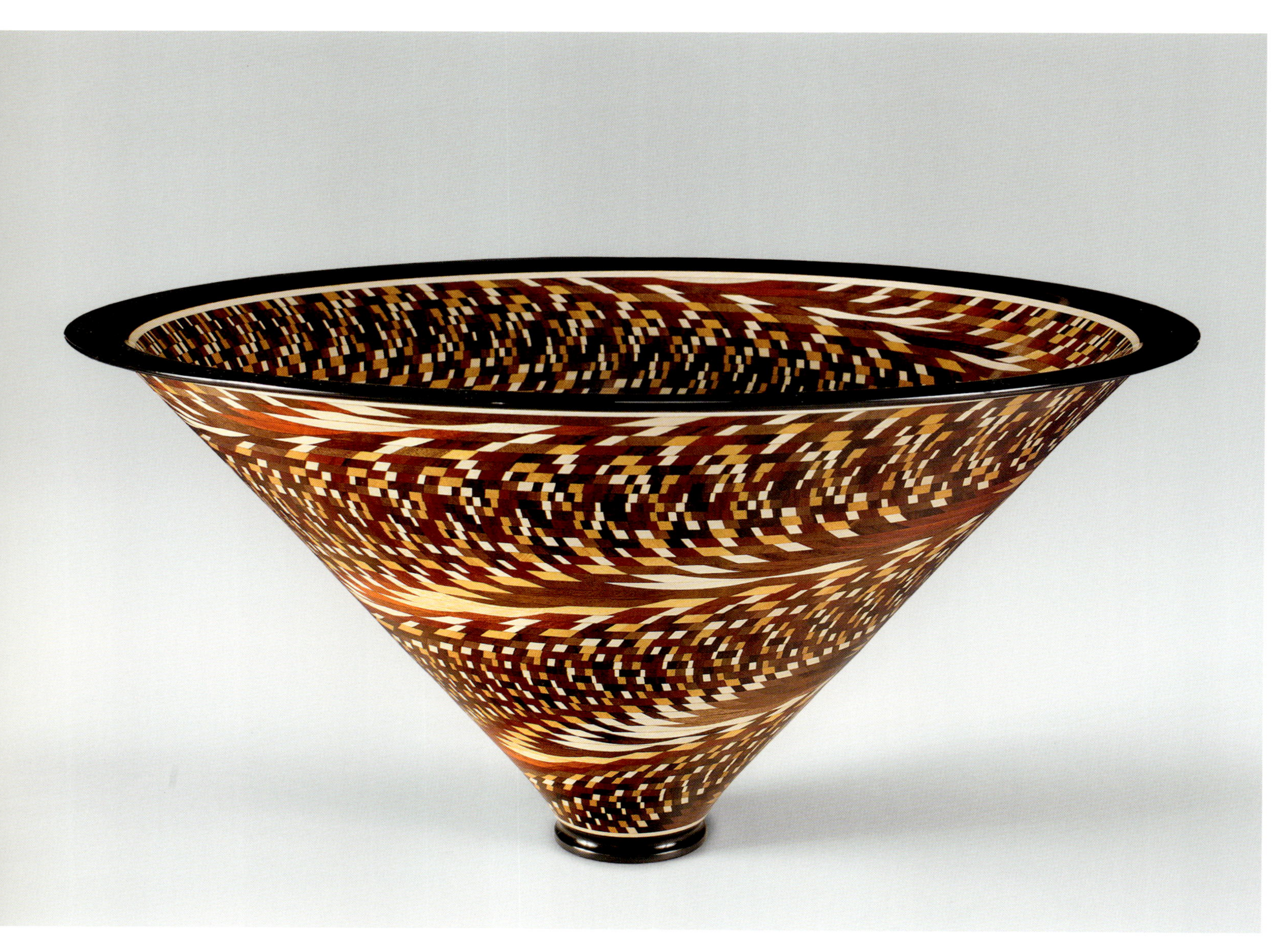

HAL METLITZKY born 1946, works Claremont, California
DOUBLE HELIX 2012, black walnut, yellowheart, pernambuco, satine, holly, imbuia, old growth East Indian rosewood, East Indian ebony (6,500 pieces of wood), 10 x 19 in. (25.4 x 48.3 cm)
Right: Detail, interior

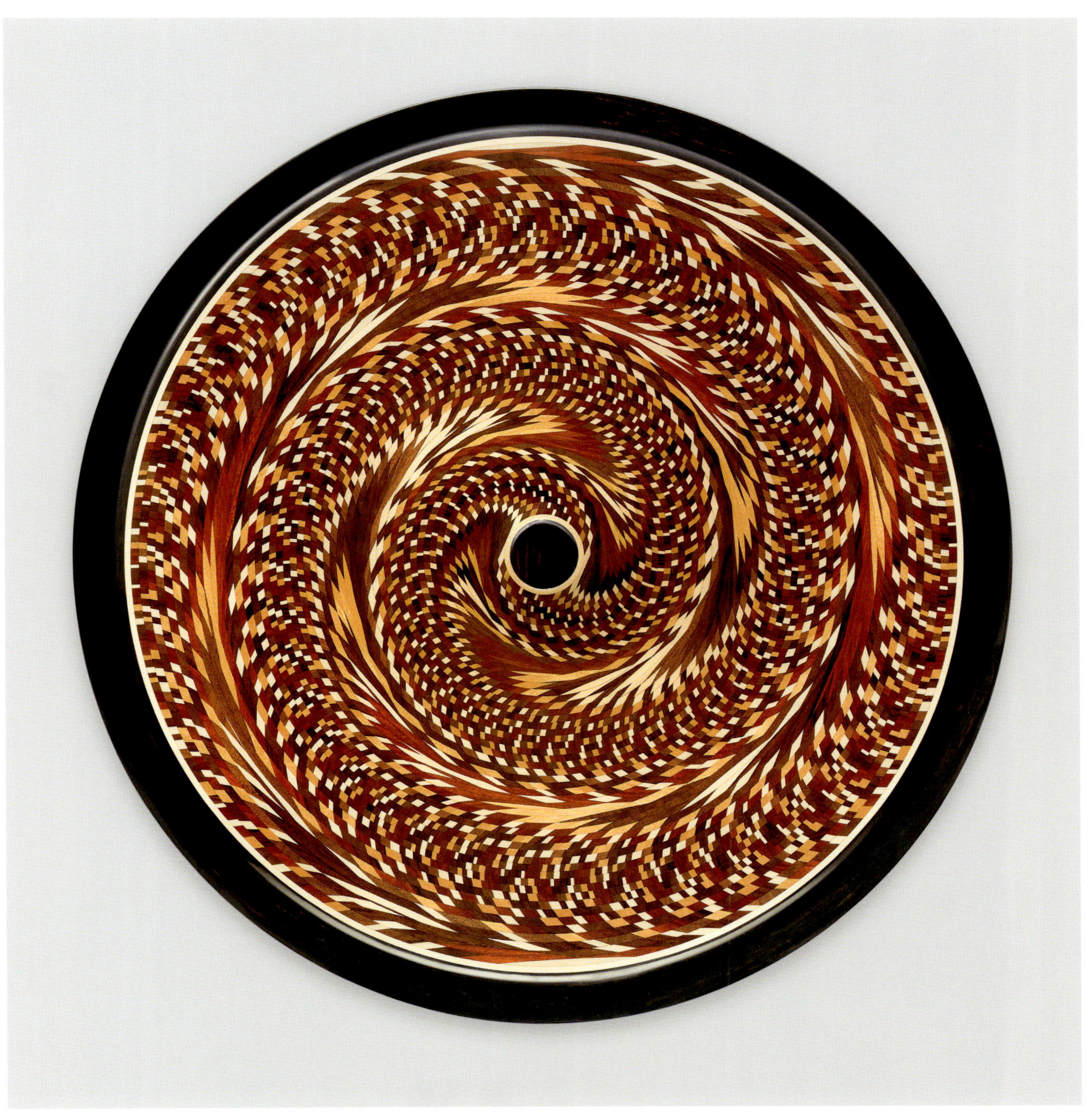

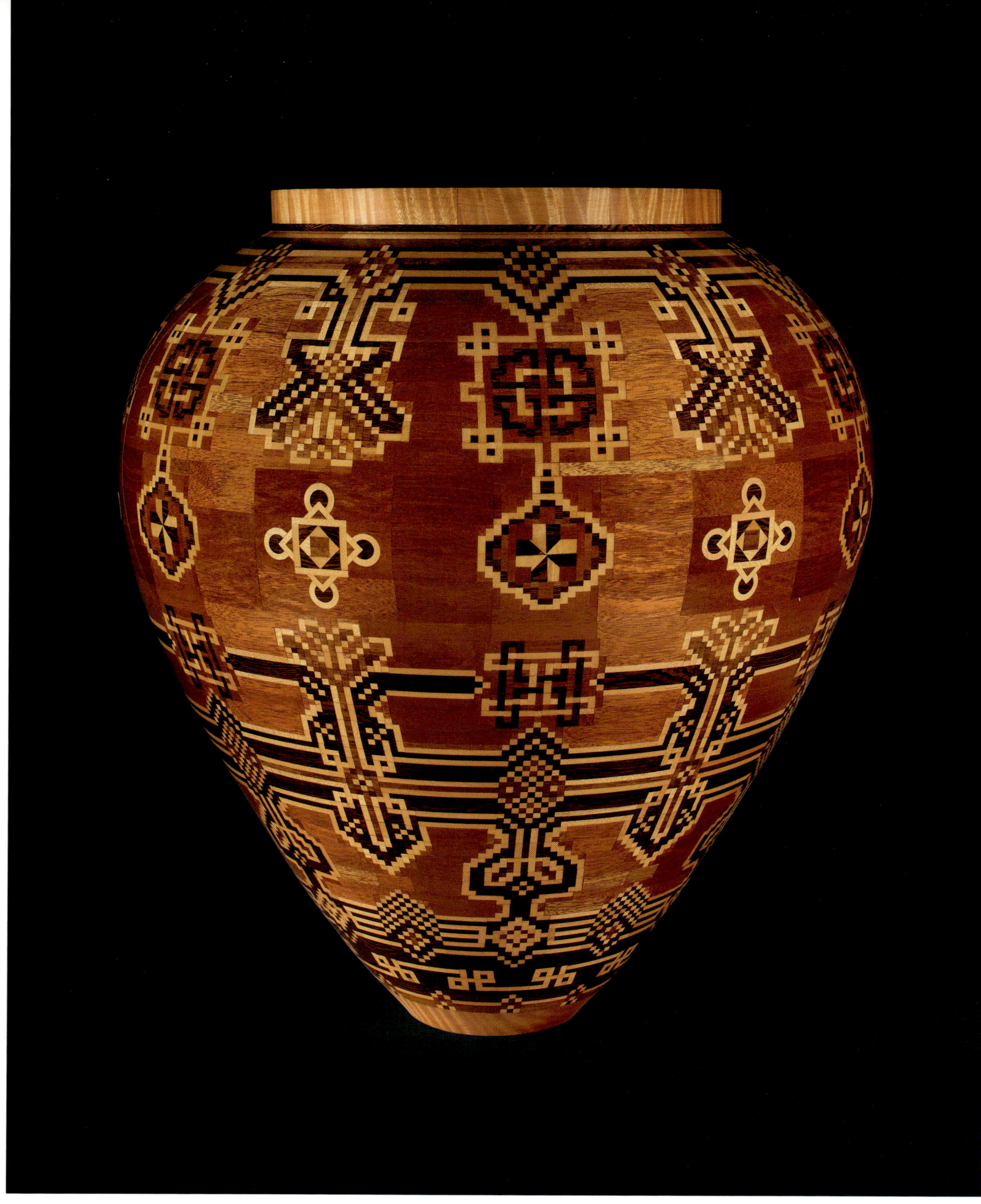

EUCLED MOORE/KAZI STUDIO born 1955, works Driftwood, Texas
UNTITLED 1999, mahogany, maple, paduak, wenge (13,400 pieces of wood), 18 $^{3}/_{4}$ x 15 in. (47.6 x 38.1 cm)

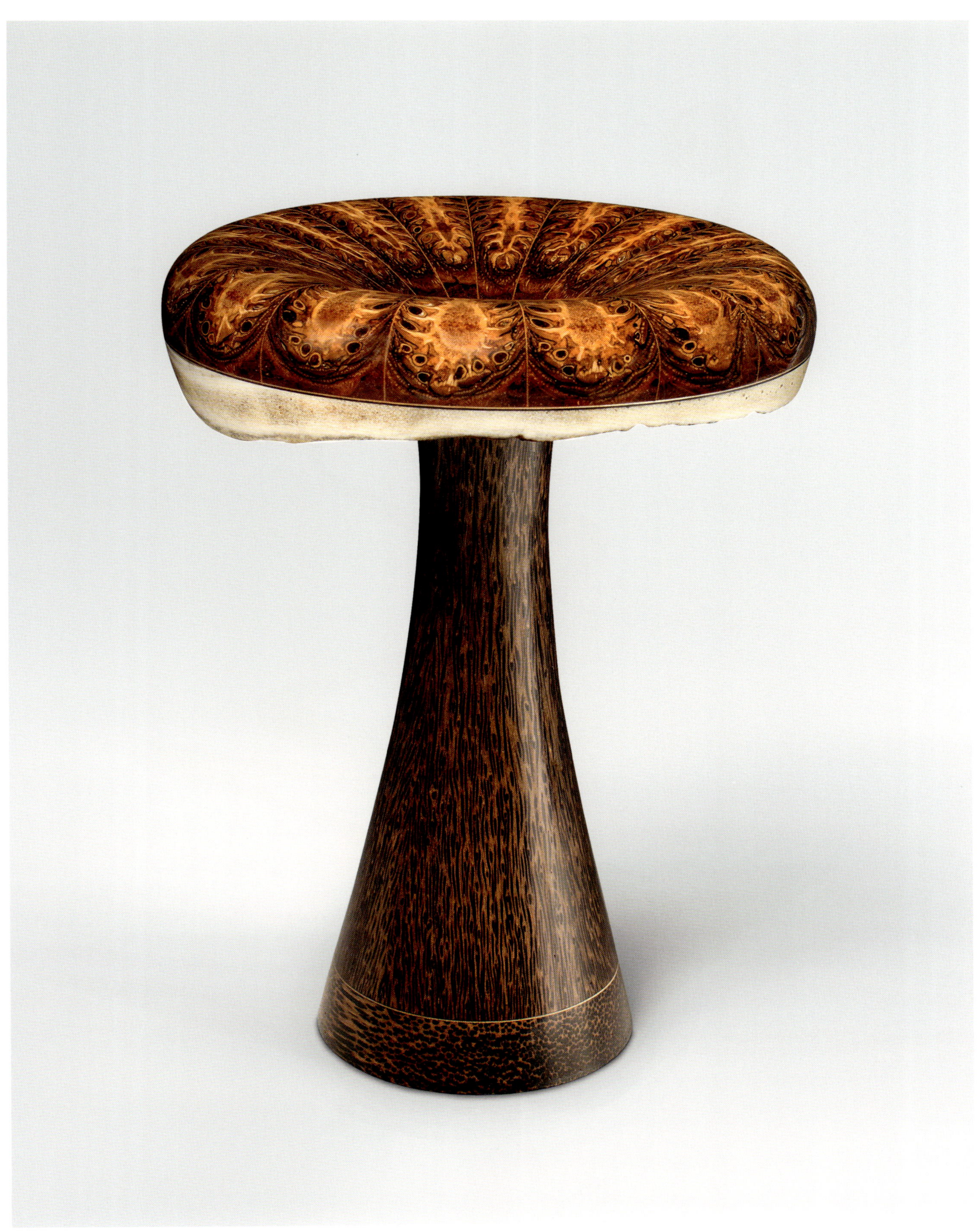

GALEN CARPENTER born 1946, works Sedona, Arizona
"01-1" 2001, pinecones, antler, maple, royal palm, black palm, 10 $^{1}/_{8}$ x 7 $^{3}/_{4}$ in. (25.7 x 19.7 cm)

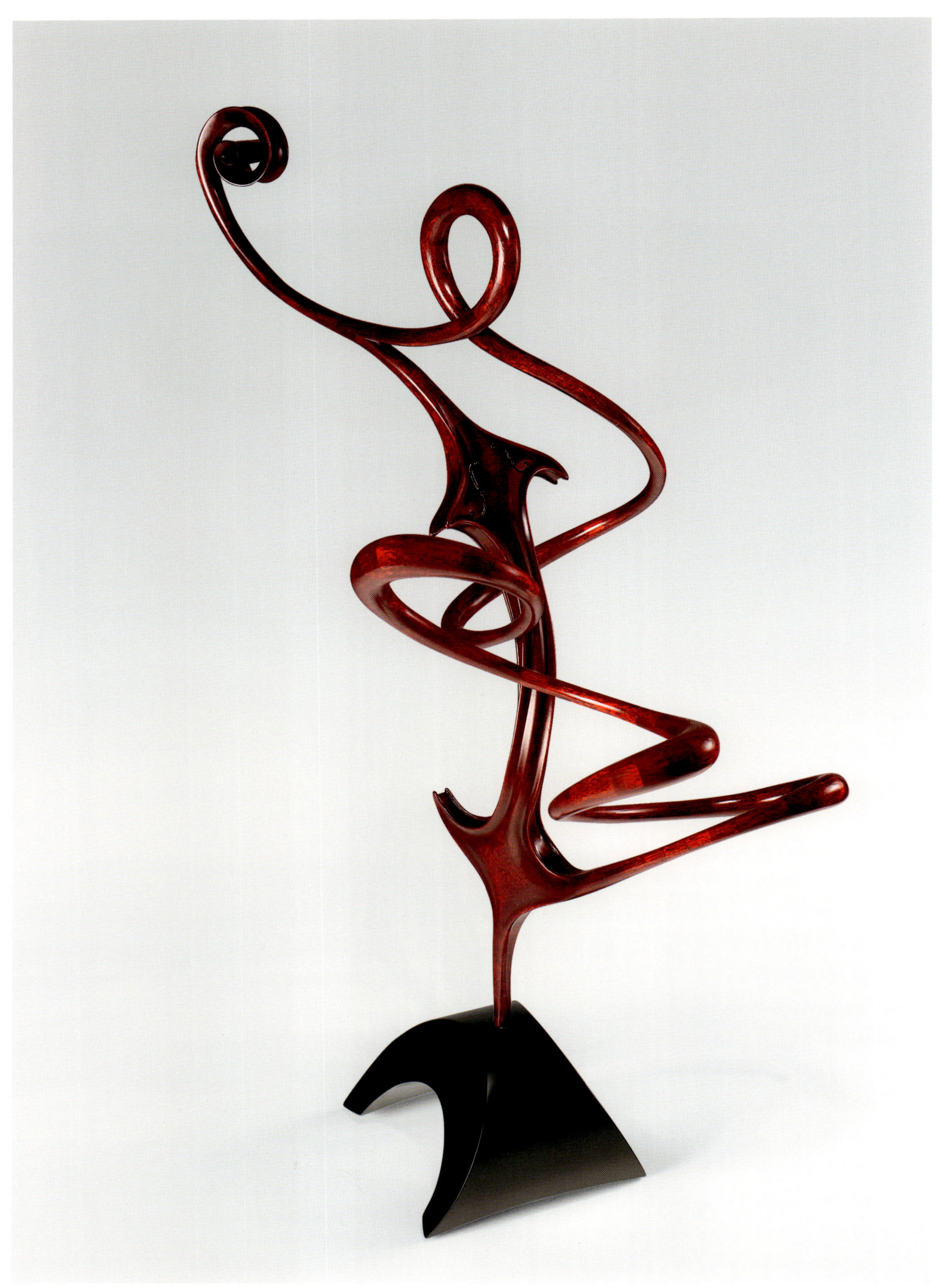

JERRY BENNETT born 1941, works Huntsville, Texas
HUMORESQUE 2011, mahogany, ebony, dyes, maple, lacquer finish, acrylic, 28 $^{1}/_{2}$ x 17 x 11 in. (72.4 x 43.2 x 27.9 cm)

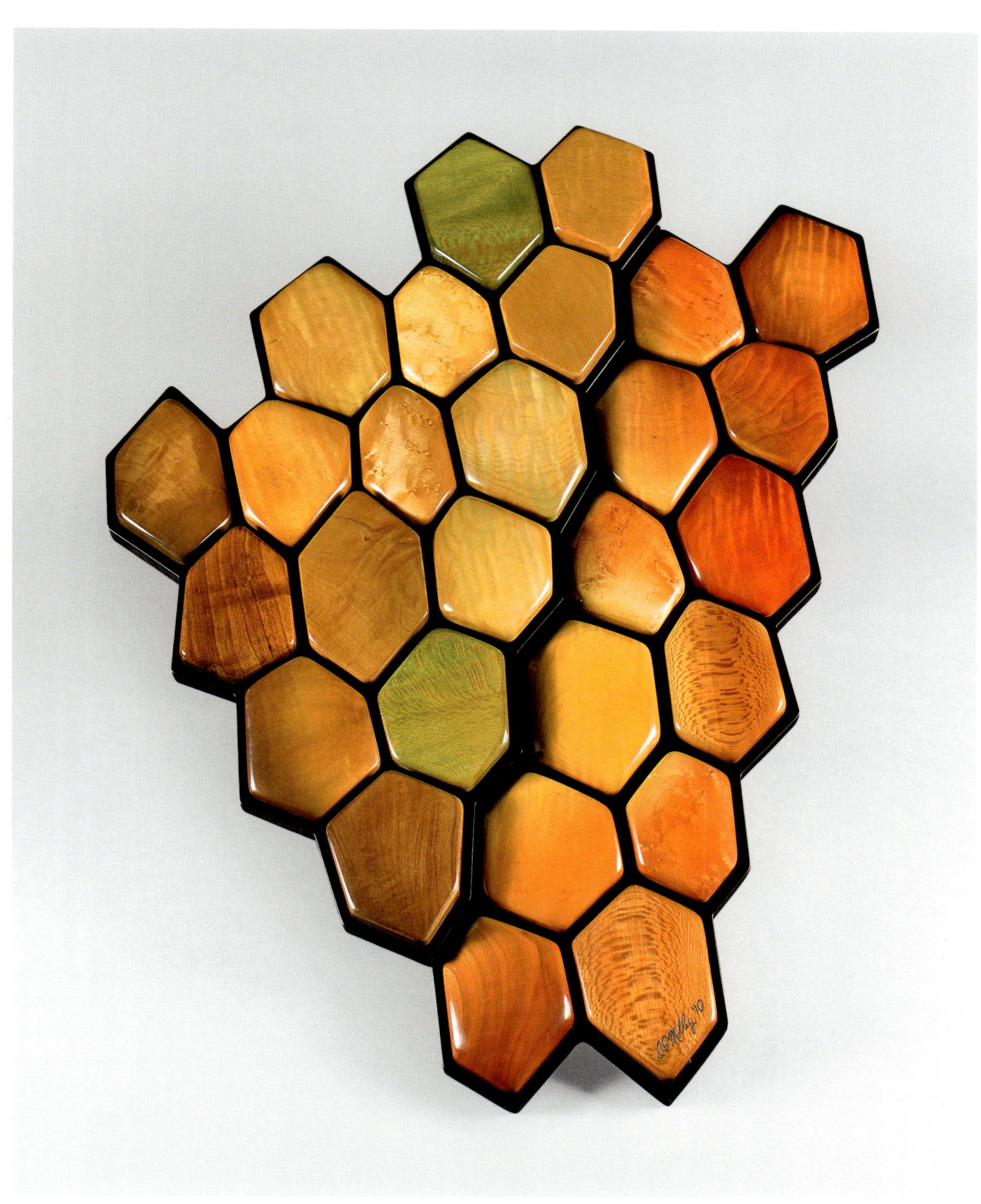

DAVID MOBLEY born 1953, works Niskayuna, New York
SURFACE ENERGY 3 2010, curly maple, birds-eye maple, sycamore, cherry, beech, apple, pear, dyes, fiberboard, 30 1/2 x 24 x 4 1/2 in. (77.48 x 61 x 11.4 cm)

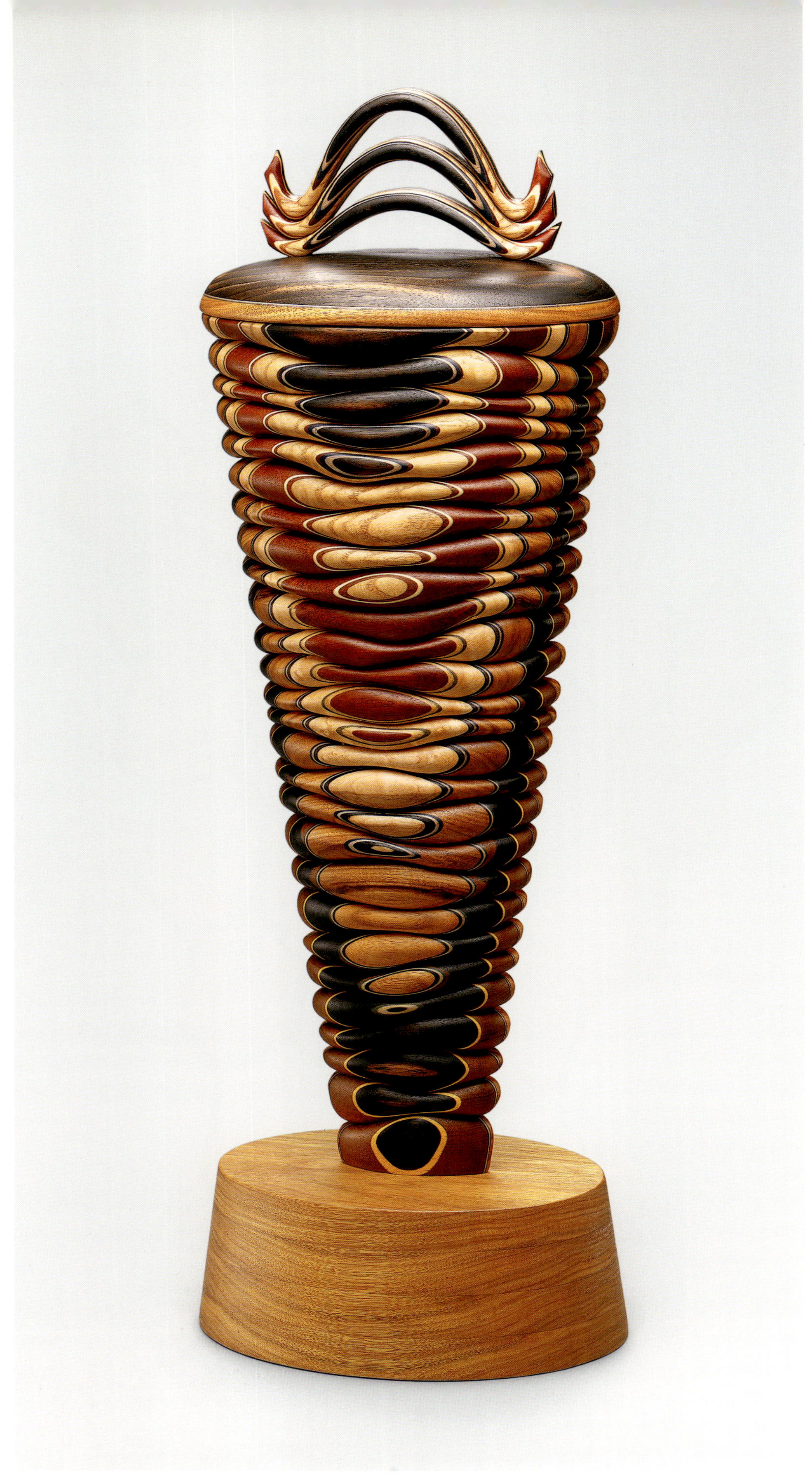

TERRY EVANS born 1951, works Overland Park, Kansas
TAPERED URN #7 2002, ebony, ash, bloodwood, canary wood, imbuia, sassafras, hackberry, 23 x 7 1/2 x 6 in. (58.4 x 19 x 15.2 cm)

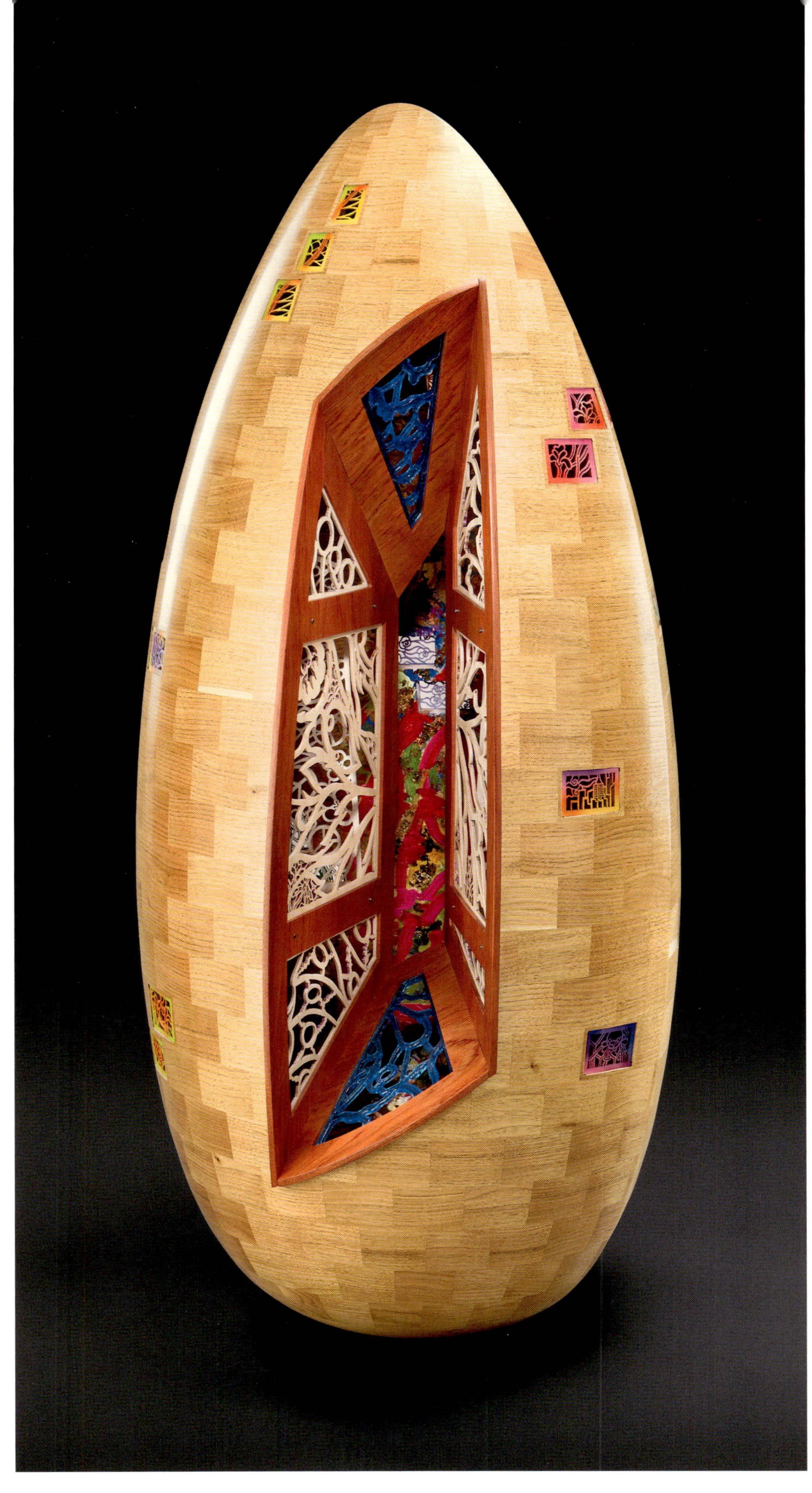

CURT THEOBALD WITH BINH PHO born 1965, works Pine Bluffs, Wyoming (Theobald); born 1955, works Maple Park, Illinois (Pho)
INNER WORLD 2014, butternut, African padauk, birch plywood, acrylic paints, cast glass, 43 x 18 x 17 in. (109.2 x 45.7 x 43.2 cm)

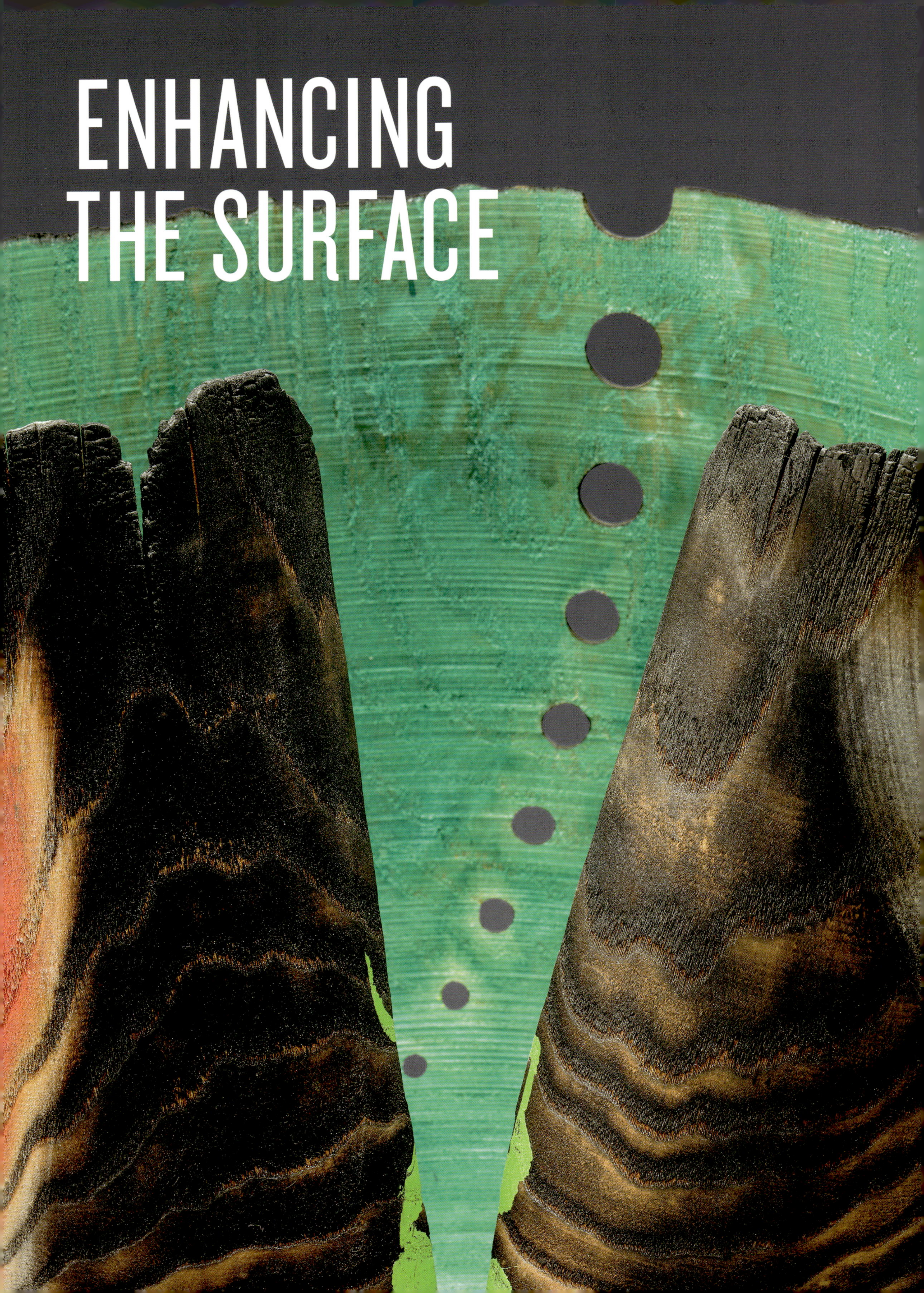
ENHANCING
THE SURFACE

Some artists add paint or texture to the surface by carving, gouging, cutting, burning, or stamping their forms. The natural characteristics of the wood become less important. Several artists go even further to achieve a surface akin to glass or ceramics. Still others have used silver for a dramatic accent or iron tacks for a novel surface.

DAVID ELLSWORTH: FREEDOM TO EXPLORE

I am constantly reminded of two important elements that surround one's creative directions: first, that it is the *process* of making, rather than the *products* produced, that remains the ultimate goal in the evolution of a creative being; and, second, that as much as we applaud the importance and the power of our technical virtuosity as crafts-people and artists, the most powerful works we make seem always to be marked with some measure of naive delight.

The evolution of the *Solstice Series* (1989-91) is a perfect example of this balance between process, product, and self-discovery. The pieces were conceived as sculpture rather than my typical vessel forms. As such, I felt at liberty to explore not only the dynamics of new forms, but also how to enhance an object's singular identity that goes beyond the natural grain patterns and colors in wood.

I began by focusing on surface enhancement through the use of fire and color, and this led to juxtaposing the intimate relationship between interior and exterior surfaces. As the process evolved, each piece retained the vitality of risk, that is, not knowing the end result before I began.

My entire forty-year career in making vessel forms in wood is a record of this journey of discovery, where the hand and the eye, left on their own and devoid of the intrusion of the head, often produce some element of collective power within an object that can only be recorded, not defined. It may not be recognized at the time of its making, even by me. Yet, these are the elements of the creative process that have the greatest meaning and that often lead makers into the next direction within their work. If these wonderfully crazy, unpredictable happenings never occurred, we might likely continue to produce only "wonderful objects."

Detail, David Ellsworth, *Intersphere,* 1991 (page 127)

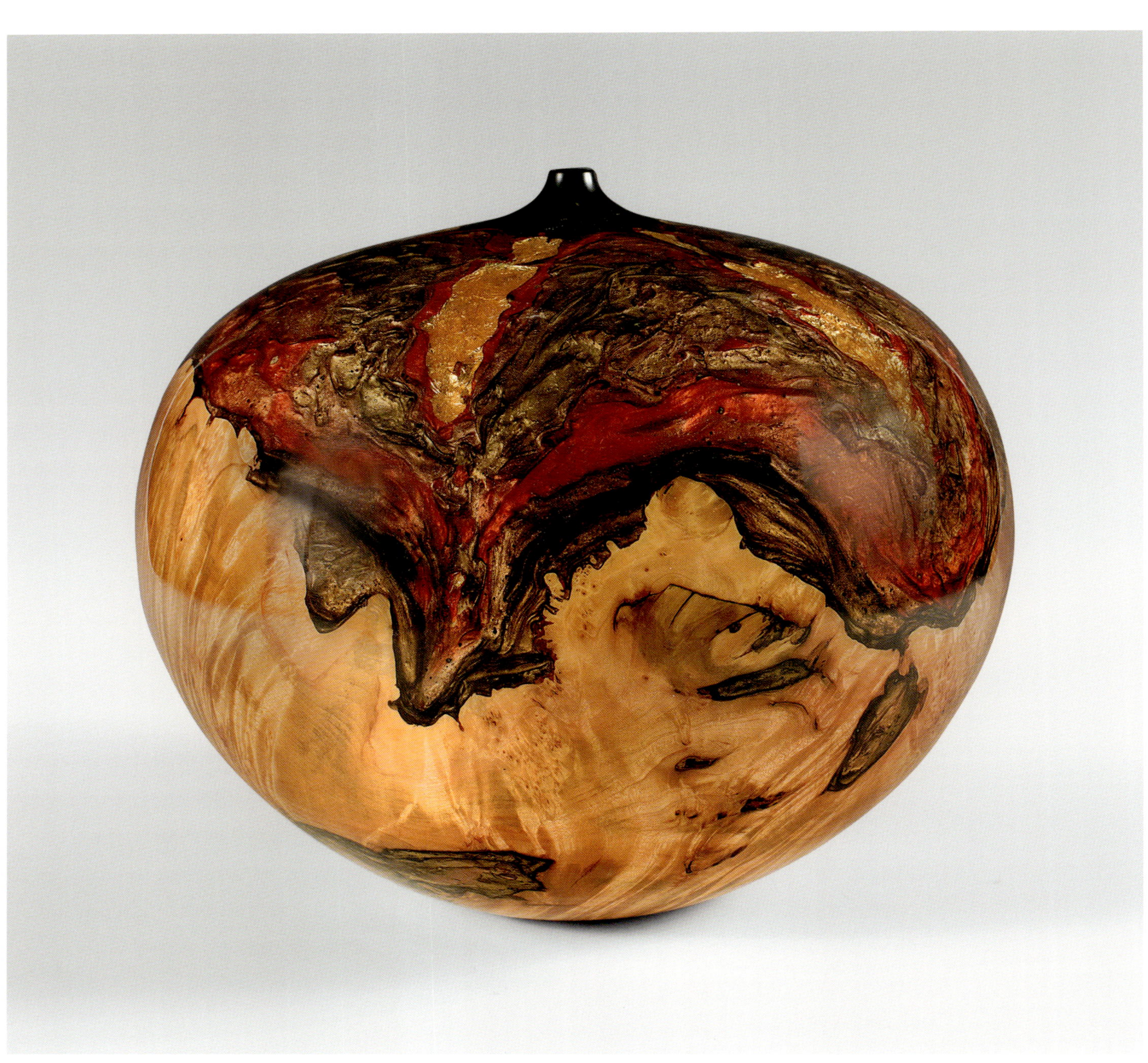

ROBERT CHATELAIN born 1945, works Huntington, Vermont

UNTITLED 1999, red maple burl, gold leaf, metallic powders, 10 x 11 $^{1}/_{2}$ in. (25.4 x 29.2 cm), Peabody Essex Museum, Gift of Lillian Montalto Bohlen

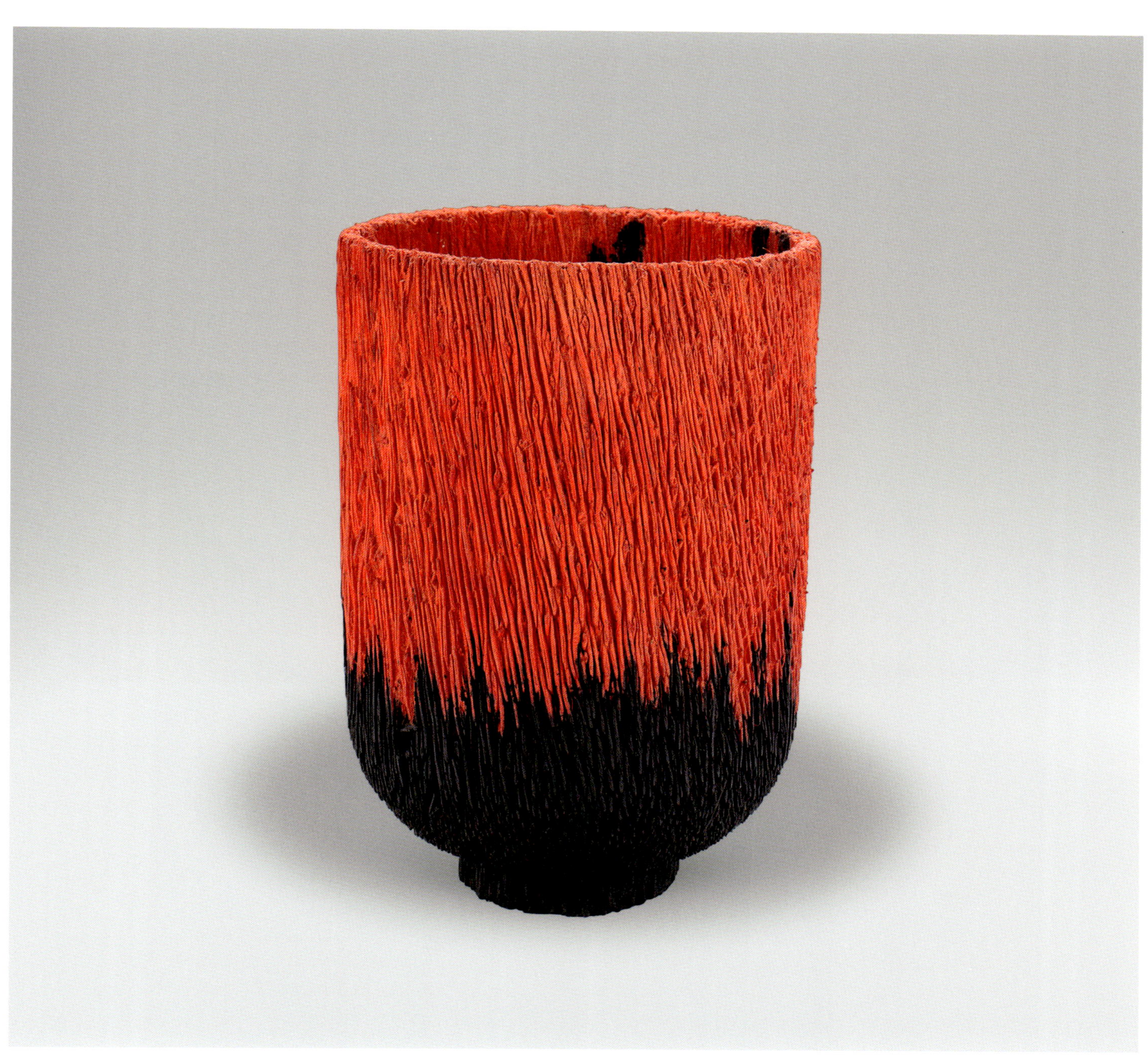

DEWEY GARRETT born 1947, works Prescott, Arizona
R AND B 1997, palm, dye, 13 1/2 x 8 in. (34.5 x 20.3 cm), Peabody Essex Museum, Gift of Lillian Montalto Bohlen

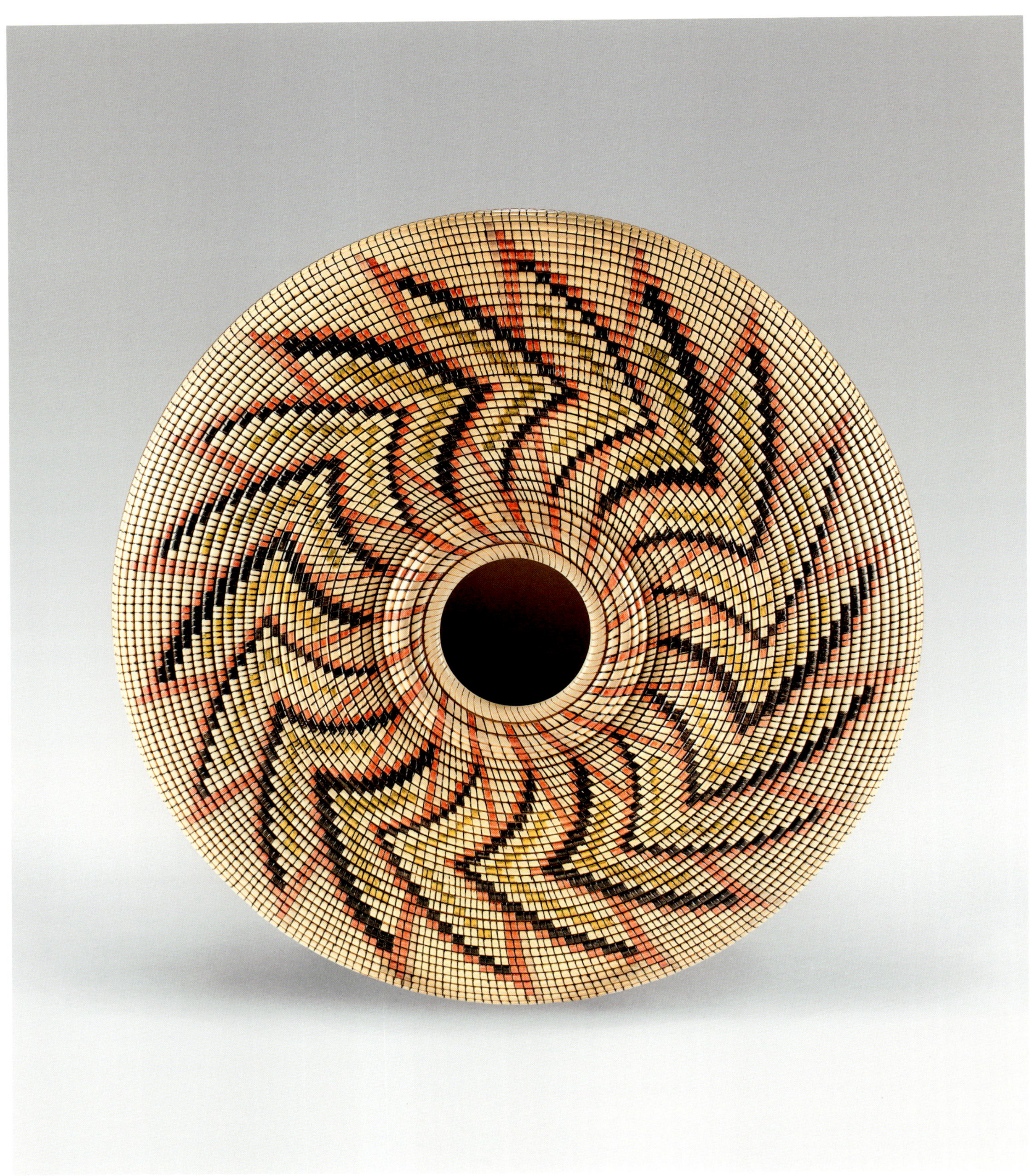

DAVID NITTMAN 1944–2014, worked Boulder, Colorado
SHAMROCK V from BODYDRUM BASKET ILLUSION SERIES 2001, American holly, 3 x 15 in. (7.6 x 38.1 cm)

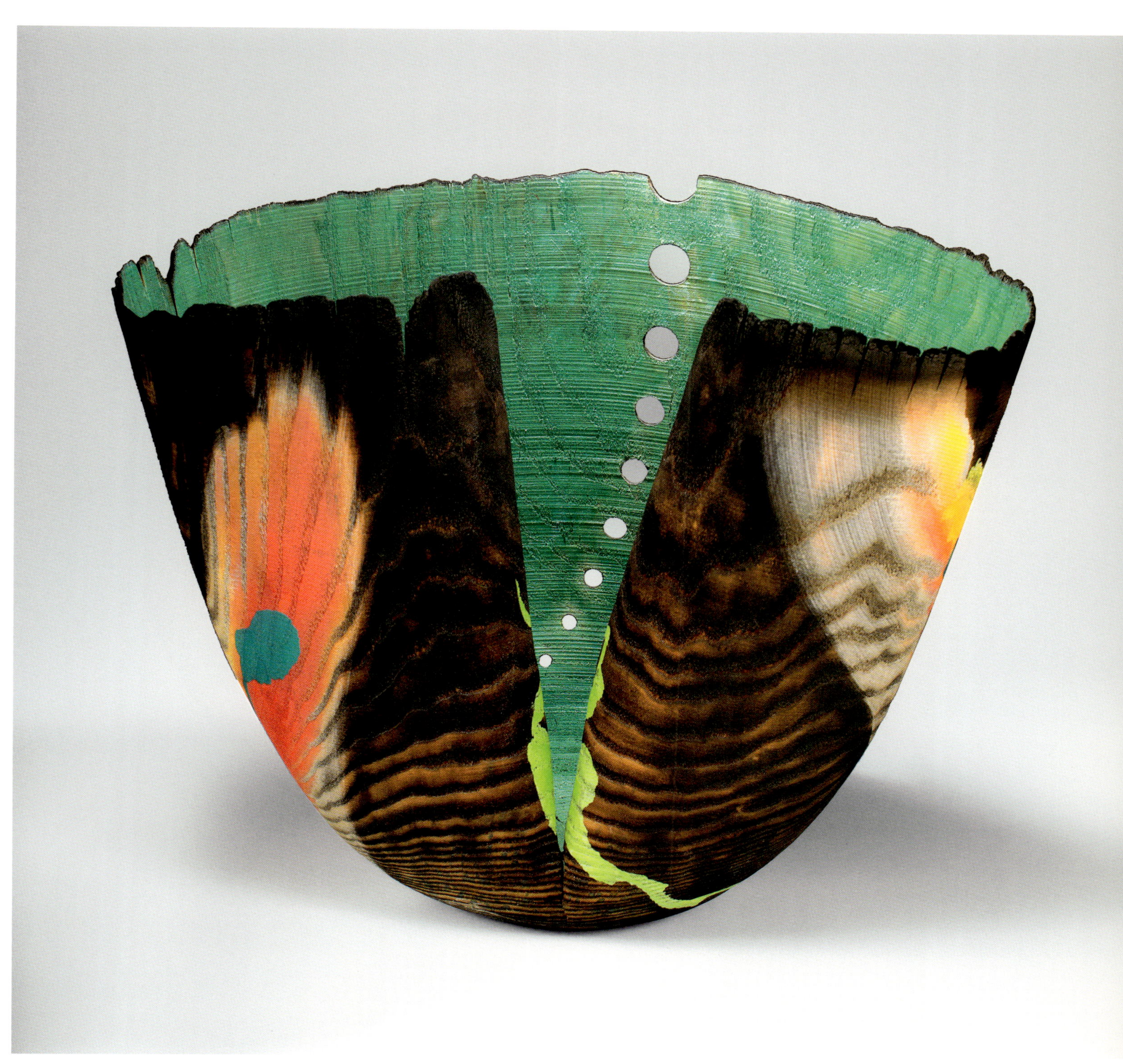

DAVID ELLSWORTH born 1944, works Quakertown, Pennsylvania
INTERSPHERE from SOLSTICE SERIES 1991, burned ash and pigment, 14 x 16 x 9 $^{1}/_{2}$ in. (35.6 x 40.6 x 24.2 cm), Peabody Essex Museum, Gift of Lillian Montalto Bohlen

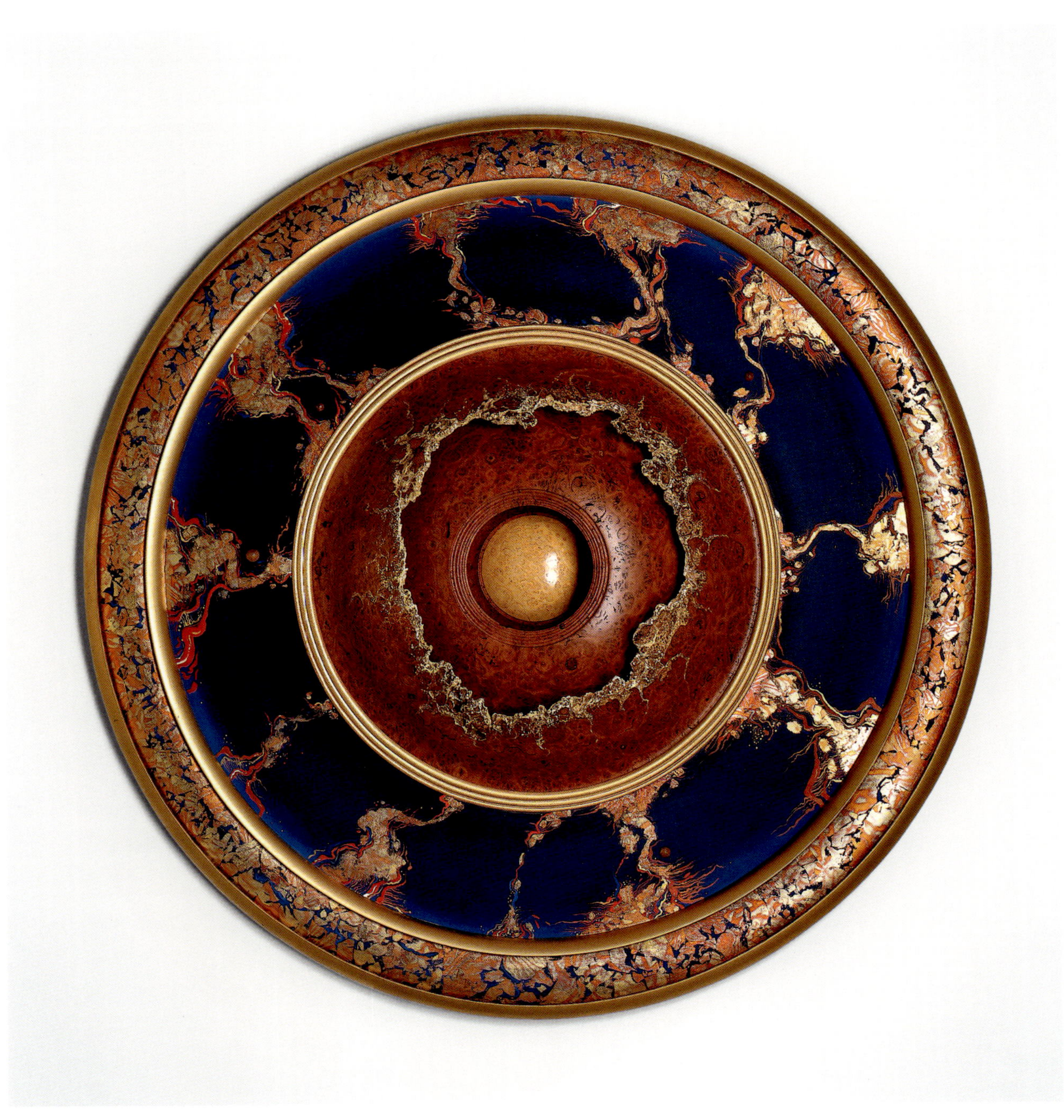

STEPHEN HUGHES AND MARGARET SALT born 1958, works Apsendale Gardens, Victoria, Australia (Hughes); born 1946, works Nungurner, Victoria, Australia (Salt)
ERUPTION SHIELD #3 1998, acrylic paint, gold leaf, jarrah burl, 47 x 47 x 6 in. (119.4 x 15.2 cm)

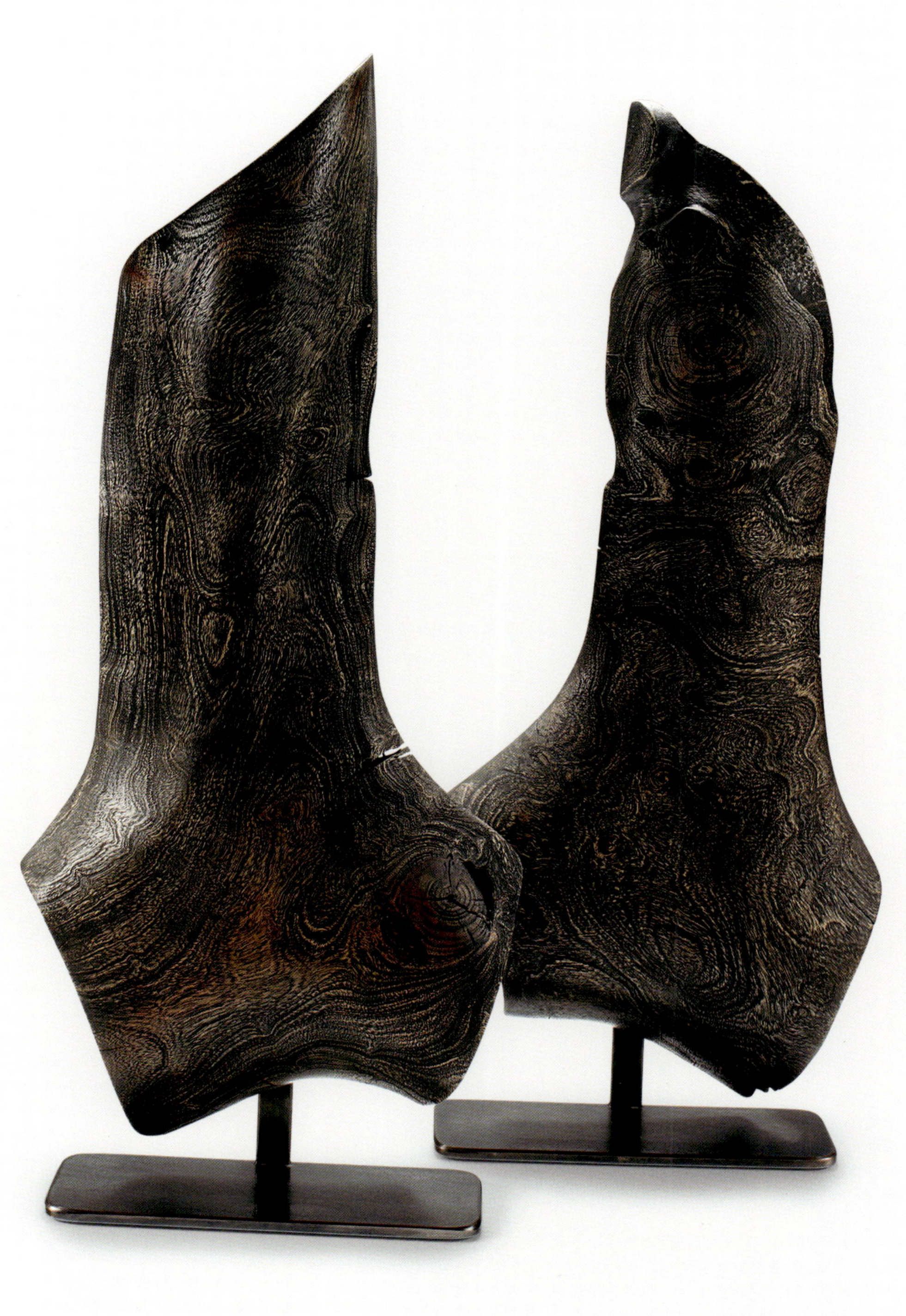

MICHAEL JAMES PETERSON born 1952, works Lopez Island, Washington
COASTAL OBJECTS 1999, carob, India ink, 23 x 10 1/4 x 3 1/2 in. (58.4 x 26 x 8.9 cm); 22 1/2 x 10 x 3 in. (57.2 x 25.4 x 7.6 cm)

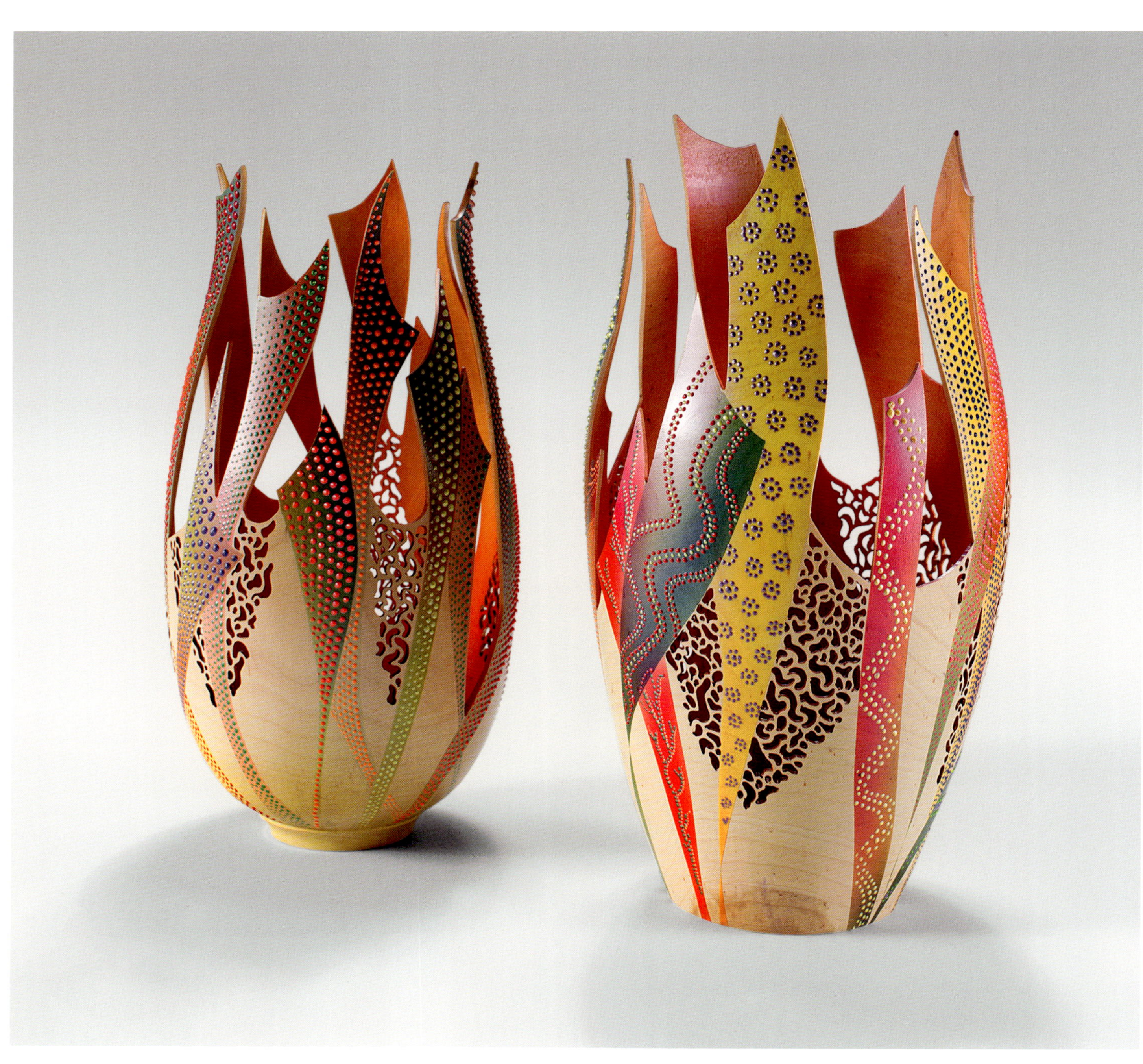

FRANK SUDOL 1933–2006, worked Paddockwood, Saskatchewan, Canada
RIBBON SERIES #3 *(left)* 2002, birch, lacquer, dye, fabric paint, 10 1/2 x 10 1/2 x 5 1/2 (26.7 x 26.7 x 14 cm)
RIBBON SERIES #2 *(right)* 2002, birch, lacquer, dye, fabric paint, 10 1/2 x 10 1/2 x 5 1/2 (26.7 x 26.7 x 14 cm), Peabody Essex Museum, Gift of Lillian Montalto Bohlen

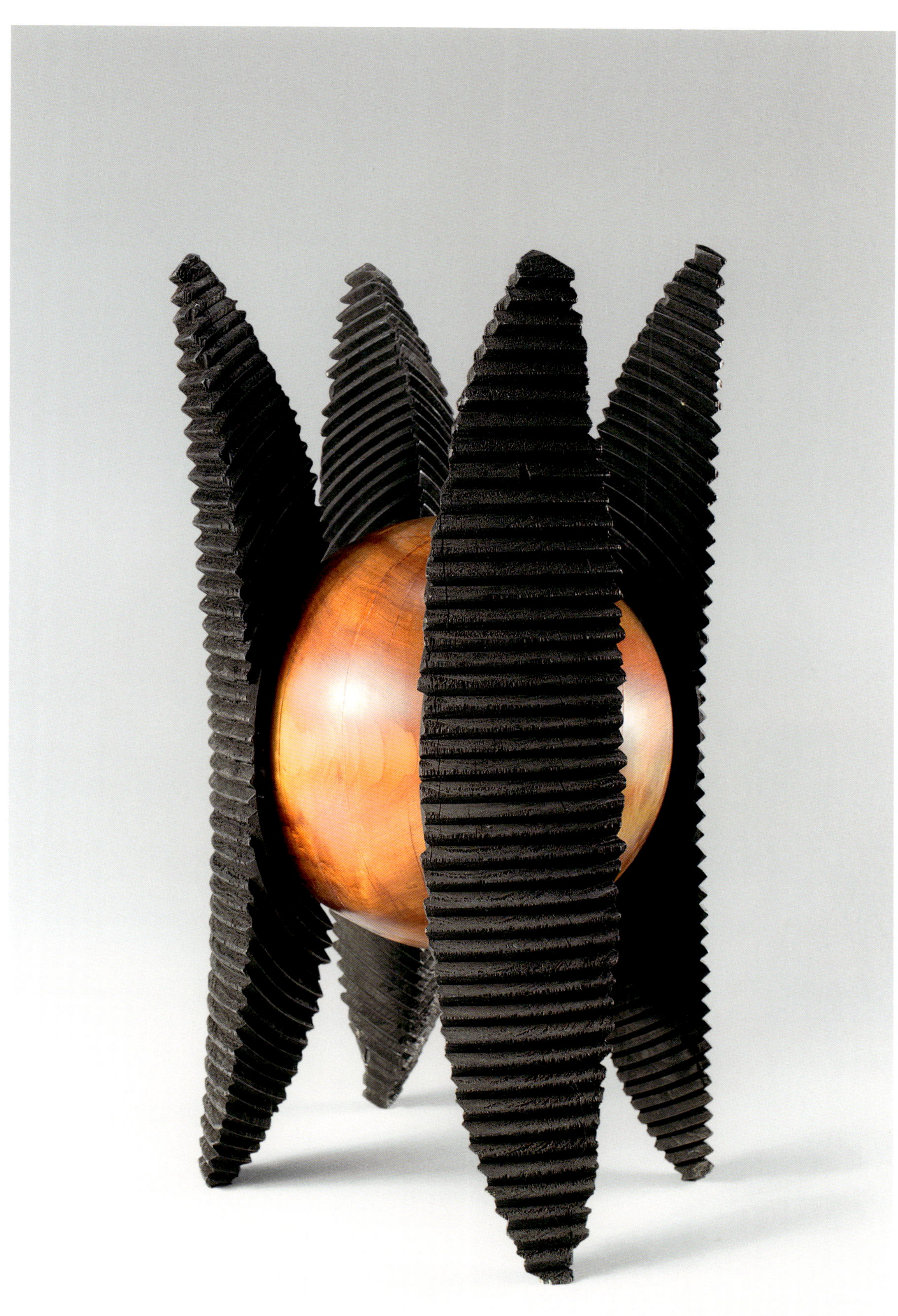

TODD HOYER born 1952, works Bisbee, Arizona
MOVING ON 1993, Arizona cedar, ink, 20 1/4 x 9 x 9 1/2 in. (51.4 x 22.9 x 24.1 cm)

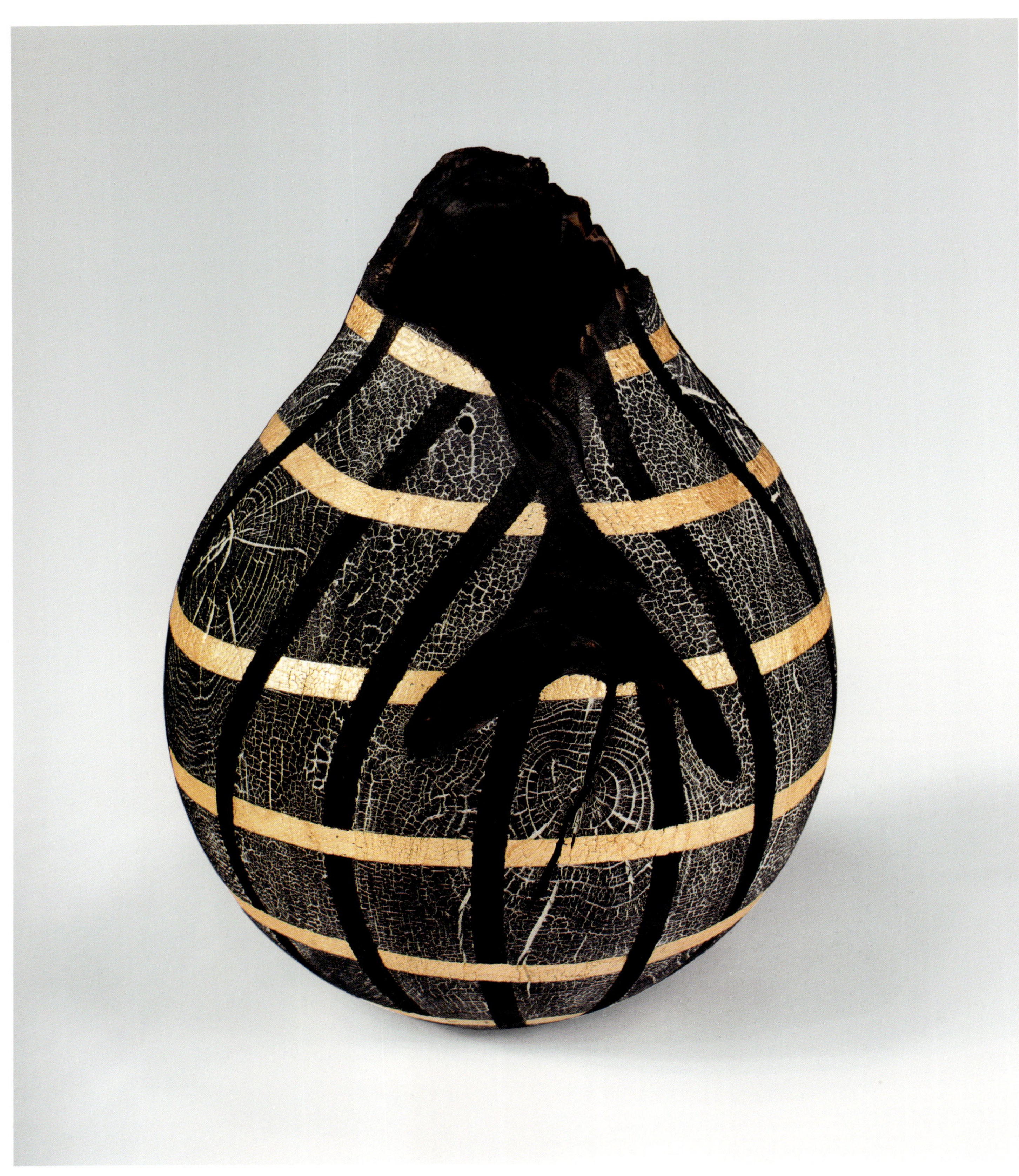

TODD HOYER born 1952, works Bisbee, Arizona
UNTITLED, RINGED SERIES 1992, burnt and gilded mulberry with tile grout, 14 x 10 in. (35.6 x 25.4 cm)

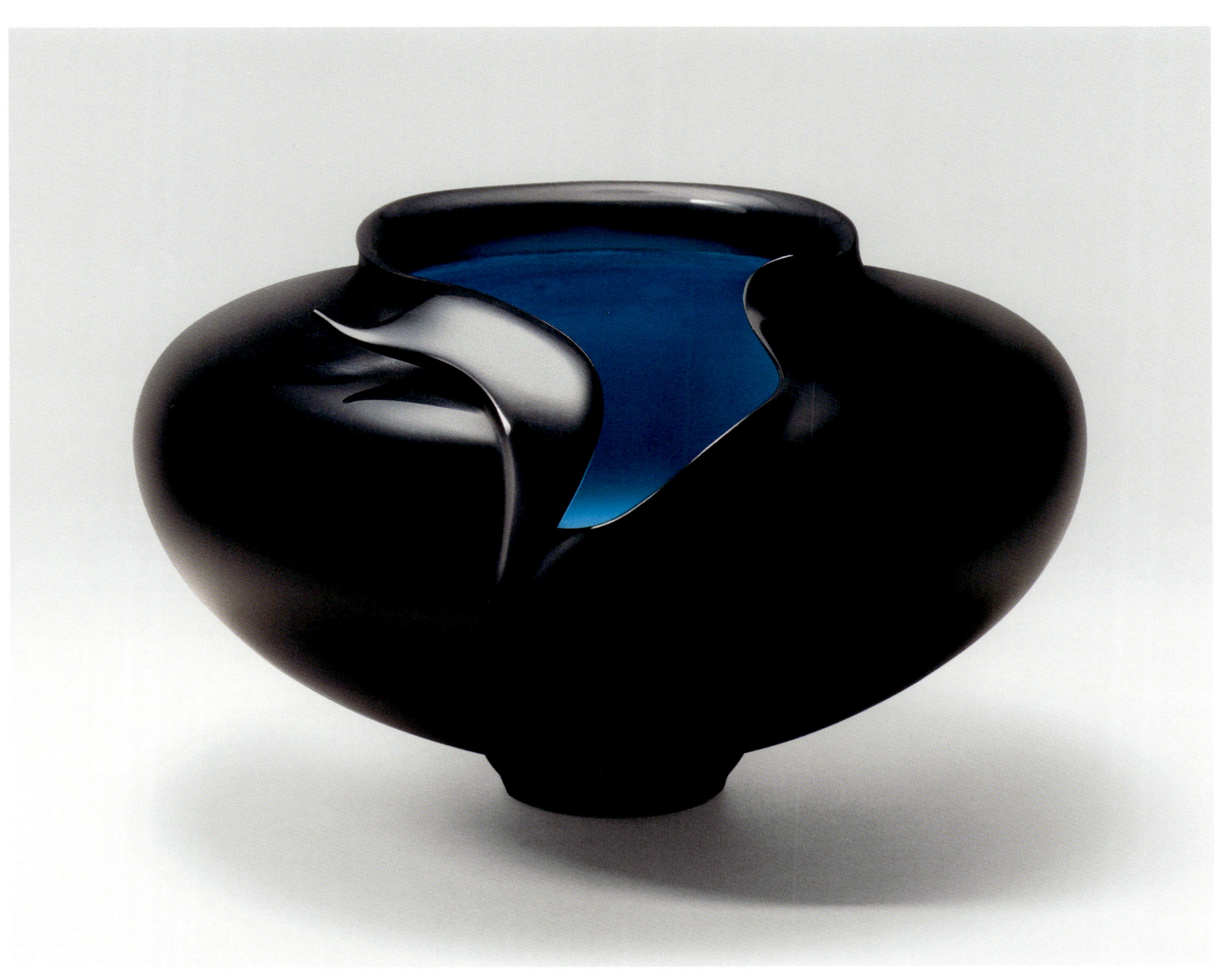

GILES GILSON born 1942, works Schenectady, New York
CAMMY-OH 2001, basswood, pakkawood, pigment, lacquer, 6 1/2 x 11 1/4 in. (16.5 x 28.6 cm), Peabody Essex Museum, Gift of Lillian Montalto Bohlen

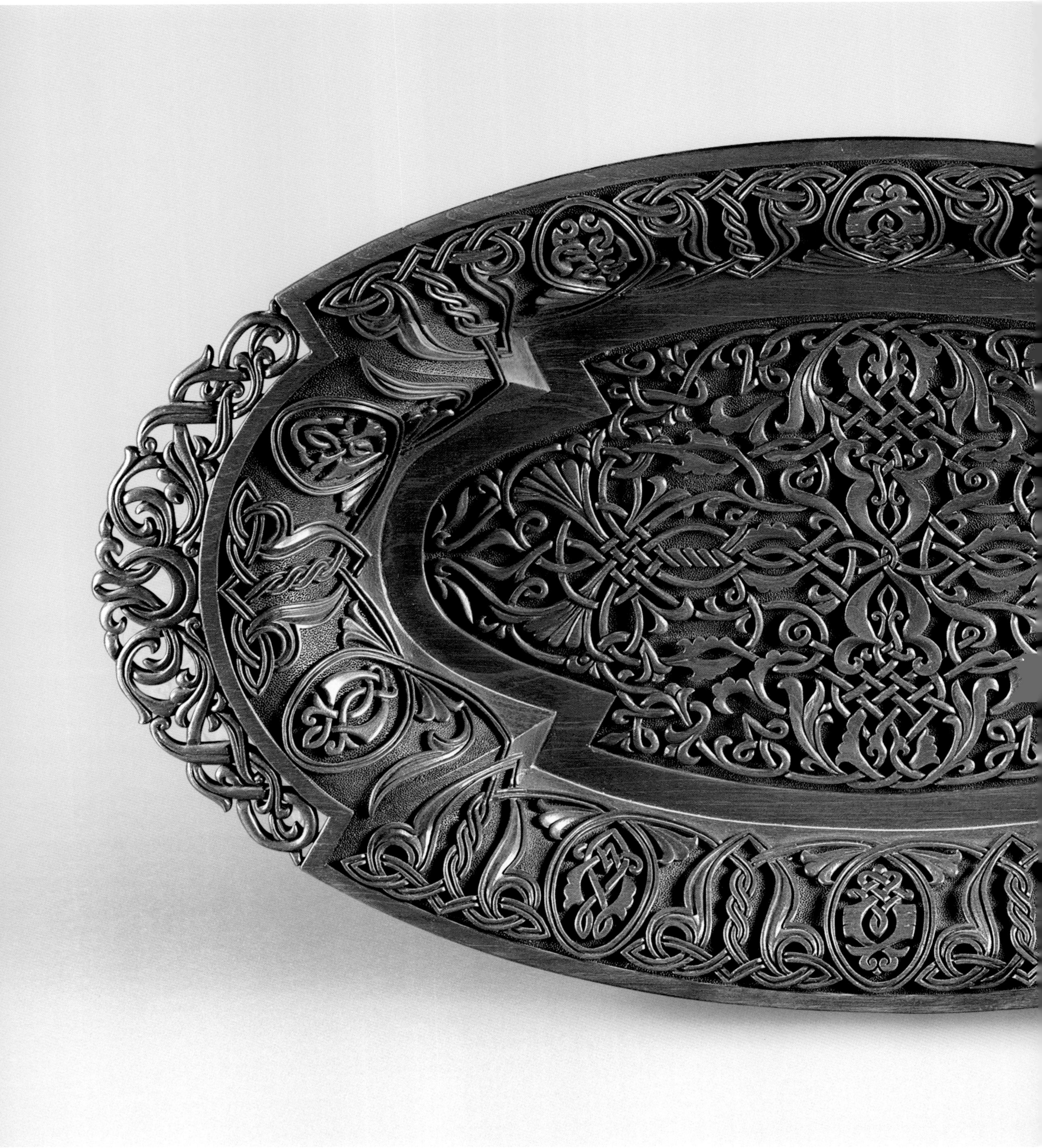

MELSIK YEGHLAZARYAN born 1946, works New York City
LUSY (TRAY) 1995, mahogany, 20 x 37 x 6 in. (51 x 94 x 15.2 cm)

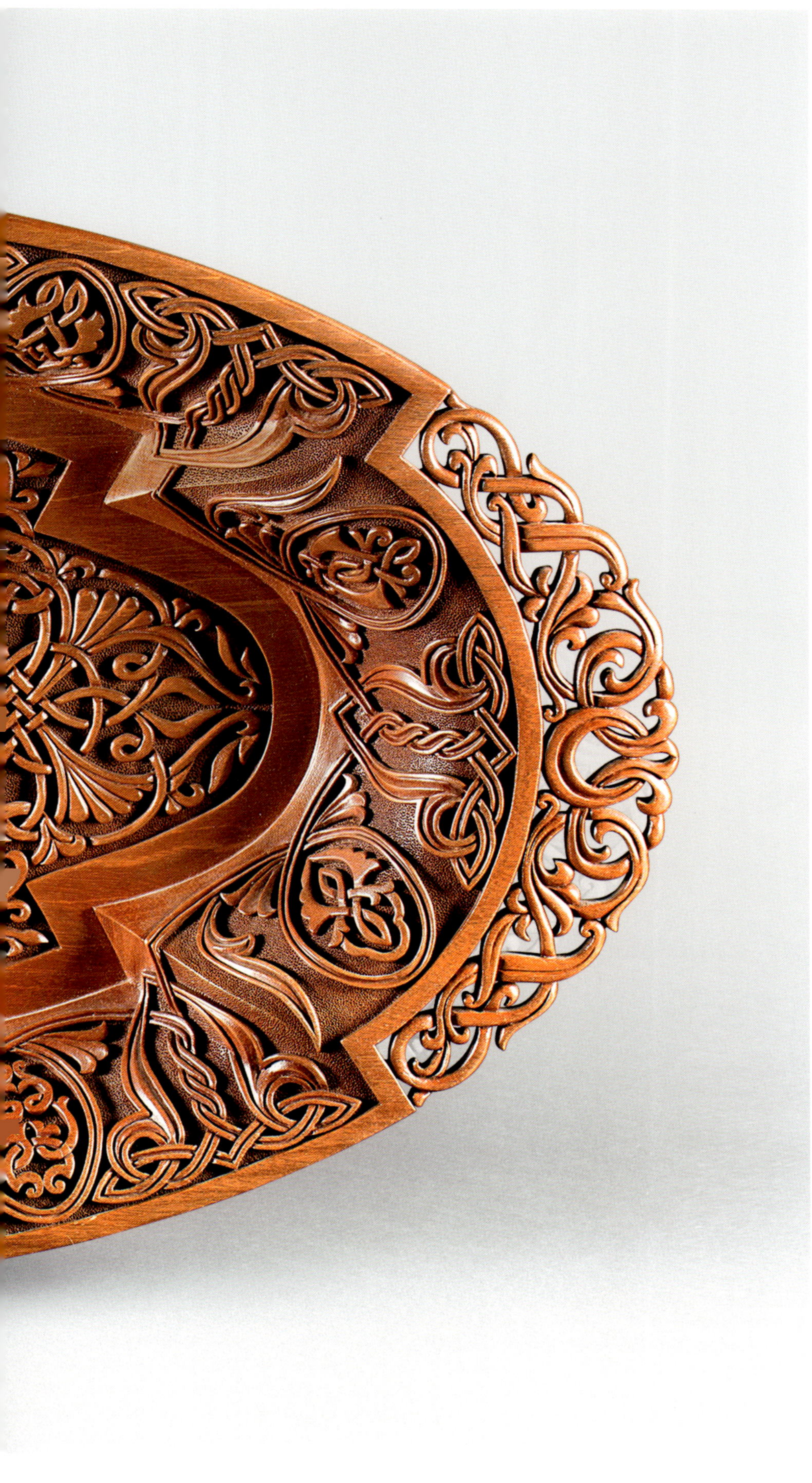

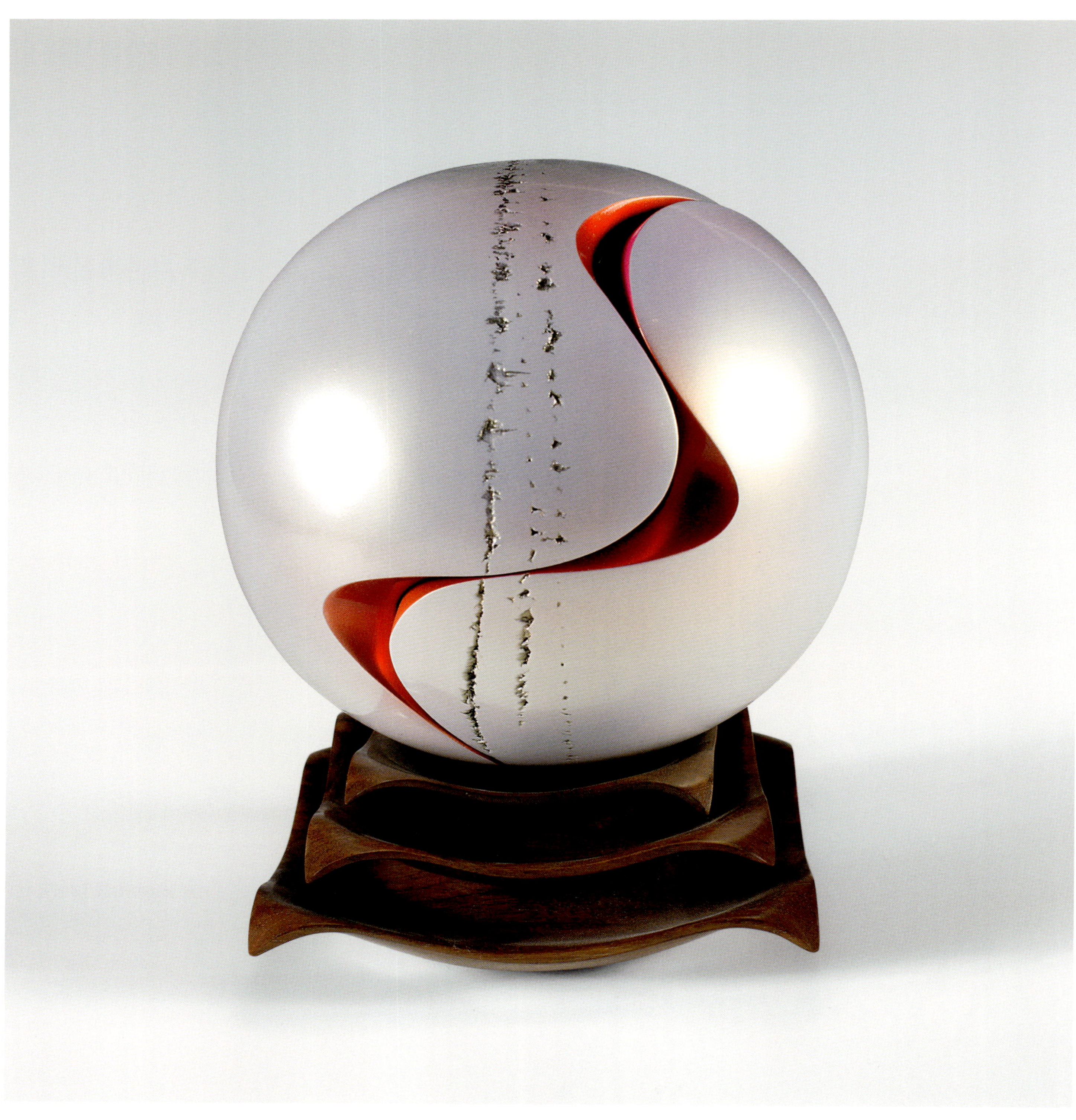

GILES GILSON born 1942, works Schenectady, New York
SNOWBALL FROM ATLANTIS 1997, basswood, walnut lacquer, 9 x 7 in. (22.9 x 17.8 cm)

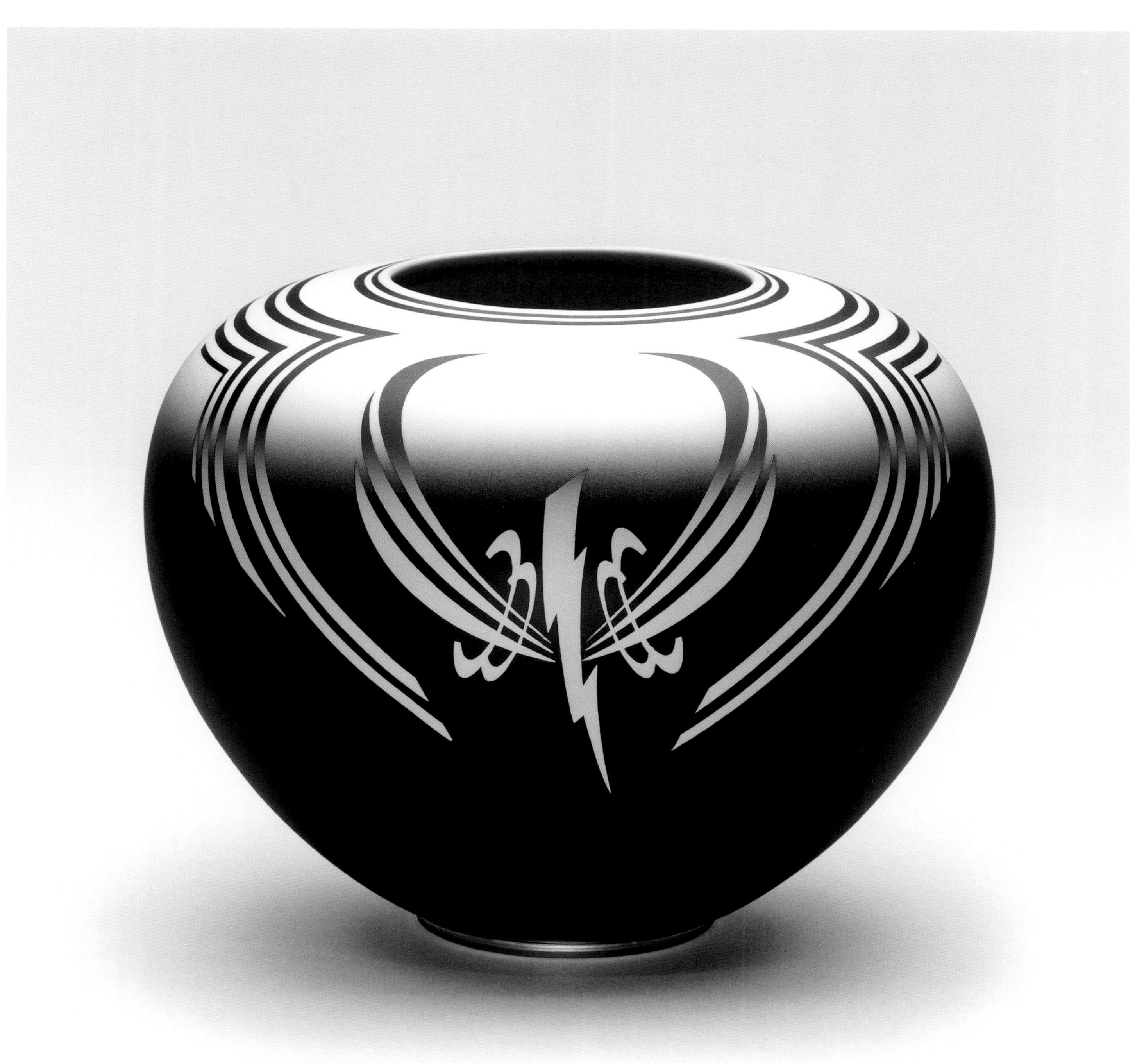

GILES GILSON born 1942, works Schenectady, New York

PSYCHOSYMMETRIC 2005, basswood, lacquer, paint, aluminum, 6 x 7 $^{1}/_{2}$ x 7 in. (15.2 x 19.1 x 17.8 cm), Peabody Essex Museum, Gift of Lillian Montalto Bohlen

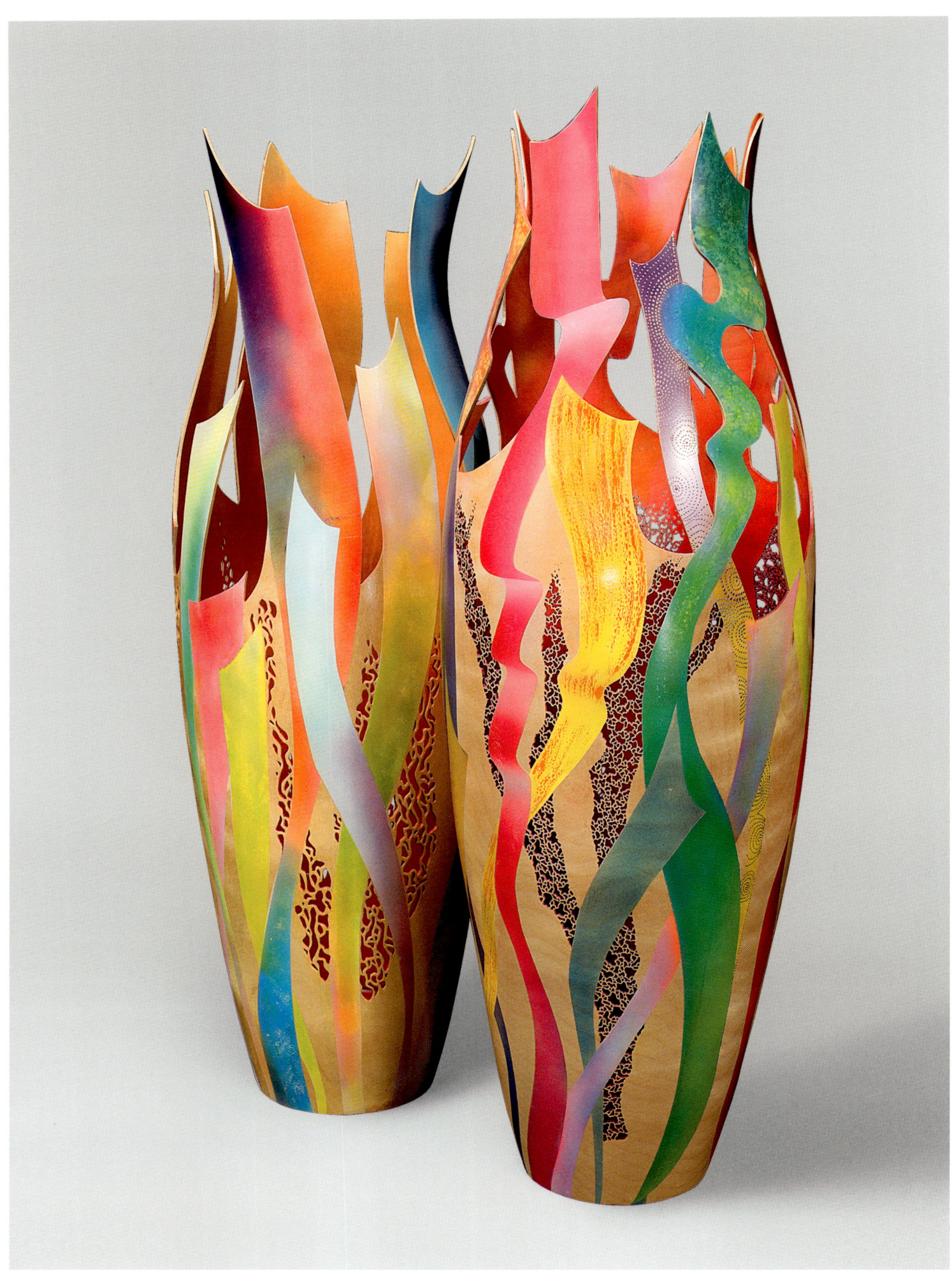

Left to right: **FRANK SUDOL** 1933–2006, worked Paddockwood, Saskatchewan, Canada
GIANT RIBBONS #2 2002, birch, acrylic paint, fabric paint, 46 x 14 in. (116.8 x 35.6 cm)
GIANT RIBBONS #1 2002, birch, acrylic paint, fabric paint, 44 x 14 in. (111.8 x 35.6 cm)

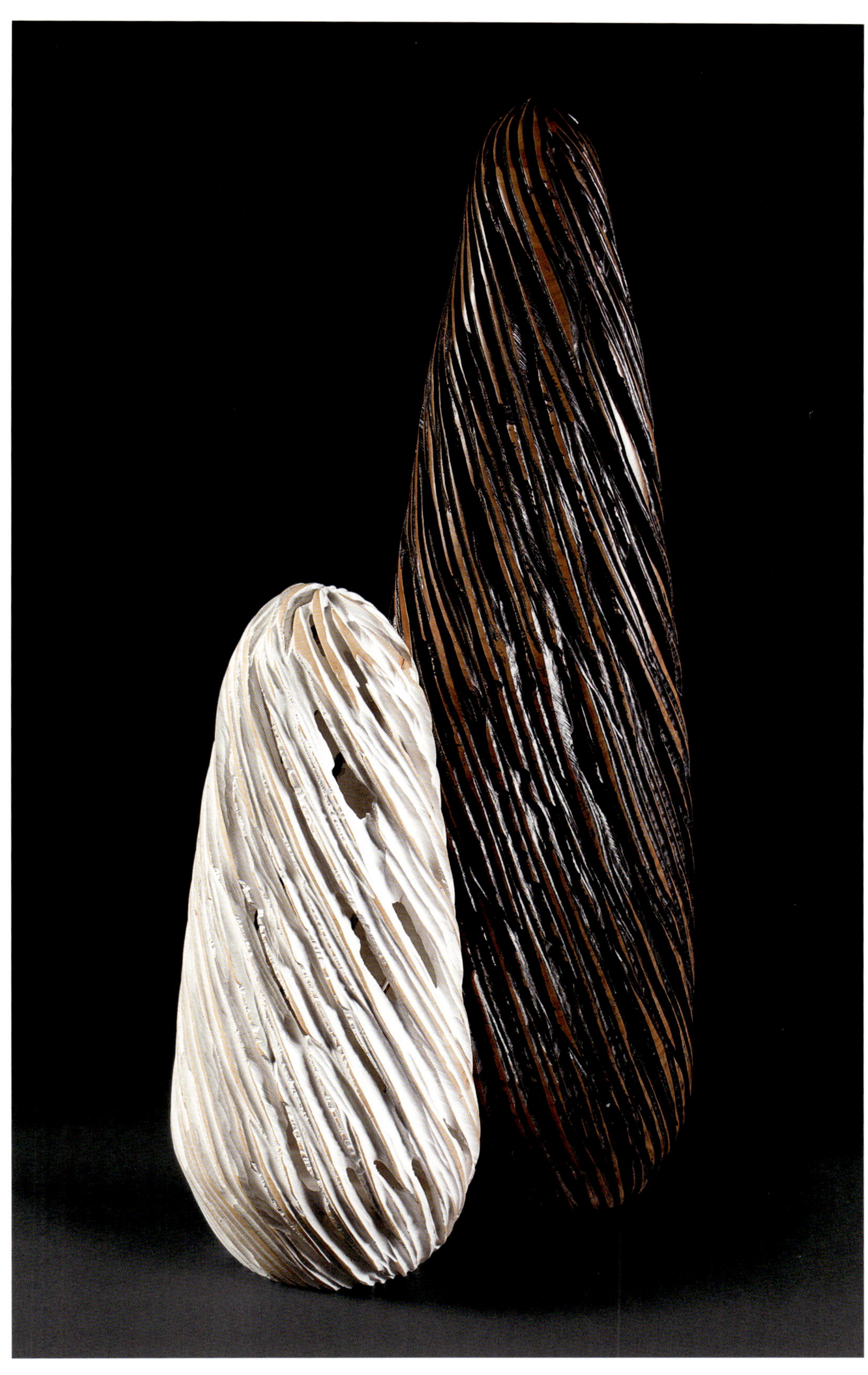

MICHAEL BAUERMEISTER born 1957, works Augusta, Missouri
BLACK TWISTED SHELL AND WHITE TWISTED SHELL 2012, walnut, maple, and tinted lacquer, white: 31 x 14 x 11 in. (78.7 x 35.6 x 27.9 cm), black: 50 x 18 x 10 in. (127 x 45.7 x 25.4 cm)

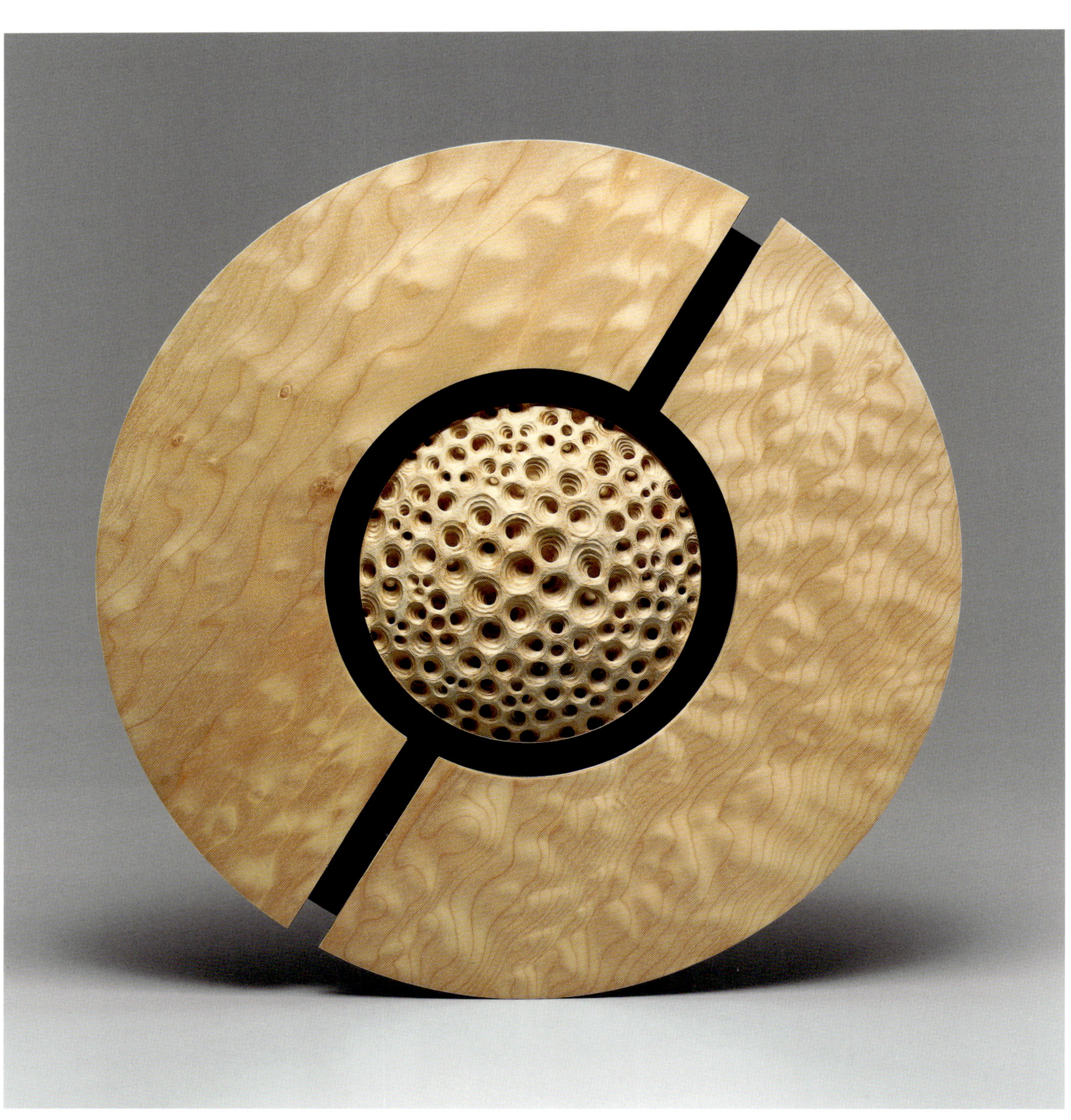

HAYLEY SMITH born 1965, works Bisbee, Arizona
WALL PIECE #1/01 2001, maple, 17 $^{1}/_{4}$ x 2 in. (43.8 x 5.1 cm), Peabody Essex Museum, Gift of Lillian Montalto Bohlen

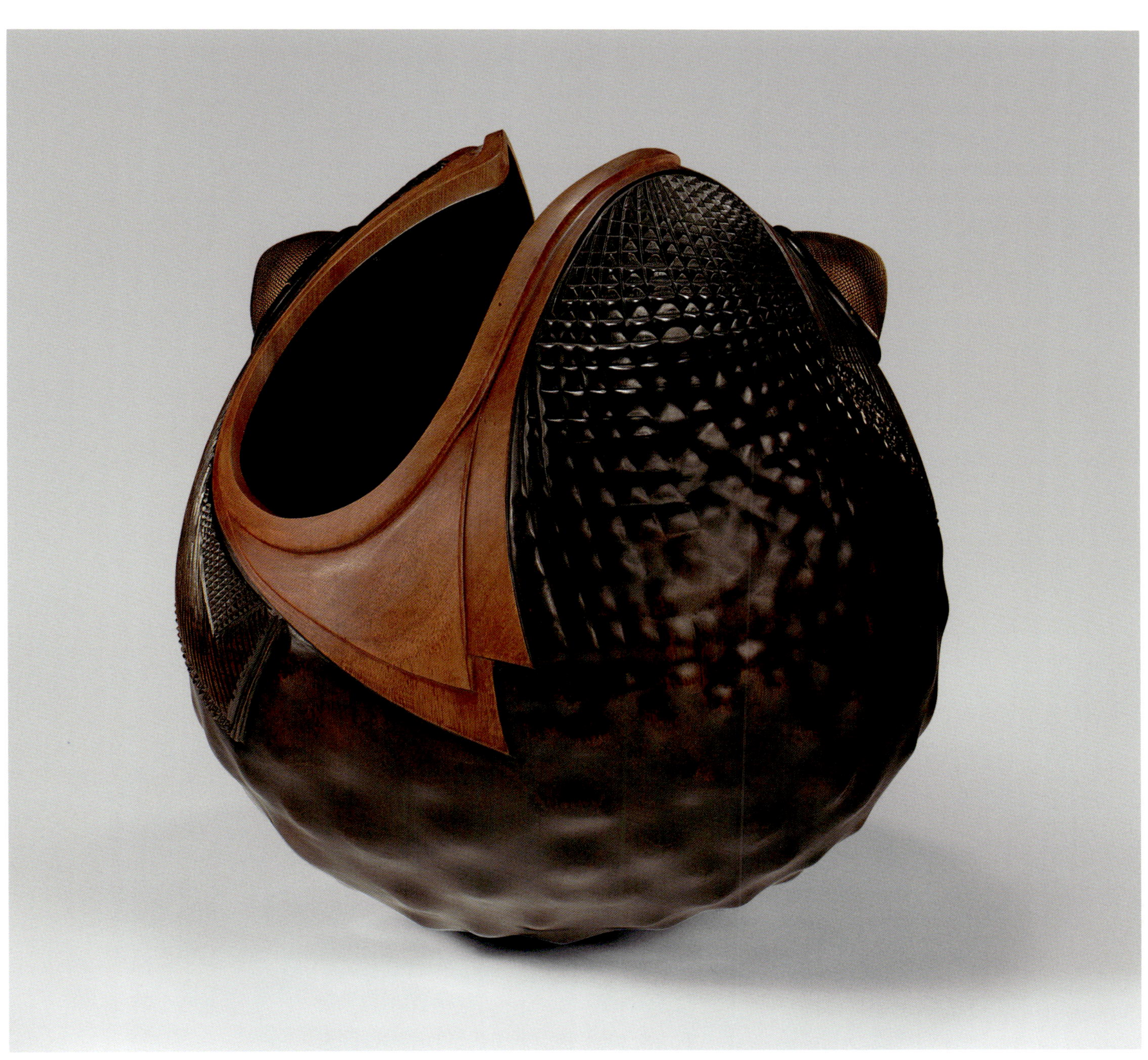

ROLLY MUNRO born 1954, works Levin, North Island, New Zealand
HAPUKU II 1998, pohutukawa wood, brass mesh, copper, epoxy, polyester resin, pigment, 14 x 13 x 12 in. (35.6 x 33 x 30.5 cm)

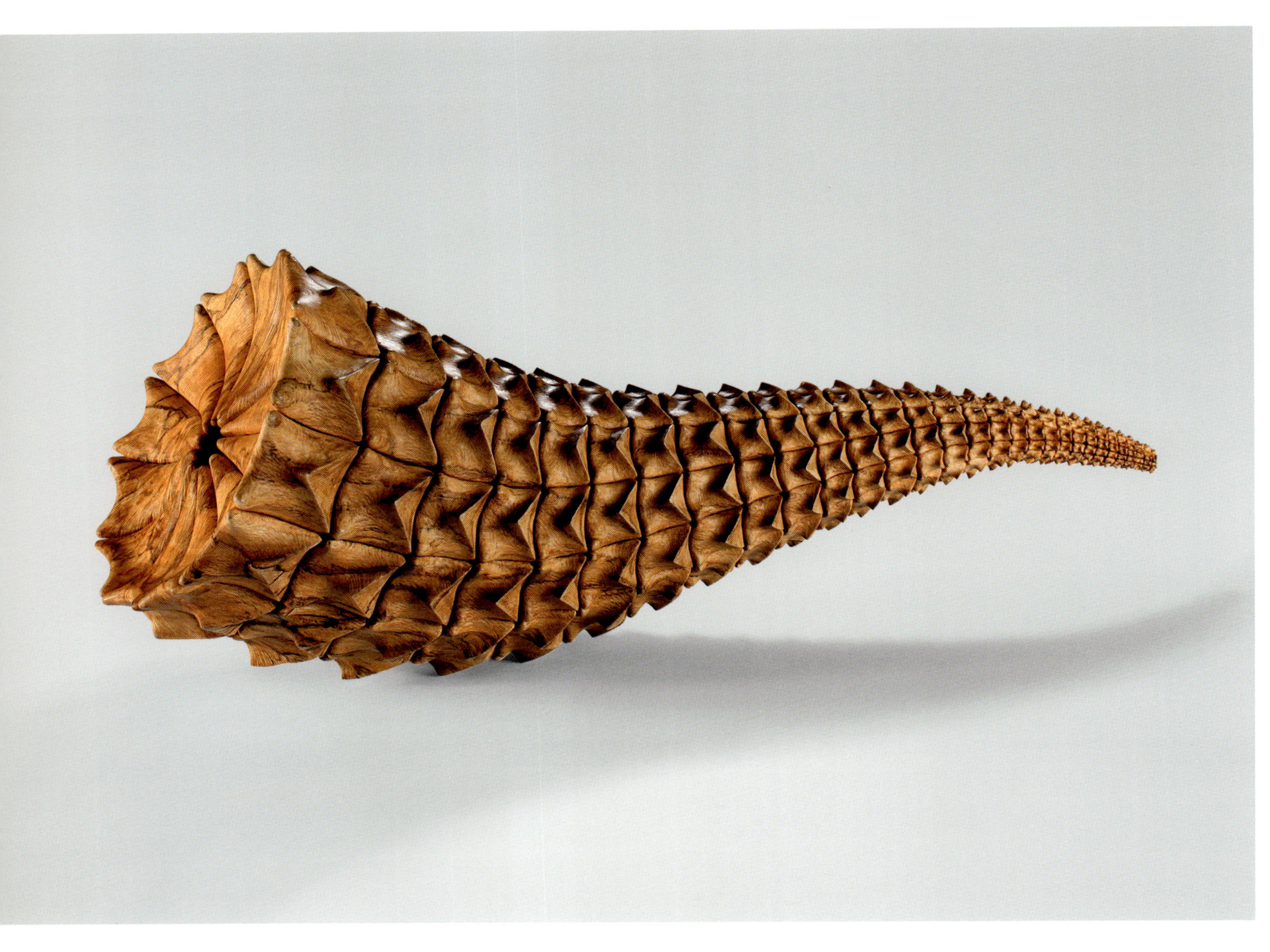

ARTHUR JONES born 1937, works Winter Park, Florida
SPINY DODECADON 1999, sycamore, 6 1/2 x 16 1/2 x 6 3/4 in. (16.5 x 41.9 x 17.1 cm)

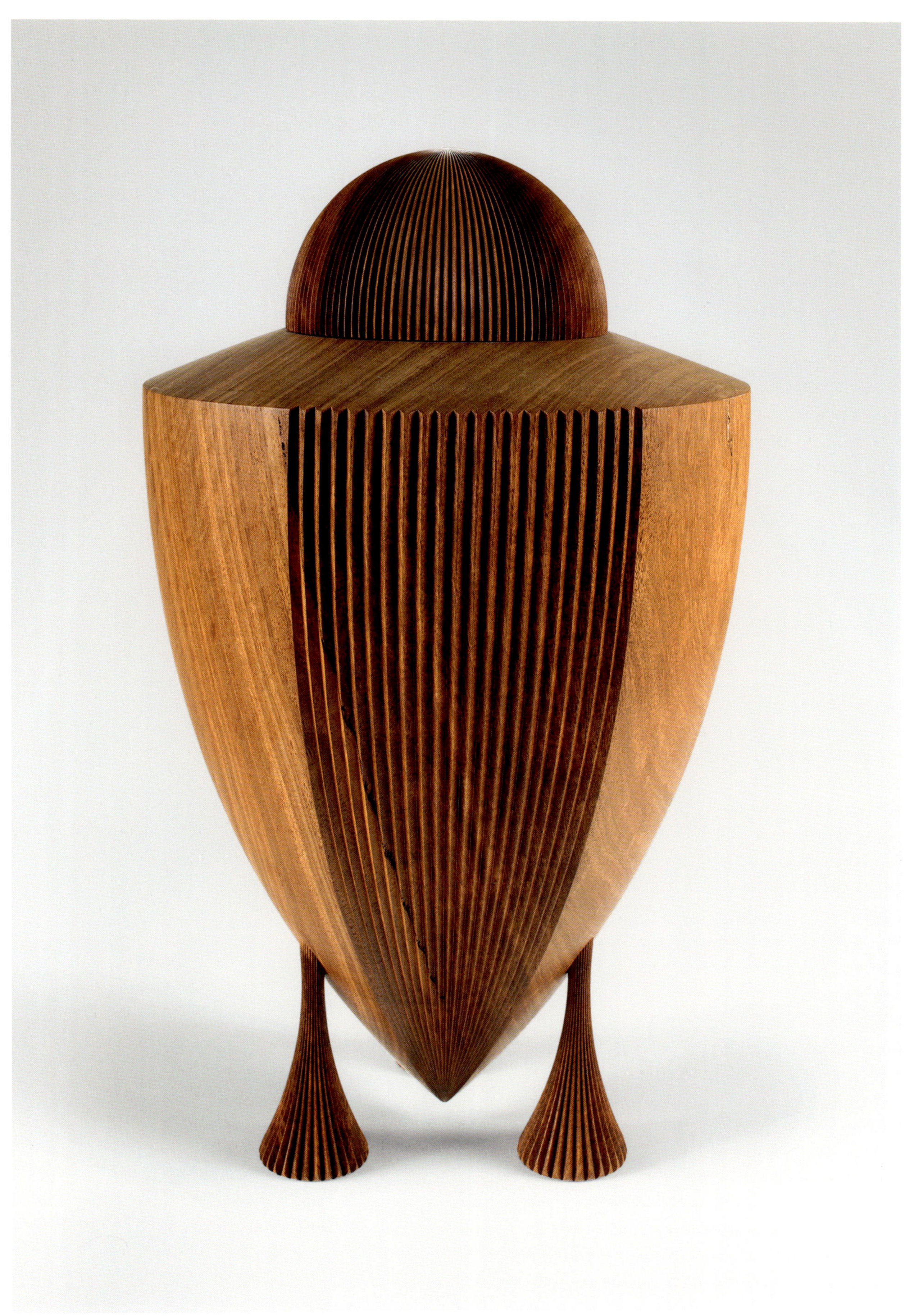

DEAN MALCOLM born 1965, works Albany, Western Australia
SENTRY JARRAH 1997, jarrah, 19 x 11 in. (48.3 x 28 cm)

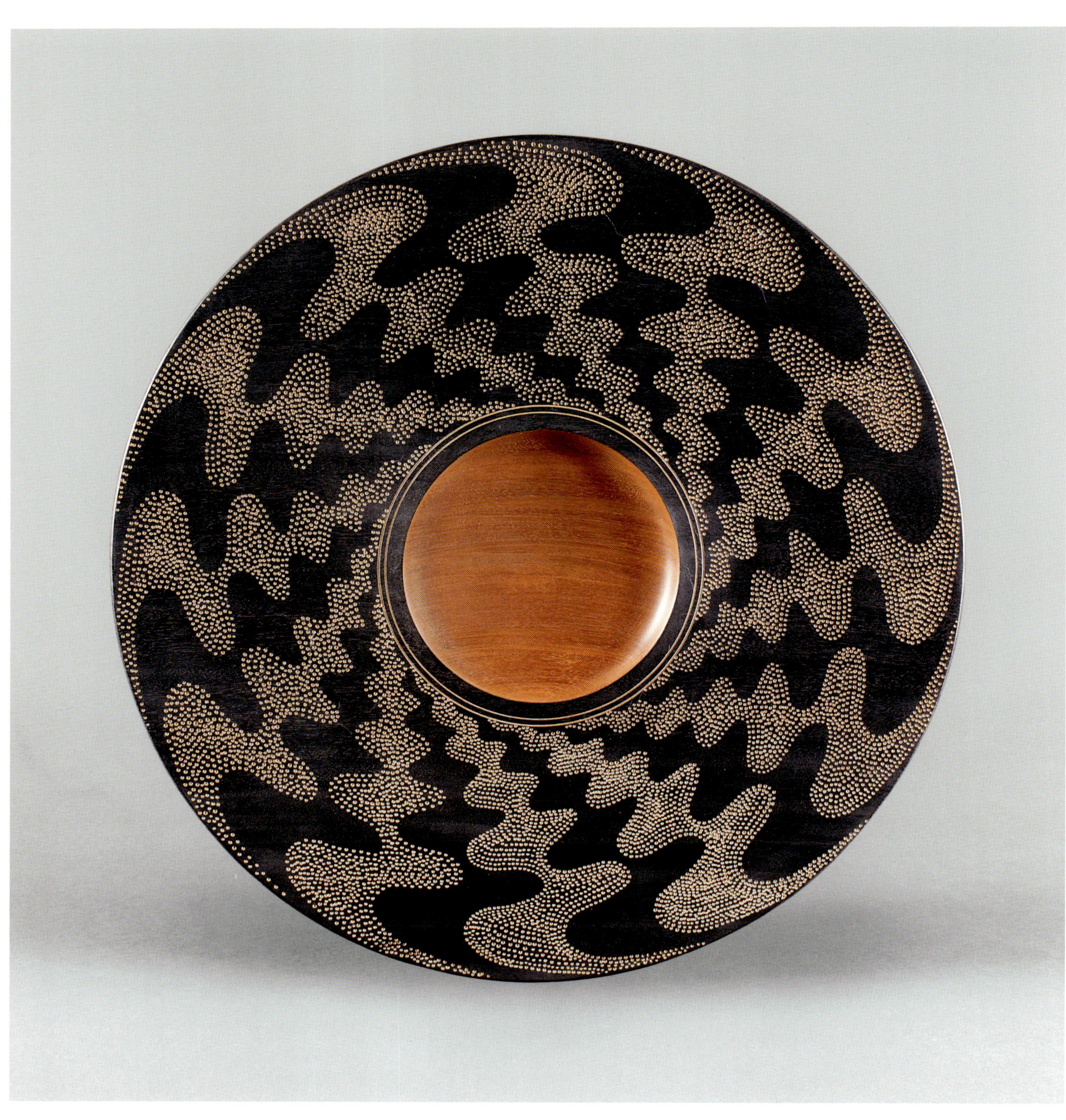

ALAN STIRT born 1946, works Enosburg Falls, Vermont
SPIRAL CERATITE 1997, mahogany, milk paint, 24 x 1 $^{1}/_{2}$ in. (61 x 3.8 cm)

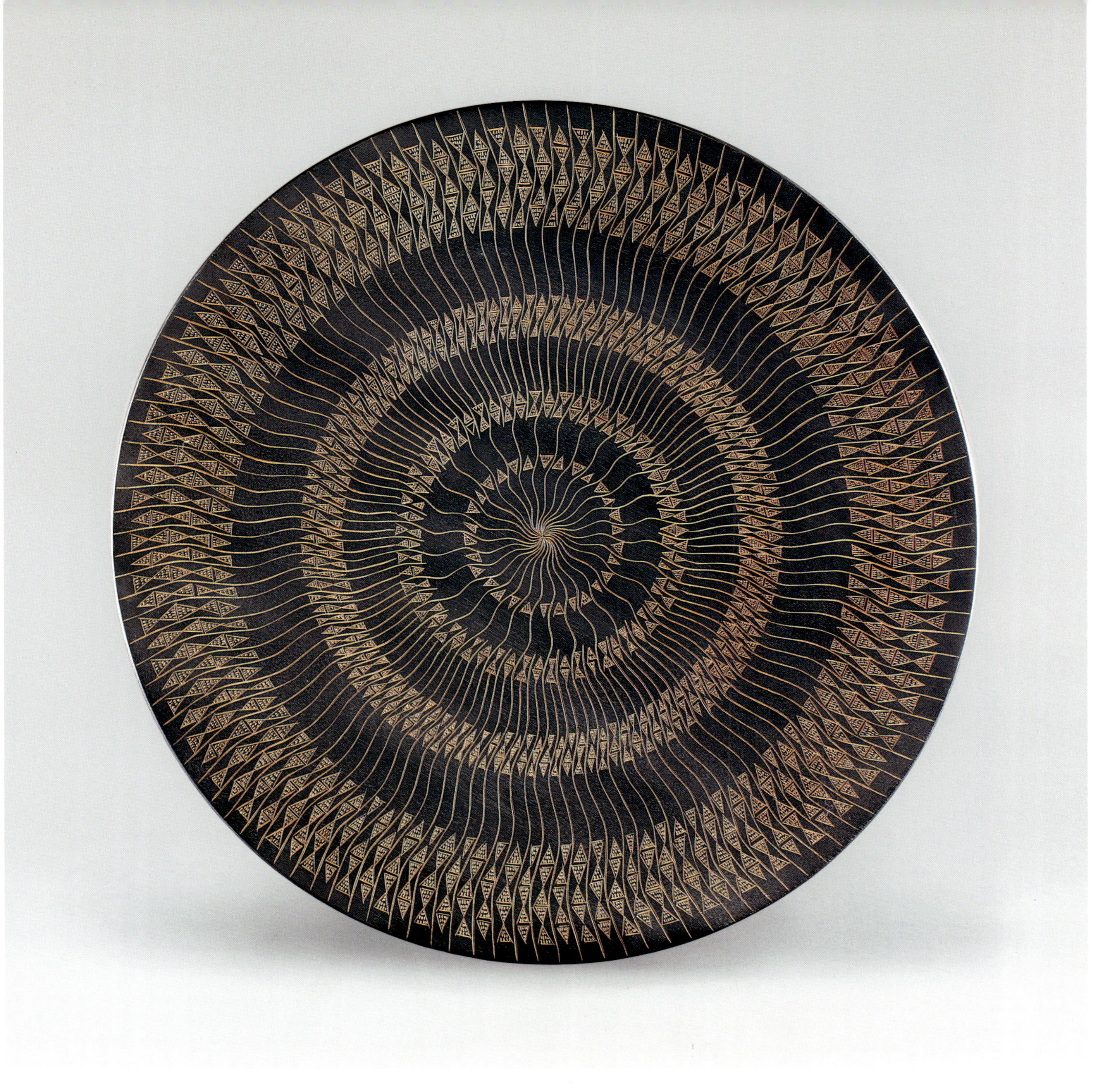

ALAN STIRT born 1946, works Enosburg Falls, Vermont
LINES AND TRIANGLES 2003, mahogany, milk paint, 24 3/4 x 1 in. (62.9 x 2.5 cm), Peabody Essex Museum, Gift of Lillian Montalto Bohlen

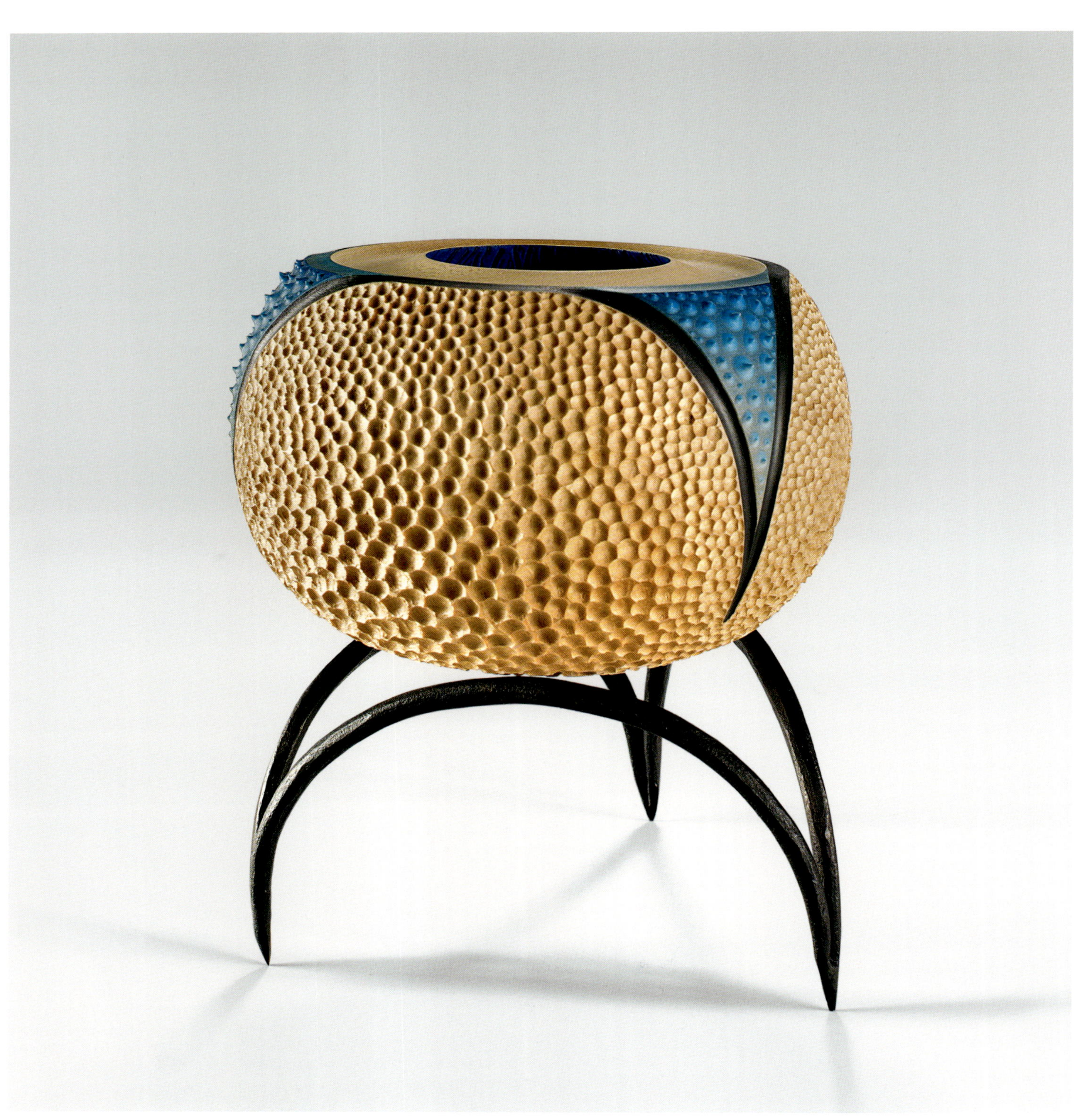

HAYLEY SMITH AND LOUISE HIBBERT born 1965, works Bisbee, Arizona (Smith); born 1972, works Llanfairfechan, Wales (Hibbert)
EMMA LAKE COLLABORATION 2000, wood, acrylic paint, forged steel, 6 x 5 1/2 in. (15.2 x 14 cm), Peabody Essex Museum, Gift of Lillian Montalto Bohlen

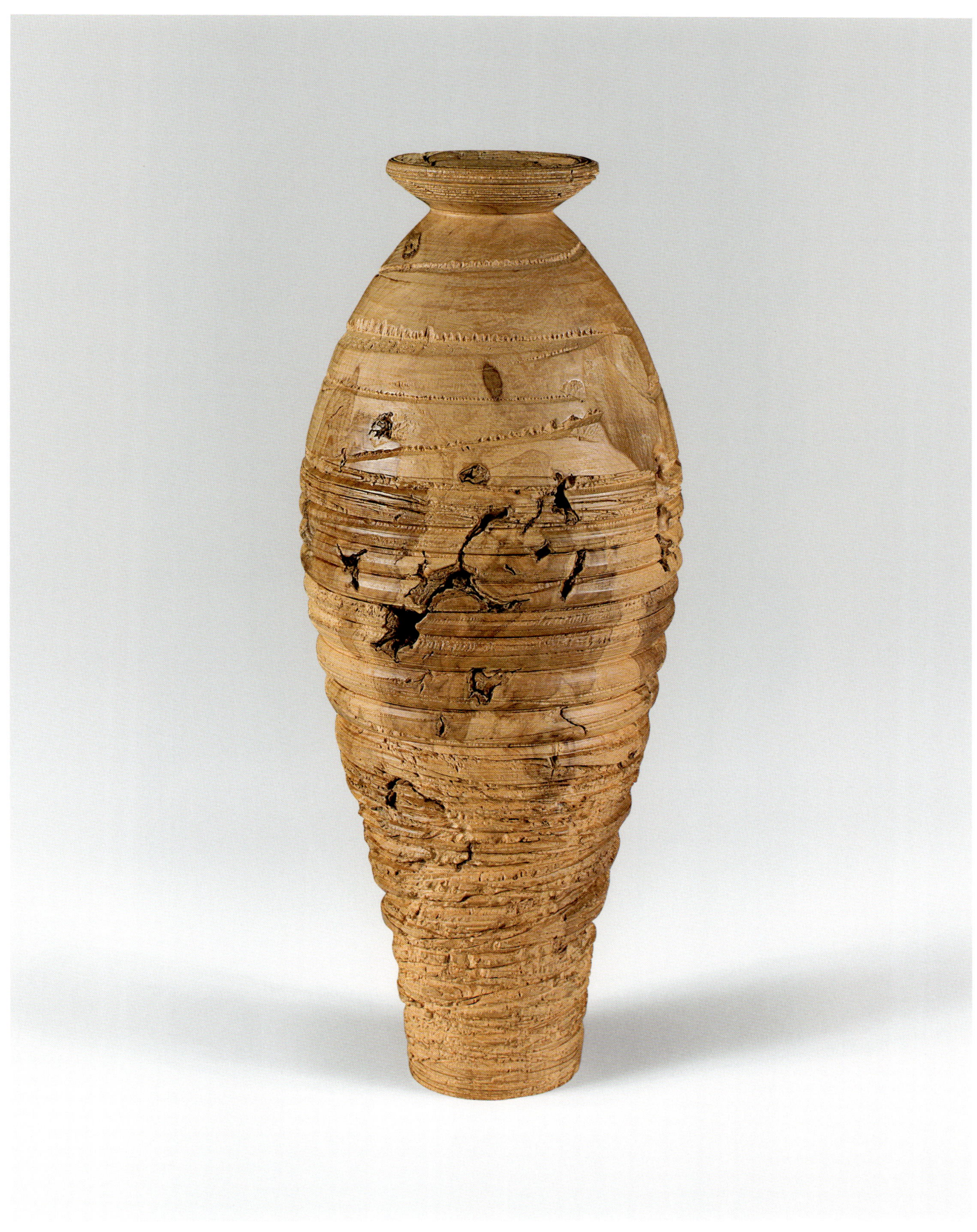

MELVIN & MARK LINDQUIST 1911–2000, worked Quincy, Florida (Melvin); born 1949, works Quincy, Florida (Mark)
ANCIENT LYRICAL VASE #2 1985, maple burl, 13 $^{3}/_{4}$ x 5 $^{1}/_{2}$ in. (34.9 x 14 cm)

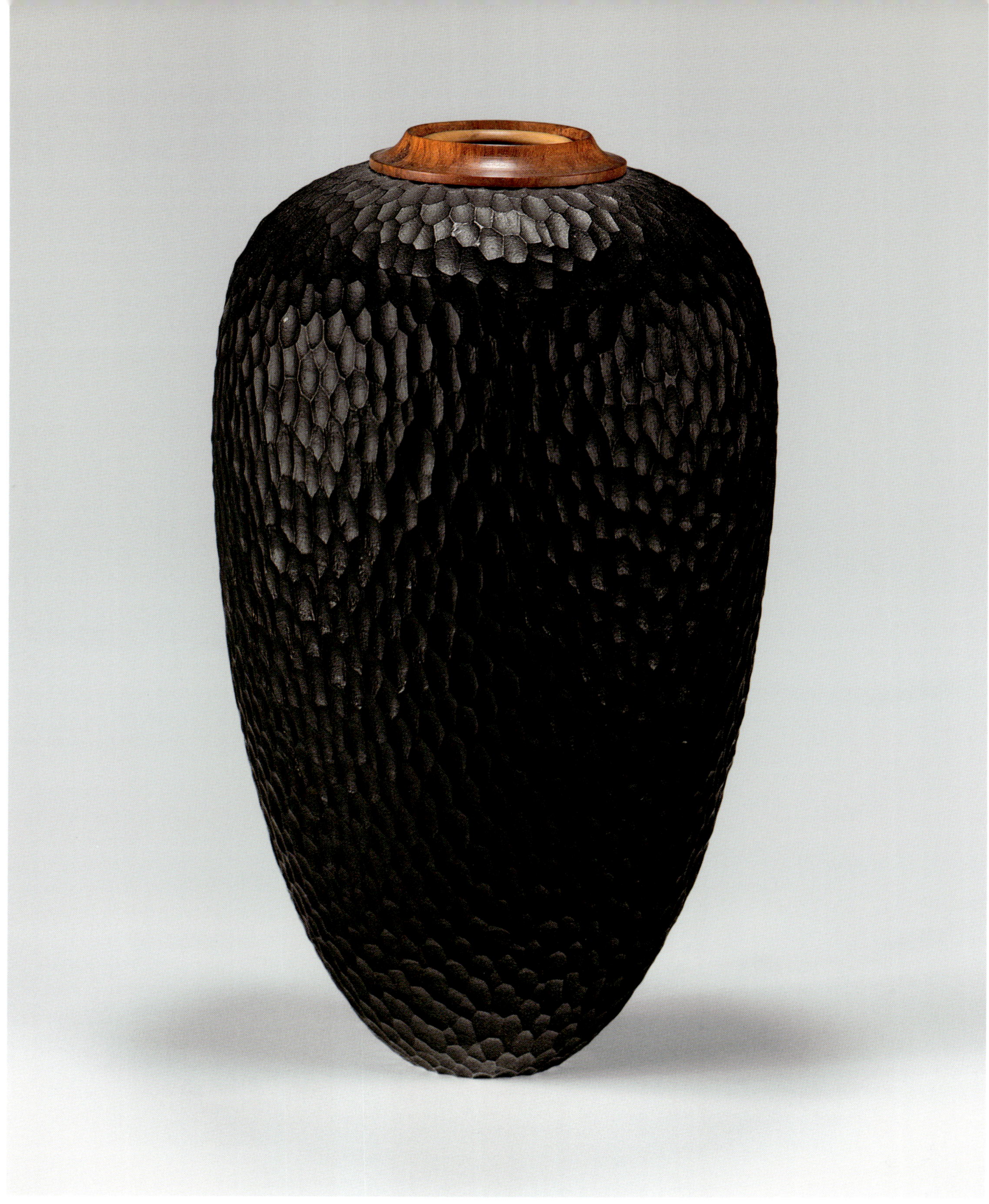

JACQUES VESERY born 1960, works Damariscotta, Maine
TRIBAL FIRE 2000, cherry, paela burl, enamel, 6 $^1/_2$ x 3 $^1/_2$ in. (16.5 x 8.9 cm)

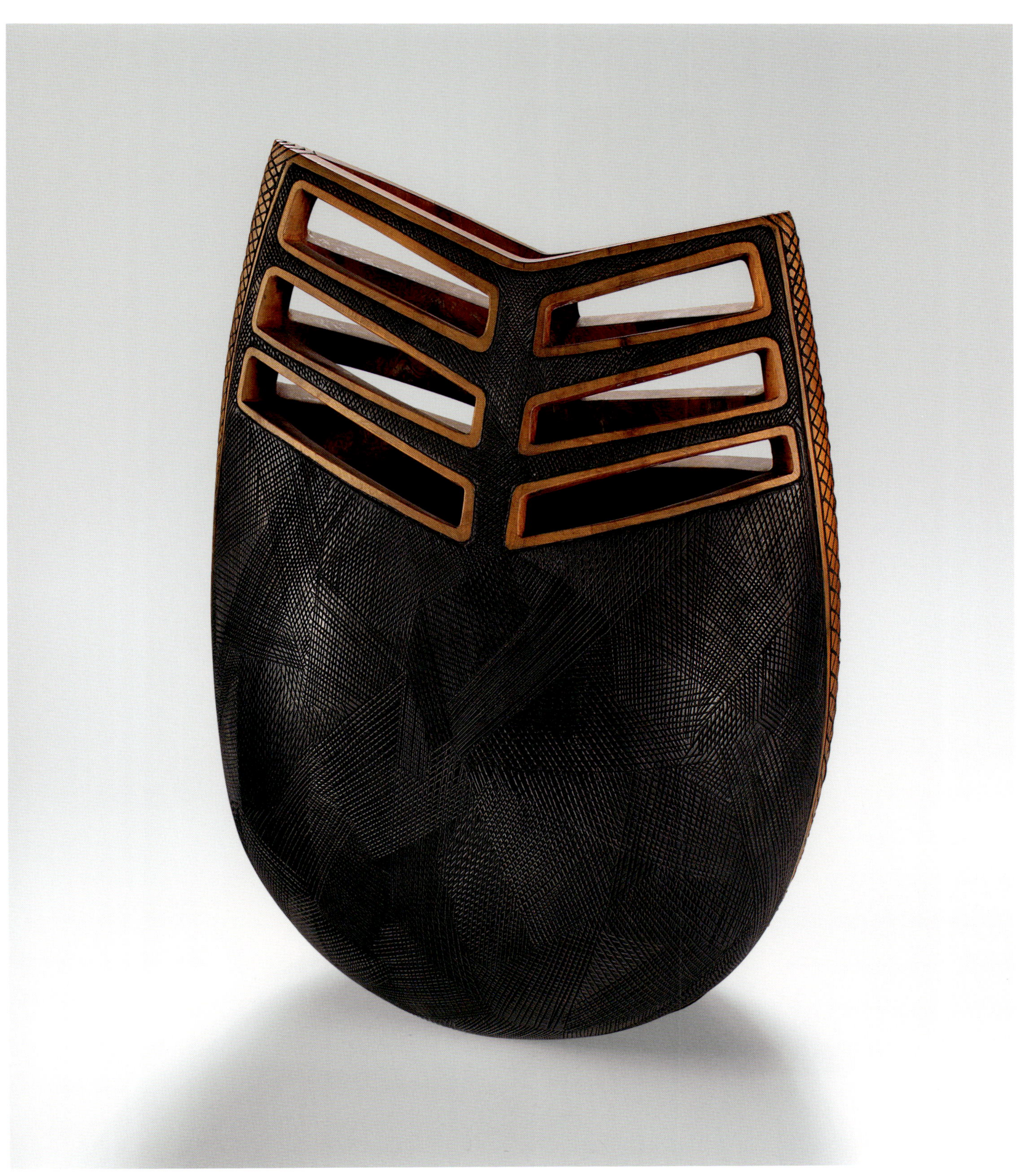

ROLLY MUNRO born 1954, works Levin, North Island, New Zealand
#2 1998, totara, 14 x 11 x 6 in. (35.6 x 28 x 15.2 cm)

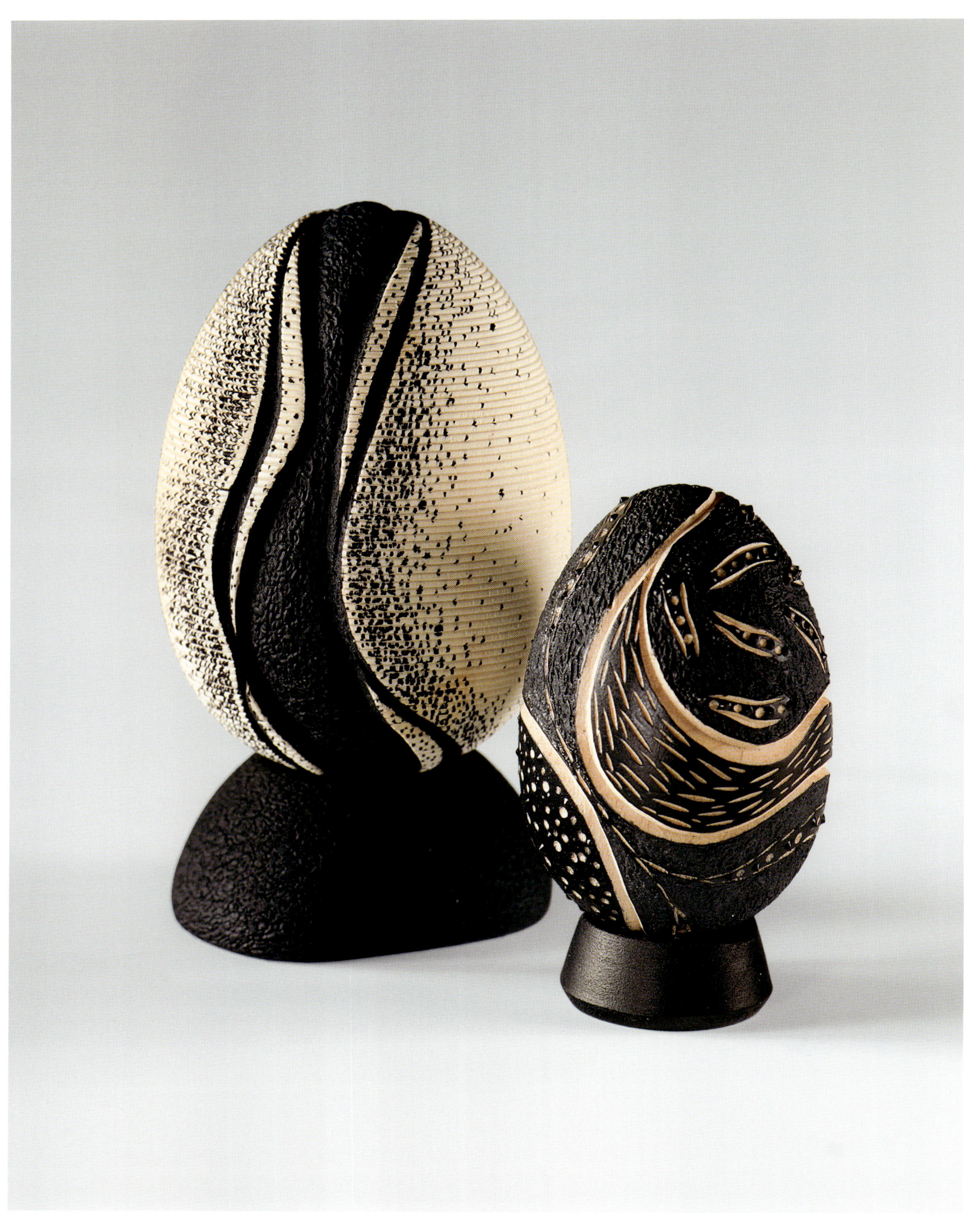

Left to right: **BETTY J. SCARPINO** born 1949, works Indianapolis, Indiana
EGG 2006, maple, bleach, ink and paint, 5 1/2 x 2 1/2 x 2 in. (14 x 6.4 x 5.1 cm), Peabody Essex Museum, Gift of Lillian Montalto Bohlen
EGG 2006, maple and paint, 4 x 2 in. (10.2 x 5.1 cm)

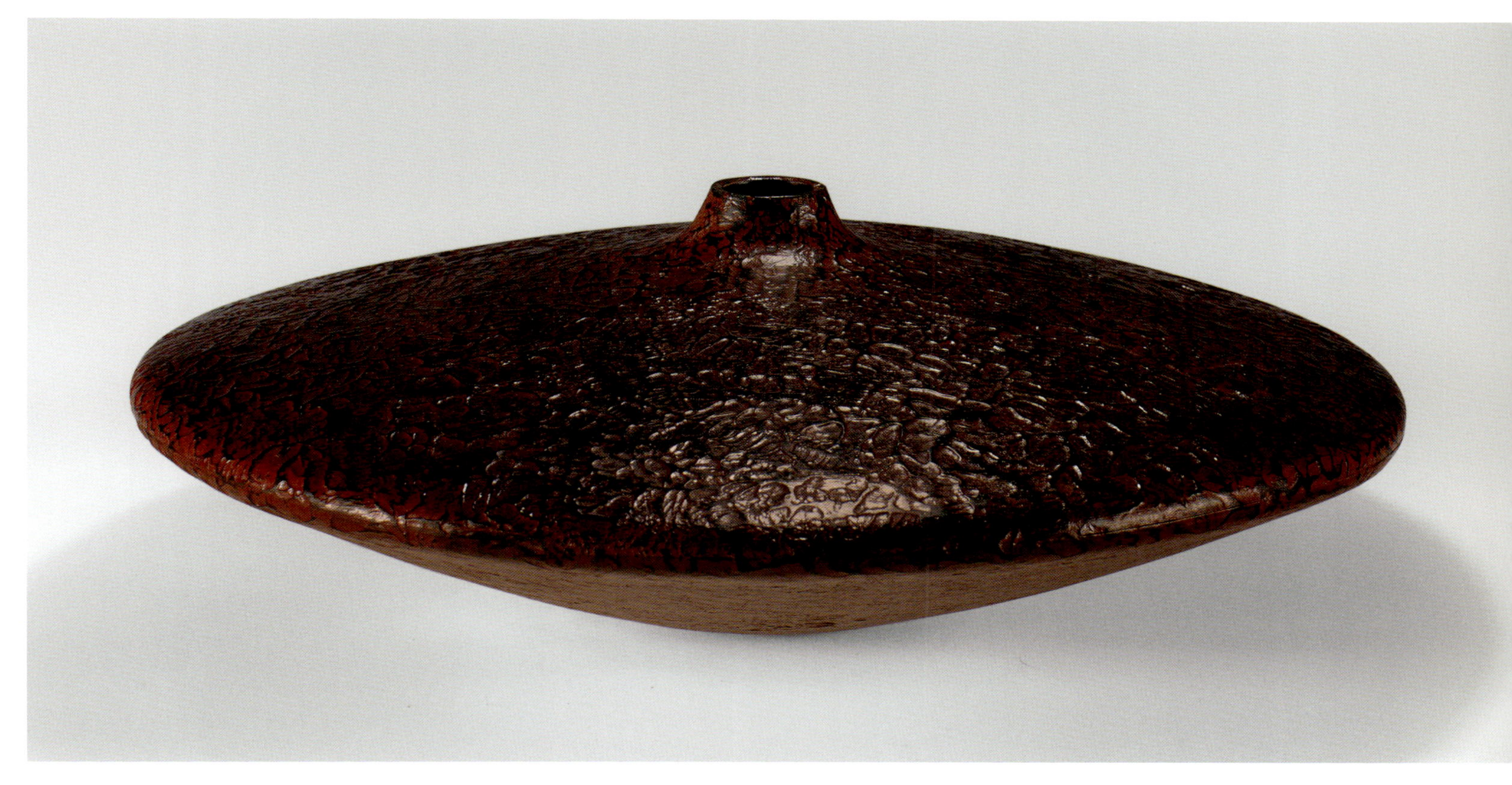

DERRICK TEPASKE born 1945, works Belmont, Massachusetts
AP RED #1 2008, cherry, red acrylic polymer, 4 $^{3}/_{4}$ x 15 in. (12.1 x 38.1 cm), Peabody Essex Museum, Gift of Lillian Montalto Bohlen

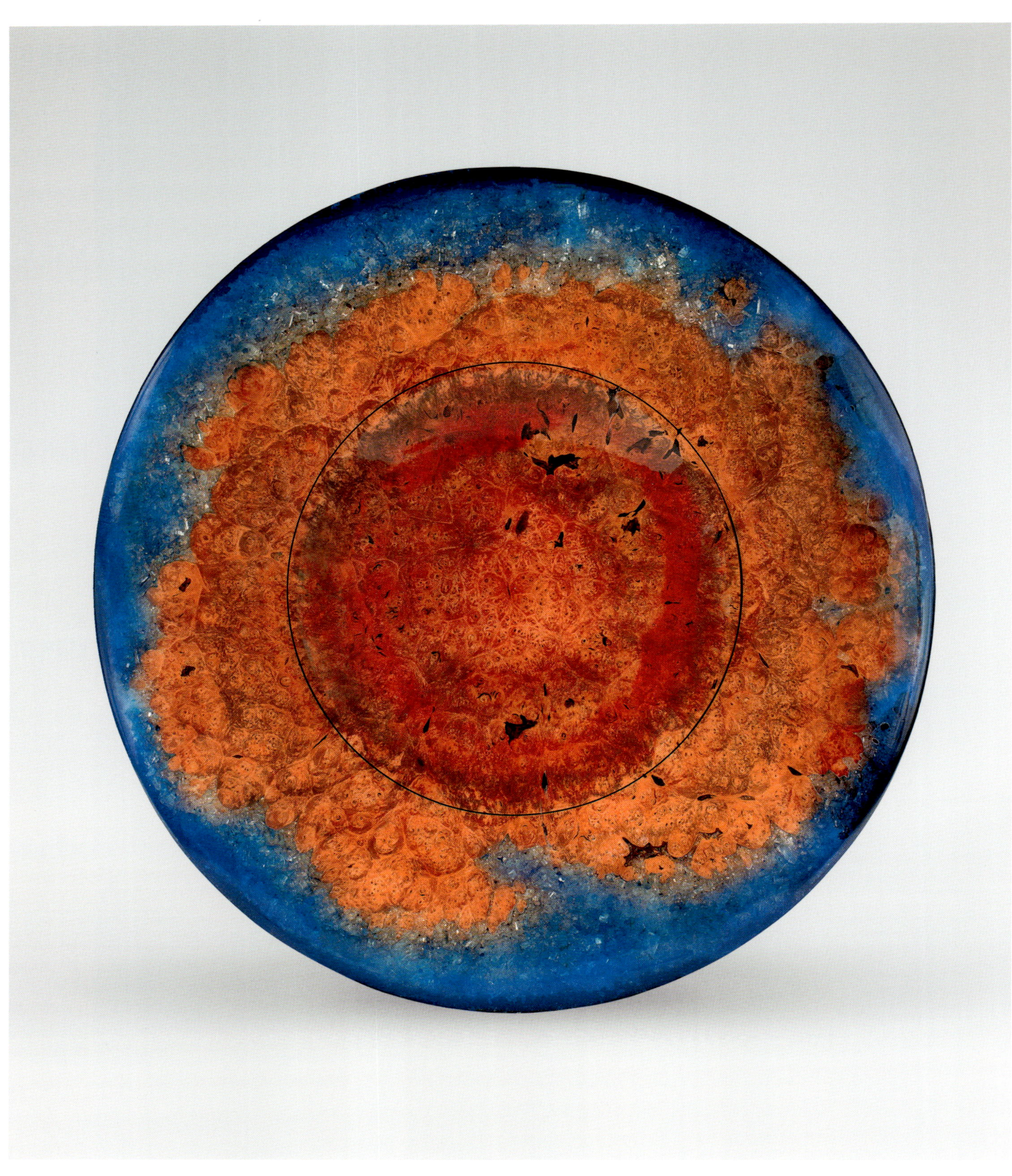

STEPHEN HATCHER born 1953, works Olympia, Washington
ISLAND CALDERA 2007, maple burl, calcite crystals in resin, transparent paint, hand-rubbed lacquer finish, 1 1/2 x 15 in. (3.8 x 38.1 cm), Peabody Essex Museum, Gift of Lillian Montalto Bohlen

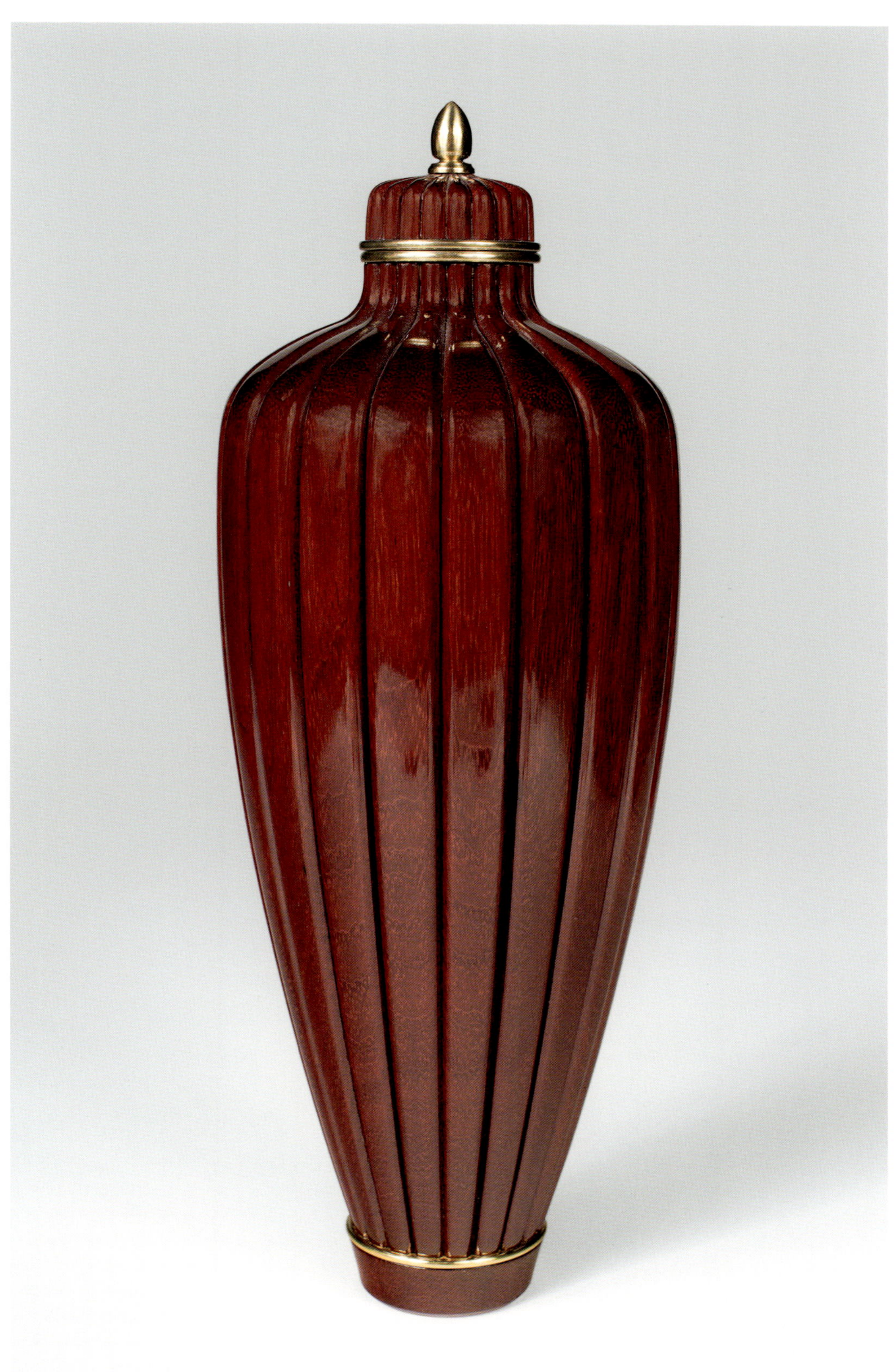

WALT COLE born 1932, works Livonia, Michigan
UNTITLED 1998, purpleheart, brass, 12 1/2 x 4 1/2 in. (31.8 x 11.4 cm), Peabody Essex Museum, Gift of Lillian Montalto Bohlen

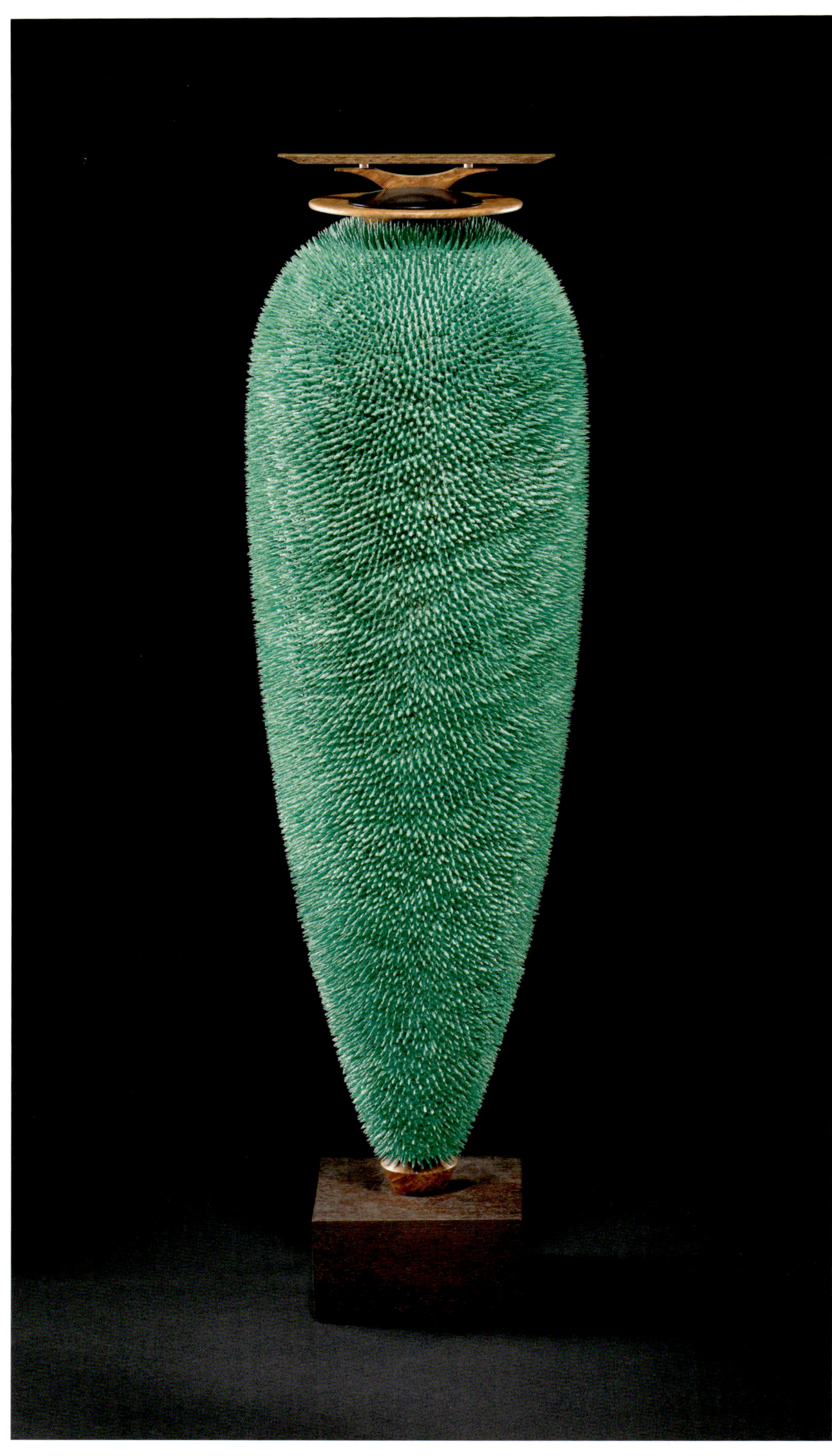

DICK CODDING born 1942, works Leesburg, Florida
UNTITLED 2009, mahogany, oxidized copper tacks, 34 x 10 in. (86.4 x 25.4 cm)

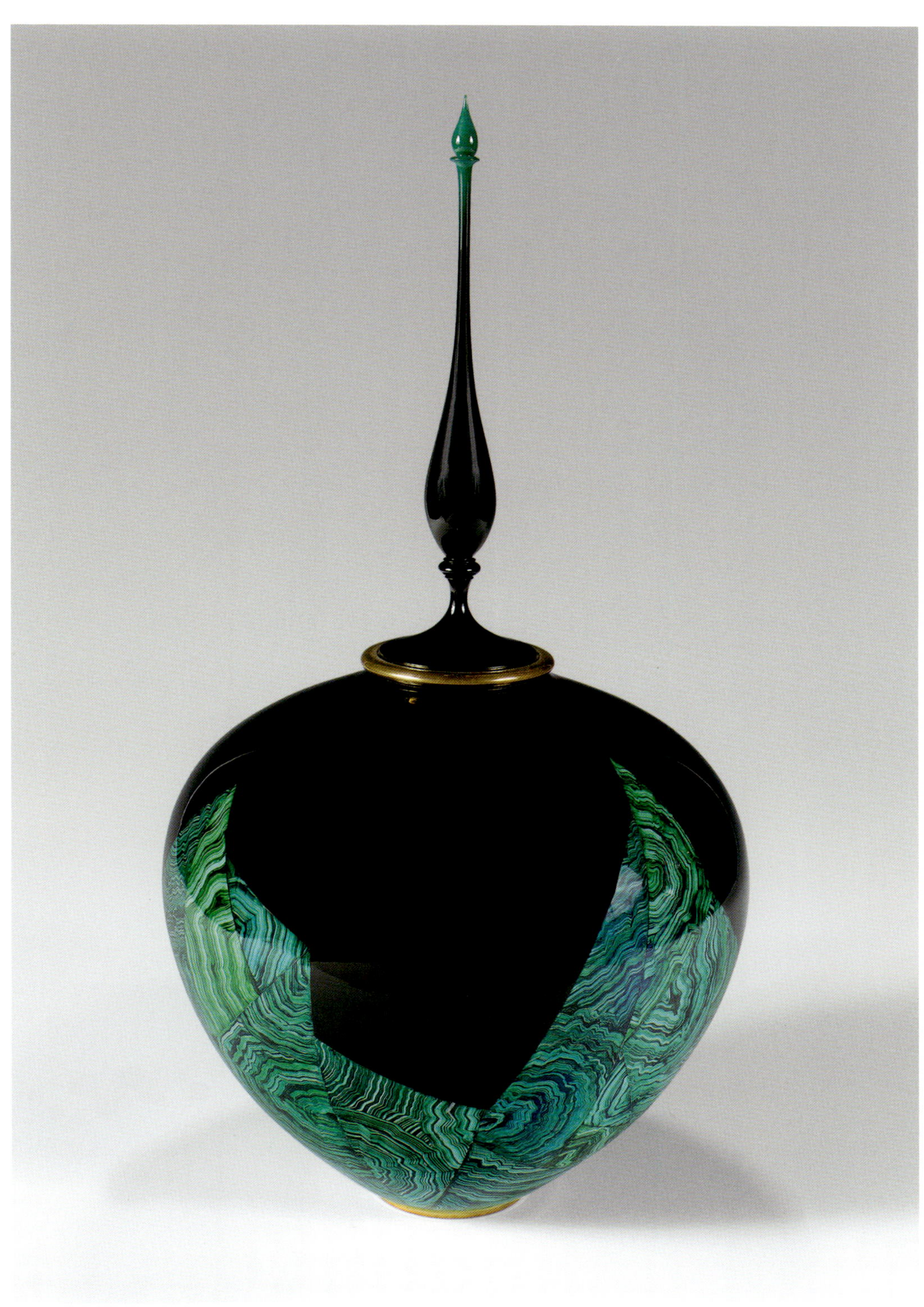

STEVE SHERMAN born 1942, works Saugerties, New York
NEUE RELIQUAIRE 2008, hard maple, bronze, paint, urethane resin, 15 1/4 x 6 1/2 x 6 in. (38.7 x 16.5 x 15.2 cm)

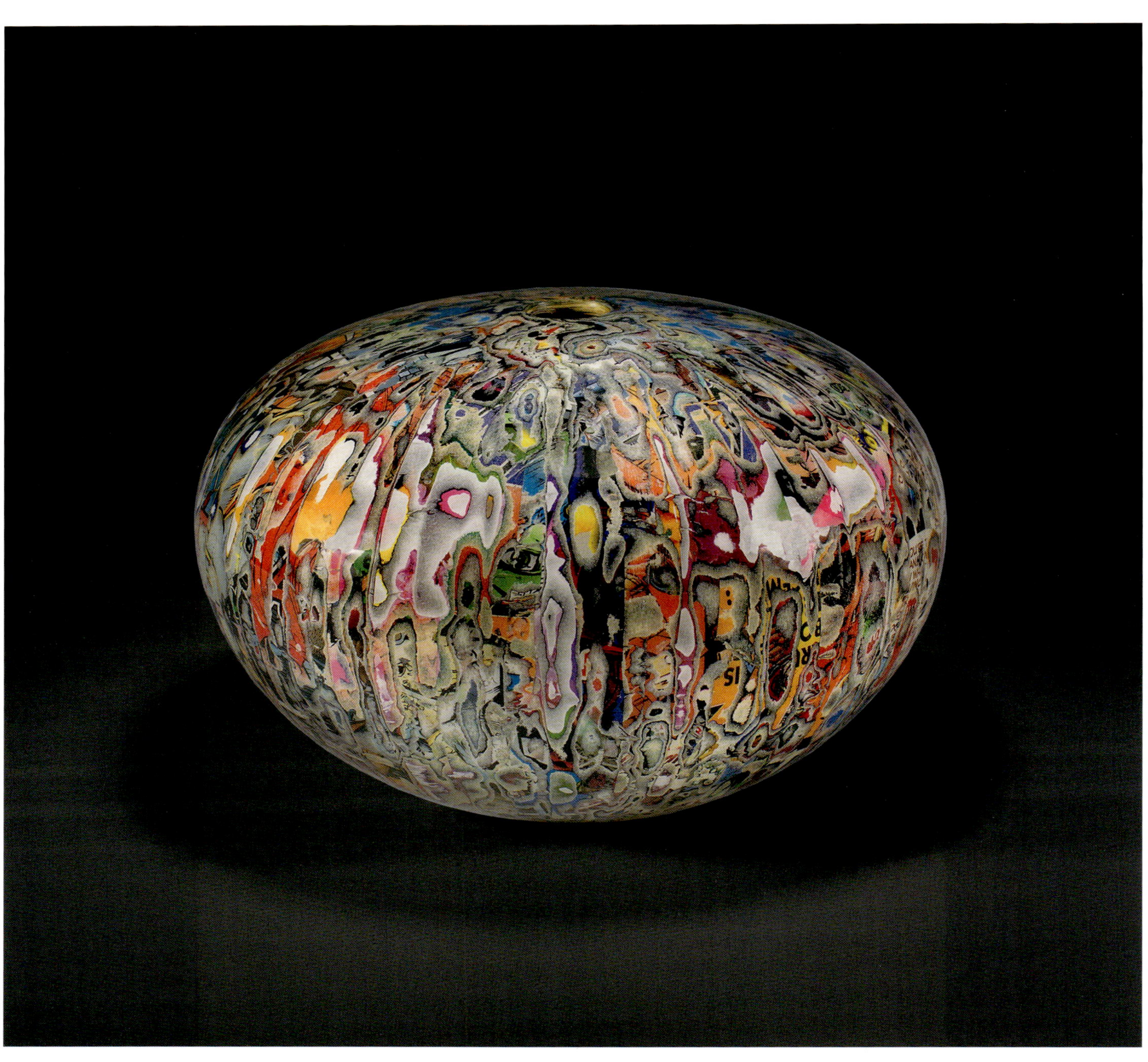

MARK BRESSLER 1951–2010, worked Santa Fe, New Mexico
SUPERMAN MINI 2009, comic books, 4 1/2 x 5 1/2 in. (11.4 x 13.7 cm), Peabody Essex Museum, Gift of Lillian Montalto Bohlen

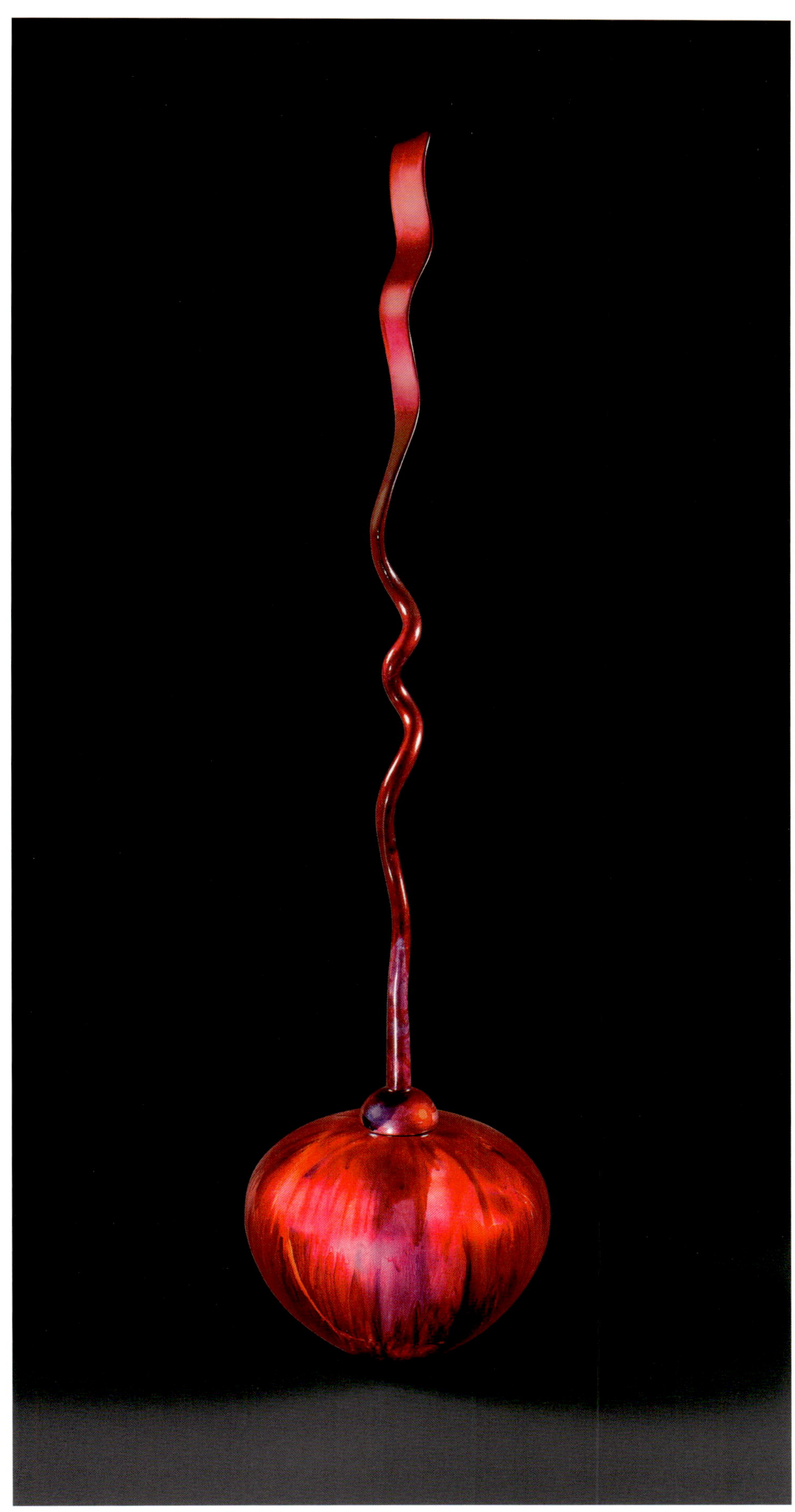

MARK BRESSLER 1951–2010, worked Santa Fe, New Mexico
CHERRY BOMB II 2006, maple, lacquer, 49 x 12 in. (124.5 x 30.5 cm), Peabody Essex Museum, Gift of Lillian Montalto Bohlen

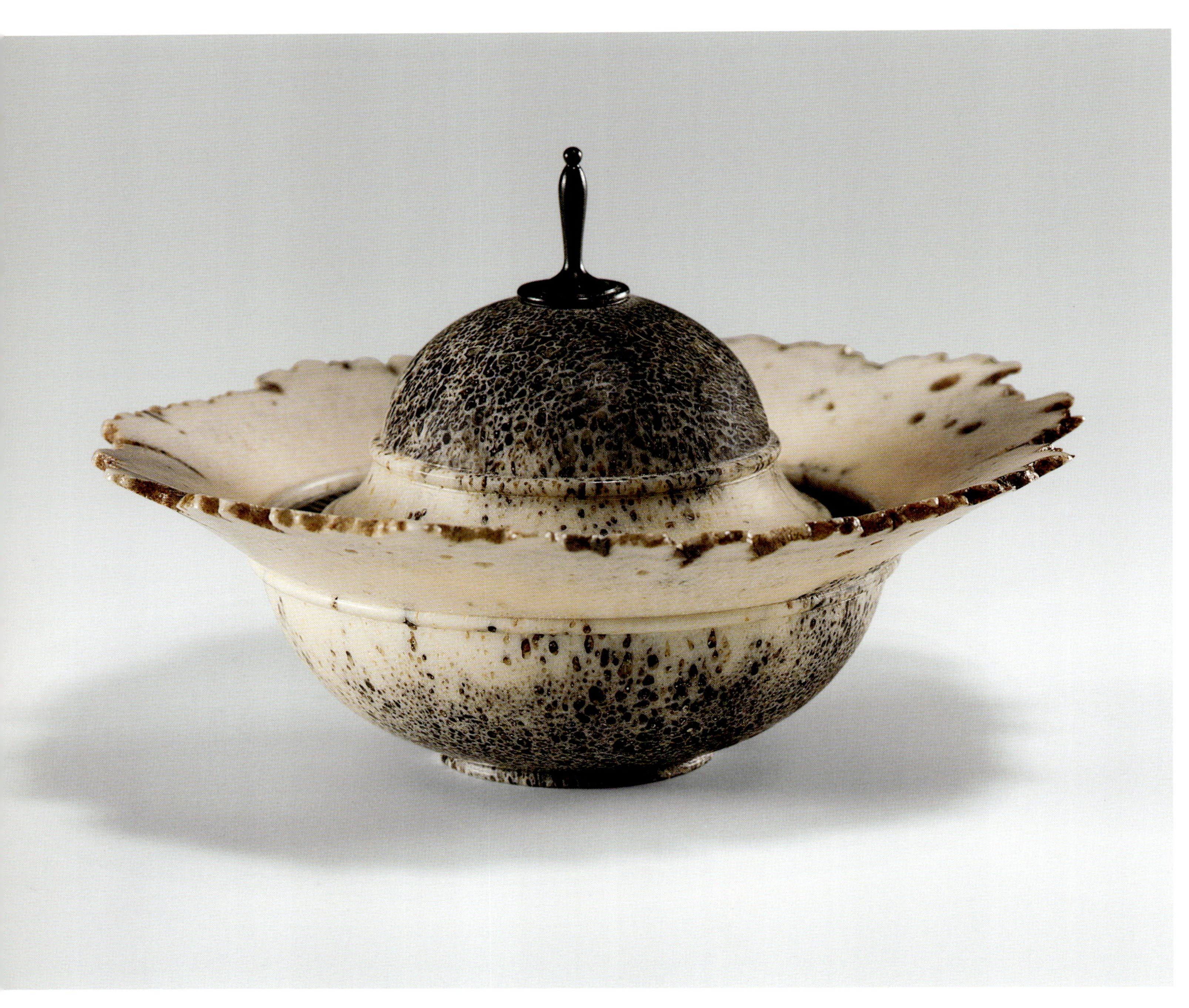

KIP CHRISTENSEN born 1955, works Springville, Utah
JEWELRY BOX 1999, elk antler, turquoise, ebony, pink ivory, 2 $^{1}/_{4}$ x 4 x 3 $^{1}/_{2}$ in. (5.7 x 10.2 x 8.9 cm), Peabody Essex Museum, Gift of Lillian Montalto Bohlen

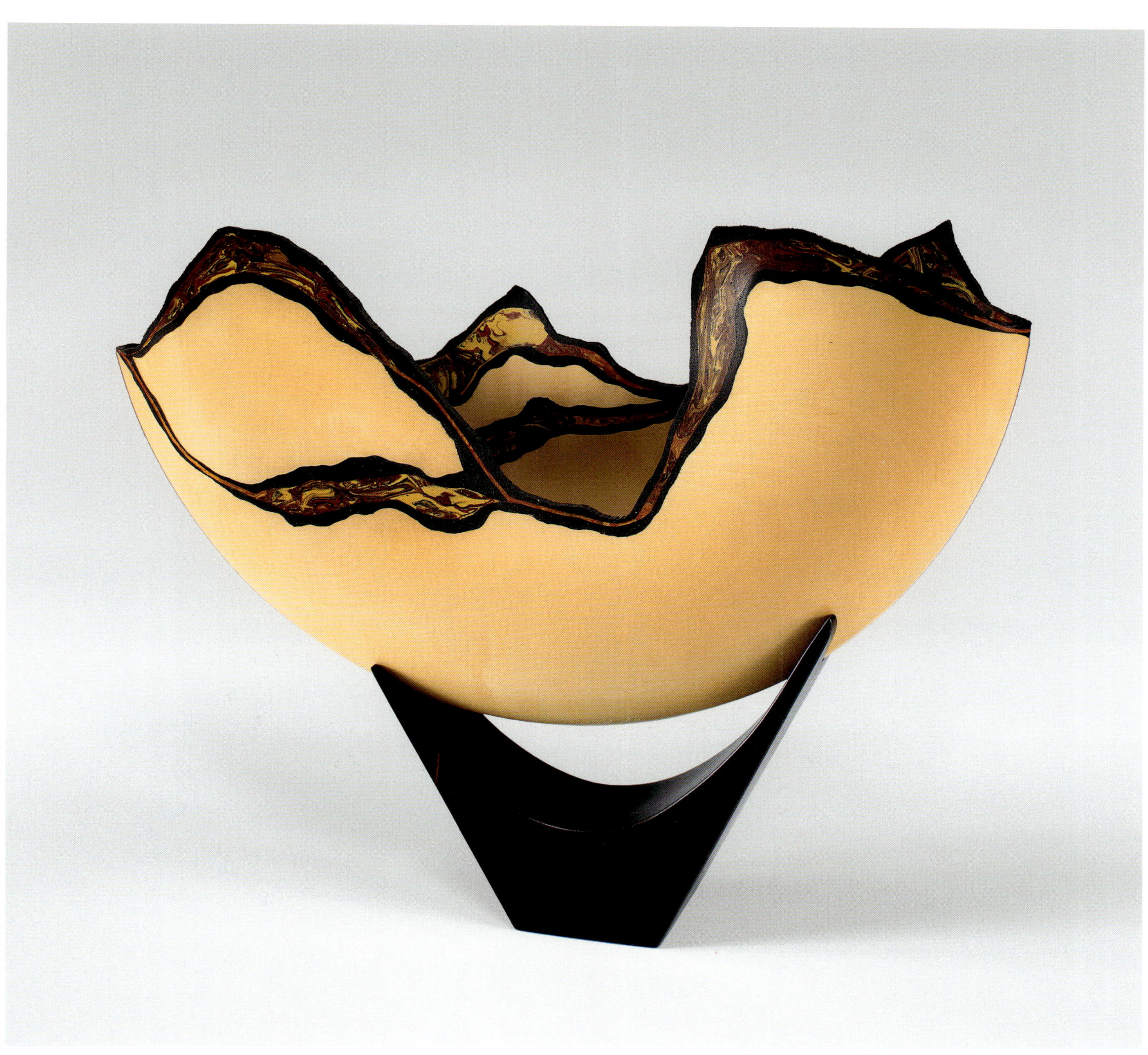

MARILYN CAMPBELL born 1951, works Kincardine, Ontario, Canada
IGNEOUS SERIES #3, RARE ELEMENTS 1999, holly, pigmented epoxy, 9 $^{1}/_{2}$ x 11 $^{7}/_{8}$ x 2 in. (24.1 x 30.2 x 5.1 cm)

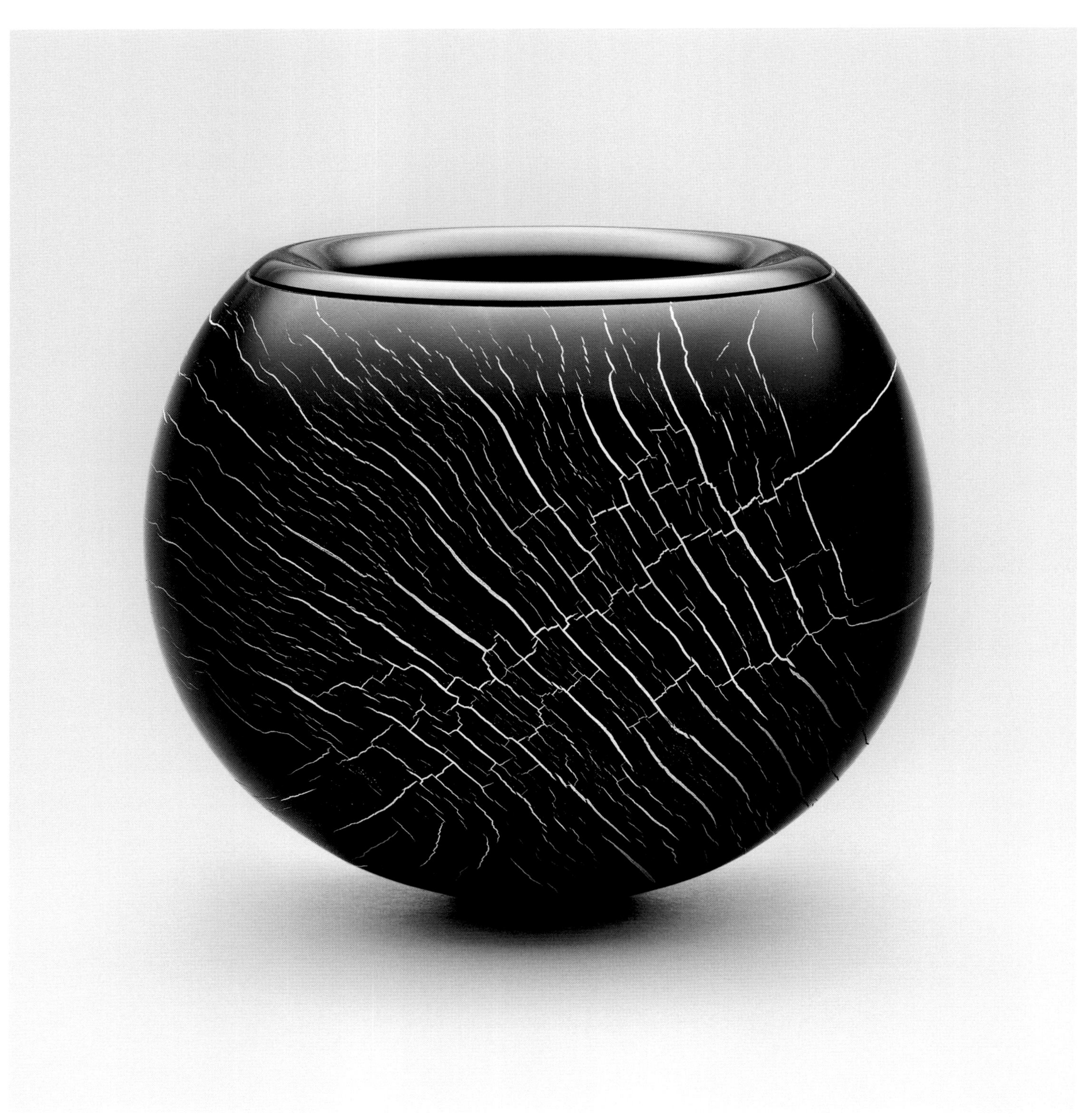

RUEDIGER MARQUARDING born 1943, works Wustrow, Germany
SPIDER'S WEB 2000, ebony, silver alloy, 5 ½ x 6 in. (14 x 15.2 cm)

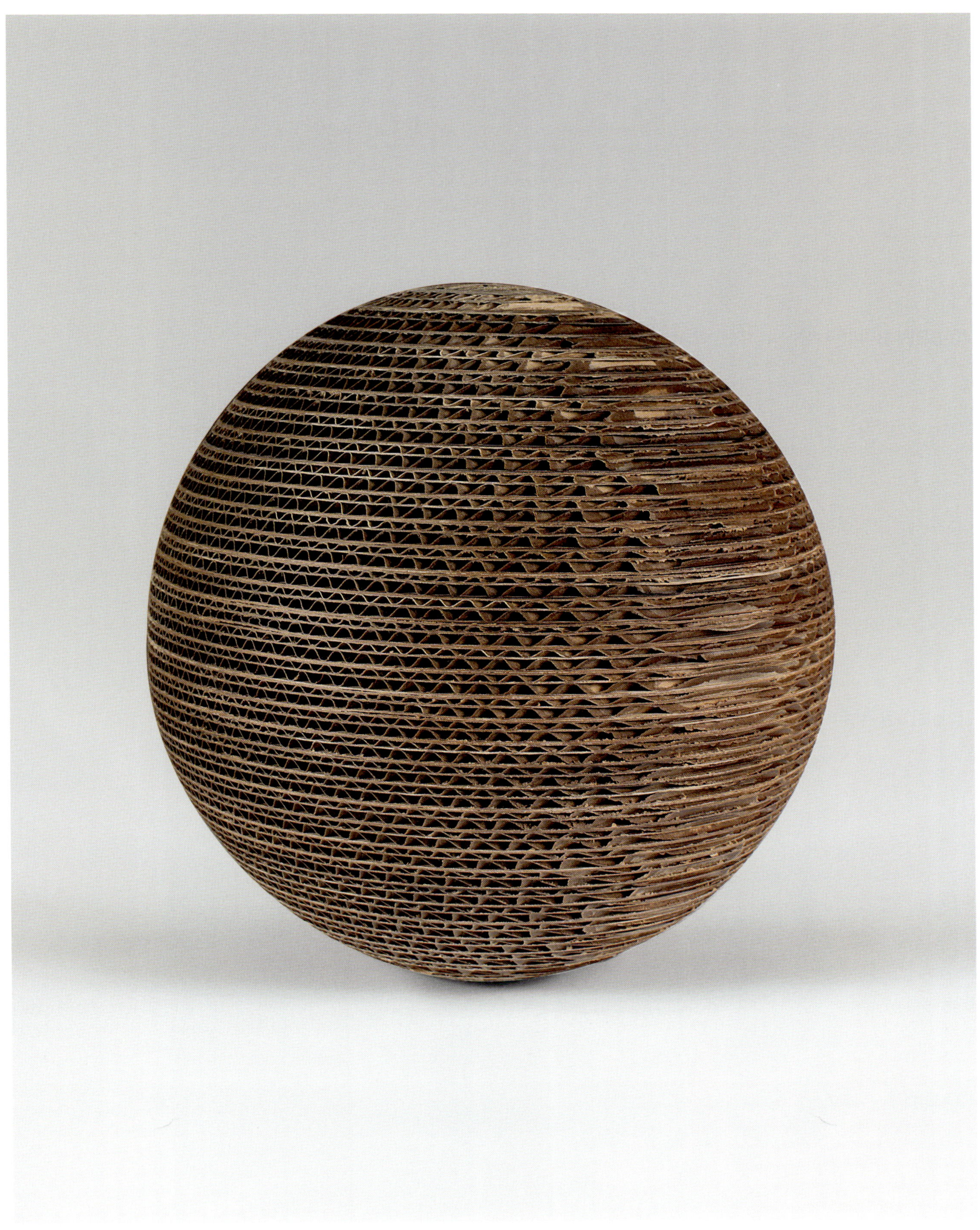

RON GERTON born 1946, works Richland, Washington
AIR APPARENT 2010, cardboard, 10 x 10 in. (25.4 x 25.4 cm)

ECHOES OF PLACE

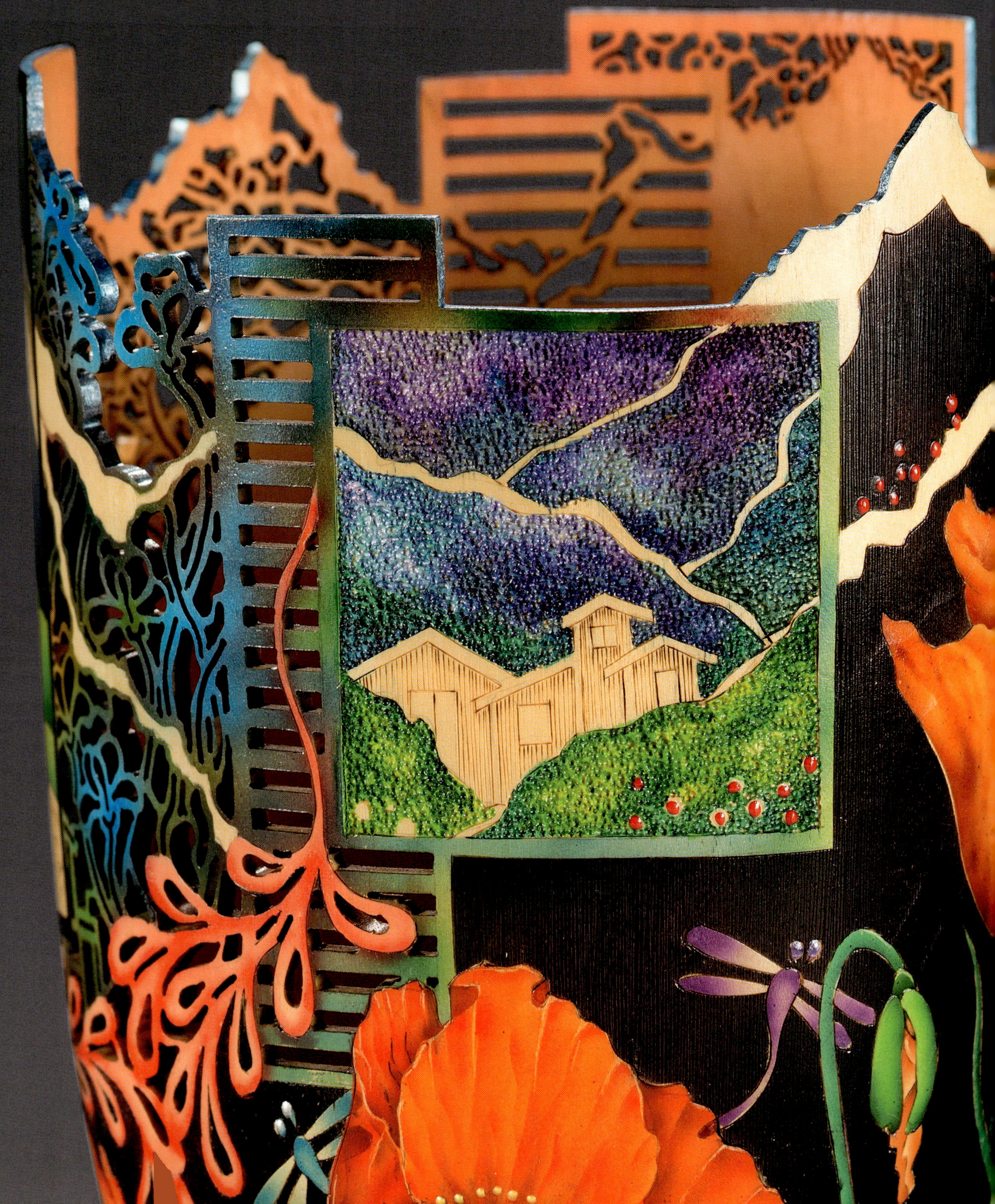

Artists seeking to tell stories through their works have incorporated realistic imagery that captures personal memories or a sense of place. Some of the artists produce three-dimensional environments filled with cultural references tied to their personal experiences. Others have produced works that have nothing to do with lathe turning, such as a trompe-l'oeil, hand-carved wooden quilt suspended on a piece of real rope. These artists are taking wood art into new areas of creative expression.

BINH PHO: HARMONIZING ELEMENTS

Wood is a living material and trees parallel human life, making wood an ideal material for self-expression.

The things that happen in life—sorrow and joy, misfortune and fortune, despair and hope—impact each of us in different ways, yet create a balance. I use color and imagery to share dreams, transformation, destiny, magic, and love.

My works are filled with symbolism—the dragonfly represents the military helicopters of my childhood in Vietnam that failed to take me to freedom, while that freedom is represented by the butterfly. The peacock feather represents the dream, poppies speak of mystery, and clouds represent change. When people become familiar with my stories—whether autobiographical or fictional—they understand my works and what I seek to share.

The work *Eternal Return* narrates the relationship between mother and child. Through different arrangements, it shows how the mother carries her dream child and remains with him or her through good and bad times.

Sinus Amoris is a set of three teapots, each created in a different medium—wood, glass, and bronze. The teapots reference the rich traditions of the tea ceremony, the sharing of dreams, and the harmonizing of the elements. The original was created in wood, which was cast to bring the glass and bronze teapots to life. The characteristics of the media are drastically different, creating both contrast and balance.

Artists Giles Gilson, Steve Sinner, and Steve Sherman embed images under a flawless, glasslike finish, so that viewers can feel the richness and glamour of the work. Frank Sudol and Malcolm Zander express their inspiration through mostly negative spaces. Ron Fleming, Joey Richardson, Derek Weidman, and Jacques Vesery incorporate their stories with three-dimensional depth; viewing their works, we sense a hidden place.

Detail, Binh Pho, *Seven Poppies,* 2009 (page 173)

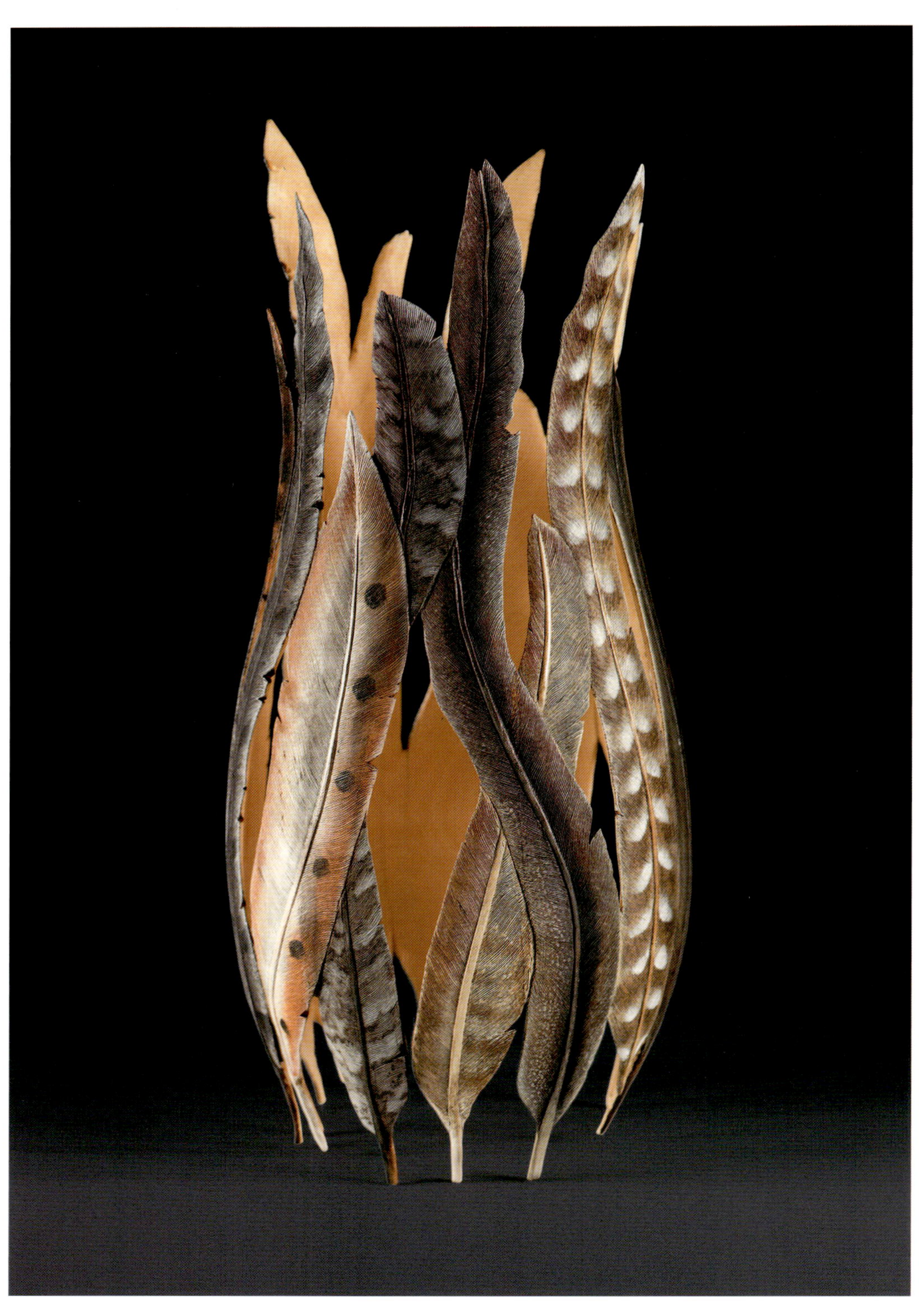

FRANK SUDOL AND CAM MERKLE 1933–2006, worked Paddockwood, Saskatchewan, Canada (Sudol); born 1957, works Martensville, Sasketchewan, Canada (Merkle)
HAWKS & OWLS 2000, birch, acrylic paint, 12 $^1/_2$ x 5 $^3/_4$ in. (31.8 x 14.6 cm)

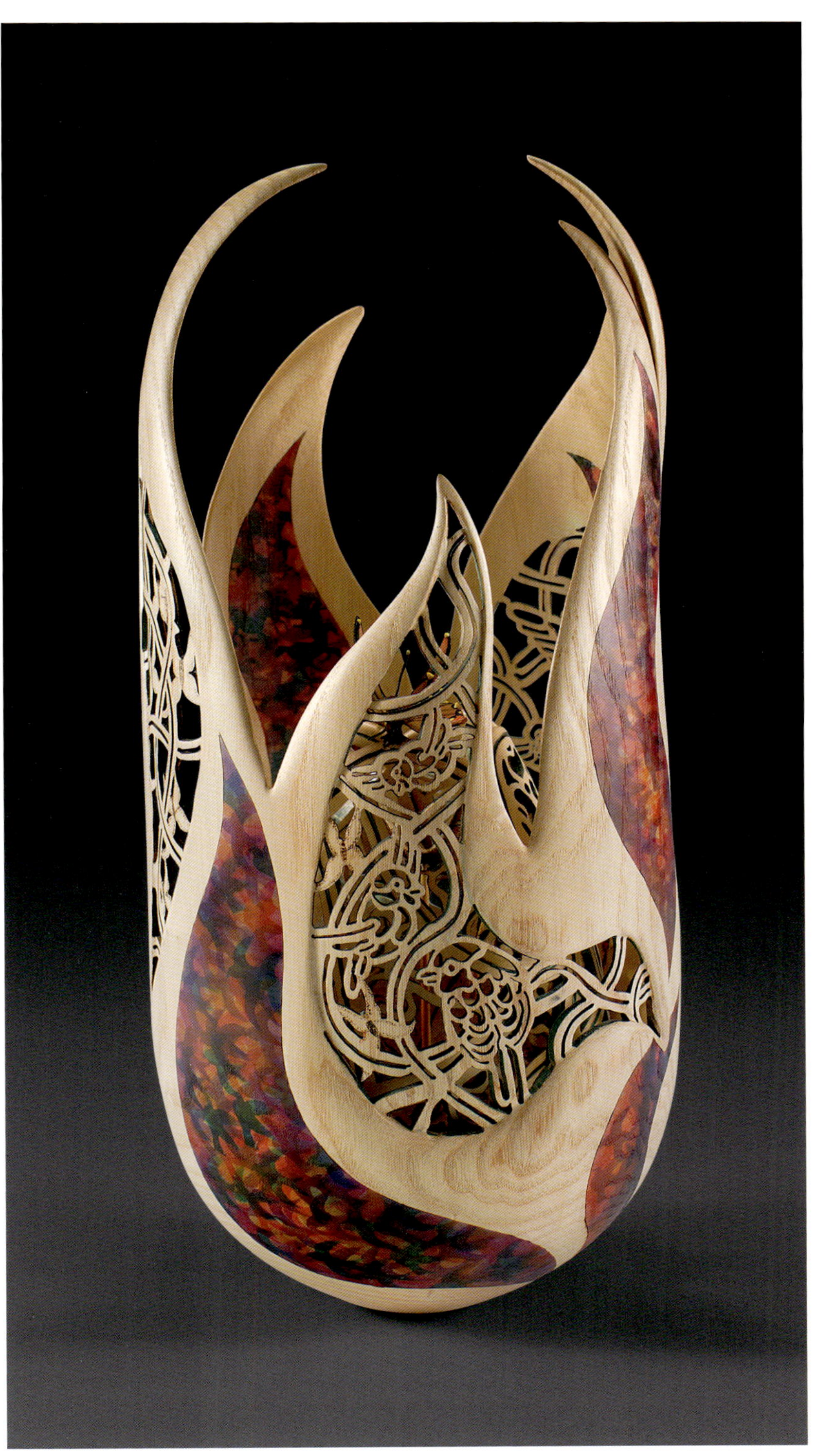

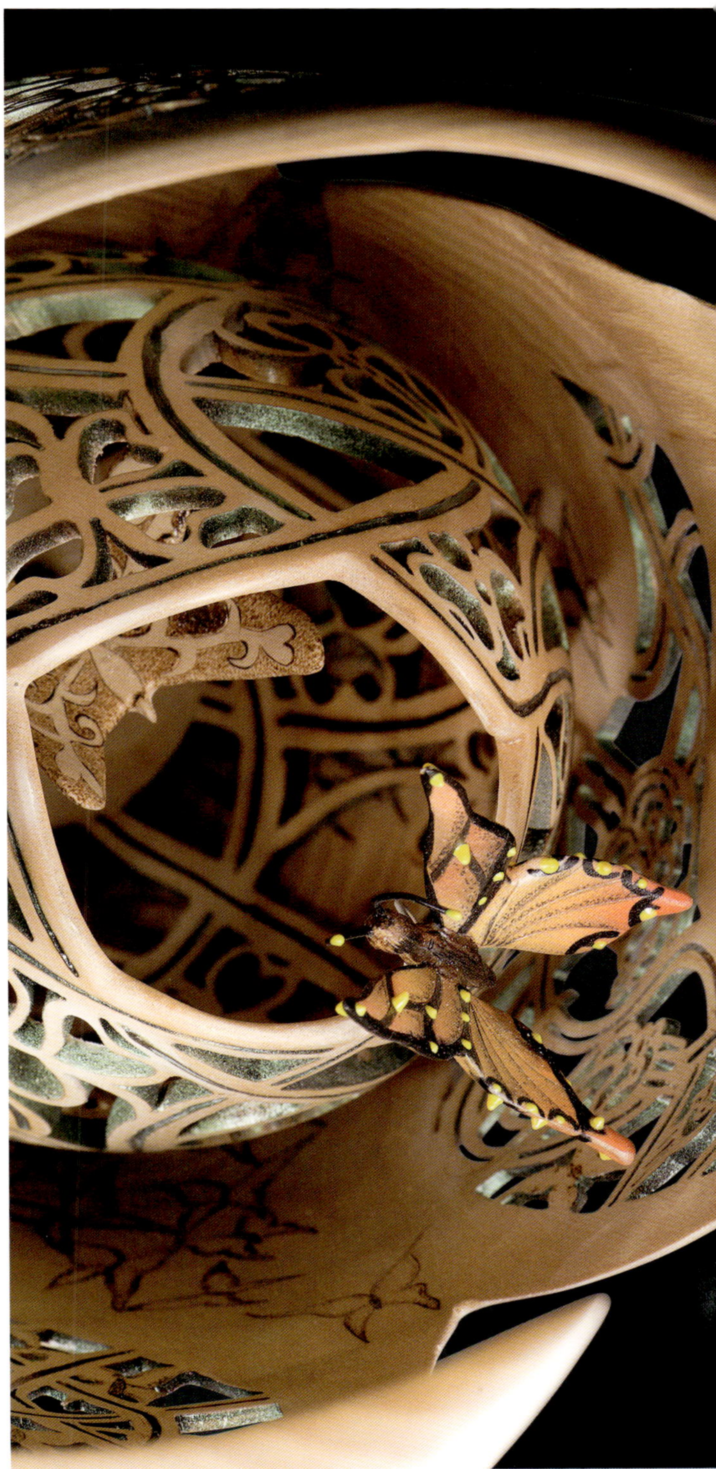

JOEY RICHARDSON born 1964, works Grimsby, Lincolnshire, England
KISS 2010, sycamore, acrylic paint, 13 1/4 x 6 x 7 in. (33.7 x 15.2 x 17.8 cm)
Right: Detail, interior

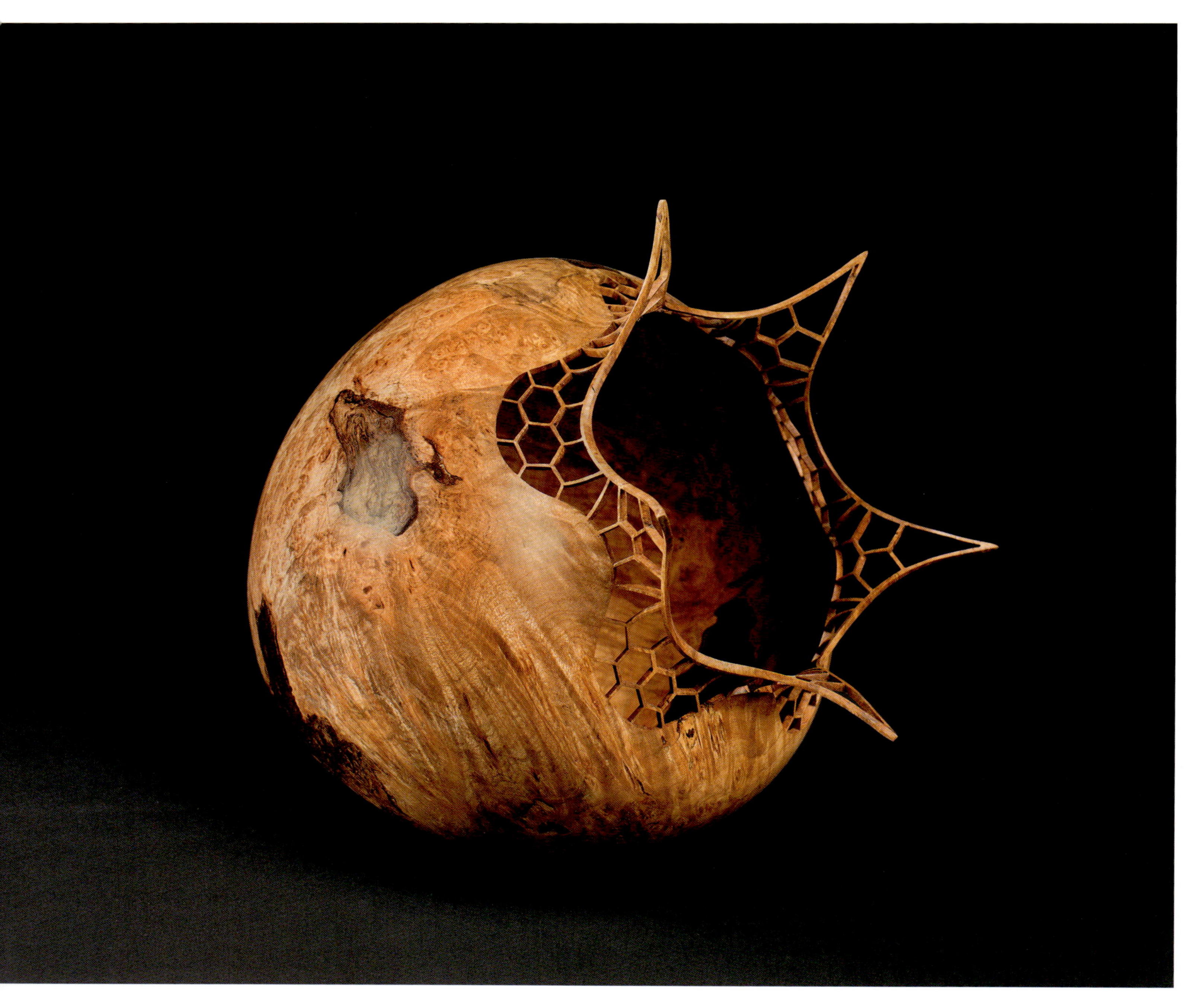

MALCOLM ZANDER born 1942, works Ottawa, Ontario, Canada
HEART OF LOVE 2011, big leaf maple burl, 12 x 12 x 9 $^{1}/_{2}$ in. (30.5 x 30.5 x 24.1 cm), Peabody Essex Museum, Gift of Lillian Montalto Bohlen

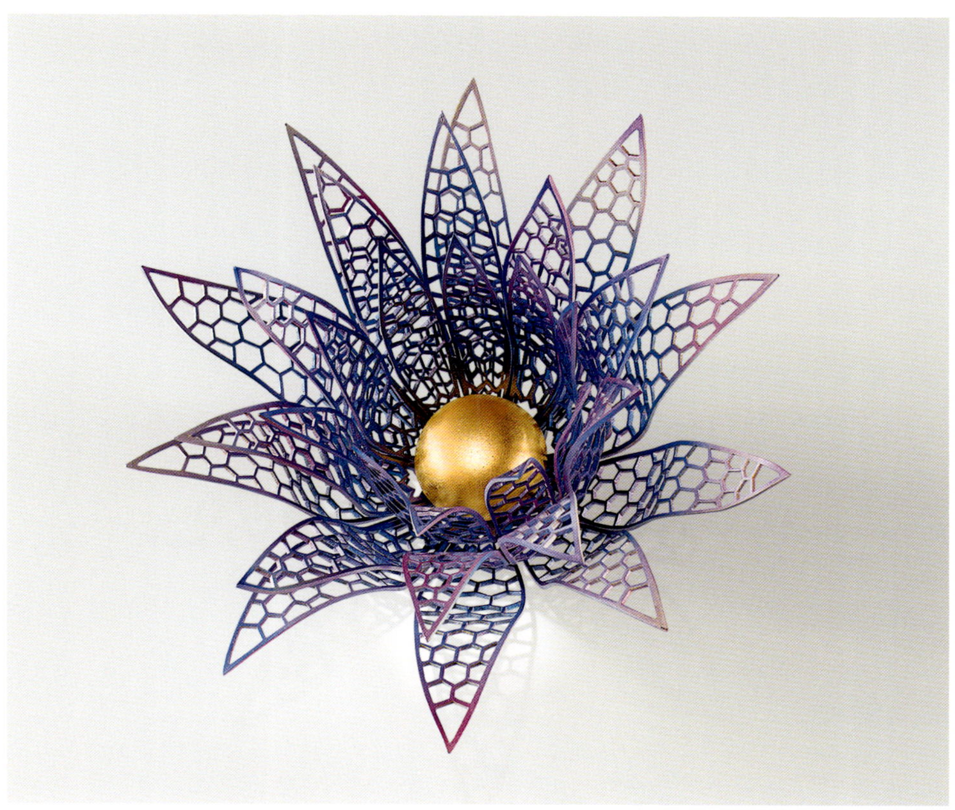

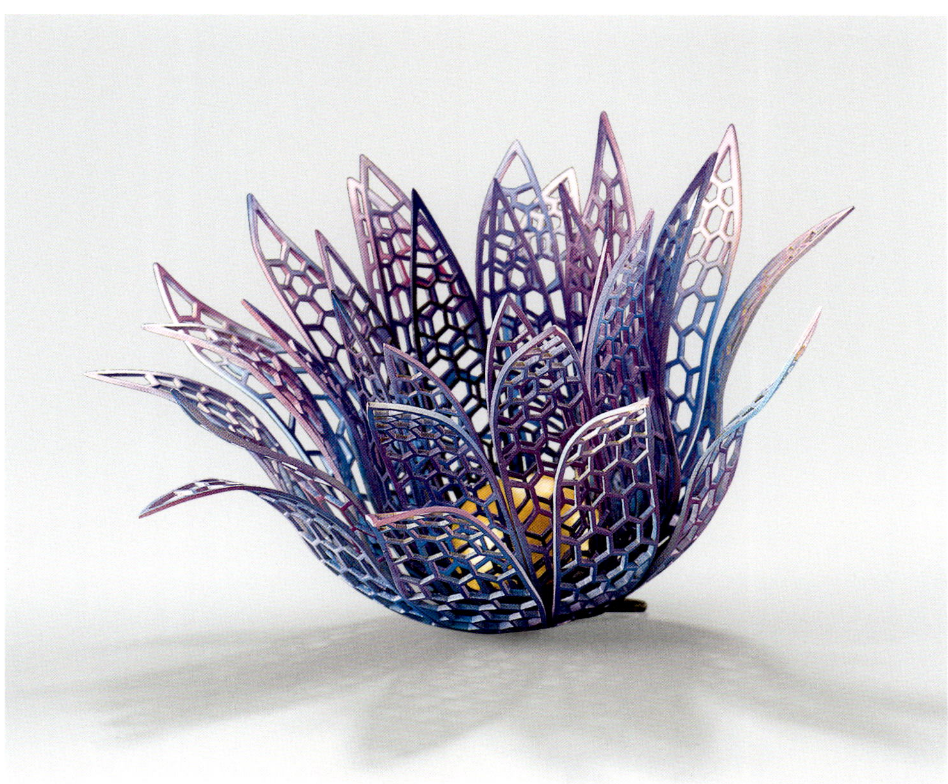

MALCOLM ZANDER born 1942, works Ottawa, Ontario, Canada
FLOWER 2010, compressed cherry wood, acrylic paint, 24k gold leaf, 5 x 7 $^{1}/_{2}$ x 8 in. (12.7 x 19.1 x 20.3 cm)

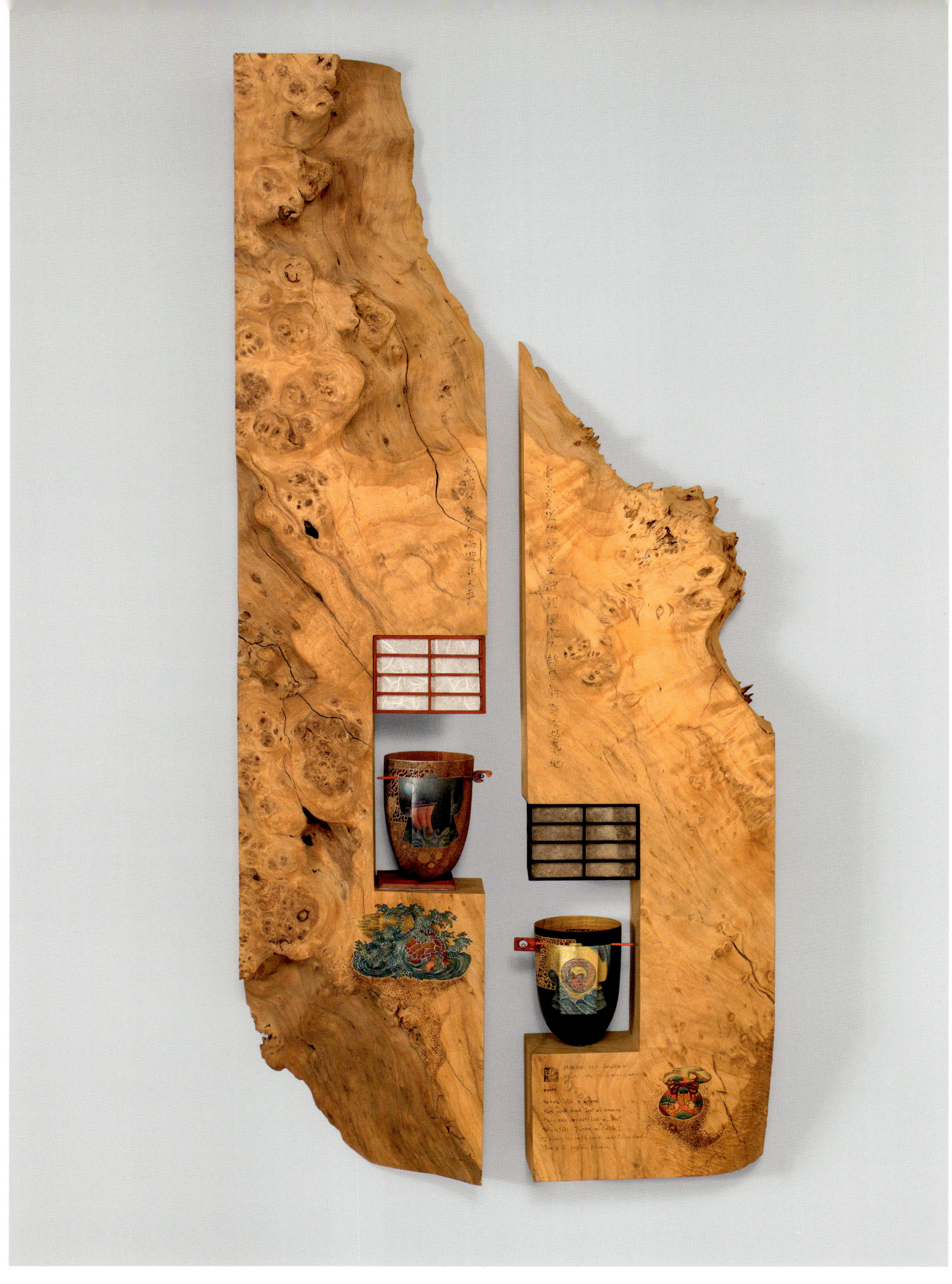

BINH PHO born 1955, works Maple Park, Illinois
OTOMINE AND URASHIMA 2002, willow burl, carob, maple, acrylic paint, 45 x 20 $^{1}/_{2}$ x 3 $^{1}/_{3}$ in. (114.3 x 52.1 x 8.5 cm), Peabody Essex Museum, Gift of Lillian Montalto Bohlen
Right: Detail

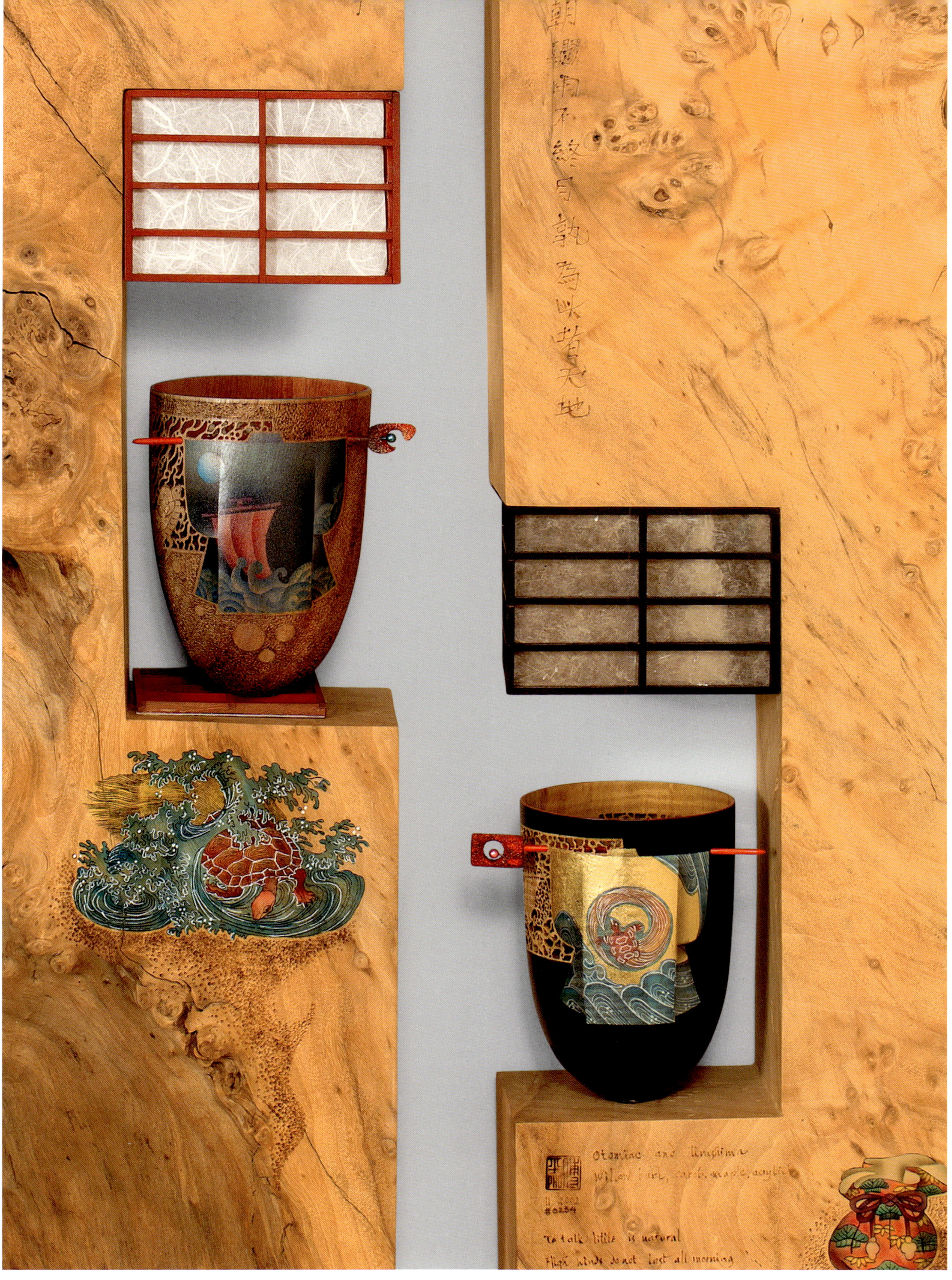
#0234
To talk little is natural
High winds do not last all morning

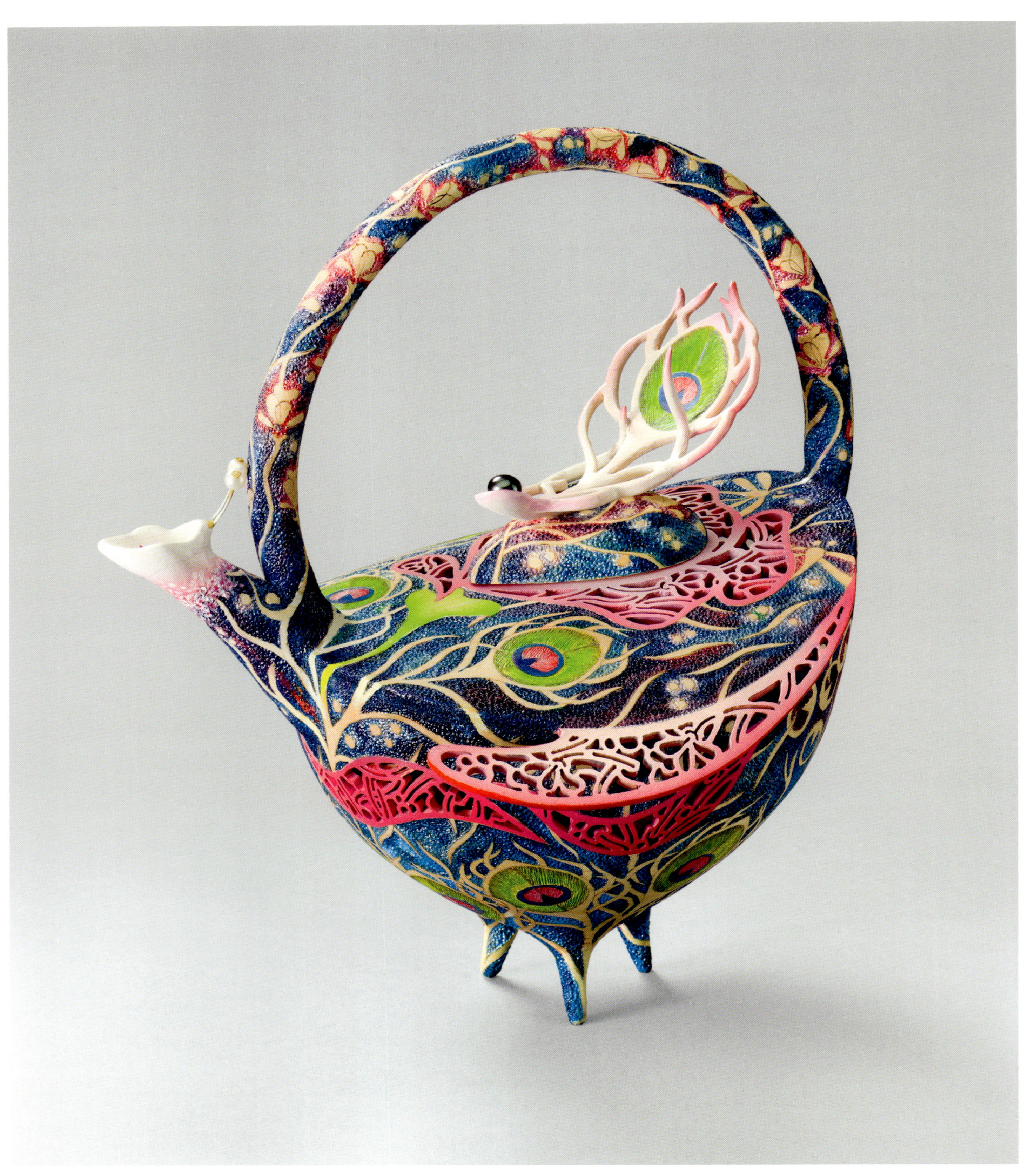

BINH PHO born 1955, works Maple Park, Illinois
SINUS AMORIS—SPRING 2011, maple, acrylic paint, pearls, 18K gold, 8 $^{1}/_{2}$ x 7 x 8 in. (21.6 x 17.8 x 20.3 cm)

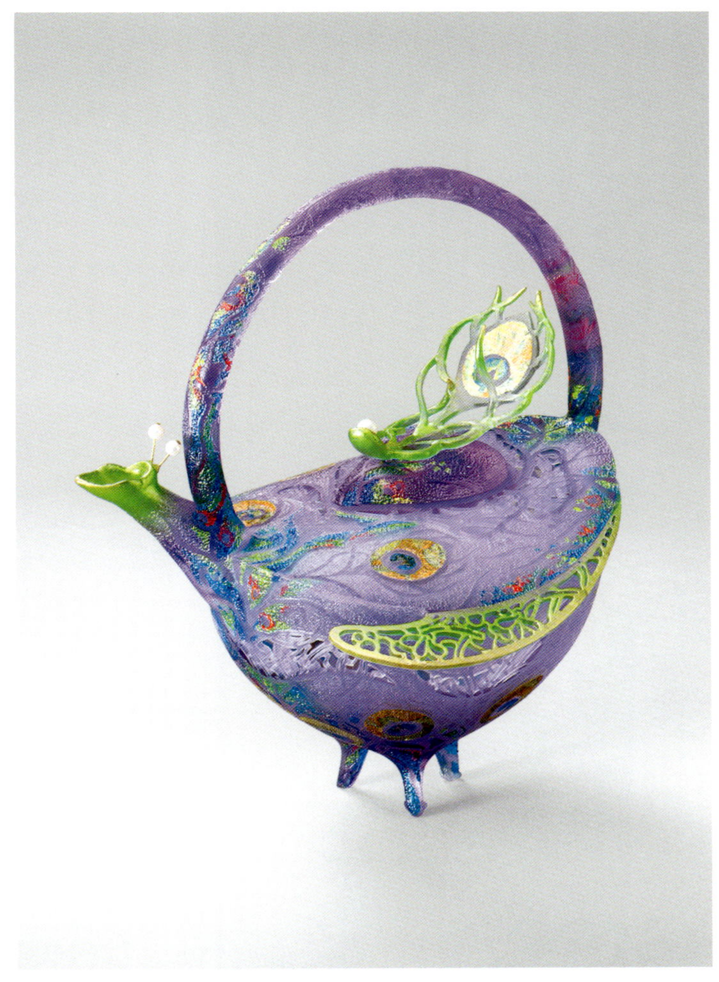

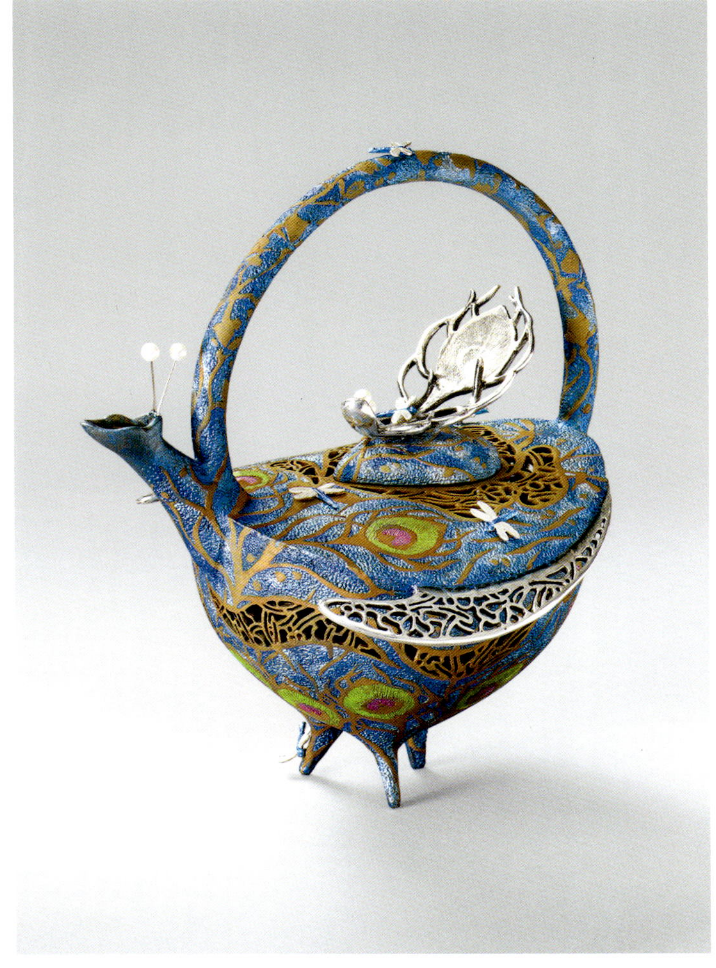

Left to right: **BINH PHO** born 1955, works Maple Park, Illinois
SINUS AMORIS—HOPE 2012, cast glass, gold leaf, acrylic paint, pearls, 8 $^{1}/_{2}$ x 7 x 8 in. (21.6 x 17.8 x 20.3 cm)
SINUS AMORIS—DREAM 2014, cast bronze, pearls, acrylic paint, 8 $^{1}/_{2}$ x 7 x 8 in. (21.6 x 17.8 x 20.3 cm)

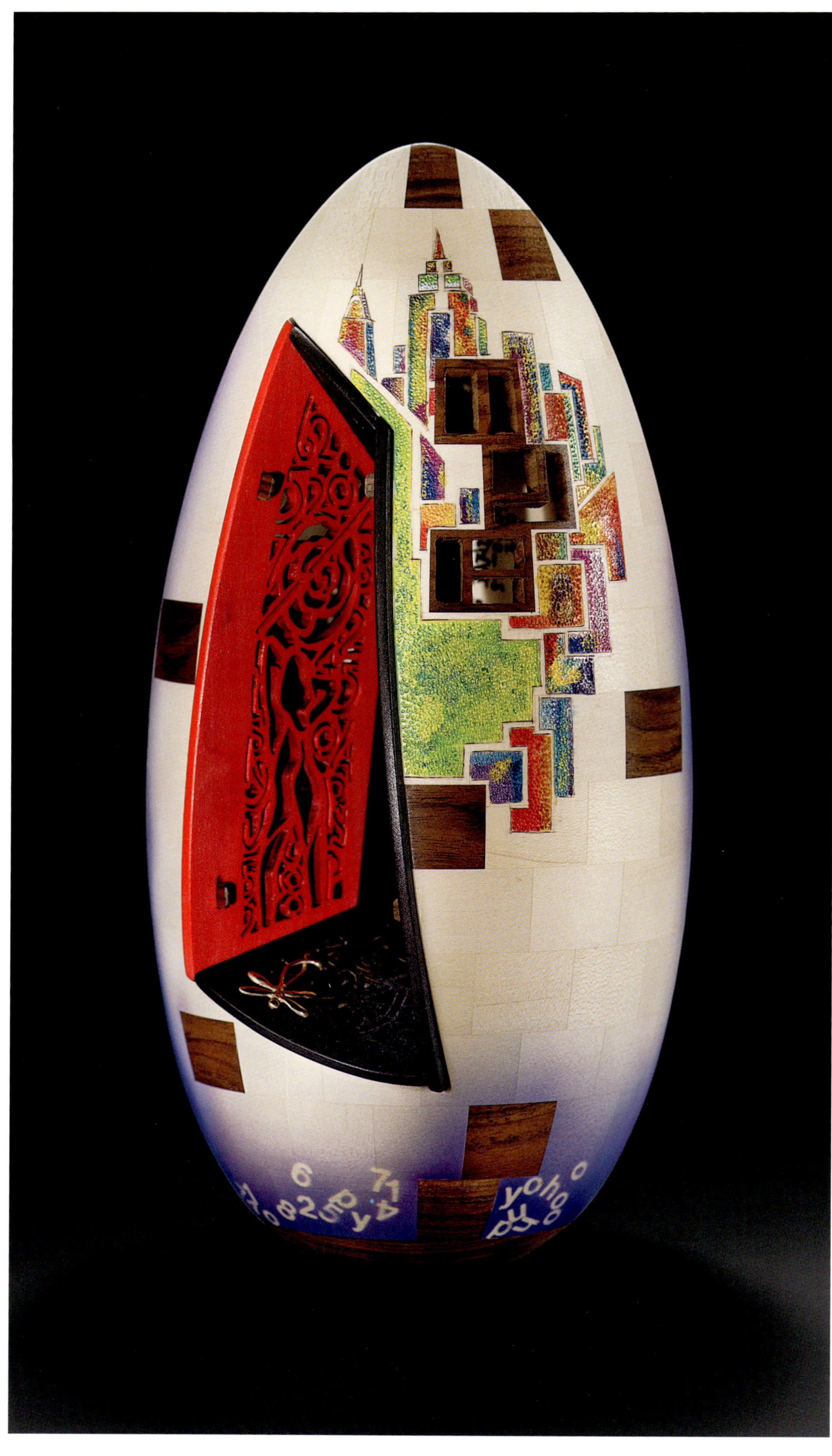

CURT THEOBALD AND BINH PHO born 1965, United States, works Pine Bluffs, Wyoming (Theobald); born 1955, works Maple Park, Illinois (Pho)
CLOAKED IN WIZARDRY 2012, holly, walnut, basswood, acrylic paints, 11 x 5 x 4 in. (28 x 12.7 x 10.2 cm)

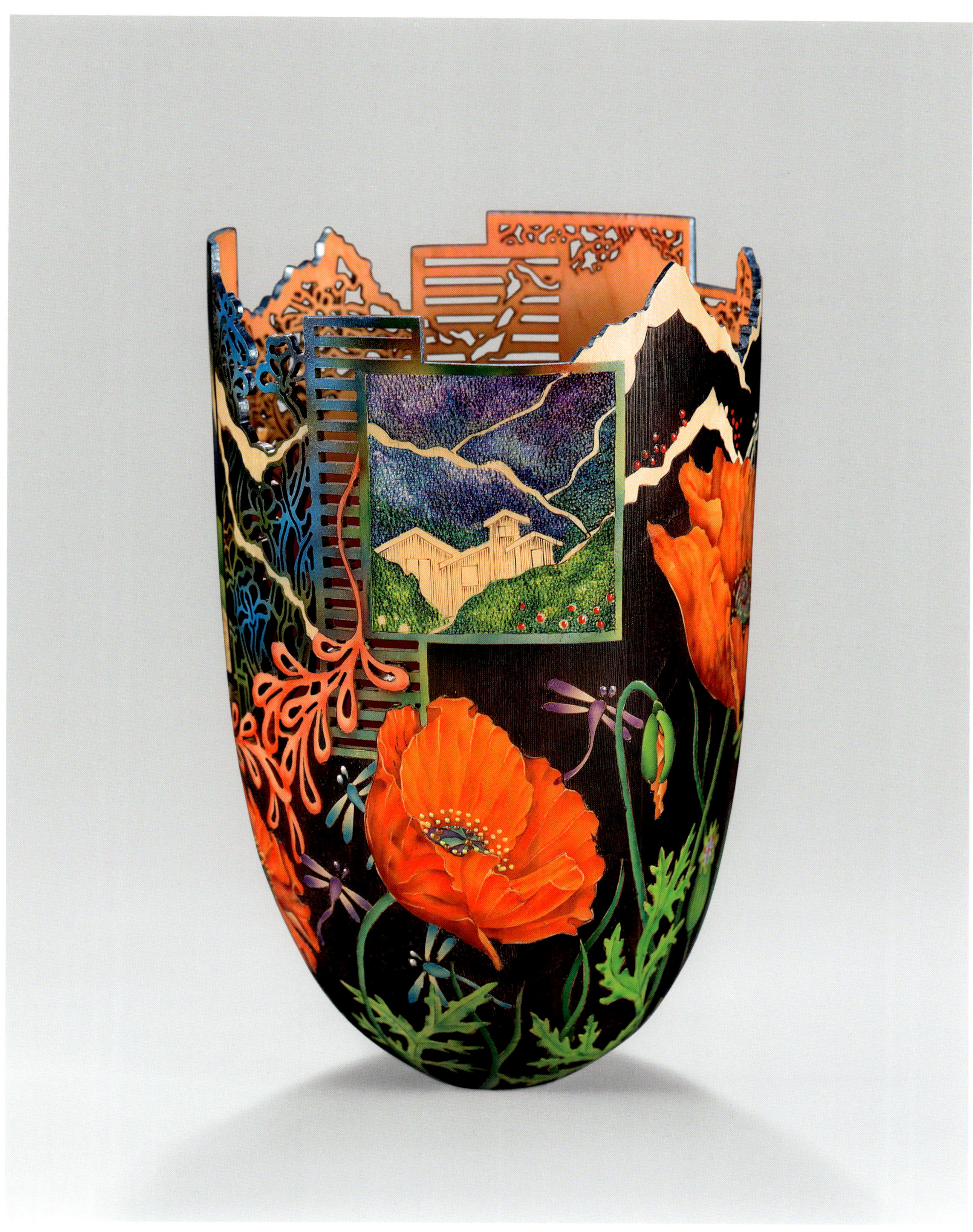

BINH PHO born 1955, works Maple Park, Illinois
SEVEN POPPIES 2009, box elder, acrylic paints, 10 x 6 x 6 in. (25.4 x 15.2 x 15.2 cm)

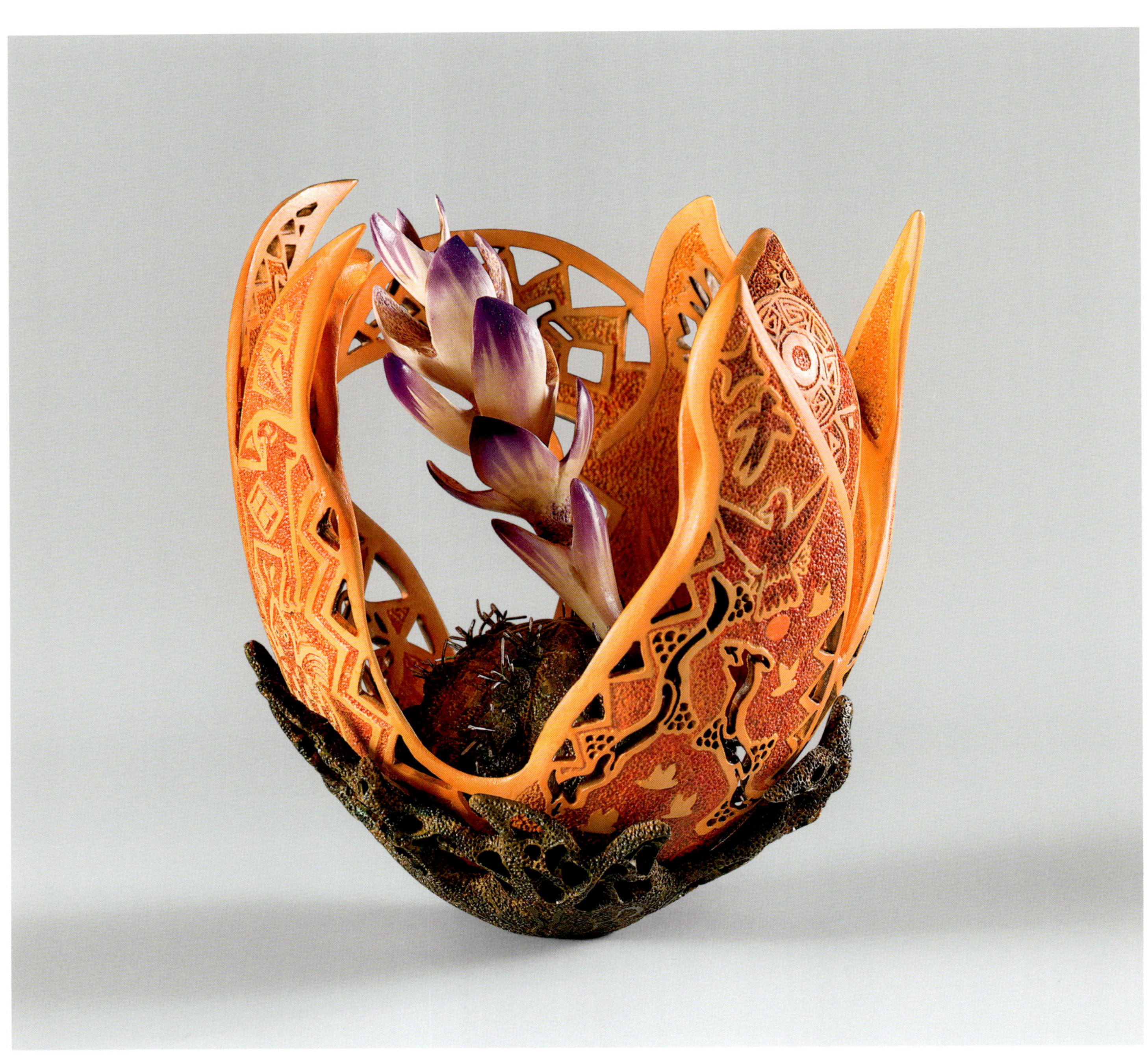

JOEY RICHARDSON born 1964, works Grimsby, Lincolnshire, England
PUEBLO BLOOM 2009, sycamore, holly, acrylic colors, 6 x 6 in. (15.2 x 15.2 cm), Peabody Essex Museum, Gift of Lillian Montalto Bohlen

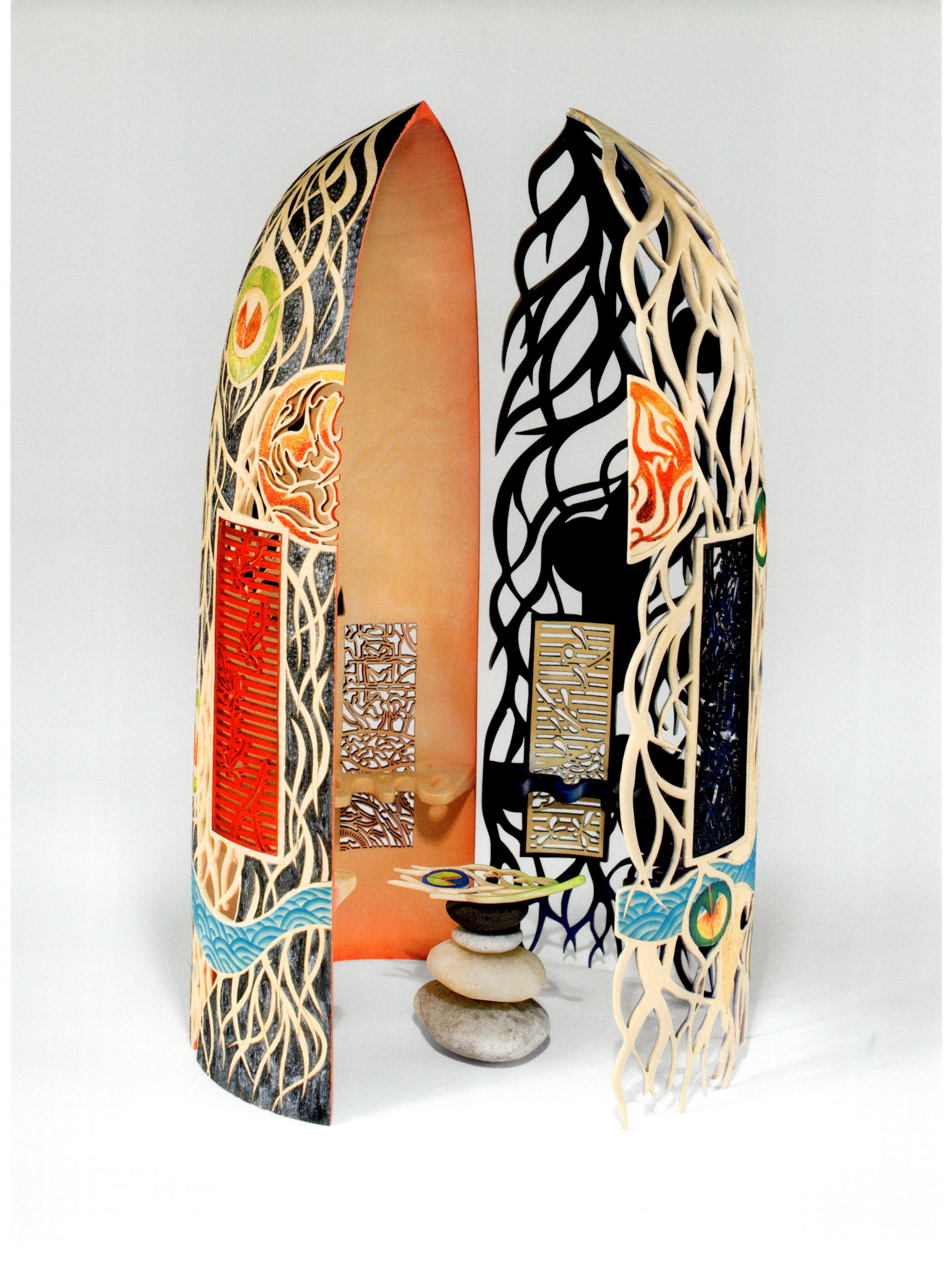

BINH PHO born 1955, works Maple Park, Illinois
ETERNAL RETURN 2010, cottonwood, acrylic paints, 17 x 12 x 10 in. (43.2 x 30.5 x 25.4 cm)

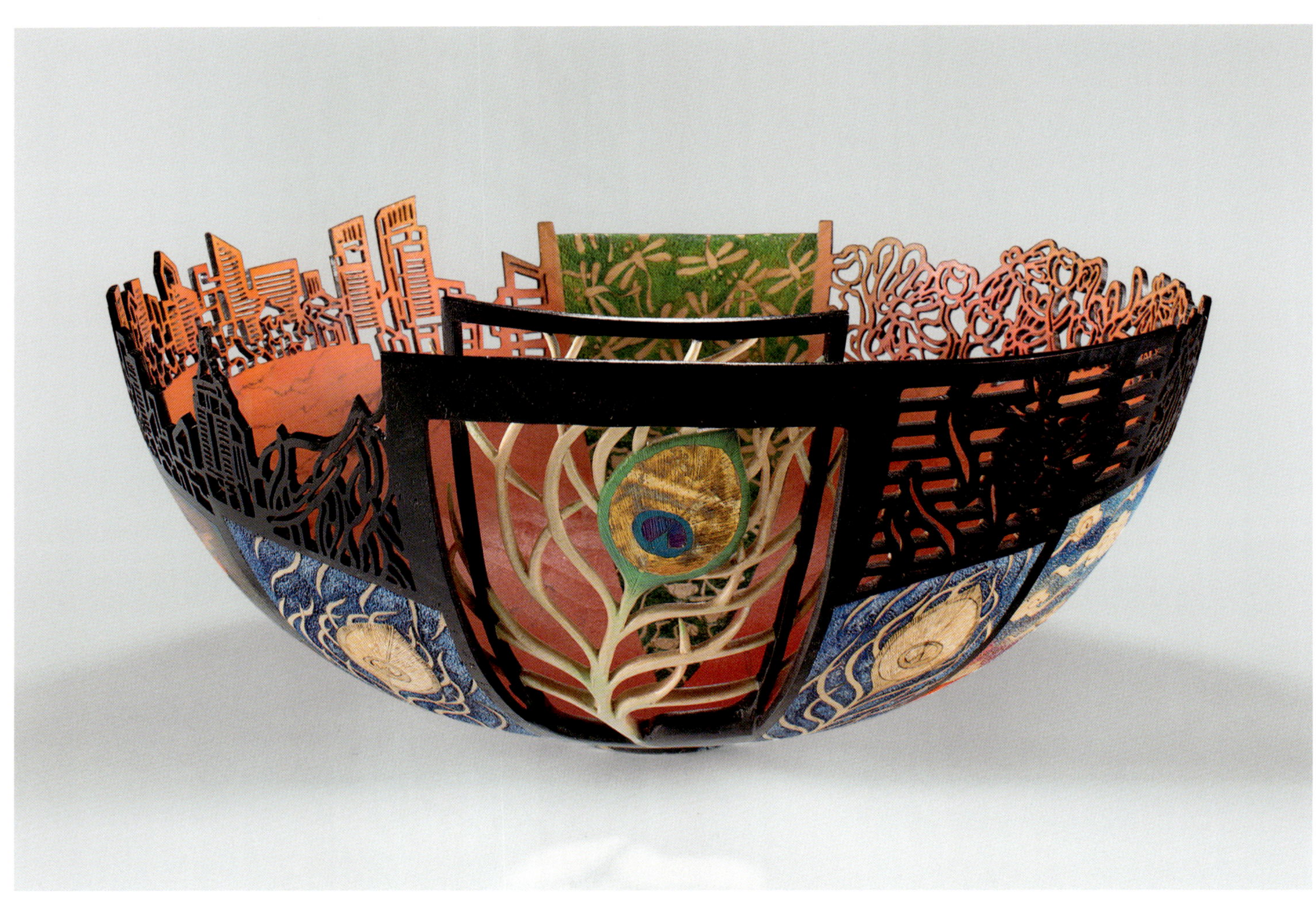

BINH PHO born 1955, works Maple Park, Illinois
GATELESS DREAM 2009, cottonwood, acrylic paints, 5 $^{1}/_{2}$ x 13 x 14 in. (14 x 33 x 35.6 cm)

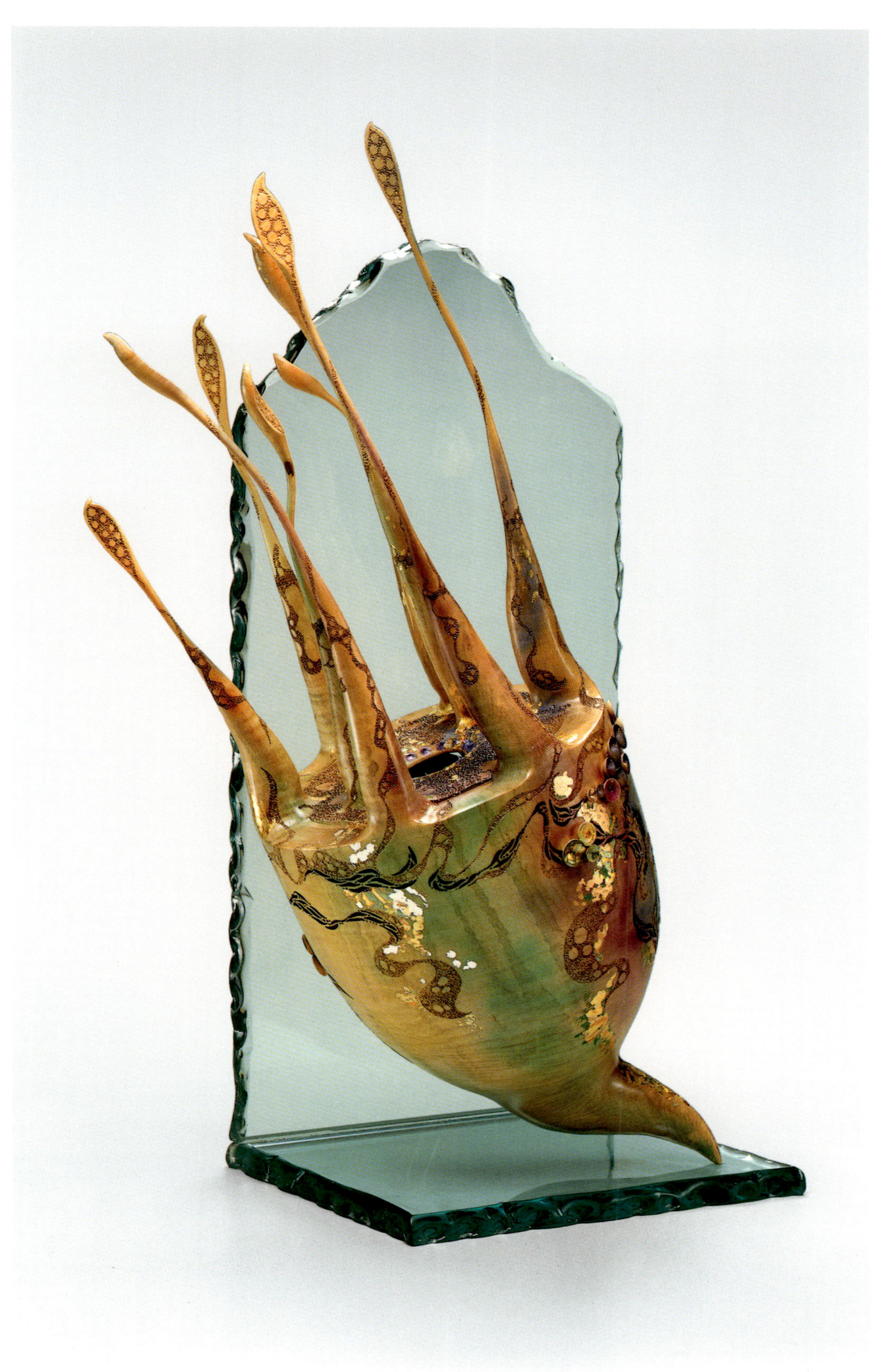

BINH PHO born 1955, works Maple Park, Illinois
WHEN MEDUSA MET CHIHULY 2001, maple, acrylic paint, metal leaf, glass, 27 $^{3}/_{4}$ x 19 x 10 in. (70.5 x 48.3 x 25.4 cm)

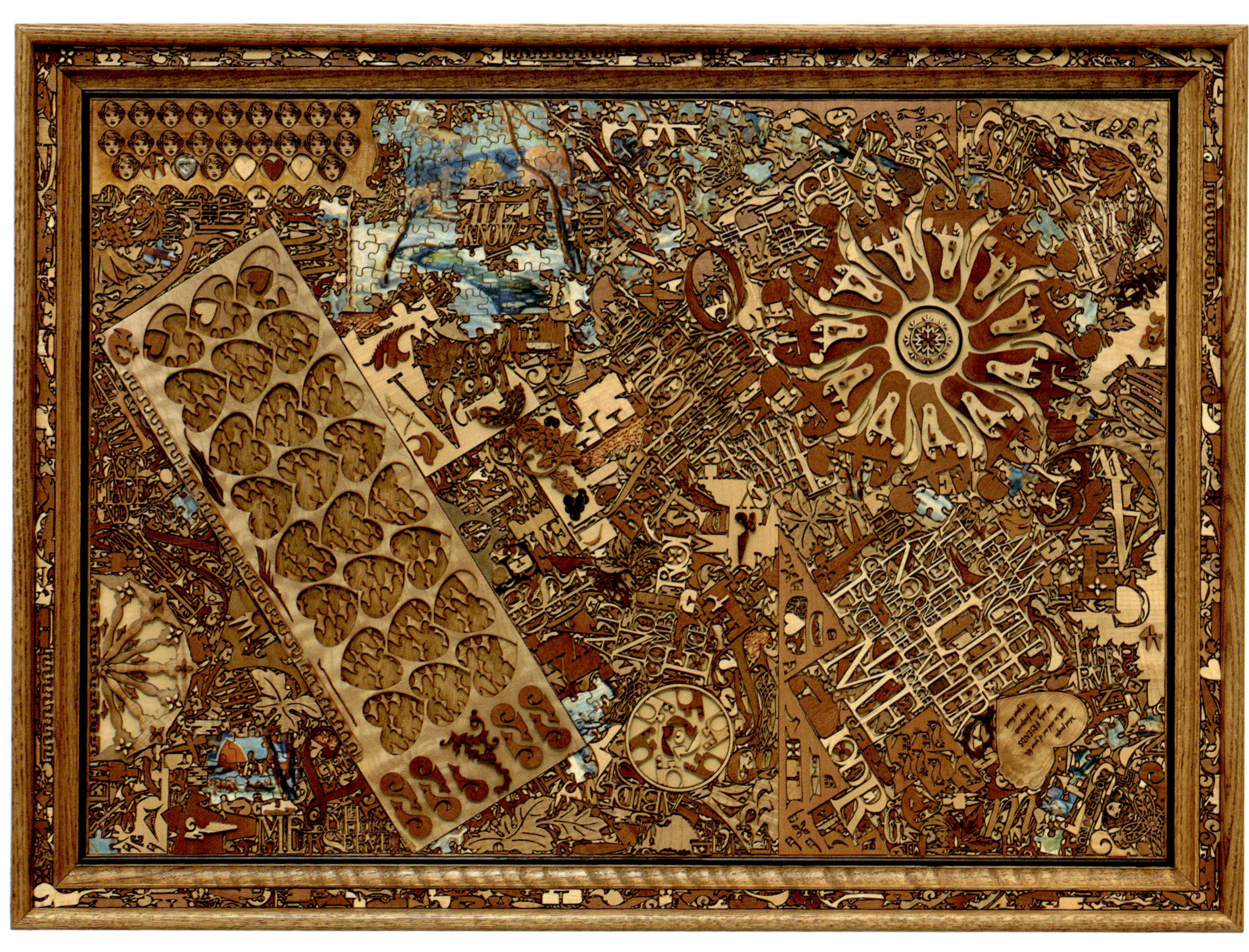

RON GERTON born 1946, works Richland, Washington
HEART AND SOULS, AN ODE TO FRANK SUDOL 2007, laser-cut wood scraps, found wood puzzle, pieces of a broken Frank Sudol vase, 33 x 44 x 3 3/4 in. (83.8 x 111.8 x 9.5 cm), Peabody Essex Museum, Gift of Lillian Montalto Bohlen

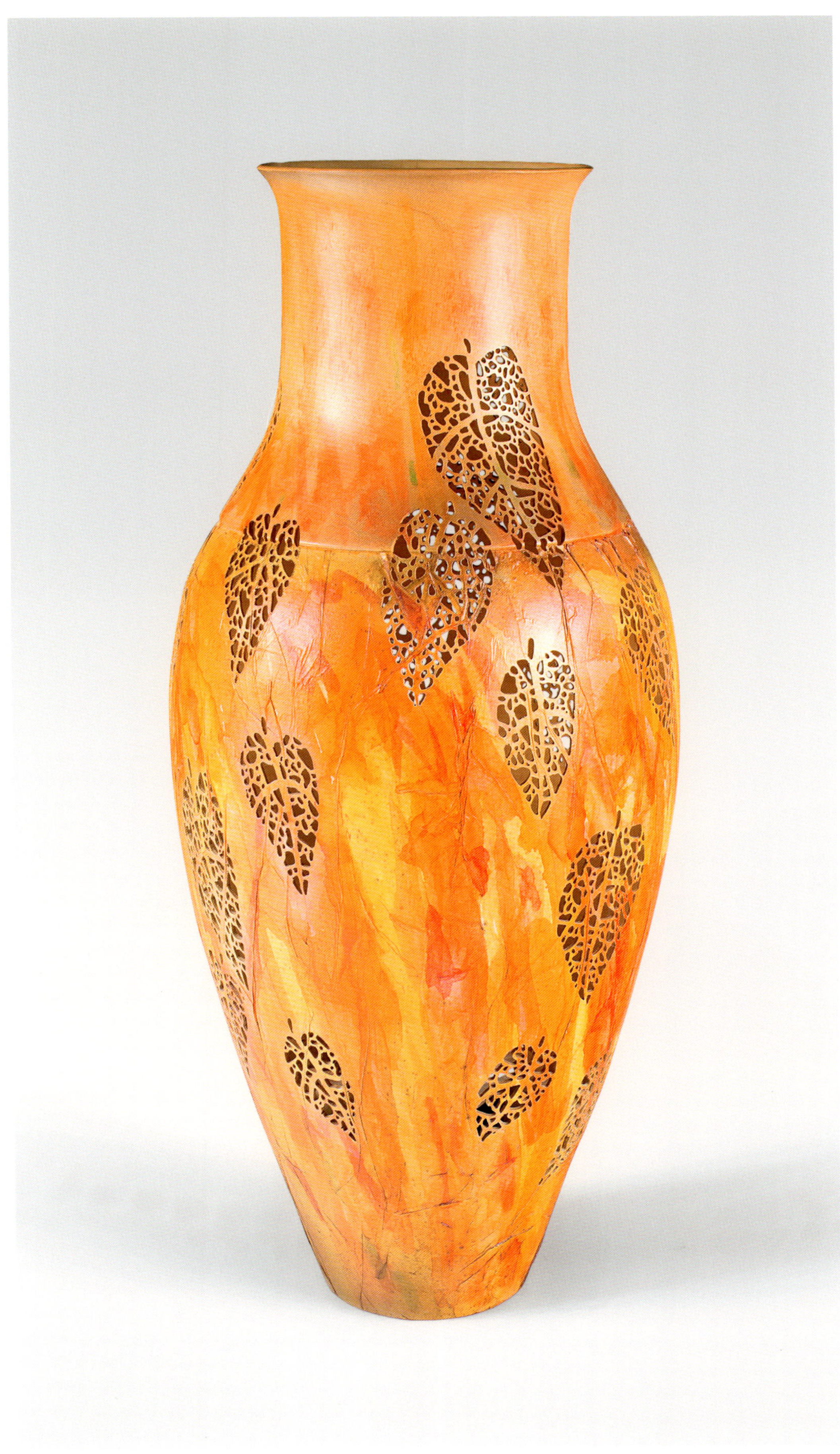

FRANK SUDOL 1933–2006, worked Paddockwood, Saskatchewan, Canada
AUTUMN LEAVES 1997, birch, rice paper, dye, 18 $^{1}/_{4}$ x 8 $^{1}/_{4}$ in. (46.4 x 21 cm)

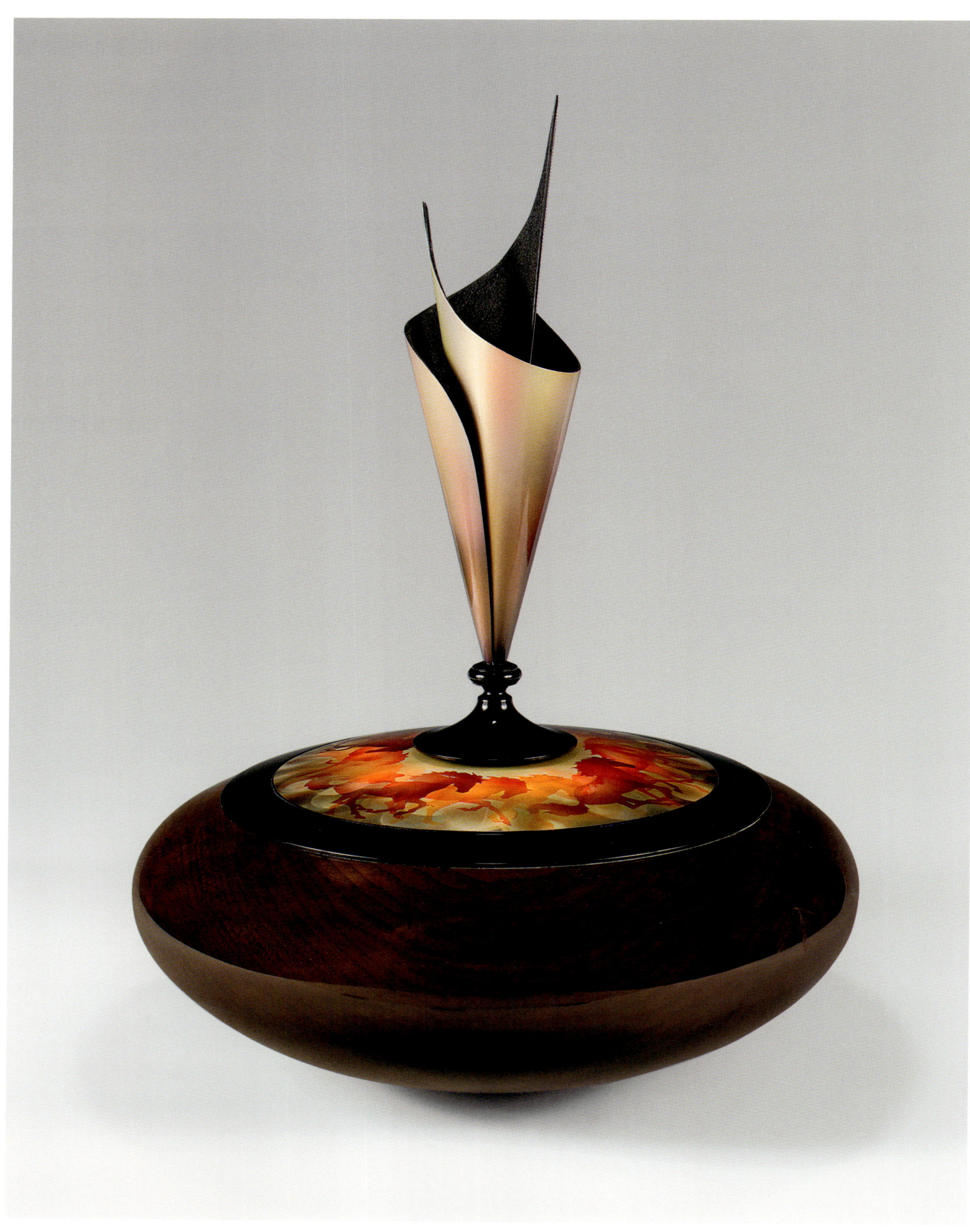

STEVE SHERMAN born 1942, works Saugerties, New York
SPIRITUS 9 2006, black walnut, hard maple, acrylic paint, hard urethanes, 19 x 14 in. (48.3 x 35.6 cm)

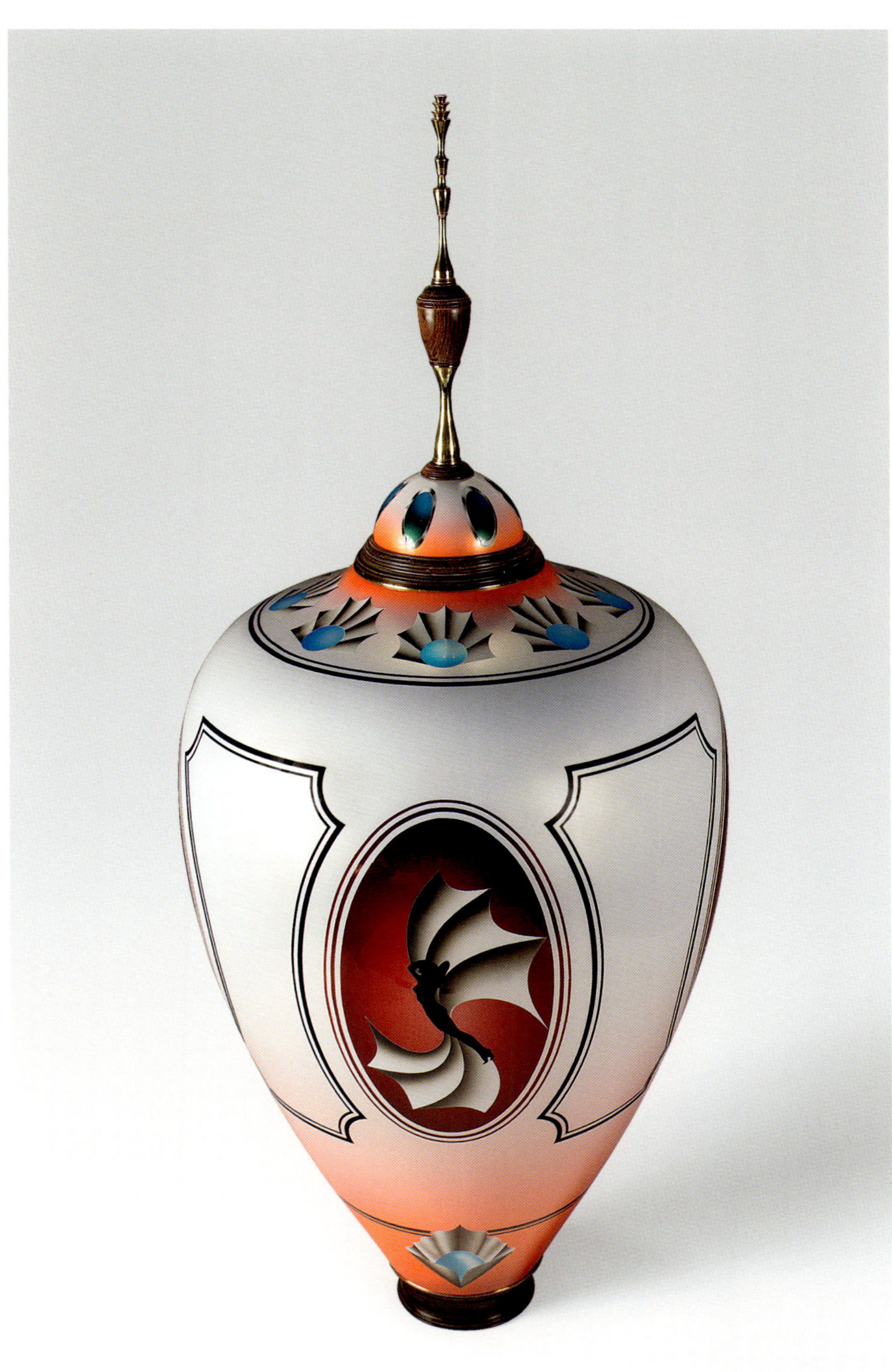

GILES GILSON born 1942, works Schenectady, New York
VENUS AND VARGAS 2006, basswood, pakkawood, 29 x 12 in. (73.7 x 30.5 cm)

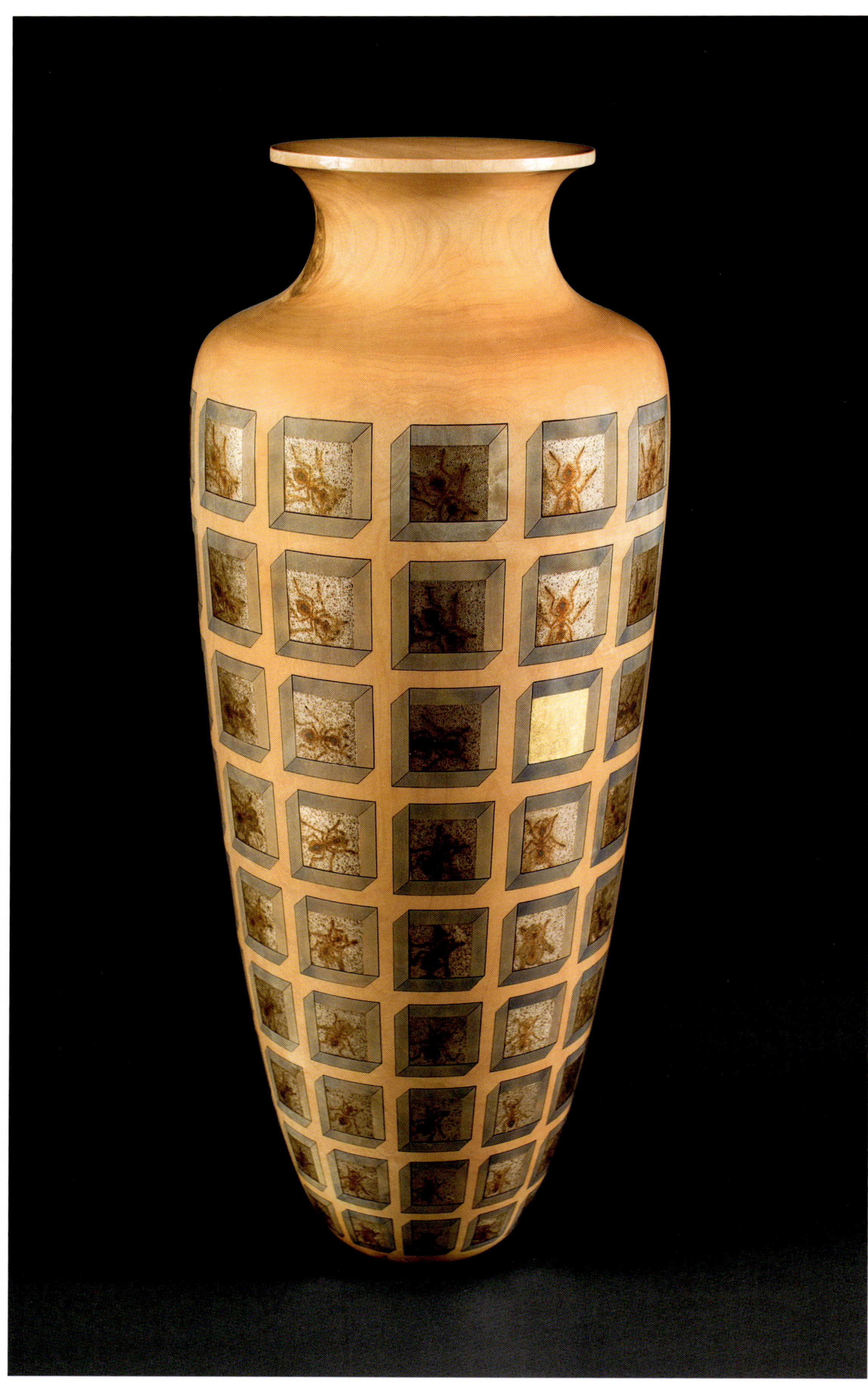

STEVEN SINNER born 1942, works Bettendorf, Iowa
ANT FARM 2001, maple, acrylic paint, ink, silver leaf, gold leaf, patina, 22 $^{1}/_{2}$ x 9 in. (57.2 x 22.7 cm)

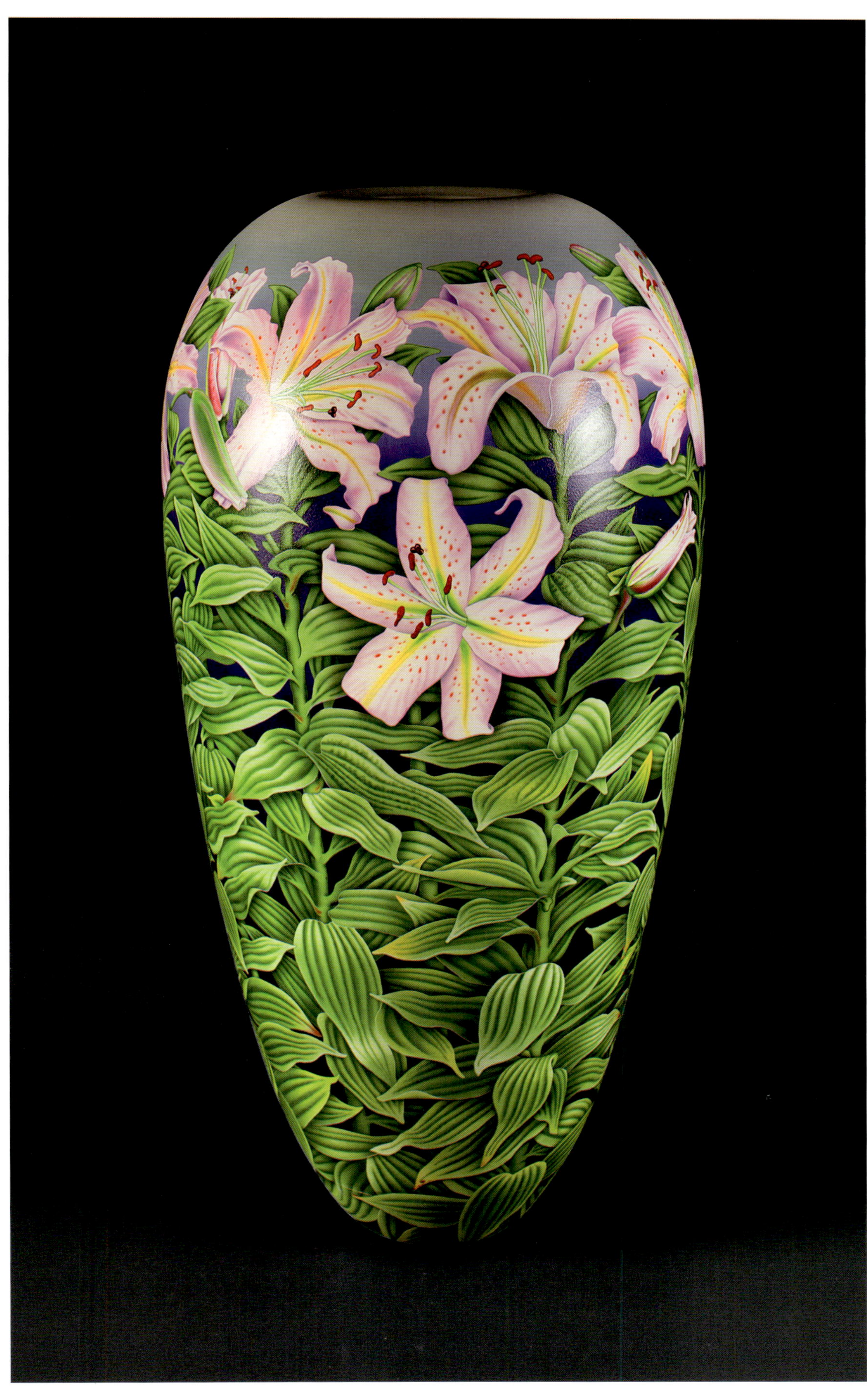

RON FLEMING born 1937, works Oklahoma City, Oklahoma
YAMA YURI 2001, basswood, acrylic paint, 36 x 17 in. (91.4 x 43.2 cm)

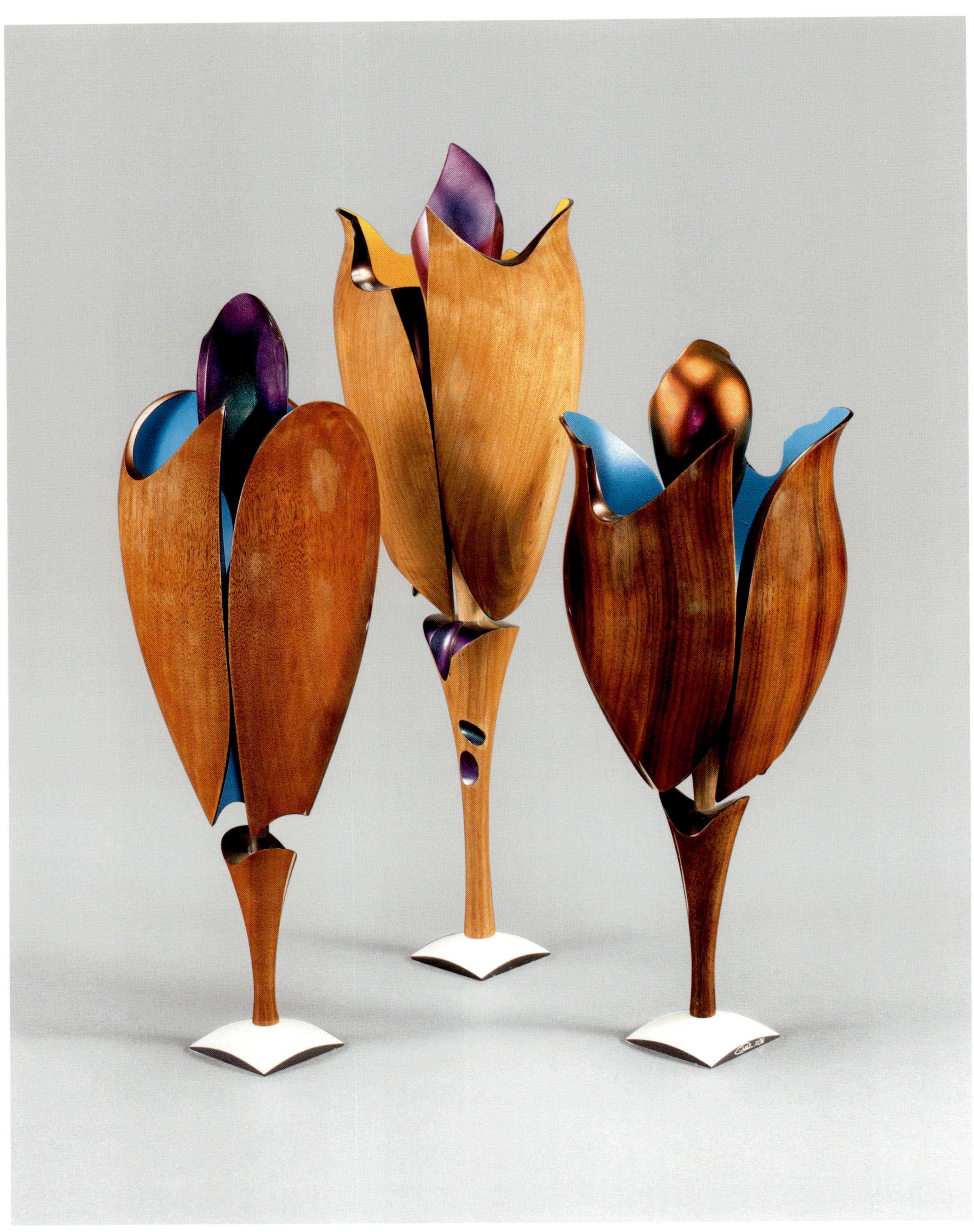

GILES GILSON born 1942, works Schenectady, New York
BOUQUET DE VIE: FLEUR DE COMPASSION, FLEUR DE SAGESSE, FLEUR DE COURAGE 1998/1999, *(Fleur de Compassion):* mahogany, pearlescent lacquer, corian, lacquer, 21 x 7 x 7 in. (53.3 x 17.8 x 17.8 cm); *(Fleur de Sagesse):* butternut, pearlescent lacquer, corian, lacquer, 24 1/2 x 7 x 7 in. (62.2 x 17.8 x 17.8 cm); *(Fleur de Courage):* padauk, pearlescent lacquer, corian, lacquer, 19 1/2 x 7 1/2 x 7 1/2 in. (49.5 x 19.1 x 17.8 cm)

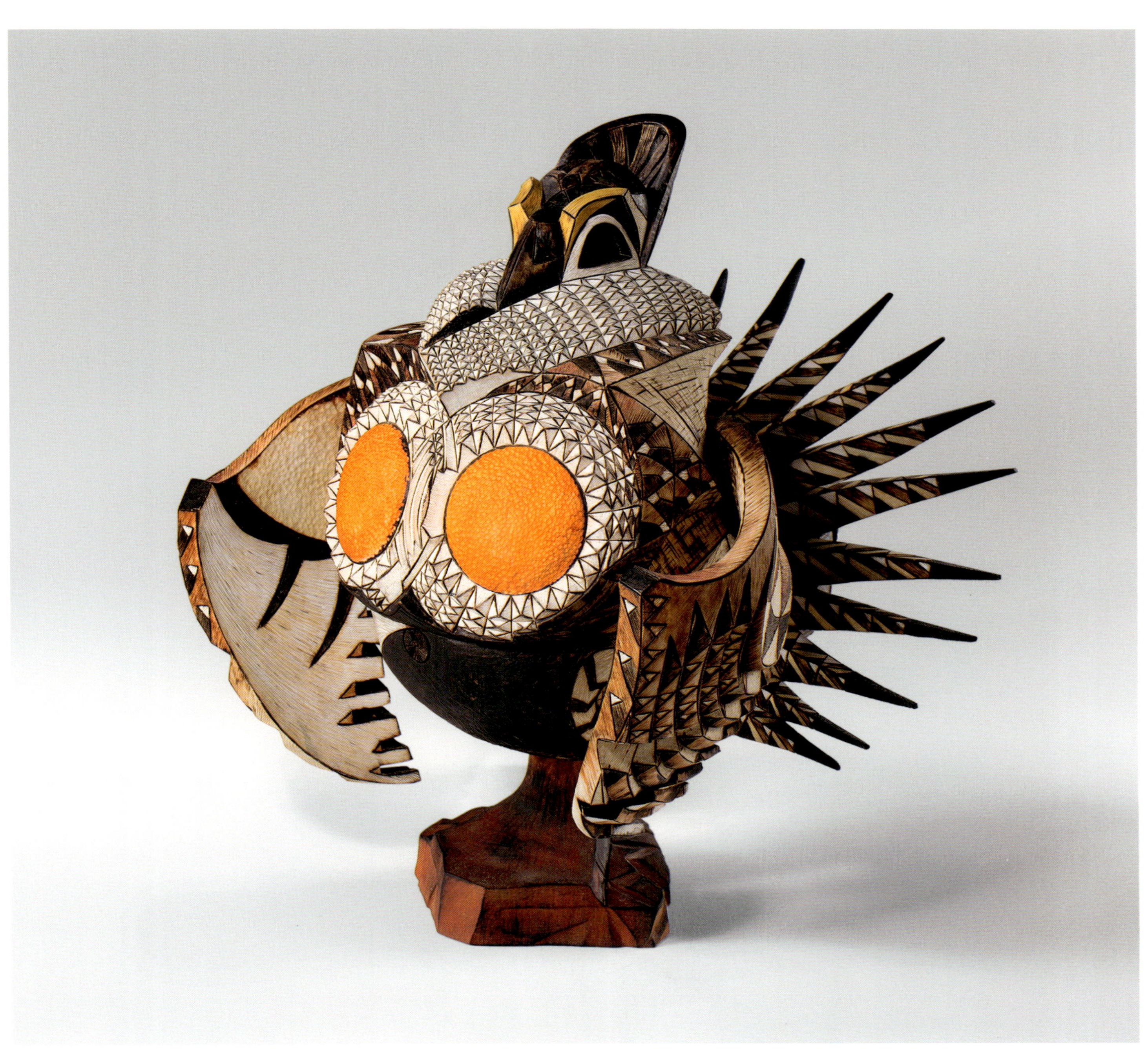

DEREK WEIDMAN born 1982, works Green Lane, Pennsylvania
SAGE GROUSE 2014, holly, ebony, redwood, pigments, 13 x 10 x 12 in. (33 x 25.4 x 30.5 cm)

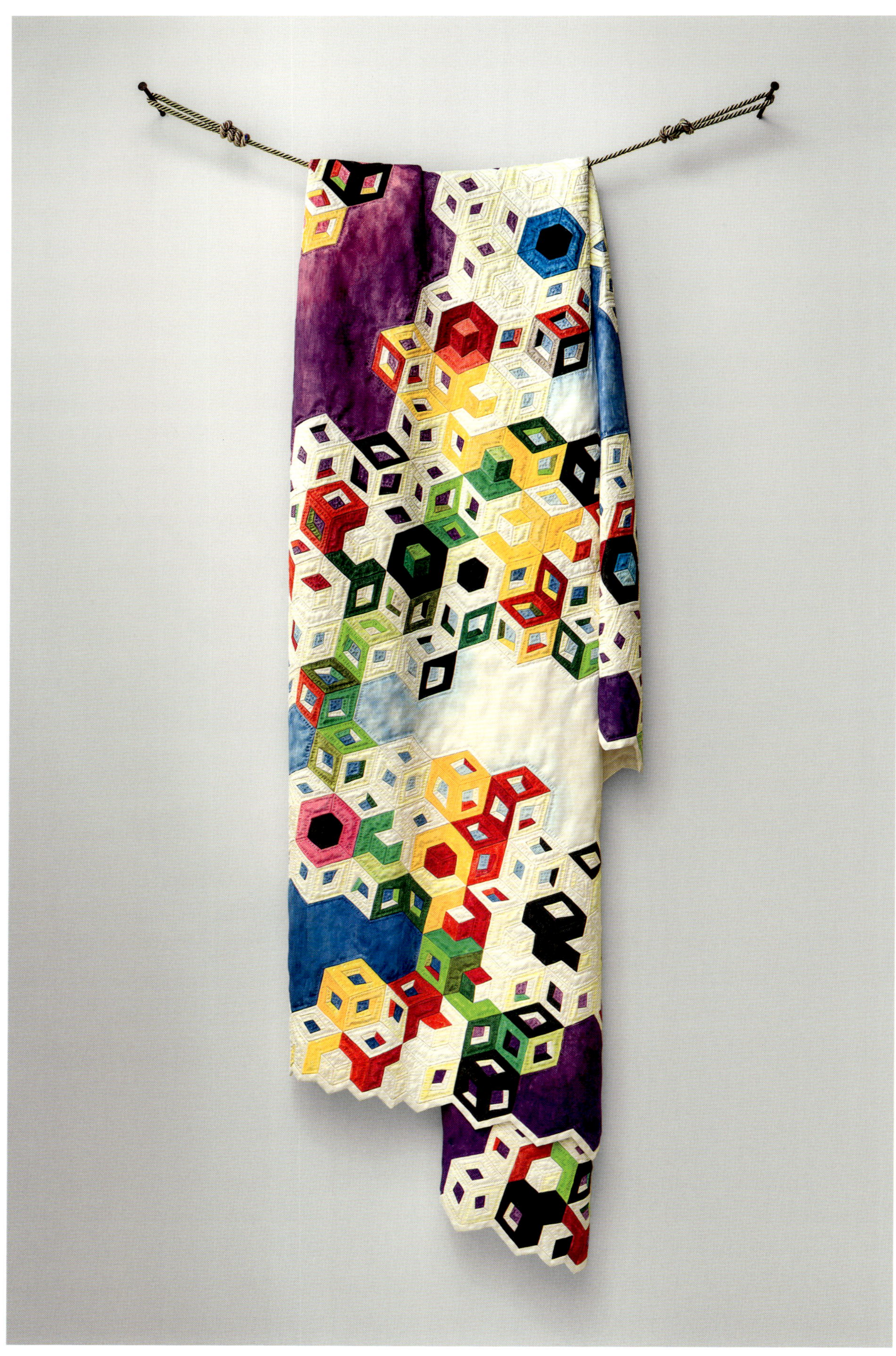

FRASER SMITH born 1958, works Tampa, Florida
THE THEORY OF EVERYTHING 2010, carved wood, silk dyes, mixed media, 68 x 22 x 4 in. (172.7 x 55.9 x 10.2 cm)

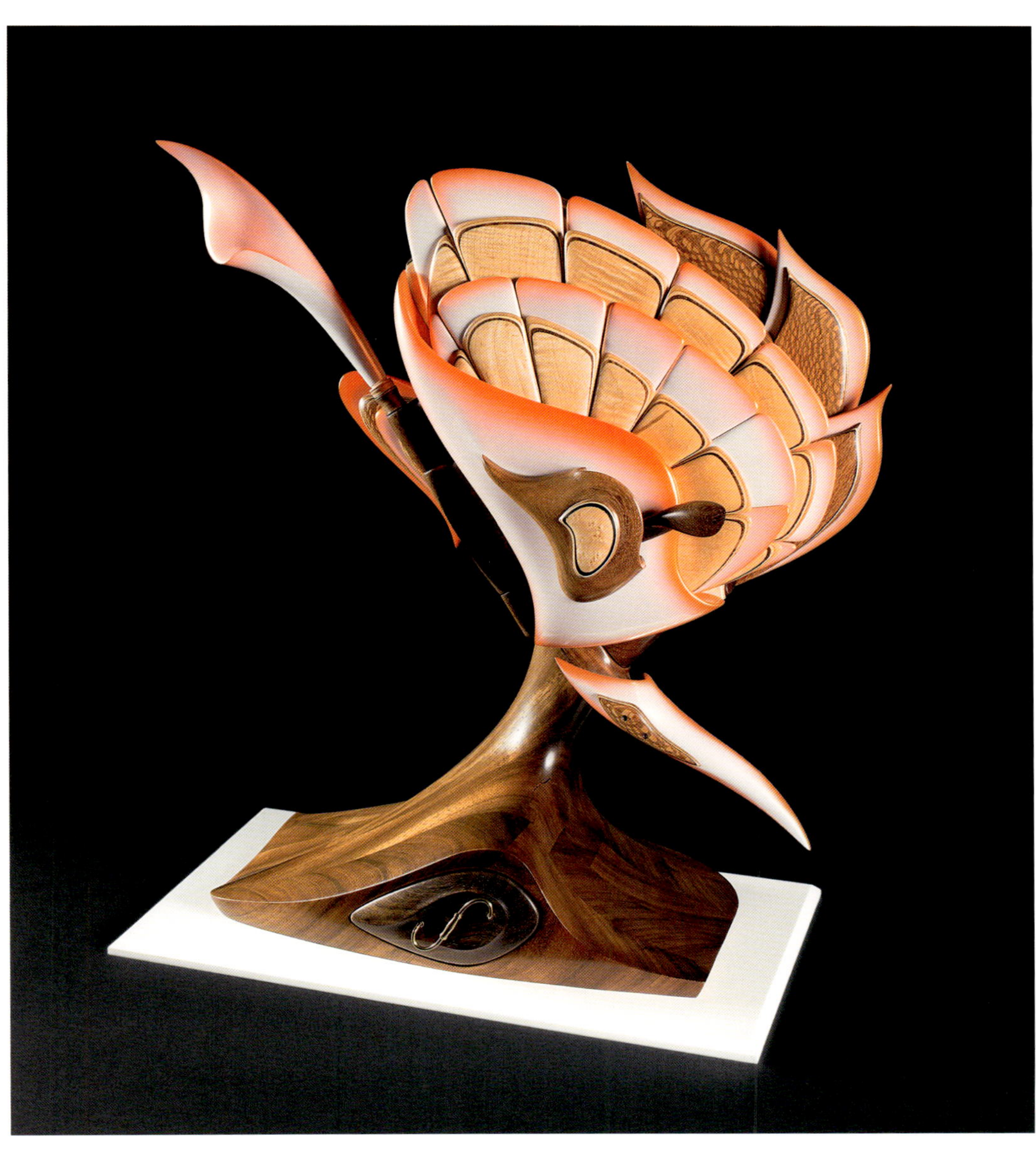

GILES GILSON born 1942, works Schenectady, New York
EARLY AUTUMN 2000, paduak, basswood, lacewood, walnut, cherry, figured maple, ebony, holly, purpleheart, brass, stainless steel, lacquer, 25 $^{3}/_{4}$ x 18 x 10 in. (65.4 x 46 x 25.4 cm)

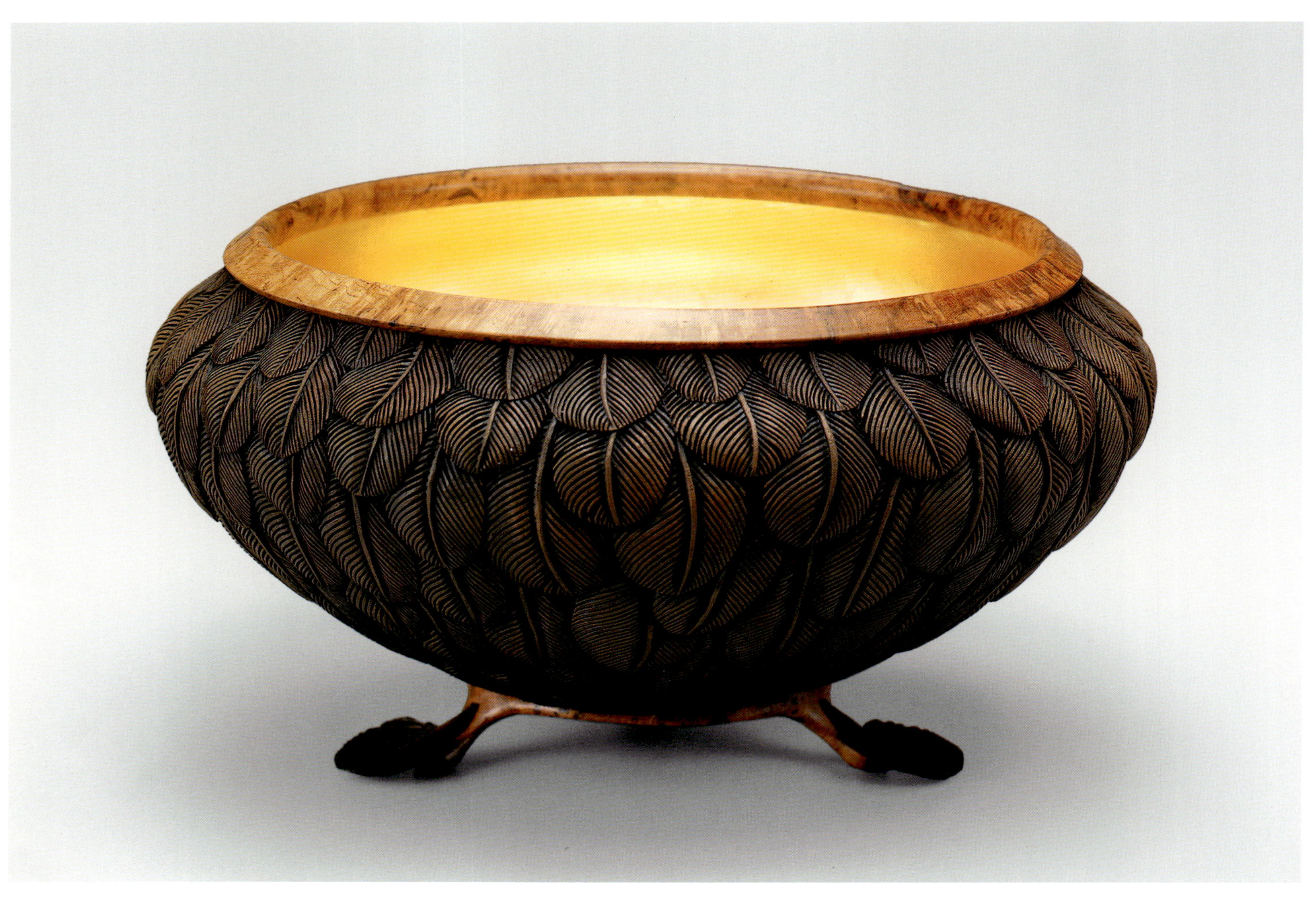

JACQUES VESERY born 1960, works Damariscotta, Maine
SEARCHING FOR THE MYSTIC WINDS 2001, box elder, cherry burl, 23.5 carat French gold leaf, acrylics, 4 1/2 x 8 1/2 x 9 in. (11.4 x 21.6 x 22.9 cm)

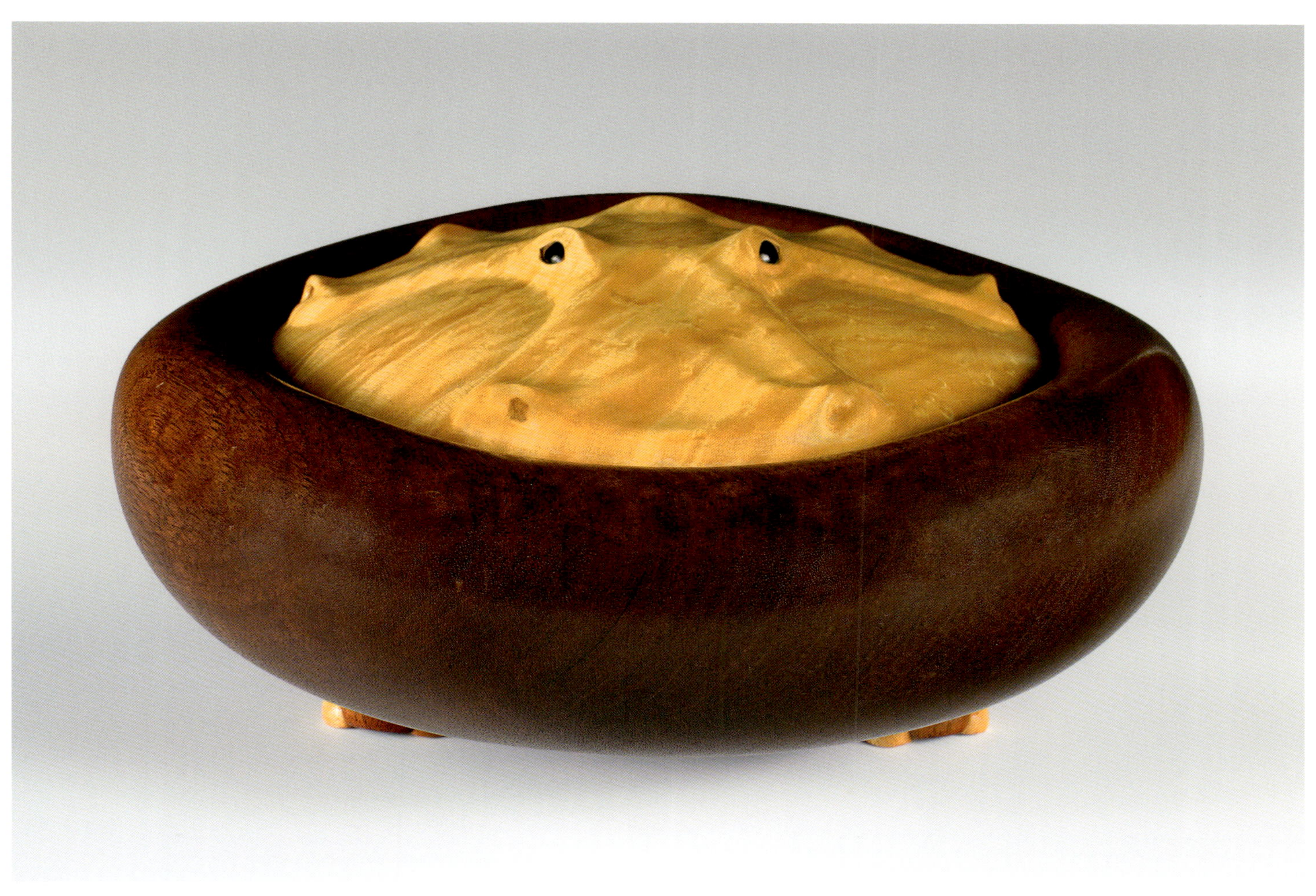

MICHAEL BROLLY born 1950, works Bethlehem, Pennsylvania
SQUATOPOTOMUS 1992, mahogany, maple, 5 x 11 in. (12.7 x 28 cm)

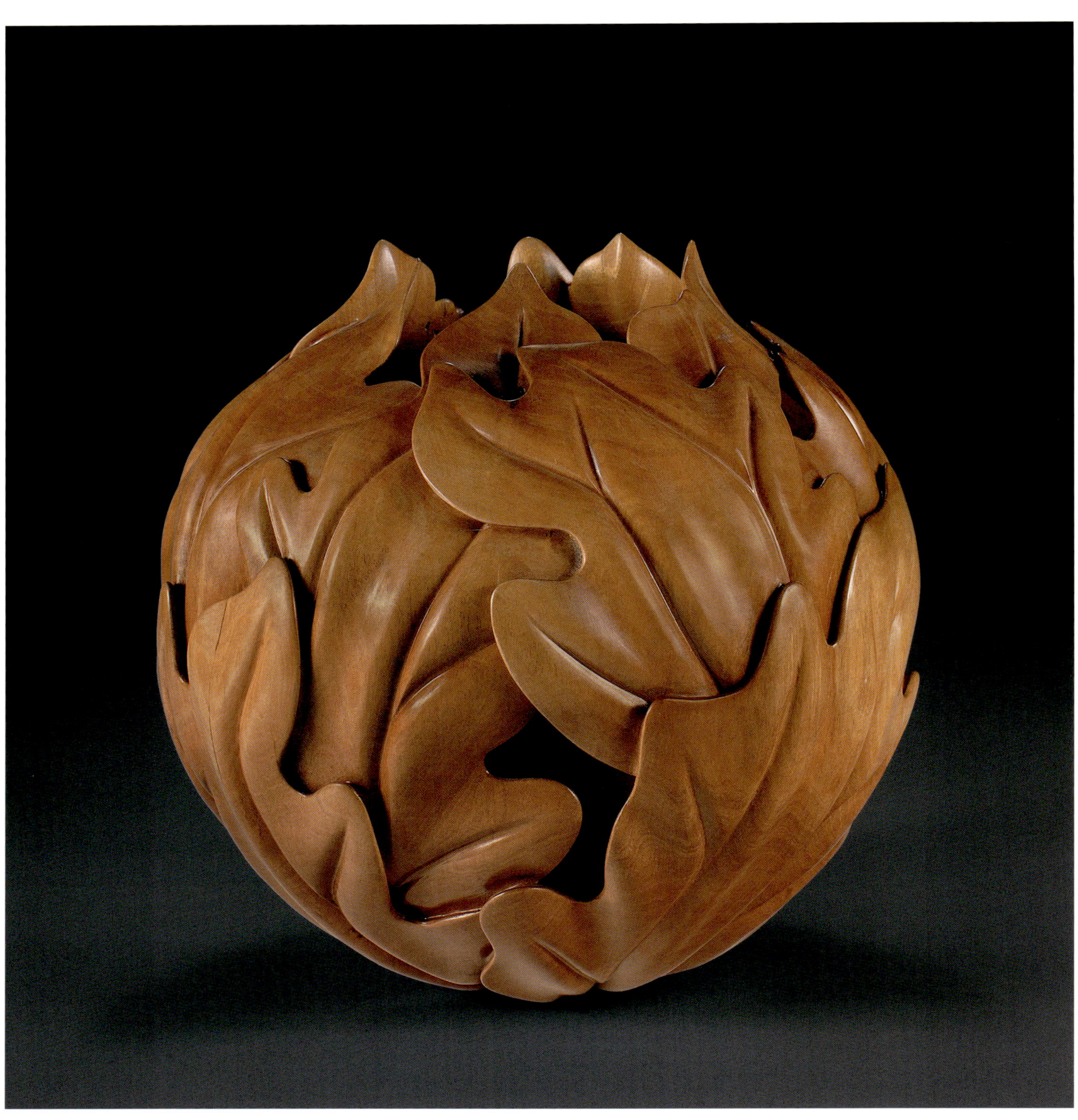

RON FLEMING born 1937, works Oklahoma City, Oklahoma
PEGASUS 1999, pink ivory, 11 x 10 in. (28 x 25.4 cm)

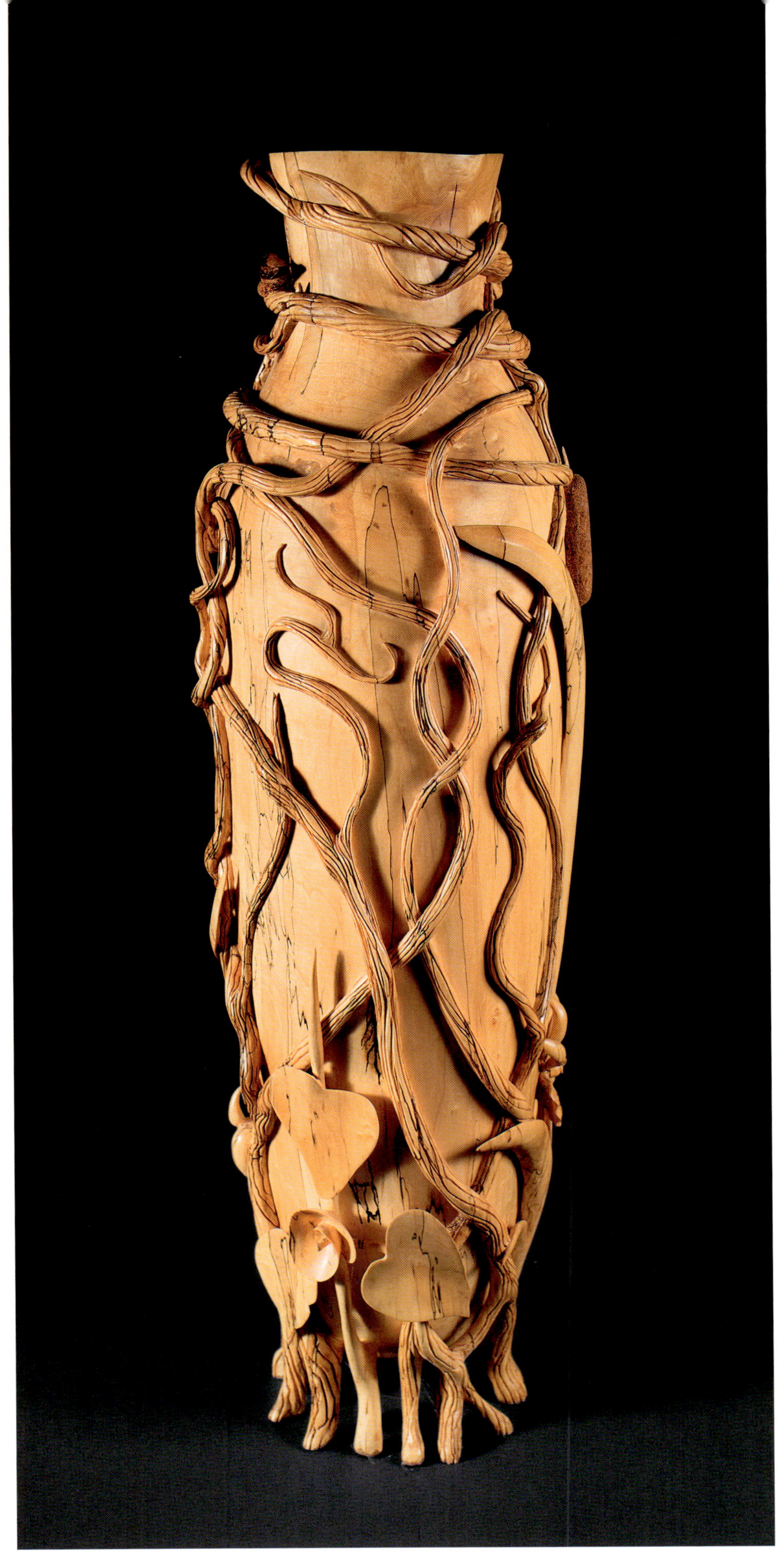

CLIFF LOUNSBURY born 1957, works East Tawas, Michigan
TANGLED IN TIME 2001, spalted maple, 50 x 14 in. (127 x 35.6 cm)

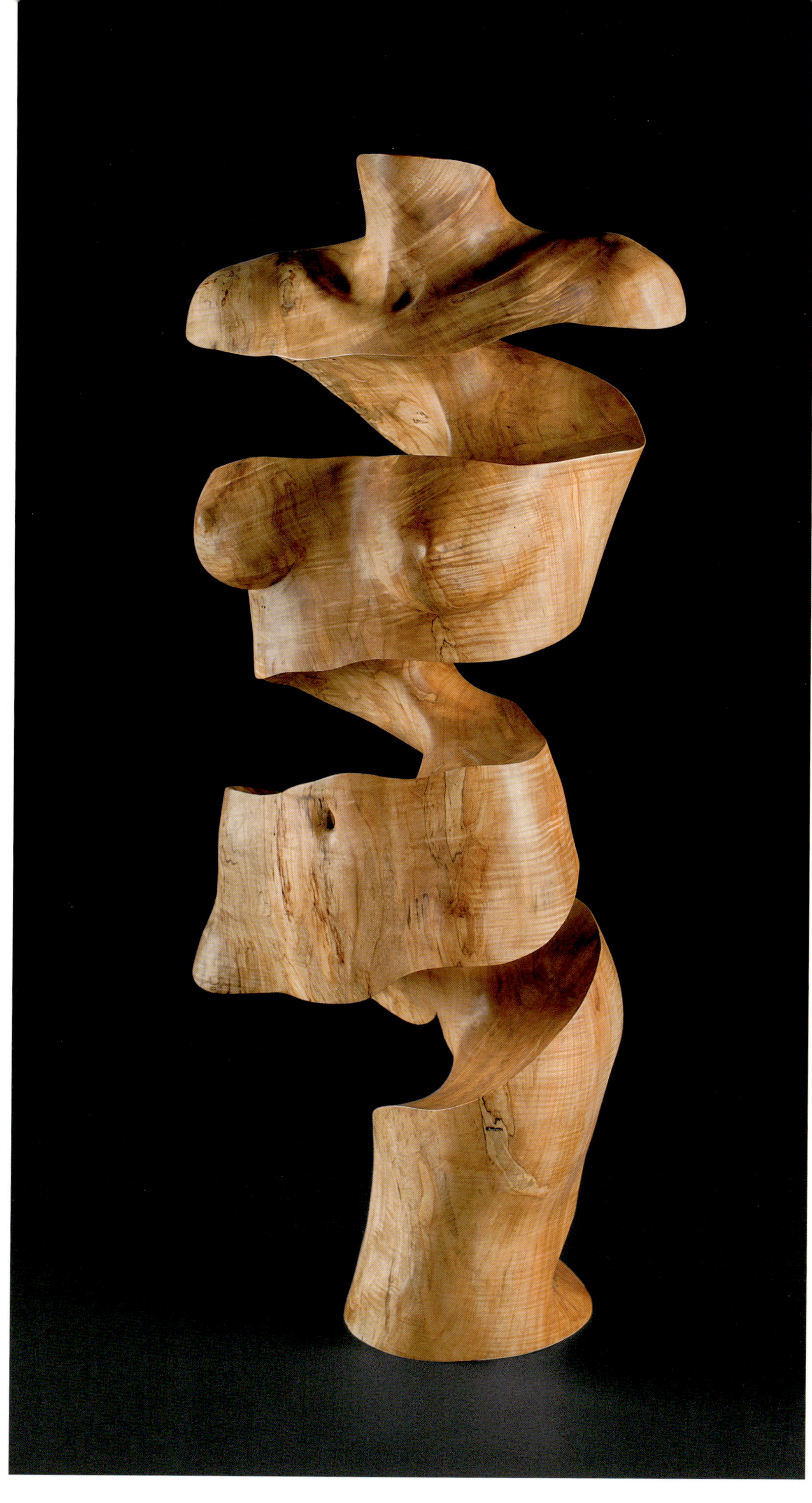

CHAD AWALT born 1958, works Tucker, Georgia
ELEOS II 2009, maple, 35 x 16 x 8 in. (88.9 x 40.6 x 20.3 cm)

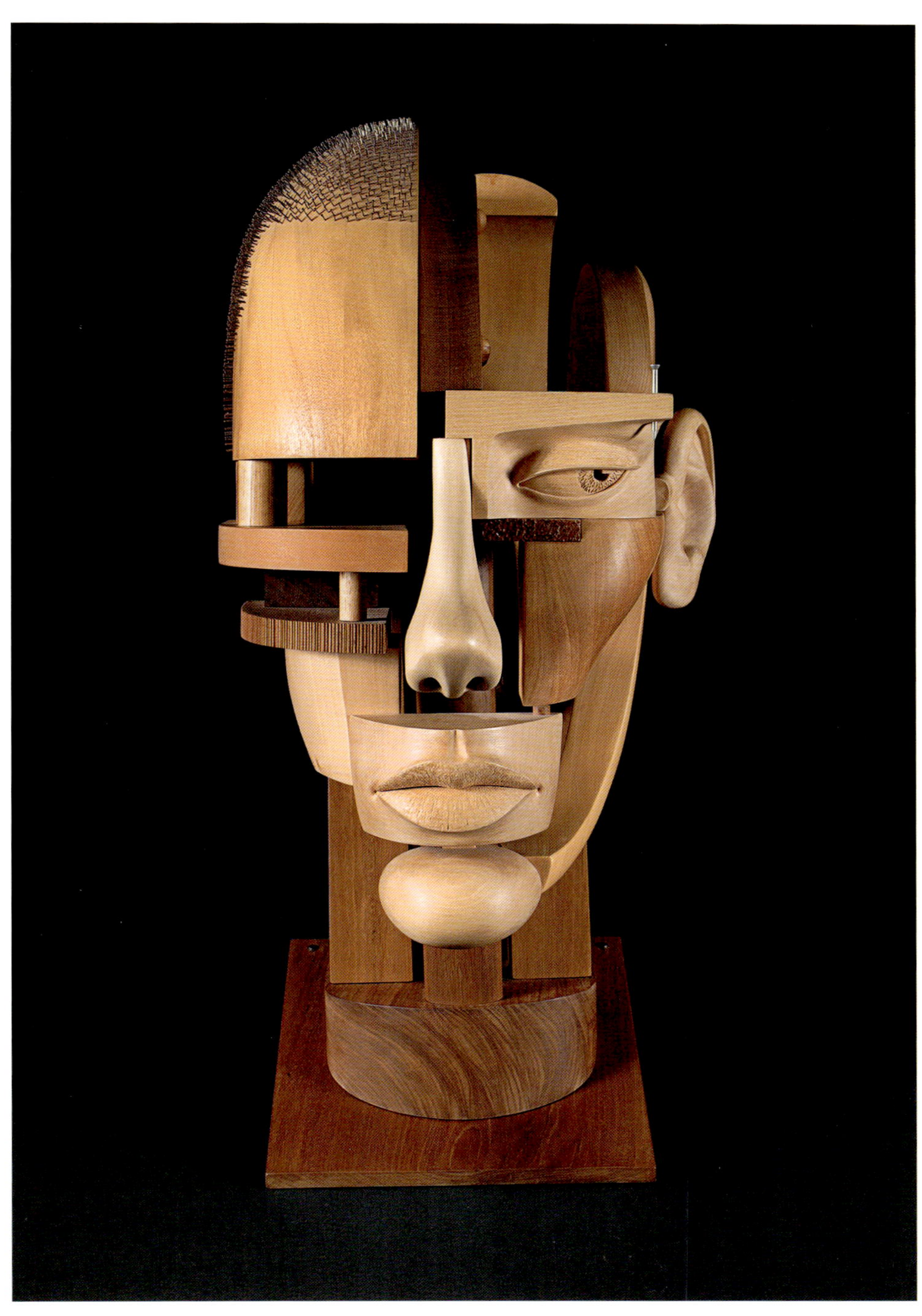

JOHN MORRIS born 1963, works Acacia Ridge, Queensland, Australia
HEAD 1999, hoop pine, Tasmanian oak, linden, jarrah, mahogany, New Guinea rosewood, kwila, nails, 32 $^{1}/_{2}$ x 23 x 16 in. (82.6 x 58.4 x 40.6 cm)

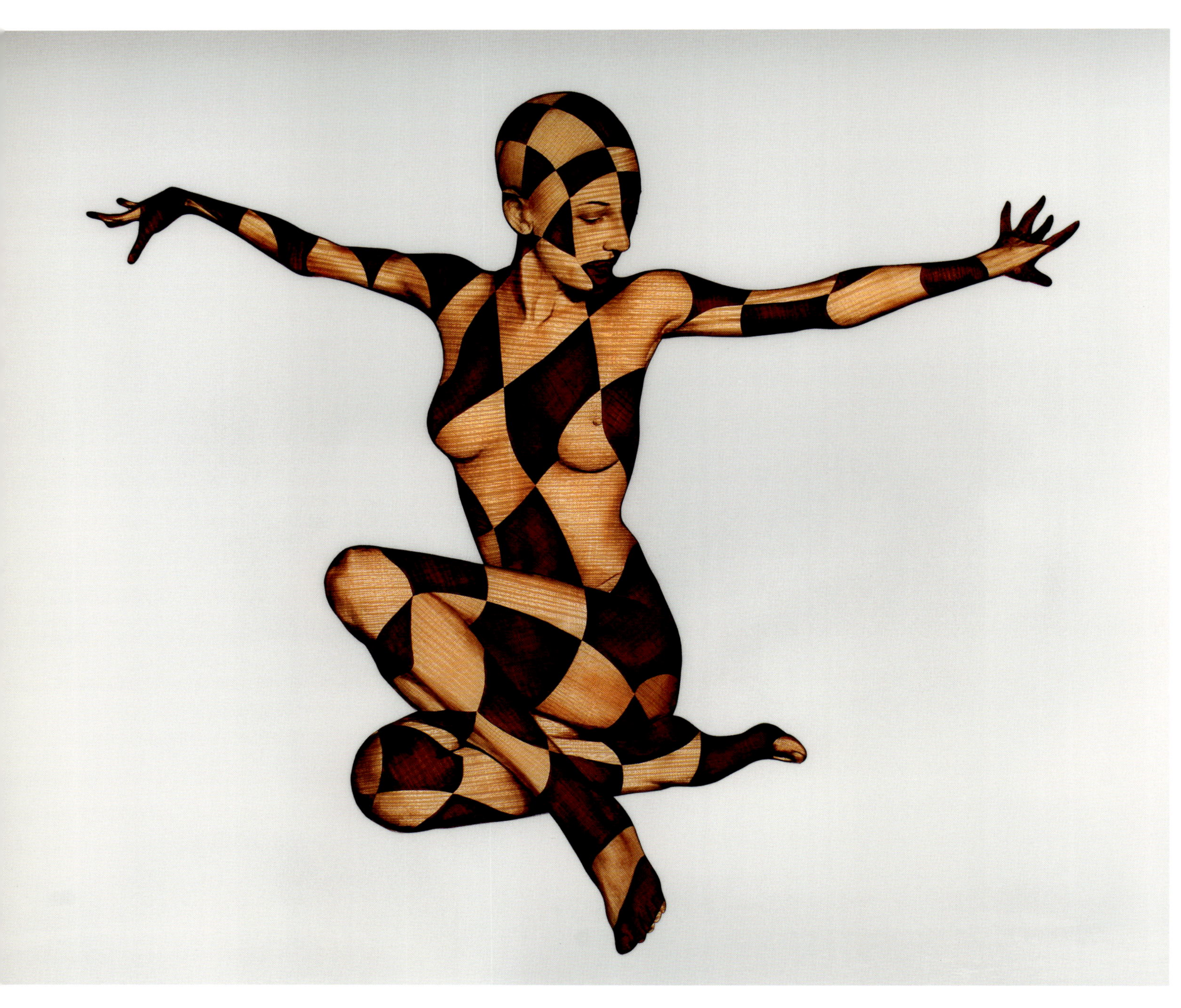

MARK CAMPBELL born 1968, works San Francisco, California
SALTIMBANQUE 2009, figured sycamore, acrylic paint, epoxy, anegre veneers, 40 x 48 x 1 1/2 in. (101.6 x 121.9 x 3.8 cm)

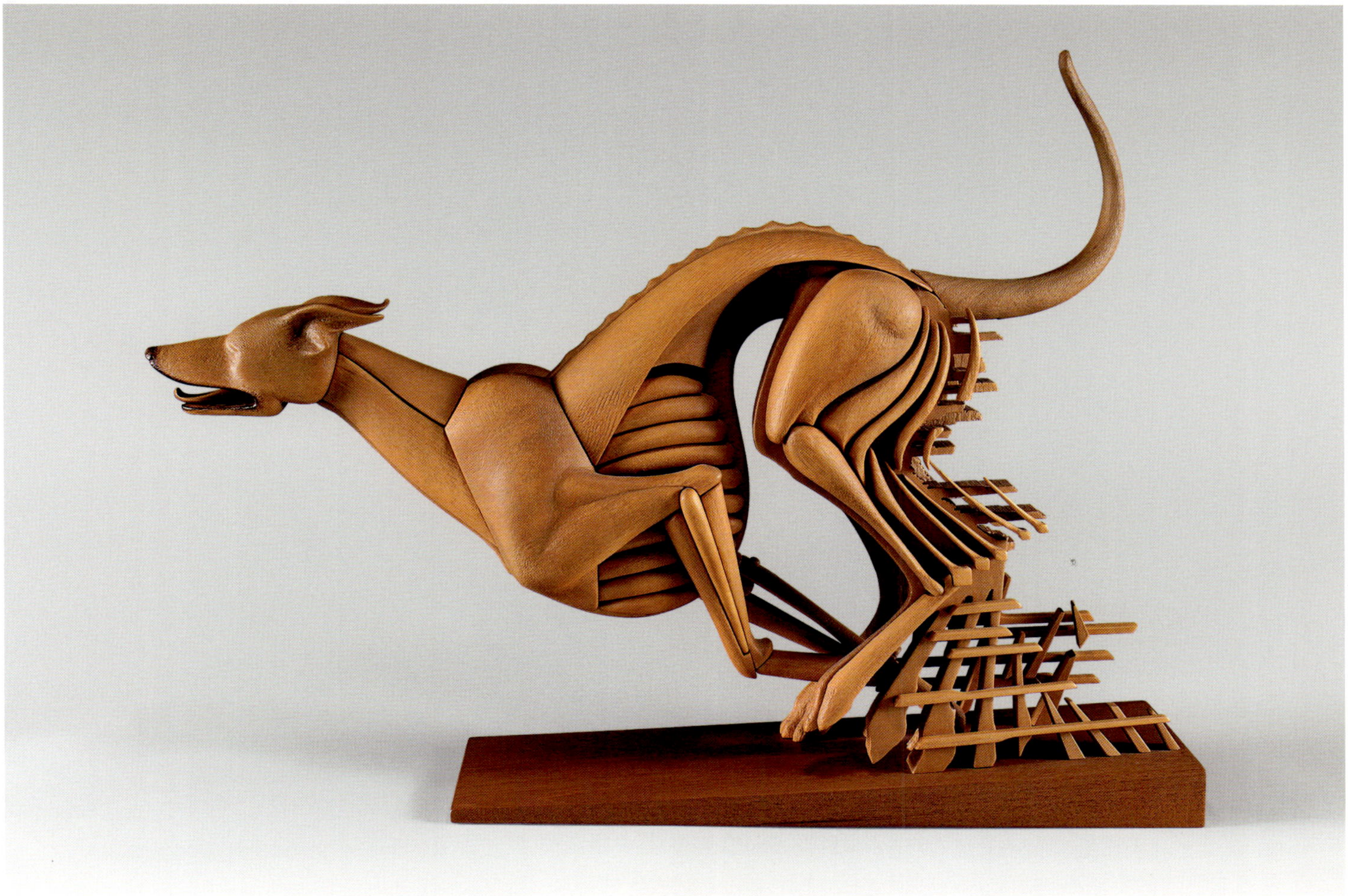

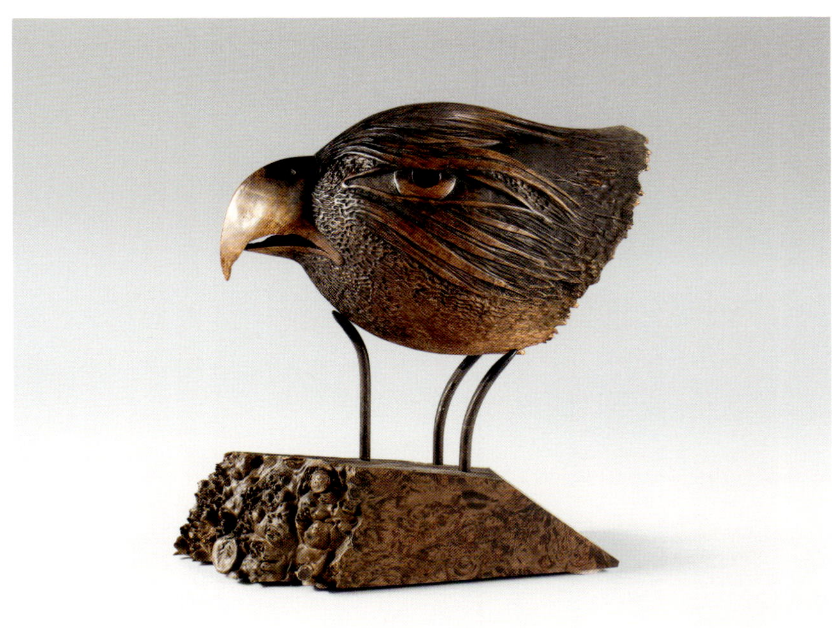

Top: **JOHN MORRIS** born 1963, works Acacia Ridge, Queensland, Australia
DOG 2003, Fijian kauri, myrtle, New Guinea rosewood, 18 x 24 x 5 $^{1}/_{2}$ in. (45.7 x 61 x 14 cm)

Bottom: **RON LAYPORT** born 1942, works Pittsburgh, Pennsylvania
MASK OF FALCON—VESSEL FROM A DISTANT DANCE 2002, maple burl, steel, paint, 16 x 13 x 7 in. (40.6 x 33 x 17.8 cm)

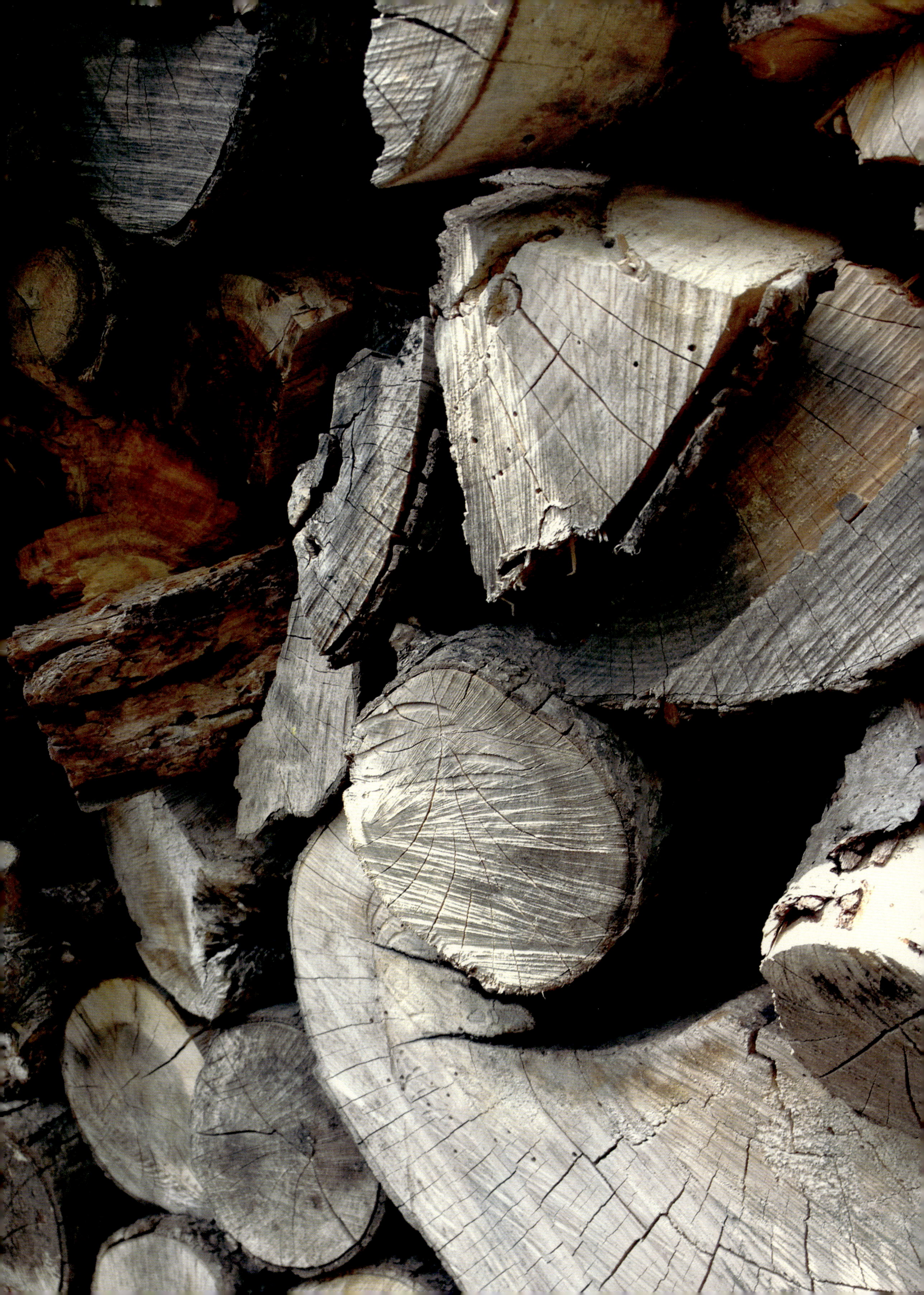

FURTHER READING

CATRINA HILL

Adamson, Glenn, Patricia E. Kane, Albert LeCoff, Christopher Monkhouse, Jennifer Komar Olivarez, Ruth Waterbury, and David Waterbury. *Conversations with Wood: The Collection of Ruth and David Waterbury.* Minneapolis: Minneapolis Institute of Arts, 2011.

Bell, Nicholas R. *A Revolution in Wood: The Bresler Collection.* Washington, DC: Renwick Gallery of the Smithsonian American Art Museum, 2010.

Burchard, Christian, Robyn Horn, Stoney Lamar, George Peterson, Michael T. Peterson, and Grant Vaughan. *Wood Now.* Philadelphia: Wood Turning Center, 2006.

Christensen, Kip, and Dale Nish. *Beneath the Bark: Twenty-Five Years of Woodturning.* Provo: Utah Woodturning Symposium, 2004.

Cooke, Edward S., Jr., Glenn Adamson, Albert LeCoff, Graeme P. Berlyn, and Andrew D. Richardson. *Wood Turning in North America since 1930.* Philadelphia and New Haven: Wood Turning Center and Yale University Art Gallery, 2001.

Dehan, Amy Miller, and Matthew Kangas. *Outside the Ordinary: Contemporary Art in Glass, Wood, and Ceramics from the Wolf Collection.* Cincinnati and Athens: Cincinnati Art Museum and Ohio University Press, 2009.

Duncan-Aimone, Katherine, Ray Leier, Jan Peters, and Kevin Wallace. *500 Wood Bowls: Bold & Original Designs Blending Tradition & Innovation.* New York: Lark Books, 2004.

Ellsworth, David. *Ellsworth on Woodturning: How a Master Creates Bowls, Pots, and Vessels.* East Petersburg, PA: Fox Chapel Publishing, 2008.

Ellsworth, David, and Sandy Blain. *Nature Takes a Turn: Woodturnings Inspired by the Natural World.* Shoreview and St. Paul: American Association of Woodturners and Minnesota Museum of American Art, 2001.

Fike, Bonita, and Mike Mendelson. *The Fine Art of Wood: The Bohlen Collection.* Detroit and New York: Detroit Institute of Arts and Abbeville Press, 2000.

Glasner, Barbara, and Stephan Ott. *Wonder Wood: A Favorite Material for Designers, Architects, and Artists.* Basel: Birkhäuser, 2013.

Hobbs, Robert. *Mark Lindquist: Revolutions in Wood.* Richmond, VA and Seattle: Hand Workshop Art Center and University of Washington Press, 1995.

Holzapfel, Michelle, Robin Rice, and Christopher D. Tyler. *Challenge VI—Roots: Insights & Inspirations in Contemporary Turned Objects.* Philadelphia: Wood Turning Center, 2001.

Kelsey, John. *Woodturning Today: A Dramatic Evolution: Celebrating the American Association of Woodturners 25th Anniversary 1986–2011.* St. Paul: American Association of Woodturners, 2011.

Leier, Ray, Jan Peters, and Kevin Wallace. *Contemporary Turned Wood: New Perspectives in a Rich Tradition.* Madison and Cincinnati: Hand Books Press and Popular Woodworking Books, 1999.

Lineberry, Heather Sealy, Joanne Rapp, Ed Moulthrop, Philip Moulthrop, and Matt Moulthrop. *Moulthrop Generations: Turned Wood Bowls by Ed, Philip, and Matt Moulthrop.* Tempe: Arizona State University Art Museum, 2007.

Martin, Terry. *Wood Dreaming: The Spirit of Australia Captured in Wood Turning.* Pymble, New South Wales: Harper Collins, 1998.

Ramljak, Suzanne, Michael W. Monroe, and Mark Richard Leach. *Turning Wood into Art: The Jane and Arthur Mason Collection.* New York: Harry N. Abrams, 2000.

Randall, Judson, ed. *Connections: International Turning Exchange 1995–2005.* Philadelphia: Wood Turning Center, 2005.

Roszkiewicz, Ron. *To Turn the Perfect Wooden Bowl: The Lifelong Quest of Bob Stocksdale.* East Petersburg, PA: Fox Chapel Publishing, 2009.

Shafto, Tiffany DeEtte, and Lynda McDaniel. *Contemporary Hawai'i Woodworkers: The Wood, the Art, the Aloha.* Mountain View, HI: Contemporary Publications, 2009.

Sims, Lowery Stokes. *Against the Grain: Wood in Contemporary Art, Craft, and Design.* Los Angeles: Renaissance Books, 2013.

Tourtillott, Suzanne J. E. *Woodturning: Major Works by Leading Artists.* New York: Lark Books, 2009.

Turner, Tran, Matthew Kangas, John Perreault, and Edward S. Cooke, Jr. *Expressions in Wood: Masterworks from the Wornick Collection.* Oakland: Oakland Museum of California, 1996.

Ulmer, Sean M., Janice Blackburn, Terry Martin, and David Revere McFadden. *Nature Transformed: Wood Art from the Bohlen Collection.* Ann Arbor and Manchester, VT: University of Michigan Museum of Art and Hudson Hills Press, 2004.

Wallace, Kevin. *The Cutting Edge: Contemporary Wood Art and the Lipton Collection.* Antioch, CA: Fine Arts Press, 2012.

Wallace, Kevin, and Terry Martin. *New Masters of Woodturning: Expanding the Boundaries of Wood Art.* East Petersburg, PA: Fox Chapel Publishing, 2008.

Wallace, Kevin, and Binh Pho. *Shadow of the Turning.* Antioch, CA: Fine Arts Press, 2012.

INDEX OF ARTISTS

Bolded page numbers indicate objects in the exhibition.

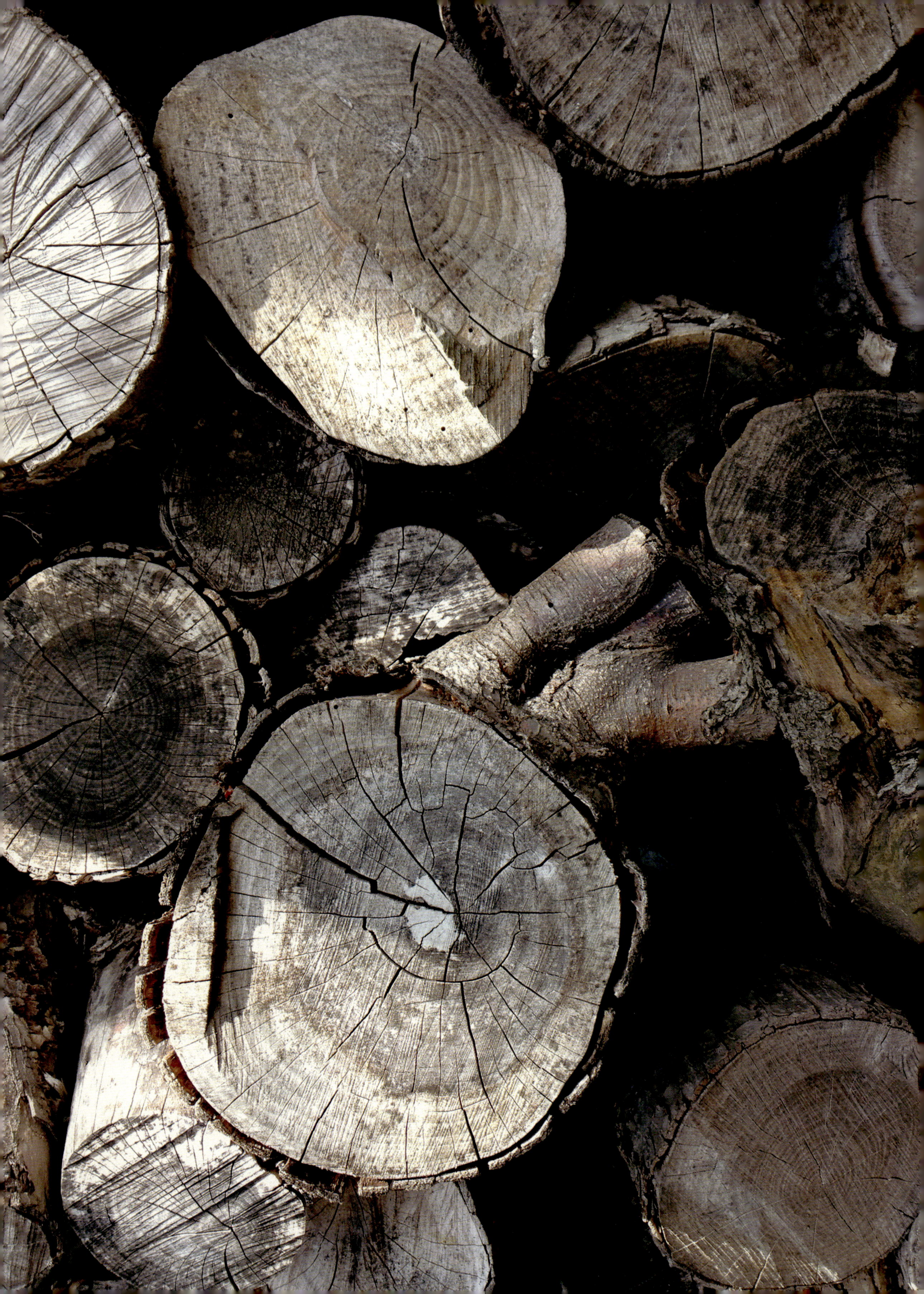